CONTEMPORARY SPAIN

A Handbook

Second edition

CONTEMPORARY SPAIN

A Handbook

Second edition

Christopher J. Ross

*Department of English, Vienna University of Economics and
Business Administration, Austria*

A member of the Hodder Headline Group
LONDON
Distributed in the United States of America by
Oxford University Press Inc., New York

First published in Great Britain in 2002 by
Arnold, a member of the Hodder Headline Group,
338 Euston Road, London NW1 3BH

http://www.arnoldpublishers.com

Distributed in the United States of America by
Oxford University Press Inc.,
198 Madison Avenue, New York, NY10016

The advice and information in this book are believed to be true and
accurate at the date of going to press, but neither the author nor the publisher
can accept any legal responsibility or liability for any errors or omissions.

British Library Cataloguing in Publication Data
A catalogue record for this book is available from the British Library

Library of Congress Cataloging-in-Publication Data
A catalog record for this book is available from the Library of Congress

ISBN 0 340 76215 2 (pb)

2 3 4 5 6 7 8 9 10

Typeset in 10/12 Palatino by Charon Tec Pvt. Ltd, Chennai, India
Printed and bound in India by Replika Press Pvt. Ltd., Kundli 131 028

What do you think about this book? Or any other Arnold title?
Please send your comments to feedback.arnold@hodder.co.uk

CONTENTS

PREFACE

Every year more and more people are taking Spanish studies in higher education. Increasingly, too, those studies are focusing on contemporary Spanish society and the use of language within it. The two aspects are inseparable. An understanding of all but the most trivial of Spanish texts, both written and spoken, requires access to the body of knowledge about their own country and society which is common to all reasonably educated Spaniards. The aim of the Handbook is to allow English-speaking students to access that same body of knowledge.

To illustrate the point, take the following (hypothetical) sentence from a UK newspaper: 'Labour's modernizers will this week tackle head-on two of the thorniest issues facing the party: selective education and electoral reform.' To understand it, the reader not only requires familiarity with English syntax and general vocabulary, but also needs to be aware of the meaning, and connotations, of the specific terms 'Labour's modernizers', 'selective education' and 'electoral reform', all of which form part of the cultural baggage of the educated UK-based English-speaker. The Handbook's primary purpose is to equip English-speaking students of Spanish with the basis of the equivalent body of knowledge and understanding about Spain.

Even more than in general language, culturally defined terminology appears to give rise to problems of interference. Again, to take an example: the party which won Spain's 1996 election habitually figures in the English-language press as the 'Popular Party'. Use of this name, taken directly from the Spanish *Partido Popular*, removes an important element of meaning from the Spanish term and is significantly misleading – as well as faintly ludicrous. It makes no more sense than to say a Spanish text has been 'traduced' into English, merely because in appearance 'traduce' resembles the Spanish word *traducir* (to translate).

The Handbook's second purpose is to help students to avoid some of the more glaring linguistic pitfalls of this type. Here a note of caution must be sounded. In some cases, English usage is too well established to be challenged. Even though 'Committees' would be much more appropriate, the trade union federation *Comisiones Obreras* is already widely known as 'Workers Commissions'. Similarly, although 'coalition' is usually applied to a government, it is already widely used in the English-language names of Spanish political parties such as *Coalición Popular*, which would be better rendered by 'People's Alliance'.

Another obvious problem in preparing the Handbook was that of selection. I have attempted to cover those concepts and terms which seem to me to occur frequently in texts, together with sufficient background explanation to allow them to be understood. The task was complicated by the change of government which occurred during the final phase of writing. Inevitably there will be increasingly frequent reference to the party and individuals who now run Spain, and less to their predecessors. Nevertheless, the Socialists had been in power for so long and through a period of such rapid development that their names and actions will remain an essential point of reference for many years to come.

The Handbook is arranged in a series of topic-based chapters, each of which attempts to introduce the main features of one facet of Spanish society and its institutions. It is intended for readers without specialist knowledge of any of the subjects concerned, and technical language is kept to a necessary minimum. Although not a reference book as such, the various sections and sub-sections are intended to be self-standing, so that readers can dip into a particular topic or aspects of it. There is frequent cross-referencing, indicated by section numbers in square brackets, to allow threads of interest to be followed across topic boundaries. Inevitably this approach makes for a degree of intrusiveness and repetition, but I have taken the view that it is desirable in the interests of easy usage.

The glossaries included after each chapter are in no sense intended to be comprehensive. They are meant to complement published dictionaries by picking out usages that I have found from experience to be difficult to locate, or potentially misleading, or both. The bracketed Spanish terms inserted in the main text are intended to give an indication of usage in context; there is no suggestion that they are the sole, or even the most usual, equivalent of the preceding English concept or phrase. Where fully assimilated English versions of Spanish terms exist, they are used in the text, e.g. Saragossa, Aragon. Where they do not, the original Spanish form is used, including any accents. This applies in particular to proper names, e.g. Felipe González.

Even more than the text as a whole, the listing of initials and acronyms is, of necessity, selective. I have attempted to include only those which are habitually used to refer to the organization or concept without further explanation, e.g. PSOE. Where sets of initials have effectively supplanted the full term, such as the radio station *Cadena COPE*, they are not included in the list.

A list of further reading is included at the end of the Handbook. It is deliberately brief, including only items which seem to me reasonably accessible to the non-specialist reader. Particular mention should be made of John Hooper's *The New Spaniards*, an outstanding work of journalism that gives an extraordinarily vivid and sympathetic picture of contemporary Spain. There is, of course, no substitute for the quality Spanish press in keeping up with events in the country; a number of titles are now available on the Internet. For more analytical material the best source is the *International Journal of Iberian Studies*, formerly the *Journal of the Association for Contemporary Iberian Studies*.

I owe a sincere debt of gratitude to various people who have helped in the production of this book. First and foremost among them are my wife and parents, for their unfailing support down the years. Second, my former teacher and colleague Diarmuid Bradley; that I could even think of undertaking such a project is due to his wisdom, inspiration and friendship. Last but very far from least, valued colleagues at Heriot-Watt University, especially Kent Sproule and Ann McFall for support and solidarity beyond the call of duty, and Graeme Lewis for his help in producing the maps. Needless to say, the errors and imbalances of the Handbook have nothing to do with any of them, but are entirely my own responsibility.

Chris Ross
February 1997

PREFACE TO SECOND EDITION

Apart from the addition of two chapters, on the European tier of government and the individual regions, and updating of others, the main change with respect to the first edition is that the list of acronyms and abbreviations has been suppressed as a separate unit. This time I have taken the view that these are best incorporated in the (expanded) index, to enable interested readers to access all the information provided on a particular item from a single point.

I should like to thank those readers who kindly alerted me to errors in the first edition; their corrections have been gratefully taken up in the new one. On the other hand, I have not attempted to do as a number of comments suggested and extend the book's coverage to wider social developments. That would have exceeded both my competence and the space available. Happily, since the first edition's appearance a number of publications have come on the market which address such aspects specifically.

Chris Ross
March 2002

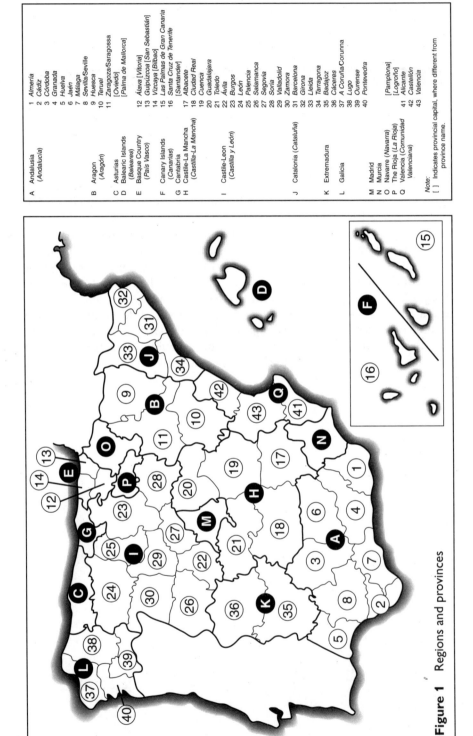

Figure 1 Regions and provinces

A	Andalusia (*Andalucía*)		1	*Almería*
			2	*Cádiz*
			3	*Córdoba*
			4	*Granada*
			5	*Huelva*
			6	*Jaén*
			7	*Málaga*
			8	*Sevilla/Seville*
B	Aragon (*Aragón*)		9	*Huesca*
			10	*Teruel*
			11	*Zaragoza/Saragossa*
C	Asturias			[*Oviedo*]
D	Balearic Islands (*Baleares*)			[*Palma de Mallorca*]
E	Basque Country (*País Vasco*)		12	*Álava* [*Vitoria*]
			13	*Guipúzcoa* [*San Sebastián*]
			14	*Vizcaya* [*Bilbao*]
F	Canary Islands (*Canarias*)		15	*Las Palmas de Gran Canaria*
			16	*Santa Cruz de Tenerife*
G	Cantabria			[*Santander*]
H	Castile-La Mancha (*Castilla-La Mancha*)		17	*Albacete*
			18	*Ciudad Real*
			19	*Cuenca*
			20	*Guadalajara*
			21	*Toledo*
I	Castile-Leon (*Castilla y León*)		22	*Ávila*
			23	*Burgos*
			24	*León*
			25	*Palencia*
			26	*Salamanca*
			27	*Segovia*
			28	*Soria*
			29	*Valladolid*
			30	*Zamora*
J	Catalonia (*Cataluña*)		31	*Barcelona*
			32	*Girona*
			33	*Lleida*
			34	*Tarragona*
K	Extremadura		35	*Badajoz*
			36	*Cáceres*
L	Galicia		37	*A Coruña/Corunna*
			38	*Lugo*
			39	*Ourense*
			40	*Pontevedra*
M	Madrid			
N	Murcia			
O	The Rioja (*La Rioja*)			[*Logroño*]
P	Navarre (*Navarra*)			[*Pamplona*]
Q	Valencia (*Comunidad Valenciana*)		41	*Alicante*
			42	*Castellón*
			43	*Valencia*

Note:
[ ] indicates provincial capital, where different from province name.

INTRODUCTION
Contemporary Spain in context

With its population of around 40 million, Spain now ranks among the world's ten largest economies. Its area of 505,000 square kilometres, while relatively modest in global terms, is the second largest in the European Union, of which it is a fully-fledged and influential member. Beyond any doubt it belongs to the select club of industrialized Western democracies. Yet little over a quarter of a century ago Spain was a relatively backward country, largely isolated from its European neighbours and ruled by a dictatorship. Even though it has since undergone immense and rapid changes, this radically distinct experience means that Spain – even more than other countries – cannot be understood without some knowledge of its history. This introductory chapter accordingly attempts to give an overview of that history, concentrating on the critical period from around 1800 which culminated in the lengthy dictatorship of General Franco. It then examines the process by which, after his death, Spain finally joined the mainstream of Western liberal democracy. Lastly it indicates the main features of the geopolitical context in which the country now finds itself, its principal ties with the outside world and their implications.

0.1 THE NINETEENTH CENTURY AND ITS AFTERMATH

Spain's situation in 1975 was the product of a long process of decline (*decadencia*) that had been in train for over three centuries. The highpoint of its history had come in the century after the crucial year of 1492, which began with the completion of the country's seven-century-long 'Reconquest' from the Moors and ended with the arrival in the Americas of Spanish ships under the command of Columbus (*Colón*). During that time it emerged as the first genuinely global power, dominating Europe and controlling vast areas in the Americas. Thereafter, however, it steadily lost political influence while stagnating socially and economically.

The crucial phase came in the nineteenth century, when most of the Western world experienced the great advance into modernity, an advance made possible by the earlier intellectual revolution of the Enlightenment (*Ilustración*). But just as that movement made little impact on Spain, so the country was barely touched by the three phenomena which together brought about modernization – industrialization, liberalism and nationalism.

Where they appeared they tended to be mutually reinforcing, and their non-appearance in Spain was similarly interlinked. The failure to industrialize was both cause and consequence of the weakness of the middle class (*burguesía*), which proved incapable of replacing absolute monarchy (*absolutismo*) with a regime based on the rule of law and individual liberties. The lack of a dynamic middle class also deprived Spain of the key factor in forging a sense of common nationhood as occurred in other European countries. Furthermore, such industrialization as did take place served to accentuate the distinctiveness of two of the country's disparate regions, the Basque Country and Catalonia. In both it triggered off important political forces whose very essence was denial of Spanish nationhood.

The result was that, while for other Western countries economic advance went hand in hand with the acquisition of colonial empires, for Spain the loss of most of its American colonies was matched by domestic stagnation. The liberal movement frittered away what little strength it had in fighting three civil wars against the ultra-traditional Carlist movement (*carlismo*). For half a century from 1820 changes in government occurred typically as the result of a military coup (*pronunciamiento*), of which there were frequent examples. In 1868 one such rising made common cause with widespread popular discontent and turned into the 'Glorious Revolution' that expelled the hapless Queen Isabel II. There followed the period of deepening chaos known variously as the six revolutionary or democratic years (*sexenio revolucionario/democrático*), which culminated in the First Republic (1873–74).

The Republic came about not because most Spaniards had rejected monarchy as an institution, nor due to widespread support for the relatively progressive ideas it embodied, but merely since there was no real alternative at the time. Not surprisingly it proved to be a disaster; at one stage the government was faced by a number of so-called 'cantonalist' revolts that demanded extensive autonomy for individual provinces or districts. Spain, it seemed, was threatened with complete collapse.

At last a further coup restored the monarchy, in the person of Alfonso XII, and put in place a political arrangement known as the Restoration Settlement. Under this, the military was kept out of politics for half a century, but at a high cost. In a caricature of democracy the Liberal and Conservative parties conspired to produce alternation in government (*turno pacífico*). Elections were subject to widespread rigging (*fraude electoral*), of which the main agents were local party bosses (*caciques*).

In 1898 this system was shaken by a graphic demonstration of Spain's international decline. In several engagements lasting a total of only a few hours, the country saw its navy destroyed by a handful of US ships, and lost the remnants of its colonial empire: Cuba, Puerto Rico and the Philippines. This 'disaster' revealed to all with eyes to see, the extent of Spanish backwardness (*atraso*), and provoked much gloomy analysis of the country's condition. But, outside the field of literature, few results were produced by the ill-defined regenerationist movement (*regeneracionismo*).

Spain's non-involvement in the First World War underlined its negligible weight in world affairs. And, the obvious advantages notwithstanding, it actually served to aggravate the country's problems in one respect. For Spain, alone of the major Western countries, did not experience the surge of unifying national feeling which, for better or worse, the war evoked. Instead, it remained deeply split. A tiny, mainly well-off, more or less educated elite had little or nothing in common with the mass of rural poor or the small industrial working class.

Politically the country became ever more sharply divided into what were often referred to as the 'two Spains'. One comprised what we would now call the right, the forces of authority and tradition: the monarchy, the Church and the military, allied with landowners, small farmers and most of the urban middle class. On the left side of the divide was ranged an even more motley collection of industrial workers, landless peasants and urban intellectuals, influenced by ideas that ranged from anarchism through Marxist socialism to liberalism.

After the First World War, control over the country swung between these two mutually irreconcilable forces. First, in 1923, General Miguel Primo de Rivera staged a coup with the tacit blessing of King Alfonso XIII, and imposed a relatively mild form of dictatorship (*dictablanda*). When his support crumbled Primo abruptly abandoned Spain in 1930, to be followed a year later by the King. For the second time in 60 years, Spain became a republic mainly because there was no obvious alternative.

During its five-year life the Second Republic itself underwent regular changes of government. Power was held first by the left, then by the right, during the so-called two black years (*bienio negro*). In February 1936 the combined forces of the left, in the guise of the Popular Front (*Frente Popular*), regained power. Five months later, on 18 July 1936, a military uprising against the elected government plunged the country into civil war. It was an unequal struggle.

The Republic, it is true, could count on considerable support from the worse off, and from the strategically vital industrial regions of Catalonia and the Basque Country. But, crucially, it received little backing from abroad. The main Western democracies, France and the UK, stood idly by; the Soviet Union, after initially providing much-needed logistic aid, abruptly withdrew its support in 1938. The uprising, meanwhile, received considerable supplies of both men and machines from the Fascist powers of Italy and Germany. Together with the support of most of the army – as well as significant sections of the people – this proved decisive, and in 1939 the Republican forces surrendered to the rebel Nationalists (*nacionales*).

0.2 FRANCO'S DICTATORSHIP

By 1939 the victorious rebels' undisputed leader (*Caudillo*) was General Francisco Franco Bahamonde. His personal power was the first key feature of the regime he created. The second was its basis in the traditionalist ideas of the Spanish right, centred on Spain's glorious military past, the Catholic Church and the desirability of strong central authority. It was this traditionalism that distinguished the Franco regime from the fascist ones of Hitler and Mussolini. Nevertheless, its third main characteristic was an important fascist element, reflected in the idea of a distinctive Spanish 'race' and a strong strain of anti-semitism.

That derived from the Falange, the party founded by José Antonio Primo de Rivera, son of the country's ex-dictator, and modelled explicitly on Mussolini's Fascist party. Conveniently for Franco, the Falange's charismatic leader was killed at the outbreak of the Civil War by Republicans, who thus converted a potential rival into a martyr for the Francoist cause. While the war was still in progress Franco forcibly amalgamated the Falange with various other groups to form the National Movement (*Movimiento Nacional*).

As well as a powerful instrument of propaganda and social control, the Falange also provided Franco with an ideological basis for his regime, the notion of so-called organic democracy (*democracia orgánica*). Allegedly this was a purer form of the doctrine than the corrupt liberal democracy of the Western powers, and also more in tune with Spanish traditions. It rejected pluralist party politics and class-based trade unions as the creators of artificial divisions in society.

In line with these ideas the Franco regime outlawed all parties other than the Movement, and required all producers in a given industry, workers, managers and owners alike, to belong to a single trade union (*sindicato vertical*). Like other 'organs' of the Francoist state these were strictly government-controlled. Vigorous efforts were made to stamp out regional culture and identity in the Basque Country and Catalonia. In reality, organic democracy was a cover for an authoritarian and often brutally repressive regime, whose fascist connotations were evident in the name it adopted for its philosophy, National Syndicalism (*Nacionalsindicalismo*) – the parallel with National Socialism was unmistakable.

Franco's closeness to the fascist powers led to Spain's international isolation after their defeat. Most importantly the country was excluded from the American-funded Marshall Plan of economic aid which triggered recovery in the rest of Western Europe. The regime made a virtue of necessity, proclaiming its belief in economic autarky, or self-sufficiency, and itself imposed restrictions on the movement of persons and goods across its frontiers.

In the 1950s isolation was somewhat relaxed. In 1953 a Concordat was signed with the Vatican; later the same year defence agreements were signed by which US military bases were established on Spanish soil. Yet Franco continued to block trade and travel, and even on occasion refused offers of outside economic assistance.

By the middle of the decade this course had proved economically disastrous. The country was near bankrupt and living standards remained perilously low; Spain was classified by the United Nations as a developing country until the 1960s. In these dire straits Franco brought into his government a group of technical experts, mainly lawyers and economists. Most were drawn from the conservative Catholic lay group Opus Dei and were unconnected with the Falange.

These experts (*tecnócratas*), of whom the best known were Laureano López Rodó and Alberto Ullastres, brought about a radical change in policy. Often identified with the 1959 Stabilization Plan (*Plan de Estabilización*), it in fact involved a range of measures adopted during that year and the following one. In essence they allowed foreign trade, tourists and investment into Spain, while allowing out those of its own people unable to find work at home. The result was the prolonged period of economic expansion, lasting up to 1974, which made the word *boom* part of the Spanish language and, allied with continued repression, served to dampen opposition to the regime.

The Franco regime itself also underwent an ideological change in its later stages. Even before the crisis of the 1950s discredited its economic doctrine of self-sufficiency, the defeat of fascism had made National Syndicalism an unhelpful concept with which to be associated. Latterly it was replaced as the regime's official ideology by so-called Catholic Nationalism (*Nacionalcatolicismo*). This lacked the overtly fascist overtones of the earlier concept, but also the more egalitarian and modernizing ideas associated with the Falange. Instead, the regime became identified ever more closely with the most conservative brand of Catholic thinking, which placed a dead hand over artistic innovation and free thought of virtually any kind.

Ironically, Catholic elements became one of the sources of discontent with the regime. The dissent of liberal lay Catholics, and some clergy, was fostered by the debates and decisions of the Second Vatican Council (*Concilio Vaticano II*). Another focus of dissatisfaction was the business community, the more dynamic sections of which were increasingly frustrated by the European Community's refusal to countenance Spanish membership so long as the regime lasted [4.2.1].

More active resistance came from two sources, the first being the industrial workforce. Organized with the help of illegal trade unions [5.2.1.1], strikes proved impossible to prevent and regularly escalated into street clashes with the police. Not infrequently the intervention of the army was necessary before they could be suppressed. The second source of active opposition was the regional nationalism which the regime had signally failed to stamp out. In Catalonia this centred on cultural issues and mainly involved the middle classes. In the Basque Country, however, it not only formed an alliance with the workers' movement and the lower clergy; it also developed an armed wing, ETA.

In fact ETA's main significance was as a catalyst which transformed Basque nationalism into a major political force [3.2.2.1]. Its actions never posed a serious threat to the regime while Franco lived. One, however, did have a significant effect on the prospects of its surviving him. In 1973 an ETA commando blew up the car carrying the first and only man to whom Franco had entrusted the office of prime minister, Admiral Luis Carrero Blanco, and a key element in plans to preserve authoritarian rule after his own death.

In one sense these depended on restoring the monarchy, an institution which commanded the loyalty of most conservative Spaniards, especially the army. Technically, the rightful claimant to the throne was Alfonso XIII's son,

Juan de Borbón, about whose reliability Franco had long harboured well-founded doubts. The dictator had therefore persuaded Juan to entrust him with the upbringing of Juan's son, Prince Juan Carlos de Borbón, whom he groomed carefully to succeed him as head of state. The machinery of government, however, would remain in the hands of loyal Francoists, to be led by Carrero Blanco had he lived. Franco himself seems to have believed that these arrangements would ensure the survival of his regime; famously, he asserted that matters were 'all tied up' (*atado y bien atado*).

0.3 TRANSITION TO DEMOCRACY

Even if Admiral Carrero Blanco had survived it is highly doubtful that this confidence would have been vindicated. Like many a dictator, Franco mistook acquiescence with his repressive regime for full-hearted support, which it had never enjoyed except among a small minority. Yet opposition remained muted by fear of another civil war, by the balm of rising material prosperity and because change appeared impossible while Franco lived. His death released the pressures that had built up during the later years of dictatorship, and which rendered virtually unthinkable a continuation of his regime (*continuismo*).

0.3.1 Pressures for change

In part, pressure for change derived from the economic progress the regime had itself stimulated. The contacts engendered by incoming tourism and temporary emigration in search of work had shown many ordinary Spaniards that, contrary to the regime's assertions, liberal democracy produced considerably higher living standards than the Francoist 'organic' variety [0.2]. To the liberal middle classes, for whom economic conditions were easier, democracy offered the attraction of greater intellectual and artistic freedom. To younger Spaniards in general it promised a more relaxed and enjoyable lifestyle.

Powerful external forces also favoured a move towards democracy. The US government had been greatly alarmed at the Portuguese revolution of 1974 and feared that an attempt to prolong dictatorship might result in Spain's turning Communist. More realistically, business interests in Western Europe were eyeing the Spanish market, to which access would only be possible if democracy were restored. Last but not least, democratic parties in Europe, especially those of the left, provided financial as well as moral support to those working actively for change within Spain.

These were divided, broadly speaking, into two camps. One was made up of individuals who, while working with or for the old regime, had come to accept that some form of meaningful democracy was necessary, even desirable, once Franco was dead. These liberalizers (*aperturistas*) were a disparate, unorganized group whose aims were in a sense negative; while they wished for change, they wished also to keep it within strict bounds.

The genuine opposition, considerably larger in numbers, covered an even wider spectrum of groups and opinions, ranging from revolutionary Maoists and Trotskyists to enlightened businessmen and liberal Catholics [0.2]. Its organized core lay in the umbrella organizations set up by the two historic parties of the Spanish left: the Democratic Council (*Junta Democrática*), headed by the Communist Party, and the Socialist-led Democratic Platform (*Plataforma Democrática*). Their aim was a complete break with the past (*ruptura*).

Exactly what that meant was unclear. Certainly it implied the establishment of a democratic regime in which those who had worked with the former regime should have no part to play. For sections of the opposition, however, it suggested rather more. Some Socialists and Communists, in particular, expected institutional reform to be accompanied by radical social and economic changes involving restrictions on the power of private capital. Such demands were anathema to other supporters of democratization, both inside and outside Spain.

After a lengthy illness Franco finally died on 20 November 1975 (*20-N*). Juan Carlos was immediately sworn in as King, and confirmed in office Carlos Arias Navarro, who had taken over as Prime Minister from Carrero Blanco [0.2]. Arias had the reputation of a timid liberalizer; in the event he proved to be more timid than liberal, taking only minimal steps towards democracy. His speeches consistently indicated an essentially authoritarian attitude that gave heart to reactionary opponents of democracy (*nostálgicos*).

Yet Arias was unwilling or unable to clamp down on pressure for change, as he was urged to do by the small group of diehard Francoists (*búnker*). Despite still being technically banned, opposition became ever more vocal and visible. In 1976 the Democratic Council and Democratic Platform came together in a Joint Platform (*Platajunta*). Even so, the opposition leaders' control over their followers was tenuous. On the streets, mass demonstrations frequently degenerated into clashes with the police. Widespread industrial unrest reflected workers' growing concern at rapidly rising prices, and at the same time served to worsen the economic situation. Events were getting dangerously out of hand.

0.3.2 Adolfo Suárez and political reform

At this crucial juncture, in July 1976, King Juan Carlos and his closest advisers took what proved to be a decisive step. Having encouraged Arias to resign as PM, they used the small room for manoeuvre left to them by Franco's complex arrangements to appoint in his place a high-ranking but relatively unknown Francoist bureaucrat, Adolfo Suárez. Their choice provoked consternation and fury from the opposition. In the event, however, it was to prove an inspired one. Effectively Suárez's appointment marks the true beginning of Spain's transition to democracy (*transición democrática*).

It was precisely Suárez's Francoist past that allowed him to move the situation forward. A former head of the regime's state broadcasting service [5.3.1] and secretary-general of the National Movement [0.2], he had immense knowledge of the operation of the old regime and many of its leading figures. That allowed him to achieve what, on the face of it, seemed impossible; to build a democratic state on Francoist laws and institutions.

The key to this process lay in the Parliament (*Cortes*), whose members (*procuradores*) had all been more or less directly appointed by the regime. Using a mixture of procedural manipulation and covert pressure on individuals, Suárez persuaded the existing Parliament effectively to vote itself out of existence. In 1976 it passed the Political Reform Act (*Ley de Reforma Política*), which provided for democratic elections to a new parliament. On 15 December 1976 the Act was overwhelmingly ratified in a national referendum.

Suárez had already ended the ban on political parties, provided they were formally approved by the government. Over the 1977 Easter holiday he took the decisive step of legalizing the Communists, thus allowing all significant elements of the opposition to contest the coming general election. It was held on 15 June 1977, and was won surprisingly but comfortably by Suárez's own party, the Democratic Centre Union (UCD) [2.2.1].

Yet the Prime Minister lacked an overall parliamentary majority, and so needed the opposition's support to undertake the further change clearly demanded by popular feeling. Moreover, the economic situation was deteriorating alarmingly. In the wake of the 1973 rise in oil prices, inflation was spiralling out of control [6.1.1]. Many workers were using their newfound freedom to strike for large wage rises, thus aggravating matters still further. Their actions increased rumblings from army leaders unhappy at the legalization of the Communists. For all these reasons Suárez was anxious to reach agreement with the left-wing opposition.

It was a desire shared by the Socialist and Communist leaders, Felipe González and Santiago Carrillo respectively, who had been taken aback by the results of the two recent polls. In the referendum their joint call for Spaniards to abstain had been almost completely ignored. Then, at the 1977 election, their parties had proved less popular than one led by a former Francoist. At the same time, they too were concerned that continued industrial unrest might provoke a coup and so rule out any further elections. And the Socialists especially were under pressure from their foreign allies and financial backers, the most important of whom were the German Social Democrats (SPD), to tone down their more extreme demands.

0.3.3 Compromise, disillusion, consolidation

These various pressures on the government and the main opposition leaders produced a willingness on both sides to make concessions in order to achieve agreement. The opposition had already done so in its decision to take part in the 1977 election, and so tacitly accept Suárez's gradualist approach. Now it was the Prime Minister's turn to back down. He abandoned his previous plan to base a new constitution on a report from government lawyers and accepted that it must be the task of the newly elected parliament.

How to draft the constitution was one of a set of agreements reached between government and opposition in 1977, known as the Moncloa Pacts (*Pactos de la Moncloa*). The other main thrust of the Pacts was economic. The opposition leaders committed themselves to ensuring that wage demands from their supporters did not push up inflation: the government promised to take measures against unemployment.

In the event, little or nothing was done to create jobs, so that the opposition – or at least its grassroots supporters – got few direct benefits from the Pacts. The government, on the other hand, gained considerably. The Pacts did much to restore the confidence of international investors in the Spanish economy, contributing crucially to its gradual improvement and to political stability. Furthermore, Suárez and his allies not only retained the largest say in formal, constitutional change, they also achieved their aim of averting broader socio-economic transformation.

In effect, the Moncloa Pacts marked the left's abandonment of the aim of breaking with the past [0.3.1]. Change, it was now clear, was to be restricted to political reform, and even that would proceed in agreement with important elements of the old regime. To cover the extent of these arguably unavoidable concessions, a new term was coined. The transition was now described as a negotiated break with the past (*ruptura pactada*) – which, given the original meaning of '*ruptura*', was a contradiction in terms. The culmination of this process, the greatest success for the spirit of compromise (*consenso*) which characterized this period, was the approval of a democratic Constitution in late 1978. From the point of view of constitutional theory, that step marked the end of the transition.

Yet in another sense the process still had some way to run. Admittedly most Spaniards were unconcerned, even happy, that the notion of radical change in Spain's socio-economic structures had been quietly dropped. But they had expected democracy to make them materially better off – and many had yet to see any such benefits. Nor did the next few years bring any significant improvement in their situation, as the country's economic difficulties continued. In fact these were only partly due to the political upheaval of transition; understandably, however, many people could not or would not see it that way at the time. Their disillusion (*desencanto*) was obvious at the second post-Franco election, held in March 1979, when turnout fell sharply.

Over the next two years such feelings were amplified by a growing sense of political instability. First, despite winning its second election victory, the ruling UCD fell into increasing turmoil and, at New Year 1981, Suárez abruptly and mysteriously resigned [2.2.2]. Then the granting of devolution to the Basque Country and Catalonia sparked off widespread demands for regional autonomy [3.1.2]; these were seized upon by some on the right as proof that Spain was in danger of breaking up. And crucially, the Basque terrorist group ETA stepped up its murderous activities, of which the security forces were by far the principal target [3.2.2.1]. Their understandable, bitter resentment was ripe to be channelled by the military's most reactionary elements.

It was well known that these were considering a coup, to be justified by popular dissatisfaction with democracy and the country's alleged ungovernability. Indeed several times their plans were discovered and foiled when already well advanced. Eventually, though, on 23 February 1981 (*23-F*) civil guards under the command of Lieutenant-Colonel Antonio Tejero Molina stormed the Spanish Parliament during the investiture of Suárez's successor as PM, Leopoldo Calvo Sotelo. For 36 hours they held its members captive, along with journalists and parliament officials. Simultaneously various army units mutinied, led by their officers; in Valencia, General Milans del Bosch ordered tanks onto the streets.

Most sections of the army, however, remained loyal to the constitutional order. Together with the police they brought the revolt under control and released the captives. Although it was some time before all its leaders were identified, the attempted coup was effectively over in a day and a half. Briefly it seemed to confirm all the worst fears that Spanish democracy remained fatally unstable: in the event its effect was to dispel them. For the coup sparked off a massive popular and political reaction. No significant public figure spoke out in its support. Instead, political leaders ranging from the Communists to former Francoist ministers headed public demonstrations in support of the new regime. The largest, in Madrid, brought over a million people onto the streets. Spaniards might have been disillusioned with democracy, but they were virtually unanimous in preferring it to the alternative offered by the military extremists.

The next eighteen months constituted a strange interlude. As his party steadily crumbled [3.2.2] Calvo Sotelo was prevented from taking decisive action to deal with the country's problems. Yet the opposition was reluctant to force him from office for fear of another coup attempt. Finally, however, his position became untenable and a third general election was called. Held on 28 October 1982 (*28-O*) it resulted in an overwhelming victory for the Socialist Party, whose leader, Felipe González, took over the reins of government in an atmosphere of complete normality. For the first time in Spanish history one freely elected government was replaced by another of a different political persuasion without any significant section of society seriously questioning the legitimacy of the change.

0.4 SPAIN IN THE CONTEMPORARY WORLD

As well as by its history, present-day Spain is conditioned by its relations with the outside world. In 1975, thanks to the nature of the Franco regime, these were extremely limited. Since then, however, they have expanded beyond recognition. That was spectacularly symbolized in 1992. During the Quincentenary of the most famous date in Spanish history [0.1], the country hosted three major international events: the Olympic Games (*Juegos Olímpicos*/*JJOO*) were held in Barcelona and the Expo World Fair in Seville, while Madrid reigned as European City of Culture (*Capital Cultural Europea*).

By far the most important of Spain's new links are precisely those with Europe, which are discussed separately in Chapter 4. But those with three other areas of the world also have considerable significance: with the USA, because of its role as dominant world power; with Latin America, for historical and cultural reasons; and with the Mediterranean, because of its geographic proximity.

0.4.1 Spain and the USA

The removal of barriers to the outside world has inevitably meant Spain's growing exposure to the influence of the country that was long the undisputed leader of the Western world, and since the collapse of Communism has been the world's sole superpower. That is a thorny issue in the country, partly because, like France, Spain is the homeland of a great world language whose status is threatened by (American) English. But in the Spanish case other, historical, factors also play a role.

For one thing, the Spanish right contains a deep strand of anti-American feeling quite without parallel in Western Europe. The United States was instrumental in depriving Spain of its last significant colonies [0.1], having actively supported the earlier independence struggles of those on the Latin American mainland. The Franco regime swallowed the resultant resentment, to sign the 1953 Defence Agreements [0.2]. Yet for many Spaniards who shared its traditionalist ideals the sight of their country reduced to the status of a US client merely reinforced the sense of bitterness.

Such attitudes found an echo in the centre-right governments under Adolfo Suárez that steered the transition to democracy following Franco's death [0.3.2]. Suárez made much of the idea that Spain's international role should be that of a bridge between the first (Western) and third (developing) worlds. This position, which amounted to a form of non-alignment (*tercermundismo*), led him on occasion to oppose US policies, especially in Central America. Certainly it seemed to preclude Spanish participation in NATO (*Organización del Tratado del Atlántico Norte/OTAN*), the American-dominated pillar of the Western military alliance.

In this sense Suárez's departure from power was crucial, since virtually the only decisive action taken by his successor, Leopoldo Calvo Sotelo [0.3.3], was to take Spain into the alliance's political structure. This move, taken behind Parliament's back, evoked furious opposition from the left, even more anti-American than the right but for very different reasons: US sustenance of a regime which had backed Hitler and Mussolini, and the impact of the 1968 movement of student unrest which, as elsewhere in Europe, had a strongly anti-US tone. Indeed, a considerable number of those who came to occupy leading positions during and after the transition were involved in, or influenced by, the events of 1968.

Among these were the Prime Minister elected in 1982, Felipe González, and many of his Socialist cabinet colleagues. During the election campaign they had savagely attacked Calvo Sotelo's decision, and supported calls for the removal of US military bases. However, once in power González came up against the realities of international politics. Executing a dramatic change of tack he now called for Spain to remain in the alliance provided certain, rather spurious conditions were met. In March 1986 he fought and won a referendum held to confirm this new position [4.2.2].

The referendum campaign once again brought anti-American feeling strongly to the surface. Thereafter, however, it became much less evident. The issue of the bases was effectively resolved by a formula under which the facilities were handed over to Spanish control but remained available to the American military. During the 1991 Gulf War the revelation that US aircraft *en route* for the combat zone had indeed made use of the bases caused some revival of anti-American feeling. But at the same time Spanish naval units were themselves involved in the conflict, which on balance marked a further step in Spain's integration into the American-led structures of Western defence. In any case, as elsewhere, the end of the Cold War was by then causing a general rethinking of attitudes.

The extent of change was underlined when, in December 1995, Foreign Minister Javier Solana was appointed NATO Secretary-General. Solana's Socialist colleagues portrayed his elevation not as a betrayal but as a feather in the country's, and party's, cap. Polls indicated that most Spaniards shared that view; even the Communist-led left-wing opposition tacitly admitted as much, attacking Solana's appointment as an ill-deserved reward. When, the following year, a new conservative government took Spain officially into NATO's military structure, there was virtually no reaction within the country. And today, while American cultural and political influence continues to evoke adverse reactions, these are on a scale much closer to that elsewhere in Europe than was the case 25 years ago.

0.4.2 Spain and Latin America

A major factor in Spain's complicated relationship with the USA is precisely its own close links with the superpower's own 'backyard', Latin America, which themselves have never been simple. While a shared language and significant elements of culture in common undoubtedly make for genuine feelings of solidarity on both sides, Spain's past role as the colonial power over much of the region has more ambiguous implications.

Some Spaniards at least still like to see their country in the role of motherland (*madre patria*) to its former subjects. But many in Latin America take a much more jaundiced view of the colonial experience, a feeling forcefully expressed at the time of the 1992 celebrations in Spain by members of Latin America's indigenous peoples (*indígenas*). Their protests had an impact in the sense that the concept of the Americas' 'discovery' was replaced by the less emotive one of a 'meeting' between their inhabitants and Europe's.

In comparison with the British version, of course, Spanish colonial domination ended relatively early. Nor was Spain's empire ever a commercial enterprise in the same sense as the UK's. Indeed, its ex-colonies have arguably had greater economic significance for the country since they obtained independence, as a destination for Spanish emigrants. Emigration was particularly marked from Spain's poorer regions; in some parts of the New World all Spaniards are referred to as Galicians. Many Spaniards have family ties in the Americas, and the wealthy returning emigrant (*indiano*) continues to feature strongly in popular consciousness.

Highest at the start of this century, emigration received a fresh boost when restrictions on leaving the country were relaxed after 1960 [0.2]. As well as allowing the Franco regime to export its unemployed, Latin America also provided one of its few sources of foreign support. Most notably, the Argentinean populist dictator Juan Perón provided invaluable food aid during the early 1950s, when famine was a real possibility in Spain. Such support gave some basis to Franco's concept of a Spanish-speaking community (*Hispanidad*), inspired by his own reactionary ideas. But by the 1970s the era of dictatorships was coming to an end in Latin America as well. And, in any case, an impoverished Spain could not begin to compete for real influence in the region with its powerful 'northern neighbour'.

After Spain's return to democratic rule in the 1970s its leaders continued to place considerable importance on links with Latin America, while significantly reassessing their nature. Now Spain came to see itself more as a model for the process of transition from dictatorship to democracy, on which many of its former colonies were now themselves embarking. Support for institutional reform became an important focus of Spanish development aid (*ayuda para el desarrollo*), almost half of which goes to Latin America. Since it joined the European Community in 1986 [4.2.1], Spain has also portrayed itself as the defender of Latin American interests within the EC, arguing in favour of greater financial support and improved trading conditions for the sub-continent.

Successive Spanish governments were aware that this approach had decidedly paternalistic overtones, which they were anxious to play down. In order to foster a sense of more equal cooperation, they promoted a new, and more concrete version of the old Francoist concept of 'community'. Its basis is the Conferences of Iberian American States (*Conferencias Iberoamericanas*), the first of which was held in 1991 at Guadalajara, in Mexico; subsequently they have become regular events. The participants include not only Spain and its former colonies in South and Central America, but also Portugal and Brazil – hence the neologism 'Iberian America' (*Iberoamérica*) – although Spain, as much the larger of the European members, clearly regards itself as the driving force behind the project. Indeed, some of its rulers seem to have seen in the 'Iberian American community' the basis of a distinctive world role for Spain, independent of its European ties, rather as some in the UK still hanker after the notion of the 'English-speaking peoples'.

In practice, though, the new 'community' has developed minimal political weight, not least because of Spain's own increasing commitment to a common European foreign policy [4.2.2]. Moreover, Spain's pretensions to serve as Latin America's advocate on the European stage have turned out to be somewhat hollow. It has done nothing to alter the EU's seeming determination to keep out developing countries' products – its own trade with Latin America remains very limited – and little to loosen restrictions on immigration from the region (other than of suitably talented football players).

In terms of aid, too, Spain's position is less altruistic than appears at first sight. Since its overall aid budget remains very low by European standards, the absolute sums – as opposed to the share – channelled to Latin America by the Spanish International Cooperation Agency (*Agencia Española de Cooperación Internacional/AECI*) are not especially large. Moreover, a high percentage of aid is cultural rather than economic, while almost all the latter is tied, i.e. it must be spent on specific projects, often carried out by Spanish contractors. In 1999, Spain's credibility as a supporter of democratization also took a severe blow when the head of the AECI's Latin American operations was himself dismissed for corruption. For these reasons, Spanish government aid efforts are often criticized by the country's own non-governmental organizations (*organizaciones no gubernamentales/ONGs*), whose international activities are also highly concentrated in Latin America.

Spanish NGOs have also been critical of the attitude taken by successive governments to human rights in Latin America. Ever since the realignment of foreign policy along pro-American lines in the 1980s [0.4.1], this has tended to be relatively cautious. Indeed, Spain has often been markedly more hesitant than some of its new European partners in condemning continuing human rights abuses in the region, most of them committed by right-wing regimes with dubious democratic credentials.

Such caution was accentuated by a desire not to disrupt the Iberian America project by antagonizing the leaders of Spain's partners in it. The only, somewhat ironic exception came in 1996, with the arrival in power of the conservative People's Party. The PP has close links with Cuban exiles opposed to the regime of Fidel Castro, and initially took a hard line against it. However, within two years official condemnations of Castro had died away. Subsequently, the government's reluctance to become involved in human rights issues was underlined by the obvious embarrassment it felt over the attempt by a member of the Spanish judiciary, Baltasár Garzón, to bring the former Chilean dictator General Pinochet to trial in the country.

Spain's refusal to speak out on human rights issues may have helped it maintain good relations with those who hold power in Latin America, but has not helped its standing among the region's population as a whole. Since the mid-1990s a new source of resentment has been added by an astonishing surge in Spanish investment in the region [6.2.1]. Again, there is a gap in perceptions here. For, while in Spain the investment flow tends to be seen as evidence of positive engagement, from Latin America it can look more like a new form of colonialism. Such feelings add an extra edge to industrial disputes in Spanish-owned firms, especially if they involve large-scale redundancies. Some major investors, such as *Telefónica* [6.4.1], have caused further resentment by trying to restrict competition from indigenous firms in their own interests, while the Spanish airline Iberia made itself particularly unpopular by its arbitrary behaviour in Latin American markets.

These sorts of practices hardly support the notion that Spanish capital represents a more sympathetic alternative to the US variety, of which there is still vastly more available. All in all, it is hardly surprising that Latin American governments and their peoples tend to regard Washington, not Madrid, as their principal foreign partner. And meantime most Spaniards have come to see their links with Europe as much more significant than trans-Atlantic ones, albeit these retain considerable emotional force.

0.4.3 Spain and North Africa

The cultural and historical basis for Spain to see itself as a bridge between Europe and Latin America is well known. Rather less so are the similar grounds – to which can be added immediate geographical proximity – for its claim to play a similar role *vis-à-vis* North Africa in general, and Morocco in particular. It is true that the Moorish presence is now a very distant memory in Spain [0.1]. But it is only a quarter of a century since the country withdrew from its last colony on the southern shore of the straits of Gibraltar, and even today a sizeable Spanish-speaking community exists there. Moreover, it still retains as an integral part of its own territory the two enclaves of Ceuta and Melilla [11.18].

Given that historical background, it is hardly surprising that the 'bridge' analogy is just as problematic in this case as in that of Latin America. Perhaps for that reason, once Spain had returned to democracy after the death of General Franco the country's new rulers attempted to subsume relations with North Africa in a broader context. The area was now to be seen as part of the Southern Mediterranean as a whole, whose political and economic development Spain was anxious to encourage. In fact there were some concrete grounds for a broader approach. Not only do a very large part of Spain's massive energy imports come from Algeria and Libya. Given its location, Spain's security is closely bound up with the stability of the Mediterranean as a whole.

Some attempts have been made to give substance to the new approach. In 1991 Madrid hosted the conference that gave rise to the Middle East peace process, having finally established diplomatic relations with Israel in the 1980s, and Spain has subsequently become one of the major donors of aid to the Palestinian territories. It also tried to interest its European Union partners in their southern neighbours, the highpoint of its efforts coming in 1995 when it promoted the first Euro-Mediterranean Conference, in Barcelona, during its presidency of the European Union [4.3.1]. But the dialogue supposedly initiated there has produced only meagre results, and of late Spain's own enthusiasm for it seems to have cooled. Its own links with the Eastern Mediterranean remain very limited, with Turkey its only significant trading partner there. In practice Spain's concerns remain focused on the Maghreb (*Magreb*), the region made up of Libya, Tunisia, Algeria, Mauritania and Morocco, and above all on the last of these countries.

Prior to 1975 relations with Morocco were strained, even though the Franco regime – somewhat bizarrely, given its militant Catholicism and underlying racism [0.2] – made much of its positive links with the Arab world in general. In reality, though, these were based essentially on common hostility towards Israel, which for Morocco was less important than the continuing Spanish presence in Ceuta, Melilla and the much larger territory to Morocco's west, then known as the Spanish Sahara. In 1975, seizing on the power vacuum in Spain as Franco approached death, Morocco's King Hassan II organized the so-called green march (*marcha verde*), a mass civilian incursion into the colony, that effectively brought it under his control. The territory's legal status remains unresolved today, but as an issue affecting Spanish–Moroccan relations it was closed, opening the way to considerable improvements in that field.

Thus Spain has aspired to act as Morocco's advocate (*valedor*) inside the EU, representing its interests in the Union's internal debates. In 1991 the two countries signed a 'Treaty of Friendship, Good Neighbourliness and Cooperation' in the Moroccan capital Rabat (this was intended to provide the model for similar agreements with the other Maghreb countries, but to date only one has been signed, with Tunisia, in 1995). Since then high-level ministerial meetings have been held on a regular basis. Plans to build a rail tunnel under the Straits are well advanced. In 2001, however, relations took a sharp turn for the worse, and at the close of the year the Moroccan authorities abruptly called off the forthcoming joint summit.

There are various causes of such friction. Most obviously, Spain's refusal to countenance withdrawal from Ceuta and Melilla is a constant irritant. When the two cities were given autonomous city status in 1994, confirming their place in Spain's new regionalized structure, relations were severely strained. Another problematic issue is that of access to Morocco's considerable fishing grounds, which are of vital importance to Spain's hard-pressed fishing industry [6.3.1]. The fact that some Moroccan products, especially fruit and vegetables, compete directly with Spanish ones implies a conflict of interests over access to EU markets. But by far the most difficult question is that of illegal immigration.

This is where geography plays a truly crucial role. The sea crossing from Morocco to Tarifa, the closest point on the Spanish side, is a mere 14 kilometres long. Its significance as an escape route from Africa's poverty was greatly increased when, in 1995, Spain signed the Schengen Agreement [4.1.3], which effectively turned the country's shores into the outer border of a large part of the European Union. Since then the numbers of those attempting to cross the Straits – who include a high proportion of Moroccans, but also many other Africans – has risen relentlessly. Another, much smaller flow exists from the African coast to the Canary Islands.

Immigration on any significant scale is not something Spain, traditionally a land of emigrants [0.4.2], is used to. As in most EU countries, it is a politically sensitive issue, and successive governments have attempted to stem the tide. Much of their efforts have been devoted to sealing off the perimeters of Ceuta and Melilla. As a result, more and more would-be immigrants are willing to brave one of the world's most congested sea passages in the tiny, unstable boats known as *pateras*, often paying large sums to unscrupulous traffickers for the purpose.

Every year an unknown number, certainly running into thousands, fail to survive, while many more are rounded up by the Spanish authorities on landing and returned to Morocco – in most cases to try again. Others are detained, in conditions that can be far from satisfactory [10.4.2]. Those who escape that fate, and remain in Spain rather than proceeding to other EU countries, face problems of discrimination and racism, of which Moroccans are the principal target [9.4.5]. Ironically, as more farsighted observers have pointed out, Spain's exceedingly low birth rate means that it is in pressing need of immigrants to supplement its shrinking workforce.

In the mind of the present conservative government, however, the fear of antagonizing the mass of voters appears to be uppermost. Its new Aliens Act (*Ley de Extranjería*), which came into effect in 2001, deliberately attempts to deter immigration by reducing still further the rights of those already in the country illegally. Leaving aside humanitarian and economic considerations, this approach seems unlikely to prove effective in achieving its aims. It also panders to anti-immigrant prejudice, which it is likely to aggravate further. Certainly it runs completely counter to Spain's supposed role of 'bridge' to its closest southern neighbour.

0.5 GLOSSARY

20-N m	20 November 1975 (death of Franco)
23-F m	23 February 1981 (attempted coup)
28-O m	28 October 1982 (election of first Socialist government)
absolutismo m	absolute monarchy, rule
acuerdos para la defensa mpl	1953 defence agreements with USA
adhesión f	accession (to EC)
alzamiento m	uprising (Francoist term for rebellion of 18 July 1936)
aperturista mf	liberalizer (at end of Franco era)
atraso m	backwardness
autarquía f	autarky, policy of economic self-sufficiency
ayuda para el desarrollo f	development aid
bienio negro m	'two black years' of right-wing government, 1934–36
búnker m	diehard Francoists
burguesía f	middle classes, bourgeoisie
cacique m	(corrupt) local party boss
cantonalismo m	cantonalist movement, series of revolts in early 1870s demanding that individual provinces or districts be given extensive powers of self-government
carlismo m	Carlist movement, ultra-traditionalist movement in nineteenth century

Caudillo m	'Leader', title assumed by Franco
clandestino m	illegal immigrant
consenso m	spirit of compromise (characteristic of transition period)
consolidación democrática f	consolidation of democracy
continuismo m	(support for) continuation of Franco regime after 1975
crisis del petróleo f	oil crisis (esp. that of 1973)
decadencia f	decline
democracia orgánica f	'organic democracy', Francoist term for regime philosophy
desencanto m	disillusion (with democracy, esp. *c*. 1978–81)
desmantelamiento m	removal (of US bases)
estraperlo m	black market (during Franco era, esp. 1940s and 1950s)
familias (del régimen) fpl	factions within Franco regime
fraude electoral m	election-rigging, electoral fraud
Frente Popular m	Popular Front (left-wing alliance in 1936 election)
Hispanidad f	Spanish-speaking community (Francoist term)
Hispanoamérica f	Spanish America (Francoist term)
Iberoamérica f	Iberian America, Spanish and Portuguese America
indiano m	(rich) returning emigrant from Latin America
indígena m	indigenous inhabitant; Latin American indian
integración f	integration; entry (into EC)
intentona (golpista) f	attempted coup (esp. that of 23 February 1981)
madre patria f	motherland, Spain seen from Latin America
marcha verde	mass intrusion of Moroccan civilians into former Spanish Sahara in 1975
movida f	Madrid 'scene' of late 1970s and 1980s
Movimiento Nacional m	National Movement, single party of Franco regime
Nacionalcatolicismo m	'Catholic Nationalism', ideology of later Franco regime
nacionales mpl	Francoist forces (in civil war)
Nacionalsindicalismo m	'National Syndicalism', ideology of earlier Franco regime
nostálgico m	reactionary
organización no gubernamental f	non-governmental organization
patera f	small boat (used by illegal immigrants from North Africa)
período transitorio m	transitional period (following Spain's accession to EC)
procurador m	member of Franco's (appointed) 'Parliament'
pronunciamiento m	(nineteenth-century) military revolt
regeneracionismo m	post-1898 regenerationist movement,
Restauración f	Restoration of monarchy (in 1876)
ruptura (democrática) f	clean break with the past (i.e. Franco regime)
ruptura pactada f	negotiated break with the past

sexenio revolucionario/ democrático m	six-year period of upheaval following 1868 Revolution
sindicato vertical m	Francoist government-controlled trade union
tecnócrata mf	technocrat; expert (adviser to Franco regime post-1960)
tejerazo m	attempted coup of 23 February 1981
tercermundismo m	vision of Spain as bridge between first world and third (esp. Latin America); non-alignment
transición democrática f	transition to democracy
turno pacífico m	system of alternation in power based on electoral fraud
valedor m	advocate (e.g. of a country's or countries' interests inside the EU)
vecino del norte m	USA (as seen from Latin America)

1

THE SPANISH STATE

The basis of a country's public life lies in the institutions and mechanisms by which it is governed, the state. The equivalent Spanish term (*estado*) is often used specifically to refer to Spain's own central government as opposed to the country's various regional governments. That distinction is followed here. The present chapter will examine the main central institutions – the monarchy, the Parliament, the political executive made up of the Prime Minister and his cabinet, and the administrative apparatus subordinate to it – leaving regional government to be studied in Chapter 3. Also dealt with in Chapter 1 is local government. Although clearly distinct from the central institutions, it shares with them one essential feature. Unlike the regions, which are the product of an open-ended process of development conditioned by the interplay of political forces over the last two decades, the structures of both central and local government derive from the new Constitution adopted in 1978.

1.1 THE 1978 CONSTITUTION

The Constitution's adoption marked a milestone in Spain's transition to democracy after General Franco's death in 1975, and the document itself was very much a product of that complex and delicate process [0.3]. The original intention of Adolfo Suárez, the Prime Minister who set change decisively in train, was that the basis of Spain's new democracy be drafted by government lawyers. But his hand was forced by the results of the 1977 election [0.3.2], which left him dependent on the goodwill of the opposition forces. And they were quite clear that the task must be undertaken more openly, by the democratic representatives of the Spanish people.

1.1.1 Constituent process

As a result, the newly elected Parliament became a constituent assembly (*cortes constituyentes*), that is, one charged with drawing up a new constitution. The Parliament, in turn, entrusted the bulk of the drafting process to a seven-man, cross-party committee whose members became known collectively as the 'fathers of the Constitution'. The draft they produced in January 1978 was then further debated and amended in both Houses of Parliament. On 31 October an agreed text emerged.

On 6 December 1978 (6-D) this text was submitted to a referendum; it received the support of 88 per cent of those who voted, representing 59 per cent of the total electorate. Only in the Basque Country was the result less clear. There, although just over three-quarters of the votes cast were favourable, the low turnout (49 per cent) meant that these represented only just over a third of the region's electorate. This fact, together with the circumstance that there had been no Basque representation on the drafting committee, was to provide an unfortunate excuse for some to question the legitimacy of the new constitutional order in the region [3.2.2.1].

Formally the constituent process was not completed until some three weeks later, with the King's ratification of the agreed text and its official publication on 29 December. Nevertheless, the date most closely associated with the 1978 Constitution is that of its popular approval, now commemorated by a public holiday, Constitution Day.

1.1.2 Structure, principles, content

The Constitution is divided into 11 parts or 'titles'; the first is an Introductory Title (*Título Preliminar*), while the remaining ten are substantive and denoted by Roman numerals. The areas covered are mainly typical of previous Spanish Constitutions and other similar documents, the main original feature being the specification in Title VII of the principles on which the Spanish economy is to be run.

The titles are themselves subdivided into a total of 169 numbered articles, organized where appropriate into 'chapters' and 'sections'. The major concerns of those who framed the Constitution are apparent in the number of articles devoted to different topics. Well over half of them cover just three areas: basic rights and liberties (46 articles), the role of Parliament (31) and provisions for regional self-government (23).

In addition to the main text the Constitution includes a number of dispositions. The last, or Final Disposition, established the date when the Constitution would take effect. A single Revocatory Disposition (*disposición derogatoria*) revoked the Fundamental Laws of the Franco regime, a series of measures which had effectively acted as its constitution. Nine transitional dispositions (*disposiciones transitorias*) covered questions relating to the introduction of various of the Constitution's provisions.

Of the four additional dispositions, the last three clarify points relating to the age of legal majority (*mayoría de edad*), the special situation of the Canary Islands, and the court system. The first declares that the Constitution 'protects and respects the historic rights' of the Basque provinces and Navarre. This seemingly anodyne statement hinted at the complex issues bequeathed by history in those two regions [3.2.2, 11.15].

Returning to the text itself, the three fundamental principles of the Constitution are set out in Article 1.1. First, Spain is defined as a democracy. This principle is reflected not only in the central role accorded to a Parliament elected by regular popular vote [1.3], but also in provision for various forms of direct participation in the operation of the state (*participación ciudadana*). Such provision, however, is often cautious – for example, half a million signatures are required before a proposed law can be presented to Parliament by a so-called people's initiative (*iniciativa popular*). In other cases, for example, direct participation in the judicial process through the institution of the jury [10.1.2], the necessary detailed legislation has been long delayed.

Secondly, Article 1.1 defines Spain as a state under the rule of law (*estado de derecho*). On the one hand, this principle means that all actions of public authorities are subject to legislation, which in turn must conform to the principles set out in the Constitution itself. On the other, it is reflected in a lengthy catalogue of rights set out in subsequent articles. They include not only basic human freedoms but also other economic and social rights whose protection poses clear problems, most notably the 'right to work' (Article 35).

In such cases the text is regarded by experts as establishing an aspiration; it is seen not as a delimiting constitution (*constitución muro*), freezing the country's institutional development at a particular moment in time, but as an enabling one (*constitución cauce*). Thus, even if the state cannot be forced to provide work, it is considered that the Constitution's provisions would prevent removal of public support for the unemployed. Equally, while discrimination of various types undoubtedly exists, by proscribing it the Constitution allows action to be taken against its overt practice by any social or economic body.

Similar considerations apply to the Constitution's third basic principle, one which has no direct English equivalent. The definition of Spain as a so-called social state (*estado social*) was inspired chiefly by the post-1945 (West) German socio-economic model, known in English as the social market economy. One aspect of Spain's adoption of this model is precisely the inclusion in the Constitution of social rights, such as that to work. The other is explicit constitutional authorization to state institutions of an active role in the country's economic affairs. Most famously, this role includes redistribution of income more fairly, not just between the country's regions [3.1.4], but also between its individual citizens. Here again, the Constitution has been observed more in the breach than the observance.

Nonetheless, the altruism of its basic principles is one reason why the Constitution has acquired an extraordinarily high status for Spaniards, especially those with access to power. The other is that its provisions are usually regarded as having resolved three fundamental conflicts that had split Spanish society for a century and more, relating to the roles of the monarchy [1.2], the Church [5.1.2.1] and the regions [3.1.1]. This perception is undoubtedly distorted. In reality, popular consensus on the first two institutions was the result of various social and political factors, while the regional question remains open even today, albeit much progress has been made [3.3.4].

That is not to say that the Constitution takes no credit for Spain's achievements since 1978. But it does suggest that its true importance lies less in any of its specific provisions than as a symbol of Spaniards' collective will to face the future rather than the past, and to place the highest priority on the concerns of the individual citizen. Precisely in that sense, however, it is worth noting that the text – like most documents of its type – has little or nothing to say on such increasingly crucial areas for the individual as the environment, the media and the activities of major corporations.

1.1.3 Interpretation

The complexity and imprecision of the Constitution's provisions mean that, even more than most legal texts, its meaning must often be officially interpreted. A mechanism for doing so is foreseen in the text itself, Title IX of which provides for creation of a Constitutional Court (*Tribunal Constitucional*). The details of the Court's membership and operation were laid down in legislation passed in 1979. This Act establishes that it shall consist of 12 members, all of whom must be experienced and respected jurists.

Of these, two are appointed by the government of the day, eight elected by Parliament with at least a three-fifths majority, and two named by the governing body of the legal profession [10.1.1]. Like their nine-year term of office this balance was designed to ensure the Court's independence of direct government influence. As in other areas, the efficacy of these legal safeguards has subsequently been called into question by political developments [1.4.1].

The Court, against whose decisions there is no appeal, is empowered to resolve two types of conflict over the Constitution's meaning. First, it adjudicates in disputes between the central government and the other bodies which enjoy legislative powers in Spain – the country's autonomous regions – over which of the two is competent to make law governing particular matters (*conflictos de competencias*). Because of their scope and, in many cases, the sensitive political issues involved, such disputes represent an important aspect of the Court's work, although they constitute only a small percentage of its cases.

The second way in which the Court interprets the Constitution is by deciding whether a particular act passed by the central or regional parliaments, or decree issued by the government, contravenes the Constitution. To this end the Court acts only on the initiative of certain authorized agencies. On the one hand, the central government, regional authorities and groupings of at least 50 members of Parliament may, within three months of a law's coming into effect, request the Court to rule on whether it complies with the Constitution (*recurso de constitucionalidad*). On the other, judges may question the constitutional status of a law applicable to any case with which they are concerned (*cuestión de inconstitucionalidad*).

Since judges may act on behalf of litigants, this second procedure allows members of the public access to the Constitutional Court, albeit indirectly. Direct public access to the Court exists in that all Spaniards may make application to it for protection of certain of the rights and freedoms established by the Constitution, where these have allegedly been infringed by a public authority (*recurso de amparo*). The rights concerned are those contained in Articles 14 to 29, as well as the right of conscientious objection to military service. Application to the Court may be made only once all other forms of legal redress have failed. It is one of the positive signs of genuine public participation that, contrary to many predictions, this type of dispute has made up the vast majority of those coming before the Constitutional Court.

Private citizens, however, have no right to request the Court for a ruling on whether new legislation is or is not constitutional. To do that they must go through the only agency outside government and Parliament to which the Constitution gives such powers, Spain's Ombudsman (*Defensor del Pueblo*). More generally he – as yet there has been no Ombudswoman – is charged with monitoring the activities of all public authorities for possible contraventions of individuals' constitutional rights. In practice he acts in response to complaints; in doing so he has the right to priority assistance from those authorities whose alleged maladministration he chooses to investigate.

The Ombudsman is also required to present periodic reports of his activities to Parliament, by whom he is appointed. While most of the complaints he receives relate to the legal system [10.1.4], one of his most important roles has been in assisting immigrants threatened with expulsion, or subject to abuses by the authorities. However, the present incumbent, former Socialist minister Enrique Múgica, caused considerable controversy when he declined to challenge the restrictive new Aliens Act passed in 2001 [0.4.3].

1.1.4 Amendment

The rules governing amendments (*reformas*) to the Constitution are laid down in Title X. They may be introduced by the same agencies as ordinary legislation [1.3.3]. However, in a reflection of the overriding concern with stability felt by the Constitution's architects, the conditions attached to their passage are extremely strict. In most cases a two-thirds majority is required in both Houses of Parliament. In addition, a referendum must be held should a group comprising a tenth of the membership of either House demand it within 15 days of such parliamentary approval.

However, an even more exacting procedure is set out for any 'fundamental' amendment affecting the text as a whole or its most important provisions: those relating to the role of the monarch and individual rights and liberties, as well as the basic principles set out in the Introductory Title [1.1.2]. Such amendments must first be approved by a two-thirds majority in both Houses, which must then be dissolved immediately and a general election held. The newly elected Parliament must then confirm its predecessor's decision, again with a two-thirds majority in both Houses. Finally, a referendum must ratify Parliament's approval of the amendment.

Hardly surprising, then, that as yet only one attempt at change has been made, in response to obligations acquired by Spain as a member of the

European Union. Given the overwhelming pro-European feelings of the country's political class [4.2.2], the success of that particular amendment, which allows citizens of other EU member states to vote at local elections, is equally unsurprising – and far from indicative, given that there is an even greater barrier to amendment than technical rules.

That is the extraordinary veneration in which the Constitution is held by the Spanish political elite [1.1.2], for whom any proposal for amendment seems akin to heresy. Even where the desirability of change in a major institution has long been generally acknowledged, as is the case of the Senate [1.3], the main parties continue to shy away, not just from agreeing a new constitutional wording but even from the obvious conclusion that an amendment is necessary [3.3.4]. The reason for their hesitancy is just as clear.

Their fear is that reopening the constitutional debate on any fundamental matter would give nationalists, especially in the Basque Country, the chance they have been waiting for, and bring the whole regional issue back to boiling point. The cynical might argue that such reticence is justified in that amendments will, in practice, rarely be needed because the Constitution's imprecision in many areas makes it highly flexible. But that ignores the text's silence on major issues for the twenty-first century [1.1.2], and the resultant need for positive amendment if it is to retain its relevance.

Here, too, there is a cynical response to hand. For, in fact, the main Spanish parties have shown that they are prepared to amend the Constitution by default if it suits them. Compulsory military service is enshrined in the text (Article 30), but was nonetheless abolished by new legislation in 2000. Arguably the same applies to those 'rights' supposedly conferred by the Constitution but which successive governments have ignored in practice [1.1.2]. Such behaviour is clearly at odds with their habitual rhetoric of respect for Spain's supposed fundamental charter (*Magna Carta*).

1.2 THE MONARCHY

The central constitutional role of the monarchy, or Crown as it is called in the text, is apparent from its inclusion among those aspects whose amendment is subject to especially demanding procedures [1.1.4]. The relative ease with which this role was accepted by the traditionally republican left was seen at the time as a key aspect of the consensus achieved during the transition [0.3.2]. Moreover, both then and more recently there has been a tendency to play up the contribution of King Juan Carlos and his closest advisers to the transition's success, not merely in the period up to approval of the 1978 Constitution but also thereafter. It is therefore important to stress that the Constitution also specifies the essentially subordinate nature of the monarch's role – and that the course of events since 1978 has repeatedly borne this out.

Thus, despite being Spain's Head of State, the monarch exercises only negligible powers of initiative in that role. It is true that operation of the state at the highest level depends largely on his signature. It is the monarch that makes senior official appointments, including that of the Prime Minister; laws are issued and justice carried out in his name. However, these, like all his actions, are essentially formal in nature, and require the endorsement (*refrendo*) of another important constitutional figure – the government, its head, or Parliament – from which the actions in practice emanate. Similarly, the monarch's endorsement of their decisions, such as legislation or the appointment of ministers, is a purely formal act.

This is not to say that the monarchy lacks significance, but rather that its importance is not real but symbolic. On one level, the monarch's involvement in key aspects of public life represents the principle of national unity; that the state acts on behalf, and in the common interest, of the Spanish people as a whole. On another, certain specific actions serve to present a particular image of the country both to the outside world and to its own citizens.

It is generally agreed, for instance, that Juan Carlos's official visits abroad (*viajes oficiales*) have been a highly effective form of 'marketing' for Spain. Internally, the deliberately ostentatious exercise of his right to vote has reminded any Spaniards who harboured lingering doubts about democracy that the contemporary monarchy is a pillar of that form of government, not an alternative to it. Perhaps, too, maintenance of a relatively modest lifestyle and royal household (*casa real*) serves to underline the constitutional aspiration to greater equality.

There are two areas in which the monarch's influence might be seen as real. The first is his role in appointing a Prime Minister following a general election. Under normal circumstances the monarch has no discretion in this regard; he calls on the leader of the largest party to form a government and, once they have received the requisite parliamentary vote of confidence, swears them in. It has been argued that after a close election, where no party enjoyed a clear parliamentary majority, the monarch's role could acquire greater importance. However, there is no evidence that this was the case after either the 1993 or the 1996 general elections, neither of which produced a decisive result.

The second way in which the monarch is seen as possibly exercising real influence is through his role as Commander-in-Chief of the Armed Forces (*Mando Supremo de las Fuerzas Armadas*). Here again there is no question of the King's exercising planning or operational control; these functions lie clearly with the appropriate institutions (government and Parliament) and, like others, require only formal endorsement by the Head of State. Nevertheless, it does seem clear that Juan Carlos has been able to exercise a degree of moral authority over military – especially army – officers, thereby preventing their hostility to democracy from spilling over into active opposition, most famously on the night of the 1981 coup attempt [0.3.3].

Yet, in so far as such authority exists, it would appear to derive less from the provisions of the Constitution than from the particular traditions of the Spanish military, and from Juan Carlos's upbringing and experience. After all, there seems little reason why officers suspicious of the constitutional order should feel loyalty to the monarch because of the role he is assigned by that order. More generally, the undoubted esteem enjoyed by the monarchy in Spain today has essentially been earned in political practice rather than bestowed through constitutional theory. To a significant degree it is not so much enthusiasm for monarchy as an institution as respect for Juan Carlos's personal exercise of the monarch's role (*juancarlismo*).

Juan Carlos assumed the throne under very delicate circumstances, not as the legitimate heir but as Franco's nominee [0.2]. Not until 1977, when the new King's father formally renounced his own rights, was the situation regularized. In terms of cementing his popular standing, however, the key event was probably his role in suppressing the 1981 coup [0.3.3]. Since then, he has shown consistent tact and no little political skill in establishing the monarchy as a bulwark of democracy rather than a threat to it.

At the same time, the fact that Juan Carlos and his consort Sofia perform many duties together, as the royal couple (*los reyes*), means that popular respect is not restricted to the King himself. It extends also in some degree to their children, who have been schooled in the same downbeat approach to monarchy. The two eldest are daughters, the Princesses (*Infantas*) Elena and Cristina. The youngest, Prince Felipe, has the title of Prince of Asturias. As the Constitution specifies the primacy of male offspring, he is also heir to the throne (*heredero*).

1.3 PARLIAMENT

Both the monarch and his heir – on coming of age – must swear an oath of loyalty. Its wording expresses the Crown's subordination to the law of the land and, above all, to the Spanish people as a whole. It is they who wield sovereignty under the 1978 Constitution, which ascribes the central role in the state to the body that makes law and represents the common will, Parliament. Indeed, the political form of the state is defined as not just a constitutional but also a 'parliamentary' monarchy (Article 1.3).

1.3.1 Election, structure and composition

The key role of Parliament (*Cortes*) in securing the fundamentally democratic nature of the state [1.1.2] derives from the fact that it is directly elected by the people. This takes place by means of a general election (*elecciones generales*), at which all Spaniards aged 18 and over may vote. The maximum period between elections is set by the Constitution at four years.

The Constitution also states that Parliament shall be organized in the form of two chambers (*Cámaras*), or Houses. The official title of the Lower House (*Cámara Baja*) is the Congress (*Congreso de los Diputados*); its members are deputies (*diputados*). The Upper House (*Cámara Alta*) is known as the Senate (*Senado*), its members being senators (*senadores*). In line with British usage, deputies are sometimes referred to in English as MPs, but strictly speaking the term 'members of parliament' (*parlamentarios*) applies to both Houses in the Spanish case.

As in the UK the term 'Upper House' is misleading, since the Senate has little real power. Its impotence is reflected in the fact that there is no team of government ministers there, as sits in the British House of Lords. Effective parliamentary influence lies almost exclusively with the Lower House. In particular, Congress alone designates the Prime Minister, and hence indirectly the entire cabinet [1.4.4], and can effectively overrule the Senate if the two Houses disagree over proposed legislation [1.3.3].

According to the Constitution, Congress must have between 300 and 400 members; current legislation sets the total at 350. After the 1996 election just over one-fifth of these were women. The constituencies (*circunscripciones*) that the deputies are elected to represent are Spain's 50 provinces; in addition, the North African enclaves of Ceuta and Melilla each elect one deputy.

The numbers of deputies returned by the various provinces are reviewed regularly. They are broadly proportional to the size of a province's electorate, subject to a constitutional minimum of two (currently, though, no province elects fewer than three deputies). This arrangement means that the smaller, rural provinces are significantly over-represented. The most populous province, Madrid, currently elects 34 deputies, roughly one for every 120,000 voters. That is over four times the figure for Soria, the province with the smallest electorate.

Rural over-representation is one reason why the results produced by the Spanish electoral system are less proportional than in any Western country except those which, like the UK, use majority systems in single-member constituencies. The other reasons are the relatively large number of constituencies, most of which return five or fewer deputies, and the requirement for a party to win at least 3 per cent of the votes to gain representation even in the larger provinces. Together these arrangements seriously disadvantage small parties, or at least those which operate throughout the country as opposed to within a particular province or region. As a result, the constitutional requirement that the electoral system for the Congress should 'respect the principle of proportionality' is met only partially, if at all.

However, criticism of the system has focused not on this point, but on the limited ability of voters to influence exactly who represents them, since they can choose only between lists of candidates presented by the competing parties. And, while the number of seats (*escaños*) allocated to a list depends on the number of votes it receives, the particular candidates elected are determined purely by their placing on the list, which is decided by the party. Over the years various proposals have been made to change this system of closed, blocked lists (*listas cerradas y bloqueadas*), by allowing voters either to adjust the order of candidates within a list or to choose candidates from several. But the present arrangement suits the major parties well, and they have had little difficulty in resisting the fairly mild pressure for change.

In any case, experience at elections for the Upper House, which are held concurrently with those to the Congress, suggests that the changes proposed would have little effect. At Senate elections voters may indeed cast their votes for candidates of several parties: in practice they opt overwhelmingly not to do so. In most constituencies, that is in the mainland provinces, voters cast three votes each for the Senate, and the four best-placed candidates are elected. Ceuta and Melilla elect two Senators each, while in the Canaries and Balearics the constituencies are individual islands or groups of islands, each of which returns a single Senator.

This system favours the rural provinces even more clearly than that used for the Congress. However, again debate about its reform has not centred on such bias. Instead it has been concerned mainly with the Senate's constitutionally defined role as a chamber of 'territorial representation'. At present that is achieved through the representatives of the various regional parliaments, which each designate one Senator, plus one more for each complete million of regional population. These indirectly elected Senators – currently there are 48 – are heavily outnumbered by their 208 directly elected colleagues. The question of whether, and how, to redress the balance forms part of wider debates on the Senate's general impotence and the developing relationship between central and regional government in Spain [3.3.4].

1.3.2 Organization and procedure

The internal organization of the two Houses is broadly similar. In each case overall responsibility for the running of day-to-day business and the maintenance of discipline lies with the Speaker of the House (*presidente de la Cámara*). He – up to now there has been no female speaker – is assisted in this task by a presiding committee (*mesa*), which he chairs. It establishes general rules of procedure for the House and the order of business for each day, that is, its agenda. Speaker and committee enjoy the support of legally trained parliamentary clerks (*letrados*).

The speaker is elected by the House as a whole at the beginning of a new parliament (*legislatura*), i.e. after a general election, together with the remaining council members. These are his four deputies (*vicepresidentes*) and four secretaries. As a rule their election is in fact the product of consensus between the main parties, which agree on a share-out of the posts.

These arrangements are typical of those in contemporary Western legislatures. The second internal organ of each House of Parliament is, by contrast, a peculiarly Spanish institution. This is the Standing Council (*Diputación Permanente*), which traditionally acted as a watchdog over the powers of the House while it was not in session. With the increasing unlikelihood of coup attempts, this role seems happily now to be outdated. In practice the Council's main function is to ratify government regulations issued after a parliament has been dissolved.

The *Cortes* differs from the British Parliament in another, more significant way. Both formally and in practice individual elected representatives have even less influence than at Westminster, and political parties correspondingly more. This characteristic reflects a general constitutional recognition of the role of parties [2.1.1]. In terms of parliamentary procedure it is apparent in the formalized role accorded to the parliamentary parties, or groups (*grupos parlamentarios*), made up of all of the House's members belonging to a single political party. These are represented on the Standing Council in proportion to their size. More importantly, it is the groups which elect representatives to the spokespersons' committee (*junta de portavoces*).

This body is chaired by the Speaker, and acts as an interface between the House as a whole and the presiding committee. In particular it enables the latter to take into account the wishes of members in organizing the House's business. The workings of the chairpersons' committee again reflect the importance attached to the parliamentary groups, since the voting power wielded by representatives on it is proportional to the size of their groups.

For these and other reasons the conditions under which such groups may be formed are crucial. In the Congress a minimum of 15 deputies are required, or five if their party obtained at least 5 per cent of the votes cast throughout Spain at the previous general election. In order not to disadvantage regionally based parties, who have, in practice, no hope of satisfying either of these conditions, five members may also form a group provided the lists on which they were elected obtained at least 15 per cent of the votes cast in constituencies where they were presented. In addition, parties may band together to form groups if they so desire. In the Senate the minimum group size is ten, and cross-party groups may be formed by those Senators representing a particular autonomous region, whether directly or indirectly elected [1.3.1].

In both Houses those members who are not in a position to join a party group, or choose not to do so, automatically form part of the Mixed Group (*Grupo Mixto*). This group enjoys the same rights as others but naturally tends to lack the political cohesion to make full use of them. None the less, both individual members of the Mixed Group, and the group as a whole, have on occasion played significant parts in parliamentary life.

In both Congress and Senate the full House (*pleno*) meets to exercise important symbolic functions, such as electing the leader of the largest Congress group as Prime Minister. Plenary sessions are also held regularly for substantive matters. However, most substantive debate takes place in committees of various types. Some standing committees (*comisiones permanentes*) may themselves pass laws. Also important are committees of investigation – known in the Senate as 'special committees' – set up to inquire into particular issues. Joint committees (*comisiones mixtas*) have members drawn from both Houses. In all cases representation on committees is in proportion to the size of parliamentary groups. A verbatim record of proceedings (*diario de sesiones*) is published for all committees, as well as for the Houses themselves.

1.3.3 Legislation

The Spanish Parliament's legislative work encompasses various different types of measure. Of these, only the most common has a direct British equivalent – the Act of Parliament (*ley ordinaria*). Spanish framework acts (*leyes marco*) and foundation acts (*leyes de base*) both set out objectives and principles to guide subsequent detailed legislation. Framework legislation relates to fields in which this latter is the responsibility of autonomous regions. Foundation acts lay down rather more specific guidelines for central government regulations (*decretos legislativos*).

In all these cases, parliamentary approval depends on a simple majority of those voting. However, for legislation dealing with certain issues of outstanding importance such as the status of autonomous regions and the ratification of international treaties, stricter conditions apply. In these cases, which are specified in the Constitution, legislation must receive the approval of a majority of members, not just of those actually voting. The same condition applies to the subsequent amendment or repeal of such entrenched legislation (*leyes orgánicas*).

A further category of legislation consists of the 'royal decree-law' (*real decreto-ley*). Such decrees may be issued by the government to deal with urgent matters, excluding certain fundamental areas such as individuals' rights and liberties and the basic institutions of the state. In this case Parliament's role is restricted to debating the measure within 30 days of its issue and deciding whether to ratify or overturn its provisions.

With the exception of this last case, the procedure followed by the various forms of legislation in their passage through Parliament is similar. Legislation is usually initiated by the government, in which case it is often preceded by a White Paper (*Libro Blanco*) intended for public consultation. It then becomes a draft bill (*anteproyecto de ley*), which is subjected to preliminary scrutiny by the presiding committees of the two Houses. If accepted for debate this becomes a government bill (*proyecto de ley*).

Non-government bills (*proposiciones de ley*) may emanate from a number of sources, including a people's initiative [1.1.2], as well as the various regional parliaments or either House of Parliament. In the last case the initial proposal may come from a parliamentary group or an individual member with the support of 15 colleagues; this latter option provides the nearest equivalent to a British Private Member's Bill.

Non-government bills are subject to several handicaps relative to government ones. They are not permitted to refer to matters requiring entrenched legislation or to tax affairs. Nor can they ever be accorded priority or emergency status. Indeed, any government with an effective majority can prevent their ever being debated, since that depends on their first being accepted by a vote of the full Congress.

Once admitted for debate, bills of both types pass first to the Congress and then to the Senate. Most discussion takes place in the appropriate committee; it in turn generally appoints a working party (*ponencia*) which prepares a report (*dictamen*) for the full committee. The bill, incorporating any amendments in committee, returns to the full House for further debate and possible amendment. In the Upper House the starting-point for this process is the bill as passed, and possibly amended, by the Congress. Senate approval for this text completes the bill's passage through Parliament.

Alternatively, the Senate may introduce amendments of its own or reject the measure in its entirety. In either case the bill is returned to the Congress, which may overturn Senate amendments merely by voting in favour of its original text. Even outright rejection by the Senate has little practical effect, since the Congress may approve its original proposal immediately with the support of a majority of its members; once two months have expired, a majority of those voting suffices. And even this minimal blocking power of the Upper House is reduced to a timespan of 20 days if either the government or the Congress itself declares the legislation concerned to be urgent.

Once a bill has successfully surmounted these various hurdles it is passed to the monarch for his endorsement [1.2]. Having thus become law, the measure – like other state documents – is published in the Official Gazette (*Boletín Oficial del Estado*).

1.3.4 Parliamentary control

Parliament's second main task is to exercise control over the government of the day, that is, to require it to account for its actions. In order to do so, both Houses have the right to demand from the executive any information they consider necessary and to require government members to appear before them. Indeed, parliamentary committees of investigation [1.3.2] may require the appearance of any witnesses they think fit. However, the most frequently used mechanisms are those which allow Parliament to demand a government response to two types of interrogation.

Questions on specific matters (*preguntas*) may be presented only by individual Members of Parliament; they may require an oral reply from a government minister. Interrogative motions (*interpelaciones*) may also be presented by individual members. However, they may in addition be asked by parliamentary groups [1.3.2]; they relate to the general conduct of government and they may result in the presentation, and possible adoption, of a resolution by the House. In these latter respects they are similar to British opposition motions.

In addition to these, and the establishment of investigative committees, Parliament has two further devices by which to exert control over the government of the day. The first is the censure motion (*moción de reprobación*) condemning the actions of a particular government member. Such motions have purely moral force, as the Constitution establishes that Parliament can only require the resignation of the government as a whole, not of individual members.

This restriction also applies to the second device, the motion of no-confidence (*moción de censura*). In addition, and following the German model, such motions must be constructive in nature, that is they must not only condemn the Prime Minister in office but also propose the name of an alternative candidate. Moreover, to be approved they require a majority of all members of the Congress, not just of those deputies actually voting, which they must do in public. Given these restrictions, and the high level of discipline exercised by Spanish parties [2.1.2], the chances of such a motion succeeding are very low indeed.

In fact only two have been presented, neither successfully. In both cases (in 1980 and 1987) the focus of the debate fell on the alternative candidate presented in the motion rather than on the record of the incumbent and his government (to the opposition's advantage on the first occasion but the government's on the second). That was quite proper, given the constitutional provisions, but hardly suggests that the no-confidence motion serves as an effective means of control over the existing government. Indeed, as in most other Western countries, and whatever the Constitution may say about its supremacy, the extent to which the Spanish Parliament can exert such control in practice is extremely limited [1.4.1].

1.4 GOVERNMENT

Under the 1978 Constitution executive power lies with Spain's government, in the narrow sense – that is, the political head of the country's governmental body, made up of the Prime Minister and his cabinet of ministers. Conscious of their country's history, the Constitution's authors had two conflicting concerns about the executive's status. On the one hand, they wished to ensure the government's subordination to Parliament. On the other, they wished to avoid paralysing its power to act. In the event, they were much more successful in achieving the second of these aims than the first.

1.4.1 Pre-eminence of government

Effective domination of Parliament by the government of the day is a cause for growing concern in a number of Western democracies. In Spain, certain features of the state mean that the executive's domination is especially marked. To some extent this pre-eminence can be traced to constitutional and legal arrangements. Thus government bills enjoy a privileged position in the legislative process [1.3.3]. Similarly, stringent conditions attach to the presentation and passage of a parliamentary motion of no-confidence in the executive [1.3.4]. By contrast, a vote of confidence (*moción de confianza*) requested by the Prime Minister himself requires merely the support of a majority of deputies actually voting in order to pass.

However, the fundamental reasons for government pre-eminence have less to do with the Constitution itself than with subsequent developments unforeseen by those who drew it up. One is the arguably lax way in which the constitutional requirement for a proportional electoral system was interpreted [1.3.1]. This has produced not the minority or coalition governments envisaged by the Constitution's architects but a succession of single-party administrations. Moreover, the leading political parties have proved to be considerably more tightly disciplined than expected [2.1.2].

In conjunction, these factors have enabled the government to establish a high degree of influence over Parliament, and also to some extent over the judiciary [10.1.1]. This was especially so during the period 1982–93, when the Socialist Party enjoyed an overall majority. Then Parliament's legislative role effectively became a mere rubber stamp, as the government steam-rollered measures through Parliament irrespective of opposition views (*rodillo*) [2.3.2].

During periods of overall majority, too, Parliament's theoretical powers to scrutinize the government's actions and call it to account for them are largely neutralized, since their exercise depends on the opposition's ability to muster a majority in at least one of the Houses. This applies, for example, to the establishment of committees of investigation, which can be blocked by the government majority. Similarly, censure motions against individual ministers are not only lacking in effective force [1.3.4]; they are also doomed to inevitable defeat and thus risk reinforcing the standing of their target rather than undermining it. During the 1980s, Prime Minister Felipe González made no secret of how little importance he attached to parliamentary control over him and his colleagues; at one stage he attended the Congress only twice in one year.

In the late 1980s the Parliament's manifest loss of power and prestige became a cause for concern about the health of Spanish democracy. In part as a result, the government showed decidedly greater attention at least to the formal aspects of its relations with the legislature. Again, however, this development owed more to political realities than to constitutional theory, in the sense that this period saw the emergence of a more coherent and effective opposition [2.4.2]. Only with the Socialists' loss of their overall majority after 1993 did real changes become apparent, and even then they were limited. One example was the opposition's success in forcing the establishment of a Senate special committee to investigate the government's alleged involvement in counter-terrorism during the 1980s [10.4.2].

However, the success was short-lived, since the committee's work was effectively stymied when the main Catalan regionalist party abruptly resumed its previous support for the government. Ironically, it was another about-face by the same grouping that effectively forced the Socialists from office [2.3.4]. But even then Parliament was not involved. Instead the Prime Minister, aware that he could no longer rely on getting legislation passed, simply exercised his right to dissolve the Houses, as he had done in both 1986 and 1989 in order to hold an election when it best suited him.

The result was another minority administration bolstered by Catalan support [2.4.3], and Parliament continued to have slightly more scope to exercise real control. Towards the end of this period, in 1999, the opposition actually succeeded in forcing important changes to a major piece of government legislation, a new Aliens Act (*Ley de Extranjería*), in parliamentary debate. But, as before, the key factor remained the political tactics of the government's Catalan ally rather than any change in the underlying conditions. At no stage did Parliament manage to channel obvious public concern about corruption and other executive abuses of power; indeed, it barely even attempted to do so. And, since the conservatives achieved an overall majority at the 2000 election [2.4.5], government domination has been as marked as during the 1980s.

1.4.2 Prime Minister

Just as the Spanish executive occupies a pre-eminent position among the country's institutions, so it in turn tends to be dominated by its head, the Prime Minister (*presidente del gobierno*). Since the adoption of the 1978 Constitution, four men have held this post. Of these, Leopoldo Calvo Sotelo (1981–82) faced political problems so great and so numerous as to make him the servant rather than master of events. His predecessor, Adolfo Suárez (1976–81), never exercised full control over his leading colleagues, who seem to have forced his eventual, abrupt resignation [2.2.2]. Yet, at least during his first three years in office, he bestrode the Spanish political scene under far from easy circumstances.

However, it is since the effective consolidation of a new political and party system in 1982 [2.1] that the extent of prime ministerial ascendancy (*presidencialismo*) has become clear. During the long premiership of Felipe González (1982–96) this was sometimes ascribed to his undoubted charisma and enormous personal popularity, which regularly exceeded that of his party [2.3.3]. His successor, José María Aznar (1996–), could not be called charismatic even today, and when first elected his personal ratings in opinion polls lagged behind his party's. Yet not only has that position been reversed with time; the extent of his authority over his government and party colleagues is certainly no less than González's once was, and may even be greater.

As with executive dominance of the state, the reasons for the PM's influence, and its gradual accentuation, derive to a large extent from political factors. In particular, the highly centralized and disciplined nature of Spanish parties, especially when in power [2.1.2], is a key factor. As in other countries the increasingly personalized media coverage of politics in general, and elections in particular, also plays a role. However, the power of the Spanish PM is also due in part to certain provisions of the 1978 Constitution which were specifically designed to prevent his becoming a lame-duck figure, as so often had happened in the country's previous history.

Thus it is the Prime Minister personally who is given the support of a new Parliament in the form of a vote of investiture. Should a change of government occur as the result of a successful no-confidence motion, then the requirement for this to be constructive means that a candidate to the post must be named [1.3.4]. If a PM were to be removed by a failed vote of confidence or a successful motion of no-confidence, then the entire government would have to resign with him. Moreover, although the Constitution dictates that certain matters of major importance must be discussed by the government as a whole, it does not specify any method of decision-making – and it is the Prime Minister who is responsible for presenting the government's view to Parliament or otherwise acting on it.

Above all, certain decisions are effectively taken by the PM alone, subject only to the formal endorsement of the monarch [1.2]. In particular this applies to ministerial appointments [1.4.4]. It applies also to the decision to call a vote of confidence, or to dissolve Parliament and thus force an early general election (*elecciones anticipadas*). Both privileges give the PM an obvious means of control over recalcitrant colleagues and his own political party.

Finally, the PM's power is further bolstered by the support he receives from two institutions. One is the separate ministry encharged with managing his own and the cabinet's business [1.4.5]. The other is his group of political advisers (*gabinete del presidente*). Together with this entourage, the Prime Minister represents a sort of government within the government, often referred to obliquely by the name of his official residence, the Moncloa Palace.

1.4.3 Deputy Prime Minister

Other than in the case of the Prime Minister the Constitution makes no distinction between the members of the cabinet. It does provide for the appointment of one or more Deputy Prime Ministers (*vicepresidentes*). Yet it specifies neither their specific functions, nor the method of their appointment and dismissal, assumed to be the same as for other ministers, that is, at the PM's behest.

During Adolfo Suárez's term of office as PM [2.2.2], his practice of this right tended to confuse the situation still further. Each of his cabinets contained several deputy premiers, none of whom was explicitly charged with deputizing for him under specified circumstances. Nor were they given responsibility for a specific ministry. Instead, they had special coordinating powers in a field covering several ministries (e.g. economic affairs, the military).

On his election in 1982 Felipe González appointed Alfonso Guerra his sole deputy. The following year the Central Government Structure Act [1.5.2] gave legal definition to the role of Deputy PM. As would be expected from the title, its functions were stated to consist essentially of assuming the PM's responsibilities should he die, be indisposed through illness or leave the country. These provisions formalized the Deputy PM's primacy over ordinary ministers in such special circumstances. The 1983 Act further strengthened his position by specifying that he, like the PM, was automatically a member of all cabinet committees [1.4.4].

During Felipe González's fourteen years as PM [1.4.2] the Deputy's post was also distinguished from his cabinet colleagues by having no specific subject responsibility. This arrangement reflected the special relationship between González and Alfonso Guerra, and the latter's key political role in coordinating the government's activities with those of the ruling Socialist Party [2.3.3]. When Guerra was forced to resign [2.3.4], to be replaced in his government post by the less influential Narcís Serra, the deputy PM's role again lost definition. Indeed, once Serra too had to resign it remained unfilled during González's final year in power.

When José María Aznar took office in 1996 he reverted to the early González practice, appointing Francisco Álvarez Cascos, the secretary-general of his conservative People's Party, as Deputy PM. However, his situation differed from that of Guerra in that he was also given ministerial responsibility for the Prime Minister's Office [1.4.5], arguably strengthening even further the party–government link. Aznar also returned to the practice of appointing a second deputy, Rodrigo Rato, who was however also given charge of a powerful joint Economics and Finance Ministry.

On being re-elected in 2000 Aznar retained the same basic model, but with minor changes. On the one hand, Finance was removed from Rato's portfolio, reducing his responsibilities and making them closer to those of a normal minister. On the other, Alvarez Cascos was replaced in both his government posts by the PP's election strategist, Mariano Rajoy. However, the following year Rajoy was moved from the PM's Office to the Interior Ministry while remaining Deputy PM, once more breaking the connection between the two jobs.

1.4.4 Cabinet

The 1978 Constitution allows for the government to include members other than ministers. However, the mechanism for doing so has never received the necessary definition through legislation, and thus does not as yet exist in practice. As a result the government, in the strict constitutional sense, consists of the cabinet (consejo de ministros). Important parts of its work are carried out in cabinet committees (comisiones delegadas del gobierno), of which the Prime Minister and his Deputy are automatically members.

In effect, the Prime Minister makes cabinet appointments and dismisses ministers, although officially this is done by the monarch on his recommendation. Indeed, ministers are clearly subordinate to the PM, since their position is totally dependent on his [1.4.2]. On the other hand, they are relatively immune from parliamentary pressure, as they cannot be forced to resign by a censure motion [1.3.4].

Ministers are not necessarily members of Parliament, although they have the right to appear before both Houses, and the obligation to do so if required. Nor are they necessarily members of the party in power; successive governments have included non-party 'independents', although typically these have subsequently entered Parliament attached to a party list. Another difference from UK custom is the absence of a ministerial team in the Upper House, a reflection of the Senate's powerlessness [1.3.1].

Technically, a change of government is considered to have taken place in the event of a general election, the replacement of an incumbent Prime Minister, or a cabinet reshuffle (crisis de gobierno). According to that definition there were 26 governments between Franco's death in 1975 and 2002, four of them appointed prior to approval of the 1978 Constitution. Thereafter Adolfo Suárez presided over four cabinets in little over two years, Leopoldo Calvo Sotelo five in one and a half, figures which reflect the political uncertainty of the time.

By contrast, Felipe González headed only 11 different teams during his 13 years in office; his first alone lasted over two and a half years. Latterly, however, González's cabinets too became more short-lived, largely due to the frequent ministerial resignations caused by allegations of political impropriety or corruption [2.3.4]. José María Aznar's first cabinet marked a return to stability, surviving unchanged as it did for over three years. Indeed, in his over six years in power to date (2002) Aznar has presided over just four different teams.

The Suárez governments of 1979–81 had between 22 and 24 members. This relatively large and unwieldy size reflected his need to balance factions and interests within his party at a time of major political change [2.2.2]. Under González cabinets were slightly smaller, with between 16 and 19 members. In his successful 1996 election campaign Aznar made much of his intention to cut alleged waste at all levels of government, and ostentatiously appointed a 15-member cabinet. But this was universally recognized to be a purely token gesture, and his fourth team, appointed in 2001, contained 17 members.

As in most Western countries these cabinets have been overwhelmingly male, especially during the transition period. Not until 1981 was a woman appointed to cabinet office, when Soledad Becerril became Arts Minister. After González's election the following year there was a six-year period of all-male cabinets, broken by the appointment of Rosa Conde as Government Spokesperson with ministerial rank [1.4.5]. Only in 1990 was a woman again entrusted with a subject portfolio.

During the remainder of the Socialists' time in power, cabinets included either two or three women, although their ministries were all relatively low-ranking ones. Aznar's first cabinet following his 1996 victory included four women, one of whom was given the relatively high-ranking Justice portfolio. But his fourth, appointed five years later, contained one fewer, again in middle- to lower-status portfolios. Admittedly, though, one of his female ex-ministers, Loyola de Palacio, had gone on to arguably higher things: the post of European Commissioner [4.3.1].

Finally in this section mention should be made of the 'Council of State', a body roughly equivalent to the British Privy Council. Councillors of state (*consejeros*) are senior figures from local, regional and central government together with representatives of such bodies as professional associations [5.4] and universities. They are either appointed by official decree – in practice by the cabinet itself – or are members ex-officio (*consejeros natos*), i.e. by virtue of the post they hold (e.g. director of the Spanish Royal Academy, or attorney-general [10.1.2]). Their remit is to provide ministers with expert advice, in particular as to whether their proposed actions are compatible with the Constitution and other legislation.

1.4.5 Ministries

Within the cabinet, each minister – except the PM and, at times, his Deputy [1.4.3] – is charged with responsibility for a particular portfolio (*cartera*), or area of policy, and heads the corresponding ministry. There is constitutional provision for the appointment of ministers without portfolio but it has not been used since the 1970s. The Constitution also requires the government to obtain

Table 1.1 Cabinet composition, 1979–2001: cabinet formed 6 April 1979 (first after 1978 Constitution)

Cartera	Portfolio
Vicepresidente primero/Seguridad y Defensa Nacionales	First Deputy PM/National Security and Defence
Vicepresidente segundo/Asuntos Económicos	Second Deputy PM/Economic Affairs
Asuntos Exteriores	Foreign Affairs
Defensa	Defence
Interior	Home Affairs
Hacienda	Finance
Trabajo	Employment
Relaciones con la CEE	Relations with the EEC
Industria	Industry
Educación y Ciencia	Education and Science
Administración Territorial	Local and Regional Government
Cultura	Arts
Justicia	Justice
Sanidad y Seguridad Social	Health and Social Security
Obras Públicas y Urbanismo	Public Works and Town Planning
Transportes y Comunicaciones	Transport and Communications
Agricultura	Agriculture
Comercio	Trade
Economía	Economy
Investigación y Universidades	Research and Universities
Presidencia	Prime Minister's Office
Relaciones con las Cortes	Relations with Parliament
Adjunto al presidente (sin cartera)	PM's personal adviser (without portfolio)

Notes: Order of portfolios as given by government sources; generally assumed to indicate status within the cabinet.
Prime Minister = Adolfo Suárez. Total membership including Prime Minister = 24 (no women).

Parliament's approval before making changes to the number of ministers or the distribution of their responsibilities. This injunction, however, has been repeatedly ignored in the frequent restructuring of ministries since 1978.

Spanish ministries are frequently referred to merely by the name of their portfolio (e.g. *Agricultura* for the Agriculture Ministry). In addition, the Foreign Office (*Asuntos Exteriores/AA EE*) is sometimes known by the official residence of its minister, the Holy Cross Palace (*Palacio de Santa Cruz*). It has existed as a separate ministry throughout the constitutional era. By contrast there have not always been direct Spanish equivalents to the other two great departments of state in British terms: the Home Office and the Treasury (see Tables 1.1–1.3).

In the case of the Home Office or Interior Ministry (*M. de Interior*) this was true only during Felipe González's last two governments in 1994–96, in which it was combined with the Justice Ministry [10.1.2]. Given the special

Table 1.2 Cabinet composition, 1979–2001: cabinet formed 5 May 1994 (final González cabinet)

Cartera	Portfolio
Vicepresidente	Deputy PM
Asuntos Exteriores	Foreign Affairs
Justicia e Interior	Justice and Home Affairs
Defensa	Defence
Economía y Hacienda	Economics and Finance
Obras Públicas, Transportes y Medio Ambiente	Public Works, Transport and Environment
Educación y Ciencia	Education and Science
Trabajo y Seguridad Social	Employment and Social Security
Industria y Energía	Industry and Energy
Agricultura, Pesca y Alimentación	Agriculture, Fisheries and Food
Administraciones Públicas	Public Administration
Presidencia	Prime Minister's Office
*Cultura	Arts
*Sanidad y Consumo	Health and Consumer Affairs
*Asuntos Sociales	Social Affairs
Comercio y Turismo	Trade and Tourism

Notes: Order of portfolios as given by government sources; generally assumed to indicate status within the cabinet.
Prime Minister = Felipe González. Total membership including Prime Minister = 17 (3 women).
* = portfolio held by a woman.

nature of the Justice portfolio this amalgamation was highly controversial, especially coming at a time when senior Interior Ministry officials had themselves been indicted for involvement in covert anti-terrorist operations [10.4.2]. The motivation seems to have been political – a desire to give a high profile to the Justice Minister Juan Alberto Belloch, one of the few cabinet members untainted by corruption allegations [2.3.4].

Similar considerations played a role in an earlier amalgamation. Up to 1982 the portfolios of Economy (*Economía*) and Finance (*Hacienda*) had been kept separate, as is common practice in a number of Western countries but not in the UK, where the Chancellor of the Exchequer has responsibility for both. However, when Felipe González came to power that year he wished to deploy his party's leading financial expert, Miguel Boyer, to best effect. He accordingly merged the two, and made Boyer a 'super-minister' in charge of the new, joint ministry.

This arrangement was maintained when Boyer was replaced by Carlos Solchaga, and later Pedro Solbes. Under them the joint ministry routinely decided on and implemented economic policy without reference to either Parliament or the cabinet as a whole. In effect it became one of the very few competing power bases to that of Felipe González as PM. On replacing González in 1996, José María Aznar placed one of his chief lieutenants, Rodrigo Rato, in the role. But once his political hand and personal prestige

Table 1.3 Cabinet composition, 1979–2001: cabinet formed January 2001 (fourth Aznar cabinet)

Cartera	Portfolio
Presidencia	PM's Office
Vicepresidente/Interior	Deputy PM/Home Affairs
Vicepresidente/Economía	Deputy PM/Economics
Asuntos Exteriores	Foreign Affairs
Justicia	Justice
Defensa	Defence
Hacienda	Finance
Fomento	Development
*Educación, Cultura y Deportes	Education, Culture and Sport
Trabajo y Asuntos Sociales	Employment and Social Affairs
*Ciencia y Tecnología	Science and Technology
Agricultura, Pesca y Alimentación	Agriculture, Fisheries and Food
Administraciones Públicas	Public Administration
*Sanidad y Consumo	Health and Consumer Affairs
Medio Ambiente	Environment
Portavoz	Government Spokesperson

Notes: Order of portfolios as given by government sources; generally assumed to indicate status within the cabinet. Placing the PM's Office above the two Deputies seems to indicate a new stress on proximity to the PM.
Prime Minister = José María Aznar. Total membership including Prime Minister = 17 (3 women).
* = portfolio held by a woman.

was enhanced by re-election in 2000 Aznar once again separated the posts, so that the equivalent of the British Treasury's functions are again split between two Spanish ministries.

In other cases, changing political circumstances have given rise to alterations in the titles and responsibilities of individual ministries. Thus Suárez's first, pre-constitutional government included ministers for each of the armed services, posts which have not figured in any cabinet since 1977. Between 1979 and 1986 all cabinets included a Minister of Local and Regional Government (*Ministro de Administración Territorial*), responsible for the delicate process of devolving power to the regions. With the process complete, the title was changed to Minister of Public Administration (*Ministro para las Administraciones Públicas*).

More recently, the term 'environment' has come to figure in ministry titles [6.3.1]. Initially it was appended to the title of what had originally been the Ministry of Public Works (*Ministerio de Obras Públicas/MOP*) before adding first Town Planning (*Urbanismo*) and then Transport to its name. In 1996 Aznar finally set up a separate Environment Ministry. The remaining functions were given to a new Development portfolio (*Fomento*), a title with distinctly Francoist overtones.

The other major change in the structure of responsibilities took place in 1980. In that year the vast Health and Social Security Ministry set up in 1977 was divided into two smaller, more manageable units – Health and Consumer Affairs (*Sanidad y Consumo*) and Employment and Social Security (*Trabajo y Seguridad Social*). Interestingly, this split foreshadowed that which took place in the UK some years later.

Especially worthy of note from a British perspective are two other ministerial portfolios, neither of which has a UK equivalent and both of which have come and gone from Spanish cabinets since 1975. The first, traditional in Spain, is the Prime Minister's Office (*Ministerio de la Presidencia*). In 1986 it was absorbed by González into a Public Administration super-ministry. However, five years later the PM's long-standing partnership with his Deputy Alfonso Guerra broke up in acrimony [1.4.3], and González was faced with the problem of building new connections between the government and his Socialist Party that bypassed Guerra's remaining power base there. His solution was to re-establish the PM's Office as a separate Ministry with an enhanced, more political role.

The Office's official remit is for protocol and the premier's personal security, although it had always had an additional importance because of the direct access to the PM enjoyed by its Head (*Ministro de la Presidencia*). In the late 1980s, however, he became an increasingly influential political figure, with responsibility for the PM's schedule of appointments, the arrangement of cabinet business and, in the role of government secretary, the recording of its deliberations and decisions.

Under Aznar the Office's status and importance were further enhanced by giving its Head the rank of Deputy PM [1.4.3]. In 2001, circumstances dictated the end of this arrangement [2.4.5]. Yet the new Head was one of the PM's closest political confidantes. And in official lists of government members he now tends to appear first, above even the two current Deputy PMs, a clear indication of how crucial the job has become.

The other Spanish cabinet post which appears rather odd to British eyes is that of Government Spokesperson (*Portavoz del Gobierno*). The portfolio was first given ministerial rank by González in 1985, initially in conjunction with that of Arts (*Cultura*), before acquiring its own ministry three years later. The move represented an unusually overt recognition of the importance of media management in modern politics; it was surely no coincidence that the post's first incumbent was the only woman cabinet minister between 1981 and 1990. Between 1992 and 2000 its responsibilities were incorporated into the PM's Office, a reflection of the latter's new political role. However, in 2000 Aznar again created a separate Spokesperson's Office (*Ministerio del Portavoz del Gobierno*) – rather ironically given that he had previously made a virtue of keeping cabinet size to a minimum [1.4.4].

1.5 ADMINISTRATION

Clearly running a modern country involves much more than the passage of laws or the operation of the cabinet. Below this top level of government there is necessarily a much larger apparatus, responsible for detailed implementation of policy and day-to-day administration. This is the task of Spain's public service (*función pública*) and its staff (*funcionariado*), a concept which extends well beyond that of the British civil service to include not only administrators in local government and quasi-governmental agencies but non-administrative public employees, such as teachers.

1.5.1 Franco's legacy

The first thing to note about this machinery is that, unlike the uppermost echelons of public life, its structure and personnel were relatively unaffected by the transition after Franco's death in 1975. To a large extent this was inevitable. After 1975 not only was there an overwhelming desire to avoid opening old wounds. Under Franco the state machinery had simply become too large and too complex to allow the sort of wholesale purge of public administration typical of previous regime changes in Spain; it would have brought the country to a standstill. Yet, while it may have been desirable for that reason alone, relative continuity within the public service has undoubtedly had serious implications for administration in contemporary Spain.

One was the extraordinarily complex arrangements which had grown up in a number of areas of government activity. Their most obvious symptom was the typically Spanish phenomenon of innumerable public counters (*ventanillas*), each with its narrowly defined area of business and idiosyncratic, often apparently arbitrary, opening hours. Another was the complex and outdated career structures of public servants (*funcionarios*), based on a series of corps which bore little relation to contemporary needs.

Moreover, the public service as a whole was imbued with attitudes typical of an authoritarian state, which were often inappropriate for dealing with citizens enjoying constitutionally guaranteed rights. Thus the lack of public scrutiny under the Franco regime encouraged practices such as the filling of jobs on the basis of contacts rather than merit (*enchufismo*) and influence-peddling (*tráfico de influencias*), that is, the allocation of lucrative public works contracts in return for money and favours. The succession of corruption scandals in the late 1980s was in part a reflection of how hard such habits die.

Most important of all, during the Franco era leading regime figures moved back and forward between the cabinet and the upper echelons of the administration. Furthermore, in both cases they were not merely permitted but obliged to join the governing party, and were equally subject to summary removal at Franco's behest. As a result a distinction which is basic to any democratic system, that between the government of the day and the permanent administration, was lost almost entirely. The situation today is, of course, very different, in that political posts are now subject to election. But some traces of it remain, in the system whereby senior administrators (*altos cargos*) are political appointees (*cargos políticos*), and often career politicians.

It should be stressed that this practice is not peculiar to Spain. On the contrary, in many democracies it is deliberately used to ensure an adequate link between two apparatuses that can otherwise become undesirably separated. Without it, many would argue, government policy which reflects the democratically expressed will of the people may simply be blocked by a reluctant civil service. But in Spain, not only does the system serve to conserve attitudes from the pre-democratic era. It further concentrates power in the hands of the cabinet and its head [1.4.1]. And it is also unusually widespread, extending to quangos [1.5.3], non-government agencies with constitutional status, such as the governing bodies of the judiciary [10.1.1] and the public television service [5.3.1], as well as administration at central, regional and even local level.

1.5.2 Civil service

The broad Spanish equivalent to what in the UK is known as the civil service – that is, the administrative apparatus of central government – is known as the central administration (*Administración General del Estado/AGE*). Other than at the highest levels it is staffed by career civil servants (*funcionarios de carrera*), appointed initially by competitive public examination (*oposición*). Subsequent promotion tends to be based on a points system, in which seniority plays a role but so also do other factors, such as in-service training.

The service's senior ranks, however, tend to be filled by political appointees [1.5.1] (and also to have potentially misleading titles for English-speakers). Their current structure was broadly laid down by the 1983 Central Government Structure Act (*Ley de Organización de la Administración Central del Estado/LOAE*), which brought together and consolidated a number of piecemeal changes introduced in the early 1980s. In particular, the LOAE introduced two new senior grades of administrator.

The higher of the two, containing the most senior non-cabinet posts, is that of Secretary of State (*secretario de estado*). It exists only in the larger ministries, and its role corresponds broadly to that of a British junior minister. That is, Secretaries of State may attend cabinet meetings but only to provide information, not to participate in discussion. That is a privilege denied to the other new grade, that of general secretary (*secretario general*), which also exists only in certain ministries. Holders of both types of post head sections of a ministry (*secretarías*), and have responsibility for a particular policy area or areas.

Intermediate between these two grades in seniority is another also filled by political appointees. Unlike the two grades created by the LOAE, however, that of Under-Secretary of State (*subsecretario de estado*) is a long-standing feature of the Spanish public service. While the post may carry responsibility for a policy area within a ministry, it has others which give it particular importance. One is the internal running of the ministry concerned, including personnel, financial and legal matters.

However, the crucial point is that it is in the interministerial Under-Secretaries' Committee (*Comisión General de Subsecretarios*) that two key types of decision are taken. The first is the allocation of budgets to the various ministries. The second is preparation of the cabinet agenda, which in practice means effectively predetermining its decisions on all but the most politically sensitive of issues. As a result, Under-Secretaries play a crucial role both in translating a ministry's projects into government action and in securing the financial means to implement them. In those ministries where the post has been abolished, the responsibilities have been assumed by a Secretary of State.

In addition to these political appointees at the head of the ministries' administrative structures (*organigramas*), all ministers, including the Prime Minister and his Deputy, have a private staff of political advisers (*gabinete*). As in the UK, these provide their masters with strategic and political advice on the work of the Ministry as a whole, rather than on particular subject fields. Unlike the British case, they are technically civil servants, the office's Director having the grade of Secretary of State.

Below these various tiers of political appointees begins the administrative structure proper. Its highest grade is that of director-general (*director general*). Such posts have tended to grow in numbers and importance in recent years with the expansion of government activity in the 1980s. They carry responsibility for a directorate-general, a particular section or sub-section of the ministry's organization. By contrast, the grade of professional general secretary (*secretario general técnico*) has declined in importance, even though every ministry continues to have at least one such post. Its task is to provide advice and support across the whole range of a ministry's responsibilities, a function now largely usurped by the minister's political advisers.

As in other countries, the so-called central administration is by no means exclusively located in the capital city; virtually all ministries need local and provincial branch offices to deliver their services. This outlying administration (*administración periférica*) expanded enormously during the Franco era. On the one hand, government activity as a whole grew considerably: on the other, local government was placed under strict central control. The key institution of what had become a very large and highly centralized apparatus was the provincial civil authority (*Gobierno Civil*) – whose name derives from the existence of a parallel military structure, also based on the provinces [5.1.1.1].

With the transition to democracy, some of the outlying administration's responsibilities were handed over to democratic local authorities [1.6]; more were later transferred to the new autonomous regions as a result of devolution [3.1.3]. In 1983, the LOAE gave the civil authority overall responsibility for all remaining central government functions within its province. This arrangement was a constant cause of friction with regionalists, especially in the Basque Country and Catalonia, for whom it smacked of a continuing desire for centralization.

Meanwhile, the Constitution and subsequent devolution had given rise to a new arm of outlying administration in the shape of the central government representative (*delegado del gobierno*) in each region. His or her official role is to represent the state at official events in the region. Informally, he or she also acts as a channel of communication between central and regional governments, a function that is particularly significant in those regions where regionalist parties are strong, notably Catalonia and the Basque Country. Additionally, representatives were intended to coordinate the work of the various governors within their region.

This situation gave rise to obvious problems, and in the single-province regions the two posts were soon effectively combined. In 1997 the new conservative government went a step further. Under the Civil Service Organization and Operation Act (*Ley de Organización y Funcionamiento de la Administración General del Estado/LOFAGE*) the post of civil governor (*Gobernador Civil*) was abolished. Its functions were transferred to new assistant representatives located in each province where there was no representative proper (*subdelegados*), and on each of the smaller Balearic and Canary islands (*directores insulares*).

This change was in line with the LOFAGE's main aims, which were to reduce the amount of administrative duplication and overlap [3.3.1] and to give Spaniards easier access to public authorities in general. From it has developed the idea of a local one-stop centre (*ventanilla única*) through which all individuals' administrative problems can be handled, irrespective of the authority – central, regional or local – which is responsible for the matter. The scheme depends on the government reaching agreements with individual authorities, and there progress has been patchy. So far nine of the seventeen regions have come aboard, but in the strongly nationalist Basque province of Guipúzcoa only one municipal council has done so. The LOFAGE also restricts certain civil service grades to career administrators – but by doing so, also implicitly institutionalizes the practice of political appointments.

1.5.3 Central government agencies

In addition to the civil service proper, Spain's central administration can also be regarded as including those bodies which are attached to ministries without forming part of their structure. What these quangos have in common is that appointments to their governing bodies are made by the Madrid government, and so are susceptible to political criteria. They are numerous and have widely varying natures and functions.

Thus the quangos include the Royal Academies of the arts and sciences, as well as the Cervantes Institute, charged with promoting the Spanish language world-wide. The Higher Council for Scientific Research (*Consejo Superior de Investigación Científica/CSIC*) is meant to encourage and oversee research activity, a task in which it has enjoyed strictly limited success [8.2.1.2]. Of particular importance are those operating in the spheres of business and economics. These include relatively new regulatory authorities, such as the National Stock Exchange Commission (*Comisión Nacional de Mercados de Valores/CNMV*) and the Competition Commission (*Tribunal de Defensa de la Competencia/TDC*) as well as longer-established bodies such as the Audit Commission (*Tribunal de Cuentas*).

Some quangos operate in fields where in other countries the initiative is taken not by the state but by civil society. Examples are the National Youth Bureau [9.4.2] and National Women's Bureau [9.4.3]. Others control very considerable budgets, including the procurement agencies (*Juntas de Compras*) attached to various ministries. A number of quangos have been involved in the influence-peddling scandals of recent decades, including the national railway board, RENFE, and the agency responsible for producing the Official Gazette [1.3.3].

Of particular interest are the Constitutional Studies Centre (*Centro de Estudios Constitucionales/CEC*) and the Social Research Centre (*Centro de Investigaciones Sociológicas/CIS*). Both of these are attached directly to the Prime Minister's Office [1.4.5]. As a result, the very heart of government's political machinery enjoys privileged access to sensitive information which has been assembled with public money, in particular the results of regular opinion polls carried out by the CIS. This situation has given rise to justified concern.

1.6 LOCAL GOVERNMENT

In Spanish, local government is often referred to as 'local administration'. This usage reflects the conditions of the Franco regime, under which local government effectively became part of the central government's outlying administration [1.5.2]. Its role was to impose central decisions locally rather than to allow local responses to local issues, far less democratic ones. Further back in time, however, Spain enjoyed a tradition of relatively independent local government, a tradition re-established by the 1978 Constitution and confirmed by the holding of democratic local elections in 1979.

1.6.1 Municipalities

The Spanish local government unit with the longest tradition is also the smallest: the municipality (*municipio*). The country's municipalities vary widely in size and nature, from the largest cities, through medium-sized towns down to single villages or rural areas containing various hamlets. They are run by municipal councils (*ayuntamientos*). Councillors (*concejales*) are elected at four-yearly municipal elections held on a single day for the whole of Spain, coinciding with those for most of the autonomous regions [3.1.3]. As in parliamentary polls, electors vote for a list of candidates [1.3.1].

The mayor (*alcalde*) is not a mere figurehead as in the UK, but the council's leader. He is formally elected by the councillors; in practice the post is almost always filled by the candidate on the list receiving most votes. In the largest authorities the mayor normally works closely with one or more deputy mayors (*tenientes de alcalde*), and with a team of senior councillors (*equipo de gobierno*). Within this, individual councillors have responsibility for the different departments (*áreas*) into which the council's administrative structure is divided. They are referred to by the name of the department concerned (e.g. *concejal de vivienda*) and correspond broadly to the committee chairpersons of UK local authorities.

Another feature of the larger authorities, with their extensive administrative structures, is the prevalence of political appointments to senior posts [1.5.2]. Apart from the very smallest councils almost all are now politicized, in the sense that councillors are elected from party lists. In the smaller ones only some, or none, of the institutions listed above are to be found. There the main weight falls on the mayor, and on the clerk to the municipality (*secretario municipal*).

The range of services which a municipality is required by law to provide is smaller the lower the population for which it is responsible. Many are very small indeed – of over 8000 in total, more than 60 per cent have fewer than 1000 inhabitants – and significant numbers lack the resources to provide even the most basic of services. One solution to this problem has been to amalgamate several councils into one. In such cases, villages deprived of their council usually retain an honorary mayor (*alcalde pedáneo*) for ceremonial purposes. Because of the difficulties posed by traditional loyalties, however, such rationalization of municipal boundaries (*concentración municipal*) has been relatively rare. As an alternative, in some areas councils have banded together in voluntary federations (*consorcios/mancomunidades*).

Structural problems are also apparent at the other end of the scale, in the largest population centres. There urban growth has meant that traditional municipal boundaries often make little administrative sense, cutting through what are now effectively single settlements. One potential means of addressing this problem would be the creation of metropolitan area authorities with responsibilities across entire conurbations. Such a solution was attempted in the Barcelona area. However, political rivalry with the Catalan regional government led to dissolution of the experimental authority.

Another way in which the largest authorities have sought to promote their distinct interests is by creating an association to do so. This is known as the Group of Seven, its members being the mayors of Spain's seven largest cities (Madrid, Barcelona, Seville, Saragossa, Valencia, Malaga and Bilbao). The Group operates alongside the organization which represents all the country's local authorities, the Spanish Federation of Municipalities and Provinces (*Federación Española de Municipios y Provincias/FEMP*).

1.6.2 Provinces

Whereas Spain's municipalities date from the Middle Ages and even earlier, the country's 50 provinces were created only in the early nineteenth century. They also differ from the smaller units in that they were originally intended as a means of extending central government control down to local level. It is at provincial level that the last remnants of the central government's outlying administration continue to operate [1.5.2]. These factors inevitably lend a touch of anomaly to the position of the provinces in post-Franco Spain.

Their continuing existence is due to the fact that, after 1975, they were given a new role as the upper tier of a democratized system of local government. In part this was done by handing over to them some functions formerly exercised by the outlying administration. However, it was also a response to the problems posed by the small size of many municipalities [1.6.1]; in such areas responsibility for some service provision was taken over by the provinces.

The body which exercises these responsibilities is the provincial council (*diputación provincial*), made up of provincial councillors (*diputados*) and headed by a council chairperson. In most of Spain council members are elected indirectly, that is by the various municipal councils within the province concerned. The various islands of the Canaries and Balearics also have their own councils (*cabildos* and *consells* respectively), in the first case directly elected.

The other special case is that of the three Basque provinces (Alava, Guipúzcoa and Vizcaya), which, uniquely in Spain, are traditional units dating back to the Middle Ages. There the administrative authority (*diputación foral*) is controlled by a directly elected provincial council (*Juntas Generales*). The Basque Country, where the provinces also enjoy relatively strong powers, displays in extreme form a problem apparent throughout Spain: the proliferation of administrative tiers and the overlap of functions between them [3.3.1].

Given their ambiguous historical role and relatively minor functions, the provincial authorities are the most obvious candidate for elimination in any attempt to simplify the situation. Indeed, this has already effectively occurred in the six single-province regions (*comunidades uniprovinciales*), where the provincial councils have been absorbed by the respective regional governments. Elsewhere, especially in Catalonia, there has been pressure to replace the provinces by districts (*comarcas*) with greater relation to traditional sentiment and/or contemporary population patterns, as well as the needs of service delivery. Yet not everywhere are there obvious alternatives to the provinces. And, in any case, their abolition would not solve the underlying problems posed by the small municipalities – as well as inflaming Basque sensibilities.

1.7 GLOSSARY

6-D m	6 December 1978 (date of referendum on 1978 Constitution)
administración periférica f	outlying administration (of central government)
alcalde m	mayor; leader of municipal council
alcalde pedáneo m	honorary mayor (of former municipality)
alto cargo m	senior public servant
anteproyecto de ley m	draft bill (for parliamentary scrutiny)
área f	department (of local authority)
asesor m	adviser
ayuntamiento m	municipal council

bicameralismo m	(system of) two-chamber Parliament
Boletín Oficial del Estado m	Spanish Official Gazette
cabildo m	island council (Canaries)
Cámara Alta f	Upper House (of Parliament)
Cámara Baja f	Lower House (of Parliament)
cargo político/de confianza m	political appointee
Carta Magna f	constitution
cartera (ministerial) f	(ministerial) portfolio; ministry
casa real f	royal household
circunscripción f	constituency
comarca f	district
comisión delegada del gobierno f	cabinet committee
comisión de investigación f	committee of investigation (of Congress)
comisión especial f	special committee (of Senate)
comisión mixta f	joint committee (of both Houses)
comisión permanente legislativa f	standing legislative committee
comisión permanente no legislativa f	standing non-legislative committee
comunidad uniprovincial f	autonomous region consisting of a single province
concejal m	municipal councillor
concentración municipal f	rationalization of municipal boundaries
conflictos de competencias mpl	central–regional government disputes over legislative competence
Congreso (de los Diputados) m	Congress; Lower House of Spanish Parliament
Consejero m	Councillor of State
consejero nato m	ex-officio councillor
consejo de ministros m	cabinet
consell m	island council (Balearics)
consorcio m	federation of adjoining municipalities to provide services
constitución cauce f	enabling constitution
constitución muro f	delimiting constitution
constitucionalización f	inclusion in the Constitution
cortes constituyentes fpl	constituent assembly
Cortes Generales (las) fpl	Spanish Parliament
crisis de gobierno f	cabinet reshuffle
(cf. *crisis en el seno del gobierno*)	(government crisis)
cuestión de inconstitucionalidad f	challenge by a judge against legislation on grounds that it contravenes the Constitution
decreto legislativo m	government regulation
Defensor del Pueblo m	Ombudsman
delegado del gobierno m	central government representative in an autonomous region
desarrollo m	detailed provision for a feature envisaged in the Constitution
Día de la Constitución m	Constitution Day
diario de sesiones m	verbatim record of proceedings

dictamen m	report (from parliamentary committee)
diputación foral f	provincial administrative authority (Basque Country and Navarre only)
Diputación Permanente f	Standing Council (of the Spanish Parliament)
diputación provincial f	provincial council
diputado m	deputy/MP; provincial councillor
director general m	director-general (highest career public service grade)
director insular m	central government representative on a particular island; assistant to the representative for that region
disposición adicional f	additional disposition (to Constitution)
disposición derogatoria f	revocatory disposition (to Constitution)
disposición transitoria f	transitional disposition (to Constitution)
elecciones anticipadas fpl	early election
elecciones legislativas fpl	general election
elecciones municipales fpl	municipal/local elections
enchufe m	well-placed contact (in an organization)
enchufismo m	practice of filling jobs on the basis of contacts
equipo de gobierno m	'cabinet' of leading councillors in local authority
escaño m	seat (in Parliament)
estado m	state; (Spanish) central government
estado de derecho m	state under the rule of law
estado social m	state whose economy is run on (German) social market lines
función pública f	public service
funcionariado m	public servants
funcionario m	public servant
funcionario de carrera m	career public servant
gabinete m	private office (staff)
Gobernador Civil m	provincial governor
Gobierno Civil m	provincial civil authority
Grupo Mixto m	Mixed Group (of deputies/senators)
grupo parlamentario m	parliamentary group/party
heredero m	heir (to the throne)
iniciativa legislativa f	right to initiate legislation
iniciativa popular f	people's initiative (procedure by which a proposed law can be presented to Parliament)
interpelación f	interrogative motion (requiring a government response to Parliament)
juancarlismo m	support for/loyalty to King Juan Carlos
junta de portavoces f	(parliamentary) spokespersons' committee
Juntas Generales fpl	directly elected provincial council (Basque Country only)
legislatura f	legislature; Parliament (period between elections)
letrado m	legally trained parliamentary clerk
ley de base f	foundation act (basis for subsequent government regulations)
ley marco f	framework act (guidelines for regional legislation)
ley ordinaria f	Act of (Spanish) Parliament

ley orgánica f	organic act (entrenched legislation)
Libro Blanco m	White Paper (for public consultation)
listas cerradas y bloqueadas fpl	closed, blocked lists (electoral system)
Magna Carta f	constitution; the Constitution of 1978
mancomunidad f	federation of adjoining municipalities to provide services
Mando Supremo de las Fuerzas Armadas m	Commander-in-Chief of the Armed Forces
mayoría de edad f	age of legal majority
moción de censura f	no-confidence motion (against PM)
moción de confianza f	vote of confidence
moción de reprobación f	censure motion (against an individual minister)
municipio m	municipality
oposición f	opposition (party); competitive public examination
organigrama m	structure (of an organization)
padres de la Constitución mpl	fathers of the 1978 Constitution; members of Constitution drafting committee
parlamentarios mpl	members of (Spanish) Parliament
participación ciudadana f	direct participation (by individuals, in machinery of government)
pleno m	plenary session; meeting of full House/municipal council
ponencia f	committee set up for a special purpose
pregunta f	question (to government minister, by individual MP)
presidencialismo m	presidential system; pre-eminence of PM in Spanish politics
presidente del Congreso/Senado m	Speaker of Congress/Senate
presidente del gobierno m	Prime Minister
proposición de ley f	non-government bill
proyecto de ley m	government bill
rango m	grade (in public service)
real decreto-ley m	royal decree-law (urgent legislation)
recurso de amparo m	application for protection of constitutional rights and freedoms
recurso de constitucionalidad m	request for ruling on compliance of a law with the Constitution
reforma (constitucional) f	amendment (to the Constitution)
refrendo m	endorsement (of action of one state institution, by another)
reyes (los) mpl	the King and Queen; the royal couple
rodillo m	(practice of) steamrollering legislation through Parliament
secretaría f	section (of ministry)
secretario de estado m	Secretary of State (approx. equivalent to UK junior minister)
secretario general m	general secretary (ministry post, grade below Under-Secretary)

secretario general técnico m	professional general secretary (senior career public servant)
secretario municipal m	clerk to municipality
Senado m	Senate; Upper House of Spanish Parliament
senador m	senator
sub-delegado del gobierno m	assistant central government representative to a region, based in a particular province
subsecretaría f	section (of ministry) headed by Under-Secretary
subsecretario de estado m	Under-Secretary of State (Civil Service grade below Secretary of State)
teniente de alcalde m	deputy mayor
término municipal m	area run by a municipal council; municipality
título m	title (primary divisions) of the Constitution
Título Preliminar m	Introductory Title
tráfico de influencias m	influence-peddling
Tribunal Constitucional m	Constitutional Court
ventanilla f	counter (in government office)
ventanilla única f	one-stop centre for government services
viaje oficial m	official visit
vicepresidente m	deputy (for full title see corresponding *presidente*)

2

POLITICAL PARTIES

Throughout the Western world political parties are central to public life. They play a major part in setting the framework within which debate on issues takes place, at national level and often locally as well. In contemporary Spain they have acquired a particular significance, due to the nature of society and state institutions, and also to that of the parties themselves. This chapter begins by examining certain features of Spanish parties in general, features which to a degree distinguish them from their counterparts in other Western democracies. The remaining sections then consider the nature and development of the three parties to have governed Spain since Franco's death, in order of their coming to power, before looking briefly at some of the minor players on the political stage.

2.1 GENERAL FEATURES OF SPANISH PARTIES

Political parties are crucial to modern notions of democracy. They are supposed to channel public opinion, in all its variety and even contradiction, into a manageable number of alternative visions of how to run the country, in the form of election manifestos (*programas electorales*). By the time Spain returned to democracy in the 1970s this bottom-up model already looked rather dubious as a description of reality because, even in countries where democracy was deeply-rooted, parties often appeared more like instruments to control public opinion than to express it. Since then, the doubts have increased. In Spain's case the situation was complicated further by tardy modernization and the Franco regime's ban on democratic politics, which together meant that in 1975 there were no parties with recent experience of such activity – and practically none with any experience at all. The result has been that the functions and behaviour of parties have tended to diverge even more than elsewhere from those described by political theory.

2.1.1 History, status and popular standing

The most obvious difference between Spanish parties and those in almost all other Western countries is their relative lack of historical tradition. The point is of contemporary importance. It is known that loyalty to a particular party, not just over the lifetime of a voter but over generations, often plays a significant part in determining voting habits. In Spain parties have had, as yet, little chance to build up a reservoir of loyalty. Indeed, in the period up to 1936 Spain remained so politically backward that there was little opportunity for the development of parties as they are normally understood [0.1].

On the one hand, those forces which favoured only gradual change or opposed it altogether – those we would today broadly term the right – controlled the country by means other than winning fair elections. As a result the parties they formed remained mere groups of notables, based in Madrid, with links to corrupt political bosses at local level (*caciques*). None developed a mass membership, and none re-emerged to play a significant role in politics after 1975. The only party permitted by Franco, the government-run 'National Movement' [0.2], was dissolved the year after the dictator's death.

On the left the position was rather different. By the 1930s both the Socialists and the Communists were established political forces, with genuine party organizations and, in the former case, considerable electoral strength. Because of Spain's late and patchy economic development, however, these were restricted to some of those few regions where industry had developed (the Basque Country, Asturias and Madrid) and to the southern countryside. What is more, for almost 40 years both parties of the left were banned and vilified by the Franco regime. In so far as they operated at all, it was in exile or underground.

As a result, of all the myriad political parties which emerged after they were legalized in 1976 [0.3.2] – the media talked of an 'alphabet soup' (*sopa de siglas*) – none had in existence a normal structure of organization and membership. With the possible exception of the Basque PNV [3.2.2.2], none possessed a network of related associations through which to establish contact with society as a whole. And neither parties nor voters themselves had recent, or in most cases any, experience of democratic politics. Moreover, in the case of the Communists, who in 1976 were widely expected to emerge as a leading if not the largest political force, there were understandable doubts about their commitment to observe the rules of democracy.

For all these reasons, those who framed the 1978 Constitution were anxious to foster the growth of democratic parties. Their concern was expressed through recognition, in the Constitution's Introductory Title [1.1.2], of parties as a 'basic mechanism of political participation'. It was again demonstrated by the speed with which this special status was regulated in greater detail. Before the end of 1978, at a time when many major matters required urgent attention, a Political Parties Act was passed.

Under this law parties were given certain privileges, in particular the right to public funding once registered officially as such [2.1.3]. In return, they were required to satisfy certain conditions. In essence, parties' statutes, their own internal 'constitutions', had to conform to certain rules. Thus their stated aims must not be contrary to the Constitution itself, and their internal structure and operation must be democratic in nature.

The first provision has on occasion been applied to regionalist parties who aspire to break away from Spain, thus infringing the country's territorial unity stipulated in Article 2. It would also appear to allow a refusal to register – effectively a ban on – fascist or other anti-democratic groups. The second has also been mentioned as a possible ground for de-registering Basque parties linked to terrorism. In general, however, the conditions imposed by the 1978 Act have had virtually no practical application.

Moreover, developments have belied the widespread fear that Spanish parties would prove sickly creatures in need of careful nurture. One indication of their robust health is the turnout at general elections (*participación electoral*) or, to use the term usually adopted in Spain, the abstention rate (see Table 2.1). After rising sharply in 1979 due to popular disillusion with the results of democracy [0.3.3], abstention fell to just 20 per cent in 1982 as a wave of popular enthusiasm swept the Socialists to power [2.3.1]. And, although turnout dropped sharply later in the 1980s, during the 1990s it once again rose to levels of which many older democracies would be proud.

Yet at the same time popular esteem for parties as institutions slumped, with the involvement – to a greater or lesser degree – of all the major ones in a long series of corruption scandals [2.1.3]. In fact, corruption allegations formed the main, indeed, almost the only plank of the campaigns mounted by the then conservative opposition at the general elections of 1993 and 1996. On both occasions the response of the Socialist government was to brand their main opponent as Franco's heir. In other words, high turnout followed extremely negative campaigns, which both reflected and aggravated the low standing of parties in general. After a rather less bitter but decidedly lacklustre campaign in 2000, turnout again fell sharply. Even so it was significantly higher than the figure recorded in the UK the following year, never mind those habitually seen in the USA.

2.1.2 Leaders and members

A key factor in shaping public perceptions of parties has been the way in which they have operated. Central to that is the relationship between their upper echelons or leadership (*cúpula*) and rank-and-file membership (*bases*). In Spain, this has been crucially affected by the context in which parties rapidly developed after 1976. At that time the two country-wide parties which already had some form of organization, the Socialists and Communists, were used to the secrecy and discipline required by underground operation. On the right and in the centre, parties were initially little more than groups of public figures; such organization as they had was inherited, unofficially, from Franco's National Movement [0.2].

As a result, all the parties shared two features to a greater or lesser extent. One was the high degree of control exercised by the leadership, the other a low level of party membership (*afiliación*). In 1979, after the initial surge of enthusiasm for democracy, neither Socialists nor Communists could claim more than around 100,000 members (*militantes*), while no force on the centre-right had any significant membership at all. Overall, the percentage of the population belonging to parties was among the lowest in Europe; only the Socialists, in some of their industrial heartlands [2.3.1], and the Basque PNV [3.2.2.2], could claim a strong presence in society.

Quite apart from general concerns about the health of democracy, the lack of members posed a very practical problem for the new parties. As well as building up their own organizations, those that enjoyed success had somehow to fill elected posts, such as MPs and councillors, as well as numerous political appointments in national, regional and local government [1.5.1]. The solution adopted by the country's first ruling party was to absorb a considerable number of politicians and bureaucrats from the former regime [2.2.1]. However, when the parties of the left took over control of many local authorities after the 1979 municipal elections, they were faced with a major difficulty.

The Socialists were particularly affected; they won more votes and thus had more posts to fill, but had fewer members and activists than the Communists in many areas. Moreover, within four years the party gained control over central government and most of the new autonomous regions [2.3.2]. Its response was, in part, to expand its membership by incorporating individuals seen as potential ministers, local councillors and political appointees. But the reverse also applied; the enormous patronage wielded by the Socialists during the 1980s attracted new members for reasons which often had little to do with their beliefs or even with any interest in politics as such. Towards the end of the decade, as the People's Party captured control over many local and regional authorities [2.4.3], it was affected by a similar process.

As a result, membership of both the main parties has risen substantially, with the PP now claiming over 600,000 members and the Socialists somewhat fewer. In view of the Communists' disappearance as a major force [2.5.2], and given the decline in political activism visible in most Western countries, that brings Spain much more into line with its neighbours in terms of membership density. However, it remains unusual in the sense that party members consist, to a quite extraordinary degree, of political office-holders (*cargos*) of one sort or another. This phenomenon, in turn, has had two main consequences.

It means, first, that a very high proportion of party members have a strong personal, often financial interest in obtaining and holding on to public office. Not surprisingly, administrations formed by the main parties at all levels of government often appear more interested in holding on to power than in using it to implement their election manifestos. Even more seriously for parties' collective standing, the situation is a significant factor in corruption.

It also leads to another form of impropriety: opportunistic party-hopping (*chaqueteo*). During the transition period, when parties were still in the stage of formation, the practice of individuals moving between them was a frequent and even understandable one. Nevertheless it caused sufficient disquiet that its most visible form – MPs crossing the floor in Parliament (*transfuguismo*) – was made the subject of strict controls; if an MP leaves his party group he or she must now either resign or join the Mixed Group [1.3.2]. Switches of allegiance at lower levels are less easy to prevent. Their effect, in terms of public cynicism about politics and politicians, can be readily surmised.

Secondly, the make-up of the main parties has tended to strengthen the degree of control exercised by their leaderships. It is they that decide on the placing of individual candidates on the party lists presented to voters [1.3.1], and they who make political appointments to senior administrative posts [1.5.2]. Media-centred election campaigning, which became the norm relatively early in Spain precisely because of low party membership, further accentuates party leaders' dominant status. And, as elsewhere, it also tends to place a heavy emphasis on party unity; dissidents can expect scant rewards.

The electoral impact of national leaders is important even at lower levels, since local and most regional elections take place on a single day and the campaign for them is to a large extent a national affair [3.1.3]. Yet local and, especially, regional leaders also play a significant role and, perhaps more importantly, now control a considerable amount of patronage in their own right. Likened on occasion to Spain's pre-democratic party bosses [2.1.1], the more powerful of these city and regional leaders provide the only real counterweight to the leadership's power within the main parties.

2.1.3 Power and money

At the time the 1978 Constitution was being drawn up, there were genuine fears that Spain's fledgling parties would prove too weak to ensure the state's democratic nature. In so far as the strength of parties is concerned, they have proved wildly exaggerated. Not only do parties monopolize participation in politics, in the sense that only the candidates they present have any realistic chance of election to public office, the widespread system of political appointments means that their influence over the machinery of government goes far further than merely the elected sphere.

As a consequence, the most commonly voiced concern today about the health of Spanish democracy is that the country has become a party-run state (*partitocracia*). The description needs to be severely qualified, in two ways. First, within parties it is the leadership, not the membership as a whole, who exercise effective power [2.1.2] – and as elsewhere, leaders tend to pragmatism rather than ideology. Second, in the case of parties in power at national or lower levels, there is a considerable degree of contact and overlap between party leaderships and those who control the machinery of government (again the Basque PNV [3.2.2.2] is the exception to the rule). Arguably, rather than parties controlling the state, in such cases it is the executive that exercises a decisive influence over parties.

Ironically, one of the measures taken in the 1970s to strengthen parties has, in practice, served to increase their subordination. That measure is the state funding (*financiación*) introduced by the 1978 Political Parties Act [2.1.1]. As in other countries, reservations were expressed in Spain about the provision when it was introduced. However, given the country's highly unusual circumstances, there was no viable alternative; parties, in so far as they existed, lacked both funds and the means to generate them. Consequently the money they received from the state immediately became the main source of income for all parties of any significance, and remains so today.

During the 1980s there was growing public concern about the operation of party funding in general. In response, measures were introduced in 1987 to regulate it in greater detail. Under them parties receive an annual sum from the state, based on their performance (votes and seats won) in the most recent election. In addition they receive special support for election campaigns on the same basis, including access to television time as well as finance. One effect of this arrangement is to intensify even further parties' concern with electoral success [2.1.2].

The 1987 legislation covers not only public funding but also income from other sources. Under this heading come, first, membership dues (*cuotas de afiliación*) and other income generated by the party itself. Given the low level of membership and activism this source is inevitably of only minor significance.

The second means by which parties may raise money themselves is through bank loans. That clearly places a premium on good links with the banking sector, and has proved a controversial issue on occasion, most notably in 1986. Then the notorious antipathy between Adolfo Suárez and the country's leading bankers – the ex-premier once referred to them as the 'evil godmother' of Spanish society – seems to have led them to discriminate, in granting loans, against the party he was leading at the time [2.2.3]. Interestingly, their action had little impact on the results.

Finally, parties may receive private donations. These are subject to limits on their quantity and to stringent conditions on how they are made. While this strict control has decided advantages in terms of clarity – it would, for example, render illegal the vast majority of the private and company donations which have proved controversial in the UK – it also poses problems of its own. These arise because, perhaps inevitably, parties find the level of funding they receive, public and otherwise, to be inadequate in practice. As a result, many of the influence-peddling scandals of recent years [1.5.1] have been concerned not with personal but with party enrichment.

The most notorious example was the Filesa affair (*caso Filesa*) of the 1980s, named after a company set up by the Socialist Party specifically to channel the proceeds of such activities into party coffers. In 1997, six party officials were convicted on related charges. To a greater or lesser degree, however, all the major country-wide and regional parties have financed themselves in this way, which represents yet another incentive, this time collective rather than individual, for parties to cling to office at all cost.

As a result of these problems, the two largest have been engaged in discussions for some years now about relaxing the strict controls on private contributions to parties. So far these have not borne fruit. The main differences have been over whether to retain the anonymity of private donors, and whether to permit companies to make political contributions. Whether or not it becomes easier for parties to receive private donations, however, they are certain in the medium term to remain dependent on state contributions as their main source of funding. Currently most are heavily in debt, above all the Socialist PSOE – which, just a decade ago, was the main target of allegations about supposed party dominance of the state!

2.2 THE CENTRE: UCD AND ITS SUCCESSORS

To some contemporary observers, the brief history of the first political party to govern Spain after 1975 confirmed fears about the country's ability to sustain viable parties. While that view proved unfounded, the fact remains that the Democratic Centre Union (*Unión de Centro Democrático/UCD*) did not survive into the contemporary era of Spain's development [0.3.3]. It is also the case that UCD (the initials are usually given without any article in Spanish) occupied a part of the political spectrum, the centre, to which no significant party in the 1990s belongs. Nonetheless, UCD continues to figure frequently in discussion, its involvement in and experience during the process of transition to democracy often seen as a point of reference – both positive and negative – for current parties.

2.2.1 Suárez and the rise of UCD

UCD emerged by a process of clustering from the bewildering array of tiny parties that sprang up after Franco's death [2.1.1]. Its nucleus was the People's Party (*Partido Popular*), a grouping founded in 1976 by José María Areilza and unconnected with the current governing party of the same name. Areilza had occupied various senior official posts under the Franco regime but had latterly been prominent among those working for limited change from within it [0.3.1]. He was considerably better known at the time than the young man recently appointed Prime Minister by King Juan Carlos, Adolfo Suárez, and seen by some – not least himself – as a suitable successor.

In January 1977 Areilza's formation absorbed another similar group, changing its name to Democratic Centre. Thereafter it swallowed up or allied with a steady stream of smaller parties. In the spring came the decisive step when Suárez climbed aboard the bandwagon, imposing two conditions for his support. First, he became the grouping's leader, Areilza being summarily ditched. And many of his closest colleagues, like him former Francoist bureaucrats, also assumed leading positions within UCD as the expanded electoral alliance was now re-christened.

Suárez's burgeoning personal standing, which he skilfully and ruthlessly promoted through privileged access to state-run television [5.3.1], was crucial to UCD's success at the 1977 general election (see Table 2.1). To the surprise of many, it won the largest share of the vote, some distance ahead of the longer established parties of the left. So swift had this process been that it was not until later the same year that UCD formally converted itself into a party in its own right.

Table 2.1 Results of principal parties in general elections, 1977–2000

		1977	1979	1982	1986	1989	1993	1996	2000
Turnout	%	79	68	80	71	70	76	78	69
Democratic	V	6310	6292	1429					
Centre	P	34.8	35.5	6.2					
Union (UCD)	S	167	168	11					
Social and	V			595	1863	1618	413		
Democratic	P			2.8	9.2	7.9	1.8		
Centre (CDS)	S			2	19	14	0		
Spanish Socialist	V	5371	5477	10,098	8887	8116	9150	9426	7829
Party (PSOE)	P	29.9	30.5	47.3	44.1	39.6	38.8	37.6	34.1
	S	110	121	202	184	175	159	141	125
People's Party	V	1439	1068	5557	5245	5286	8201	9716	10,320
(PP)[a]	P	8.4	6.1	25.9	26.1	25.8	34.8	38.8	44.5
	S	16	9	107	105	107	141	156	183
Spanish	V	1710	1940	845					
Communist	P	9.3	10.8	3.9					
Party (PCE)	S	20	23	4					
United Left (IU)	V				930	1859	2254	2640	1254
	P				4.7	9.1	9.6	10.5	5.5
	S				7	17	18	21	8
Convergence	V	515	483	767	1012	1032	1166	1152	965
and Union	P	2.8	2.7	3.6	5.0	5.0	4.9	4.6	4.2
(CiU)[b]	S	11	8	12	18	18	17	16	15
Basque Nationalist	V	296	275	397	309	255	291	319	352
Party (PNV)	P	1.7	1.6	1.8	1.5	1.2	1.2	1.3	1.5
	S	8	7	8	6	5	5	5	7

Notes: [a] Prior to 1989, variously People's Alliance (AP), Democratic Coalition (CD), People's Coalition (CP).
[b] Leading Catalan regionalist party.
V = votes (in thousands); P = per cent poll; S = seats.
Source: Interior Ministry

Its 1977 victory allowed UCD, and above all Suárez, to steer the process of transition over the next few crucial years [0.3.2]. In particular it had the largest representation (three members out of seven) on the committee which drafted the Constitution [1.1.1]. Yet there as in other forums the government genuinely consulted with the chief opposition parties. In part this was forced, as UCD never enjoyed an overall parliamentary majority. But its openness to dialogue seemed also to be genuine, motivated by awareness among its leaders of the delicacy of the transition process. In that sense it set the tone of compromise which marked the key period of the transition.

2.2.2 UCD: decline and disintegration

UCD's second general election victory, in March 1979, seemed to crown its astounding rise to prominence. In fact, however, it marked the start of an even more spectacular decline, sparked by internal divisions that success had papered over but not removed. At one level they were personal. UCD's origins meant that it was a party of factions headed by one or more powerful 'barons', each jealous of their own status and many resentful of Suárez and his closest advisers, a group referred to as the 'plumbers'. Since the party had virtually no organizational structure or mass membership the leadership was highly dependent on the barons at election times, and even to control its own MPs. It was in the parliamentary party that divisions between supporters of different barons came together, explosively, with those between the party's four main ideological factions.

The first was closely linked to the Catholic Church, which nonetheless had denied it support in forming a separate party [5.1.2.1]. These Christian Democrats were correspondingly conservative on social issues, but favoured the state intervention typical of the German model of a social market economy [1.1.2]. The liberal faction, by contrast, favoured a greater degree of social change, being less influenced by the Church if not mildly anticlerical. Economically they were concerned to remove the many restrictions imposed on business by the former regime, and were accordingly much less enthusiastic about the 'social' aspects of the German model. The Social Democrats, the third main grouping, were largely in agreement with the liberals on social issues but strongly opposed to them on economic ones. There they wanted to see not reduced state intervention but an expansion in welfare state provision and economic planning.

The last of UCD's factions was a group of former Francoist bureaucrats. Apart from Suárez himself its most prominent member was Rodolfo Martín Villa, a key figure in successive UCD cabinets. Not known as liberalizers before Franco's death [0.3.1], their concern seems to have been above all with avoiding insurrection by either the left or the military – with the process of transition rather than with its ends.

By 1979 that process was largely complete in terms of institutional change. With the rules of political play established in the Constitution, attention moved to more detailed and controversial issues. This change was fatal for UCD. In particular, the attempt to regulate divorce opened up splits between the Christian and Social Democrat factions which proved unbridgeable. Lacking strong discipline, the parliamentary party began to disintegrate, with individual deputies, or small groups led by a particular baron, defecting to parties to both right and left.

In the midst of this process, in January 1981, Suárez resigned, for reasons which seem to have been connected with pressures from the barons. Thereafter UCD was kept in power, indeed in being, only by the opposition's fear that overthrowing the government would provoke a second coup attempt like that which took place during the inauguration of Leopoldo Calvo Sotelo as the new Prime Minister [0.3.3]. Under his leadership UCD's disintegration continued inexorably. By summer 1982 it had lost a third of its deputies, forcing Calvo Sotelo to call an early election. UCD suffered a catastrophic defeat and was reduced to a mere 11 seats in the Congress it had previously controlled. Within a year it had been dissolved.

2.2.3 Collapse of the centre

By the time of the 1982 election UCD's driving force, Adolfo Suárez, had left the party and set up a new one, the Social and Democratic Centre (*Centro Democrático y Social/CDS*). The 'and' is important; the oft-repeated intention of UCD's former leader was not to found a left-of-centre social democratic party but to re-occupy the centre ground of politics he felt his old one had latterly abandoned. The CDS fared very poorly at the 1982 election, but considerably better four years later (see Table 2.1). Indeed, with the right-wing People's Alliance in seemingly endless crisis [2.4.1], it briefly appeared to have a real chance of becoming the main opposition to the ruling Socialists.

However, in 1988 Suárez made a crucial tactical error. In a number of major cities the CDS joined with the Alliance to oust Socialist administrations which lacked an overall majority. This step effectively undermined its claim to represent a pure centre (*centro-centro*), distinct from both left and right. Thereafter its electoral fortunes deteriorated rapidly; at the 1993 general election it failed to win a single seat. By then Suárez himself had admitted defeat and retired from active politics. Without its founder the party effectively withered away.

The 1986 election at which the CDS made its apparent breakthrough was remarkable for the fact that not one, but two parties contested it on explicitly centrist platforms, the other being the Democratic Reform Party (*Partido Reformista Democrático/PRD*). Set up in 1983, the PRD contained a number of leading figures from UCD's liberal faction [2.2.2]. However, its real driving force was the Catalan regionalist party Convergence and Union [3.2.1.2], whose deputy leader Miquel Roca was the PRD's effective head. One of the 'fathers of the Constitution' [1.1.1], Roca enjoyed considerable prestige throughout Spain. However, the PRD was unable to capitalize on this, or on the favourable treatment it received from the banks when granting loans for the 1986 campaign [2.1.3]. It captured only 1 per cent of the votes, failing to win any seats, and was thereafter quietly dissolved.

The demise of the PRD and the CDS has left Spain without an explicitly centrist party. Instead, the country has moved towards a two-party system (*bipartidismo*), in which both major contenders seek to occupy the centre ground from the right and left respectively. Especially given the nature of the electoral system [1.3.1], it is unlikely that a successor to UCD will emerge in the foreseeable future. Nonetheless, the party remains an important point of reference in Spanish politics for a number of reasons.

On the one hand, its fate serves as an awful warning to others of the dangers of factionalism, a warning that has clearly been taken to heart by the country's leading parties in their insistence on strong internal discipline [2.1.2]. On a more positive note, the willingness to compromise associated with UCD is often compared positively to more recent political practice, both by commentators and in responses to opinion polls. Significantly, both during its rise to power in the mid-1990s [2.4.3] and once established in office [2.4.4], the People's Party has attempted to cast itself not only as a party of the centre but, quite explicitly, as heir to the UCD tradition.

Most commentators would see such claims as spurious, in that the PP remains recognizably a party of the right. But, more importantly, they miss the point that UCD was the child of very special circumstances, in which the term 'centre' itself had specific connotations quite different from those in democratic politics generally. On the one hand it denoted those who wished to bring about democracy without radical change, a group which straddled the divide between Francoists and their opponents. And, on the other, it was associated with the person of Suárez. For both these reasons it makes no sense to see UCD as the prototype of a twenty-first-century centre party – whatever that might be.

2.3 THE SOCIALIST PARTY

In its role as the governing party UCD was succeeded by the Spanish Socialist Party (*Partido Socialista Obrero Español/PSOE*). In power from 1982 to 1996, the PSOE has undoubtedly exercised more influence over Spain's contemporary development than any other party. It is also by some way the country's oldest, having been founded in 1879. Prior to 1982 it had spent almost its entire history in opposition or underground, most recently during the Franco era, and was associated in the popular mind with the strict personal integrity and rigid Marxist beliefs of its founder and first leader, the Madrid printer Pablo Iglesias. In this, as in other regards, the PSOE's lengthy period in office was to change it as much or more than it changed Spain as a whole.

2.3.1 From the underground to office

During the Franco era the PSOE's leadership went into exile, and largely refrained from promoting underground opposition to the regime. Its attitude provoked growing resentment among members within Spain. In 1974 a group of these took control over the party at its 25th Conference (*Congreso*), held at Suresnes in southern France. A young lawyer, known by the code-name of *Isidro*, was elected leader. Together with his closest colleagues – most of them either from the Basque Country or, like himself, from Seville – he was to dominate the PSOE's development for the next two decades. His real name was Felipe González.

The strength of his grip on the party became quite clear in 1979. At that year's 28th Conference delegates rejected a proposal to drop the term 'Marxist' from the party's self-description, a step its leader considered vital if the party was to avoid scaring off potential voters. González promptly resigned. Before the year was out he had been overwhelmingly re-elected, and his proposal approved, at a special Conference hastily convened when it became clear that his opponents could offer no alternatives.

By 1979 the Socialists had already established themselves as Spain's second largest party, having clearly won the struggle with the more fancied Communists for left-wing votes (see Table 2.1). That same year they won

control over most of Spain's important towns and cities at the first democratic local elections. In many councils their control depended on a mutual-
support agreement with the Communists (*pacto municipal*). This agreement
indicated the thrust of the PSOE's strategy at the time; to harness the support
of all those who felt that under the then UCD government social and economic change had been too slow and too limited.

Already, in 1977, the PSOE had absorbed the smaller People's Socialist
Party (*Partido Socialista Popular/PSP*), whose former leader Enrique Tierno
Galván was a popular and successful Mayor of Madrid from 1979 to his
death in 1986. When UCD's social democratic faction broke away in 1980
[2.2.2], it too was absorbed into the PSOE. Its leader, Francisco Fernández
Ordóñez, who had served under both Franco and Suárez, later concluded his
career as González's Foreign Minister. The Socialists also received a steady
flow of prominent defectors from the Communists, by now in seemingly permanent crisis [2.5.1]. Crucially, the PSOE also now attracted a large proportion of their support, particularly young, educated professionals previously
influenced by the Communists' role in opposition to the Franco regime. Such
voters proved highly susceptible to the PSOE campaign at the 1982 general
election. Its slogan *Por el cambio* ('Vote for change') captured perfectly the
image of non-ideological radicalism assiduously cultivated by González.

Along with the collapse of UCD [2.2.2], the attraction of former
Communist voters was the key to the PSOE's sweeping 1982 victory; not
until 2000, by when the electorate was considerably larger, was its total of
over 10 million votes exceeded at a Spanish election. Although just less than
half of those cast, they were converted by the electoral system [1.3.1] into a
handsome overall parliamentary majority. The election date, 28 October 1982
(*28-O*), marks a watershed in Spanish politics. Not only did it confirm that
the transition was over [0.3.3]. It also ushered in a period of 14 years during
which the PSOE dominated Spanish government and politics to an extraordinary degree.

2.3.2 A party of government

The PSOE's dominance was strengthened in 1983, when it increased its hold
on local government and also won control of most of the newly created
autonomous regions. Indeed, for almost a decade thereafter the troubles of
the other main country-wide parties [2.4.1, 2.5.1] meant that the Socialists
faced no effective nation-wide opposition. In any case, the country's new
institutional structure, and specifically the relationship between parliament
and government [1.4.1], had been designed on the assumption that no party
would enjoy an overall parliamentary majority. Even a strong opposition
would have been hard pressed to exercise effective control over a party as
disciplined and dynamic as the PSOE of the 1980s.

In that situation, the PSOE leadership fell into practices that verged on the
anti-democratic, showing scant regard for any opinions other than its own, and
repeatedly steamrollering legislation through Parliament with only formal

debate (*rodillo*). On the other hand, it also provided the sort of strong, active government UCD had so patently been incapable of providing after 1979. During the 1980s, enormous and badly needed progress was made on a variety of fronts; taxation [6.2.3] and education [8.2] were reformed, industry was restructured [6.1.2], the welfare state overhauled [9.1.2, 9.2.1] and infrastructure, especially new roads, constructed on a vast scale. In effect, the PSOE presided over Spain's belated socio-economic modernization, one of two words which increasingly dominated its discourse. The other was Europe, by which was meant specifically entry into the European Community, an objective achieved in 1986 [4.2.1].

The emphasis on modernization and EC entry to the exclusion of more traditional Socialist concerns brought a considerable change in the PSOE's image and nature. The party increasingly sought to portray itself as the defender of national interests, a very different stance from its traditional claim to represent the interests of manual workers. For many of these the policies pursued by González's Economics and Finance Minister Miguel Boyer – himself a leading banker – had severe consequences [6.1.2]. Their resentment was reflected in the progressive estrangement between the PSOE and the Socialist trade union confederation, the UGT, which reached crisis proportions with the 1988 general strike [5.2.1.2].

An important milestone in the PSOE's transformation was the reversal of its opposition to Spanish membership of NATO, a decision prompted by the paramount importance placed on EC membership [4.2.2]. The U-turn added to the concern felt by some in the party at the direction of government economic policy. However, the leadership view prevailed not just within the party but also at the referendum held in March 1986. The comfortable 'yes' victory, won in defiance of opinion polls, provided striking evidence of both the PSOE's discipline and its ability to carry public opinion with it.

It also further strengthened González's position in the party, enabling him to crush any signs of incipient dissent within it. He seized the chance to sack Fernando Morán, his left-leaning Foreign Secretary [4.2.1]. Boyer's simultaneous departure to return to the banking sector was a mere sop; his successor as economics supremo, Carlos Solchaga, was equally firm in pursuing policies closer to Thatcherite neo-liberalism than traditional socialist ideas. Although left-wing party dissidents formed an organized faction known as Socialist Left (*Izquierda Socialista*), they never became more than a minor irritant to the leadership.

González also exploited the boost to his prestige from EC entry and the NATO referendum in electoral terms. Calling a general election somewhat earlier than necessary, in June 1986, he won another overall majority. Three years later he again led the PSOE to victory, in an election called almost a year early to benefit from the economic boom that followed EC entry [6.1.2]. By then the PSOE's vote had been eroded to the extent that it won exactly half the Congress seats, thus technically losing its overall majority. Nevertheless, with the opposition split, this was a purely academic consideration. Having reasserted its hold over much of local and regional government in 1987, the

PSOE ended the 1980s as it had spent most of the decade – in unassailable command of the political scene.

2.3.3 *Felipismo* and the González–Guerra partnership

Just as in the UK, domination of politics in the 1980s by one party and its leader brought a new word into the language. Unlike Thatcherism, however, *felipismo* is not associated with a clearly defined political or economic doctrine. To its supporters it suggested dynamic pragmatism, untrammelled by outdated ideology; to its opponents, unprincipled opportunism. For both groups, the term is associated above all with the person of Felipe González, whose tight control over the PSOE represented the other key feature of *felipismo*.

This hold was the result of the party's tight discipline and strong organizational base. In the main industrial areas, where the PSOE branch office (*Casa del Pueblo*) had long been a feature of local life, this was well established. Elsewhere, it was rapidly built up during the 1980s. Especially in these areas of newer Socialist activity, the increasing proportion of members dependent on the party for their political future and even livelihood made it relatively easy for the leadership to exercise control [2.1.2], especially when it proved so successful electorally. As a result, while remaining technically a federation of regional sections, the PSOE became a highly centralized party; only the Catalan and, to a lesser extent, the Basque sections retained a significant degree of autonomy [3.2.1.1, 3.2.2.3]. The entire apparatus was strictly controlled by the National Executive (*Comisión Ejecutiva*), and above all by González as its general secretary and charismatic leader.

Particularly in the early years of his leadership, however, he was heavily dependent on his close partnership with a single colleague. Like González from Seville, Alfonso Guerra became deputy general secretary of the party in 1974. He soon proved himself a consummate party manager; it was his manipulation of the party apparatus which ensured González's victory in the second 1979 Conference [2.3.1]. In 1982 Guerra was appointed Deputy Prime Minister, with no ministerial portfolio [1.4.3]. This left him free for another task: ensuring that party and government worked together, under the orders of their common leader. It also gave Guerra access to unprecedented powers of patronage, which he used to strengthen even further his vice-like grip over the PSOE.

The other aspect of Guerra's key importance was electoral. On the one hand, he masterminded all the PSOE's election campaigns from 1977 to 1989. On the other, he himself was a major electoral asset, adept at appealing to traditional Socialist voters with biting attacks on the better-off. Such rhetoric provided a vital counterbalance to González's talk of modernization and Europe. In this as other respects, the PSOE's two leading personalities complemented each other in a well-matched partnership (*binomio*).

Hence the importance for the PSOE of the breakdown of their relationship. It began with a scandal involving one of Guerra's brothers. Despite holding no government or even party post, Juan Guerra had used official premises in Seville while acquiring a considerable fortune with suspicious ease. When this Guerra affair (*caso Guerra*) first broke, González threatened to resign if his deputy were obliged to do so. However, as political and media pressure increased, the premier backtracked. In 1991 he accepted Alfonso Guerra's resignation as Deputy PM.

As a result, even though Guerra remained deputy general secretary of the party, he lost his key role of link between it and the government. What is more, relations between the two partners deteriorated rapidly. Guerra increasingly aligned himself with those in and close to the PSOE who were unhappy with the government's policies, especially in the economic sphere [2.3.2]. At the same time, his break with González prompted those who resented Guerra's hold over the party apparatus to challenge it. The resultant internal struggles pitted this group, known as modernizers (*renovadores*), against those loyal to Guerra (*guerristas*).

The situation was complicated by the fact that some modernizers were also worried about the PSOE's apparent lack of ideological direction. They accordingly became involved in a grandiose review of party policy, carried out under Guerra's overall direction. However, the product of this process, the so-called 'Programme 2000', proved to contain little in the way of new ideas. Thereafter the modernizers' aim was increasingly seen to be control over the party apparatus.

For that González's personal support was crucial, and the general secretary long refused to give it. However, in early 1993 criticism of the government from Guerra's supporters became so overt that it forced González to act. He exercised his power to dissolve Parliament and call a general election. This in itself forced the party to unite behind the government, especially given the concentration of Guerra's supporters in elected or other political posts. Moreover, in an unprecedented step, González took personal command of the campaign, bypassing Guerra's traditional election-time role.

The surprise victory won by the Socialists in 1993 [2.3.4] was thus, even more than the 1986 NATO referendum, a personal triumph for González. Thereafter he threw his enhanced prestige behind Guerra's opponents. At the 33rd party Conference later in the year they lost their control over the party executive; the same process was later repeated at regional and local level in most of the country. While Guerra himself was still deputy general secretary his power had been broken, although his supporters did retain control over several regional sections.

2.3.4 Corruption and crisis

In the early 1990s the PSOE faced mounting problems. In addition to the rift between González and Guerra it had effectively split with its traditional trade union ally [5.2.1.2]. The economy was entering a severe downturn [6.1.3]. Most importantly of all, the Juan Guerra affair [2.3.3] had proved to be only one in a continuing line of damaging corruption scandals. These successive affairs (*casos*) involved mainly the abuse of public funds but also security matters. They forced the resignation not only of senior administrators linked to the Socialists, but also of several ministers. The PSOE's own apparatus was also directly implicated because of its involvement in a number of related party-funding scandals [2.1.3].

Corruption formed the focus of opposition attacks at the 1993 election, by which time an economic recovery was under way. González's response was to distance himself from the party apparatus, both through the tone of his speeches and by running the campaign personally [2.3.3]. He also offered a public and personal apology for party and government misdeeds, and promised a 'new beginning' if re-elected. He further infuriated Guerra and the party apparatus by placing on the PSOE's slate of candidates a number of 'independents', public figures previously unconnected with the party, the most prominent being the jurists Juan Alberto Belloch and Baltasár Garzón.

These star signings (*fichajes*) apparently boosted the PSOE's appeal. Defying the opinion polls, the party once again emerged victorious from the election, for the fourth time in succession. However, its latest success was won at a considerable cost. This was less because González's approach to the campaign had widened the breach with Guerra; in fact, his victory helped him to break his old partner's hold over the party apparatus [2.3.3]. More important was the subsequent behaviour of one of his signings, both of whom were given important government posts.

Belloch was put at the head of a new 'super-ministry' formed by merging the Interior and Justice portfolios [1.4.5]. His rapid rise inevitably provoked jealousies among some of his colleagues. Nevertheless he remained a considerable asset for the party, which he soon joined. Garzón proved more problematic. Spain's best-known judge, he had become famous through his success in breaking up Galician drug-smuggling rings. Young and photogenic, Garzón played a central role in the PSOE's 1993 campaign, since González indicated that he would be given a free hand to deal with corruption if the party were returned to power. With the election won, however, the hand turned out to be less free than the public and Garzón himself had been led to expect.

Despite being given a senior post in Belloch's new ministry with 'special' powers of his own, Garzón found his investigations blocked once they threatened senior figures in the PSOE. This applied in particular to alleged government involvement in the 'dirty war' waged against ETA by the shadowy group known as the GAL [10.4.2]. A frustrated Garzón resigned, and resumed his former career as an examining magistrate attached to the High Court [10.1.3]. His subsequent investigations brought the GAL affair into the very heart of the government, culminating in the arrest in 1995 of former Interior Minister José Barrionuevo. Speculation mounted that the 'Mister X' with ultimate control over the GAL had been González himself.

In another respect, too, its 1993 election victory proved a poisoned chalice for the PSOE. For the first time the party was forced to govern without an effective overall majority, and thus to seek parliamentary support from other parties. One option, favoured by Guerra and his supporters, was to renew the Communist alliance of the late 1970s [2.3.1]. However, not only was this effectively ruled out by the attitude of the Communists themselves [2.5.2]; it would also have meant changes in economic policy which González was not prepared to contemplate.

The Prime Minister opted instead for an agreement with the principal Catalan and Basque parties, the first of which became the government's main bulwark over the next two years. Although Convergence and Union refused to enter a coalition, as González would have preferred, a parliamentary pact (*pacto legislativo*) secured its support in Congress, enough to give the PSOE an overall majority. But Catalan backing on policy issues did not always extend to matters of parliamentary control, and it permitted the creation of several committees of investigation [1.4.1] whose work provided further evidence of financial and other irregularities by senior Socialists.

The government's political woes were made even worse by its determination that Spain be among the EU members to qualify for the first wave of Economic and Monetary Union [4.2.2]. The austerity measures it adopted to ensure this, got off to an embarrassingly poor start and, once they began to take effect, hit hardest at the PSOE's own supporters [6.1.3]. Understandably, González's Catalan allies became increasingly alarmed at the implications of associating with an ever more unpopular government. In autumn 1995 they moved to distance themselves by refusing to support the following year's budget estimates.

As a result, González was forced to call an election for the following spring. Having previously stated that he would not stand for re-election as PM, he was eventually obliged to do so by a party conscious that he was still enormously popular with wide sections of the electorate. Even with the GAL allegations hanging over him, he once again proved a formidable campaigner. His efforts meant that the PSOE did not suffer the comprehensive defeat that was generally expected, but they could not prevent it from losing power at last [2.4.3].

2.3.5 Return to opposition

So pleasantly surprising was the PSOE's showing at the 1996 election that González and others were prompted to speak of a 'sweet-tasting defeat'. This attitude both reflected and reinforced the attitude prevalent in the party that it had, indeed, become the natural party of government, and that its removal from power would prove a temporary aberration, even a useful opportunity to recharge batteries exhausted by the demands of office. In the event such complacency has proved almost comically misplaced.

It was caused partly by failure to acknowledge that the People's Party had emerged as a formidable opponent in its own right. But above all it reflected the effects of the PSOE's strategy while in power, and a seeming inability to grasp their implications for the party now it found itself in opposition. Most obviously, the PSOE's support base had changed radically since its historic 1982 victory [2.3.1]. That had been won by extending its traditional base among manual workers – especially the industrial workforce – anxious to improve their material living conditions, to young, better-off urban dwellers who were attracted by the Socialists' image of social progressiveness. For both these groups the party's record in power had ultimately proved disappointing.

Material prosperity had risen, but workers, especially in older industries, had not been among the main beneficiaries. Since the legalization of abortion, under strict conditions, in 1985 the party had undertaken few major social reforms; while Spanish society had undoubtedly become much more relaxed, that was not primarily due to legislation and was in any case taken for granted by the new generation of voters who had no memory of the Franco era. Furthermore, the PSOE's progressive image was badly tarnished by controversial law-and-order legislation in the 1990s [10.4.2]. Corruption scandals [2.3.4], as well as its long hold on power, made it appear to many voters as the party of the establishment, an old party.

In fact these perceptions contained a considerable element of truth. In 1996 the PSOE relied disproportionately on the votes of two social groups. One consisted in the employees of a public sector vastly expanded under its rule, and possibly threatened by a right-wing government. The other was the elderly, who have come to form a very significant part of the Spanish electorate, and one which the PSOE had been careful to cultivate through allocation of state benefits [9.4.1]. The same applied, on a lesser scale, to the rural poor of the south [6.2.4.1]; it was no coincidence that the three southern regions of Extremadura, Castile-La Mancha and Andalusia were the only ones in which the PSOE topped the poll in 1996. But they also remain the most economically backward in the country, and the concentration of Socialist votes there underlined that the PSOE was now the voice of the least dynamic elements in Spanish society – in stark contrast to the 1980s, when it had been the party of modernization [2.3.2].

To be fair, some in the PSOE were aware of its plight and in the wake of its 1996 defeat they could be heard calling for complete overhaul of the party (*renovación total*). Their demand proved problematic, however. For one thing, it implied admission of past irregularities, financial and otherwise [2.3.4], on a scale far greater than the party's upper echelons were prepared to concede. It also implied González's replacement as leader – just when the 1996 results had confirmed him as the party's prime electoral asset, and when the only obvious successor had been ruled out by Javier Solana's appointment as NATO Secretary-General [0.4.1]. As González himself had pointed out before the election, and repeated thereafter, he was 'both a problem and a solution' for the party.

In the event he resolved the immediate dilemma by presenting his resignation, unannounced, at the party's 1997 Conference. But it became clear at once that his move was designed not to initiate but to thwart any wider change. With its proponents caught unaware, González's own choice of successor, Joaquín Almunia, was easily elected to replace him. Worthy but stolid, Almunia had been an ever-present in the Socialist cabinets of the early

1990s, and was clearly not about to undertake a serious critique of their performance. In any case, a mere change of personnel could not solve the PSOE's underlying problem: that for over a decade it had effectively been led from government [2.3.3], and had lost the capacity to lead itself.

2.3.6 In the wilderness

Lacking González's position and charisma, Almunia could not hope to establish the authority of his former boss. Hoping instead to pacify discontent, he made one concession to demands for a new approach. To the concern of many in the old guard, he agreed that the party's prime ministerial candidate for the next election should be chosen by a one-member-one-vote election, on the lines of an American presidential primary (*elecciones primarias*). When it was held, in 1998, his colleagues fears were borne out, with Almunia losing to the younger, more charismatic José Borrell.

Borrell was also a survivor of the González governments. Indeed, he had initially made his name as an efficient implementer of policies disliked by much of the party's rank and file [2.3.2]. In opposition, however, he was the only leading Socialist to attack the new government on overtly left-wing grounds, a stance which enabled him to exploit the widespread but poorly articulated discontent among PSOE members.

His choice sparked an immediate 'Borrell effect'; the party's morale rose perceptibly, as did its opinion poll ratings. But his mildly radical views and open sympathy with regionalist ideas in his home region of Catalonia rendered him unacceptable to much of the party leadership. And, for all the party leader's patent willingness to make it work, 'cohabitation' with Almunia proved difficult. Then, in 1999, Borrell was distantly implicated in a minor scandal uncovered in one of his former ministries. Although the affair was trivial by recent Spanish standards he resigned immediately from his position as candidate, giving the distinct impression that he was relieved to be rid of a thankless task.

With a general election now looming the PSOE had no option but to fall back on Almunia to run for PM, a candidate who was not even the choice of his own party members. But that was the least of the Socialists' troubles. For one thing, as a political machine the PSOE had become caught in a vicious circle. Its former effectiveness had depended heavily on the party's strong grip on power [2.3.3], but that was now a distant memory. Even before 1996 it had lost control of most of local and regional government [2.4.3]. With the accompanying powers of patronage and opportunities for graft [2.1.2, 2.1.3], the party had lost both funding and members, as well as the main means of maintaining discipline among those that remained. The results were increasingly apparent in an internal and, eventually, a singularly ineffective campaign when the election finally came, in March 2000.

Matters were not helped by the fact that the PSOE had failed utterly to develop a coherent programme or strategy with which to confront a government buoyed by economic success [2.4.5]. Its bankruptcy was laid bare shortly before the campaign got under way. For the best part of two decades the PSOE had treated anyone to its left with ill-disguised contempt, deriding the communist-led United Left (IU) as unrealistic and naïve; IU, for its part, had been relentless in its attacks on the Socialists, on occasion even tacitly allying with the PP against them [2.5.2]. Yet now the two parties agreed on a loose 'electoral pact', and a joint programme which lambasted the PP's record in power as irredeemably reactionary – conveniently forgetting that in many respects its policies were indistinguishable from those pursued by the PSOE up to 1996 [2.4.4].

The pact proved a disaster. In a complete reversal of events in 1993 and 1996, the PSOE fared much worse than predicted by opinion polls. IU may have lost proportionately more votes, but the PSOE's relegation to a distant second place was an equally traumatic result. Almunia, characteristically, assumed full responsibility for the defeat and resigned immediately as party leader. The election to replace him was held at a special conference a few months later. It was won by a virtually unknown forty-year-old, José Luis Rodríguez Zapatero, who narrowly defeated the leadership's favoured candidate, José Bono, the long-serving prime minister of Castile-La Mancha.

The new leader did not enjoy the support of any organized faction within the party. Instead, he succeeded in channelling widespread, if unfocused, grassroots discontent. The confusion in the party was then underlined by the conferences subsequently held in the party's several regional sections, most of which were dominated by personalized struggles for power; in some regions, notably Madrid and Asturias, the followers of Alfonso Guerra [2.3.3] retain a strong hold. Moreover, especially in those regions where the Socialists still controlled the regional government, there was a growing tendency for local party leaders to act and speak on the basis of their own political needs, with little or no concern for nation-wide party policy.

Not surprisingly, Rodríguez Zapatero has found it hard to impose his authority, nor has he yet defined a clear policy line. Perceived broadly as further to the left than his predecessor, he has nonetheless concluded several cross-party agreements with the government on individual issues [2.4.5]. The one major policy change so far adopted is the decision, taken in late 2001, to support Spain's conversion into a genuinely federal state, as long advocated by the PSOE's Catalan section [3.2.1.1]. The move is a radical break with the party's centralist traditions, not to mention the wishes of some of its most powerful regional 'barons', and there must be doubts as to its acceptance by both party members and voters. Certainly it will not be enough on its own to retrieve the fortunes of what continues to look a distinctly rudderless party, doomed to a lengthy period in opposition.

2.4 THE PEOPLE'S PARTY AND ITS FORERUNNERS

The People's Party (*Partido Popular/PP*) is currently Spain's ruling party, having first been elected to office at the general election of 1996; it is not to be confused with the short-lived party of the same name which formed the nucleus of UCD [2.2.1]. In direct contrast to its Socialist predecessor in power, the present-day PP is an extremely young party, having adopted its current name only in 1989. Even its direct forerunner, People's Alliance (*Alianza Popular/AP*), was founded little more than 20 years ago. Yet in many respects the past has been just as important for the PP as for its main rival – in some even more so.

2.4.1 People's Alliance and People's Coalition

The reason why the past weighs so heavy on the PP is to be found in the origins of AP. This was set up in 1976 as an alliance of seven small right-wing groups, none of which was a party in any meaningful sense. Instead they were the personal followings of their respective leaders, parodied as the 'magnificent seven', all of whom had been prominent in the previous regime. Their leader was Manuel Fraga Iribarne who, though he counted as one of the regime's liberalizers [0.3.1], had served in several of the dictator's cabinets.

Nor were AP's links to the old regime merely a question of personnel. Fraga himself favoured a strictly controlled form of democracy. His party campaigned for the 1977 election on a platform of minimal change. Its crushing defeat showed clearly that this line was out of touch with popular feeling (see Table 2.1). Thereafter AP and its few deputies took part in the process of drawing up the 1978 Constitution, of which Fraga himself was one of the 'fathers' [1.1.1]. Yet despite this, doubts remained about its commitment to democracy. All its leading figures were wont to express reservations about the changes under way and a number of its MPs failed to vote for the Constitution. AP was particularly outspoken in its criticism of the constitutional arrangements for devolution [3.1.1], which it long remained committed to amend if elected.

For the 1979 election AP changed tack radically. It attempted to establish a more moderate image by allying with a number of groups and individuals unhappy with or excluded from UCD. This 'Democratic Coalition' performed even worse than AP had done in 1977. The setback prompted Fraga to abandon the idea of trying to compete with UCD as a centre-right option. Over the next few years he set about building a broad party of the right (*gran derecha*). His model was the British Conservative Party and his aim to make AP what the Tories then were – a natural party of government (*mayoría natural*).

Considerable efforts were made to improve AP's organization, and, indeed, to create a party structure for the first time in much of Spain, with limited success. In fact, the crucial factor in changing the party's fortunes was the disintegration of UCD [2.2.2]. AP profited from this process, first by a steady stream of defections in Parliament, then by a large increase in its vote at the 1982 election, when for the first time its lists of candidates were not dominated by figures from the old regime. As a result it was transformed from a minor player in the political spectrum into the main country-wide opposition to the triumphant Socialists – indeed virtually the only one.

This in itself allowed AP to reap further benefits, such as the effective support of the Spanish Employers' Confederation, the CEOE [5.2.2]. AP also attracted into a new electoral alliance two splinter parties which had emerged from the wreckage of UCD. They were the Christian Democrat People's Democratic Party (*Partido Demócrata Popular/PDP*), led by Oscar Alzaga, and José Antonio Segurado's tiny Liberal Union, later Liberal Party (*Partido Liberal/PL*). Together with AP these made up the People's Coalition (*Coalición Popular/CP*).

The new recruits gave a modest boost to CP's appeal, but they also imported into it the problems that had destroyed UCD [2.2.2]. From the outset CP had within itself organized currents of opinion with differing political beliefs and mutually suspicious leaders. It proved unable to fix on a coherent line of opposition to a government whose unpopular economic policies were broadly in line with its own views. Most notoriously, in the 1986 NATO referendum [4.2.2] Fraga called on his supporters to abstain, even though he and his party were staunch supporters of Spanish membership, merely to avoid siding with the Socialist government.

Such inconsistency made it easy for the government to play down attacks from CP as opportunistic. At the same time, CP suffered from a lingering impression among large sections of the electorate that it would seek to return to the policies of the Franco regime, especially by restricting individual freedoms. These reservations were linked particularly to the person of Fraga. When CP failed to advance at the 1986 election, commentators spoke of an electoral ceiling (*techo electoral*). By this they meant a level of support (around 25 per cent of the electorate) through which no party led by Fraga could hope to break.

Almost immediately following the 1986 election the PDP withdrew from CP. Its leaders criticized CP's policies for being too right-wing, and declared that only a more moderate line offered hope of defeating the PSOE. When, in November, CP performed disastrously in a Basque regional election, Fraga resigned, publicly and emotionally, as AP leader. And in January 1987 CP effectively ceased to exist when the PL also abandoned it, leaving AP alone as well as leaderless.

2.4.2 From AP to PP

It was widely expected that Fraga would be succeeded as party leader by his experienced deputy, Miguel Herrero de Miñón, who before joining AP had been one of UCD's representatives among the 'fathers of the Constitution' [1.1.1]. However, at a special party conference held in January 1987 Herrero's supporters were outmanoeuvred by those of a younger, relatively unknown challenger. Previously AP regional leader in Andalusia, Antonio Hernández Mancha was elected chairman, his choice clearly reflecting a desire among delegates for a fresh start.

This the new leader of the AP attempted to provide by changing the line of its attacks on the government. Whereas Fraga had concentrated on opposing liberal social policies, in areas such as abortion and education, Hernández Mancha focused on the impact of the Socialists' economic policies on less well-off voters [6.1.2]. For an essentially conservative party this was a radical departure which could only have been carried off by a strong, established leader, which Hernández Mancha was not. In addition, his populist line alienated the leadership of the business community.

Given these continuing travails, AP's poor results in the 1987 regional elections were predictable. They also added a further problem for the party; the advance of a number of regionally based parties of the right and centre-right [3.2.3]. In some areas – notably Aragon and Navarre – these even threat-ened to eclipse AP completely, and so undermine its credibility as a truly national party.

By 1989 Hernández Mancha's support had vanished and he did not even stand for re-election as leader. In desperation, it seemed, the party turned again to Fraga as its chairman. The impression of stagnation was reinforced at the 1989 election, when AP again failed to improve on its 1982 perform-ance, despite the PSOE's deteriorating support. However, two significant changes had indeed taken place. AP no longer existed, having metamor-phosed into the People's Party. And for the first time Fraga had not been his party's candidate for Prime Minister.

Both changes had been agreed, on Fraga's recommendation, at the fore-going party conference. Their first intention was to remove the 'ceiling' imposed by his own past [2.4.1]. But they also aimed to resolve the dilemma addressed by UCD and CP in different ways but with equal lack of success, the question of how to bring together the three main strands of the Spanish centre-right: conservatives drawn from the Francoist old guard, liberals and Christian Democrats [2.2.2, 2.4.1]. The change in party name was a clear sop to the latter, 'People's Party' being the designation adopted by Christian Democrats internationally; Fraga also agreed that the party's MEPs would join the Christian Democrat group in the European Parliament [4.3.1]. At the same time he brought Marcelino Oreja, an internationally known Christian Democrat and former UCD minister (see Table 4.2), into the party leadership.

These various moves were intended to give the newly-born PP the image of a modern, mainstream European party, linked to successful Christian Democratic parties in Germany and other EU countries. Yet in terms of eco-nomic policy, if anything the PP shifted away from Christian Democratic ideas towards more liberal ones, a move which enabled it to regain the sup-port of the CEOE [2.4.1]. The resultant mix of social conservatism and eco-nomic liberalism brought the PP ideologically close to the British Tories, but in their contemporary, Thatcherite guise rather than the traditional brand Fraga had always admired.

The problem of Fraga's own person was solved by removing him with honour from the national political scene. In 1989 he headed the PP's slate at the Galician regional election; winning an overall majority he withdrew to govern his own home region. At his party's 1990 Conference – the first held under the initials PP – he was elected to the special post of founding chairman (*presidente fundador*). He was replaced as party leader by the man Fraga himself had chosen to be PP's candidate for Prime Minister the previous year, José María Aznar.

2.4.3 Aznar and the PP's rise to power

Under Aznar the PP began a slow but steady recovery. The new leader had three factors in his favour. The party's disastrous financial situation had been greatly eased by the new provisions for state funding introduced in 1987 [2.1.3]. Having committed a fatal tactical error the PP's only real rival for centre-right votes in most of the country collapsed into obscurity [2.2.3], leaving the PP as the only real alternative to the PSOE. And the Socialists' own increasing problems made them much more vulnerable than before [2.3.4].

On the debit side, Aznar experienced considerable difficulty in establishing himself as a credible leader in his own right. Although he was judged to have won the first of his televised debates with González during the 1993 general election campaign, he continued to lag behind the Prime Minister in popular esteem. Given the highly personalized focus of Spanish politics, this inevitably made it hard for the PP to turn itself into a genuine alternative government (*alternativa de poder*). That, in turn, was one important reason why it failed to confirm opinion poll forecasts by winning the 1993 general election. Even so, its results were by far the best achieved by the party or any of its predecessors.

The other main factor in the narrow 1993 defeat was the PSOE's strategy of insinuating that the PP was still closely linked to the Franco regime, in its ideas and also in its personnel. In response, Aznar stepped up his efforts to bring forward a new generation of leaders, like himself too young to have been involved with the previous regime. At the same time, he continued working to give the PP the strong, country-wide basis AP had never fully established.

In conjunction with PP general secretary Francisco Alvarez Cascos he achieved considerable success in this task. Party membership rose markedly and the party's youth wing New Generation (*Nuevàs Generaciones*) flourished. At the same time, the PP succeeded in marginalizing many of the regional centre-right parties which had emerged in the mid-1980s [2.4.2]. With the two largest, in Aragon and Navarre, it reached agreements to present joint lists for general elections. By the mid-1990s the PP was firmly established as a major political player in all the regions with the exception of the Basque Country and Catalonia, where most voters were still deeply suspicious of it.

Even so, the fact that a basically conservative party remained stronger in the large cities, especially Madrid, than the rural areas and small towns pointed to continuing gaps in the party's organization relative to that of the PSOE. But above the local level, which in any case is of declining importance in an age of media politics, a strong structure was built up. Its nature is such as to centralize power within the party in the hands of the 'National Executive Committee' and, above all, of the party chairman (*presidente*). In that post Aznar now exercised a hold over his party every bit as powerful as Felipe González's over the PSOE [2.3.3] – without the benefit of his rival's charisma.

Aznar's efforts first began to bear fruit in 1994, when the PP outpolled the PSOE in elections to the European Parliament, its first victory in a Spain-wide contest (see Table 4.3). At the following year's regional and municipal elections it enjoyed further success, taking control of 12 out of 17 regions, and all the large cities except Corunna and those in the Basque Country and Catalonia. This triumph also had a knock-on effect in that it brought to public notice a whole series of the party's regional leaders who had previously been largely anonymous. Unlike the old UCD barons [2.2.2], though, they have been kept clearly subordinate to the party's Madrid leadership.

Avoiding the errors of both AP and UCD has been a clear priority for Aznar. On the other hand, in the run-up to the 1996 general election – a time when the twentieth anniversary of Franco's death brought the transition into the spotlight – he was at pains to identify his party with positive memories of UCD [2.2.3]. Its conference held in January of that year was dominated by the notion of the PP as a 'centre' party. While that may have had positive effects, it also allowed the PSOE once more to exploit the past in the subsequent campaign. On this occasion the focus of Socialist innuendo was the influence allegedly exercised over the PP by the Opus Dei organization, whose close involvement with the Franco regime is notorious [5.1.2.2].

The tactic succeeded to the extent that, while the PP did win the 1996 election, its victory was much narrower than predicted by the polls. Aznar had no overall majority, and for a while it looked as though he might fall at the final hurdle of securing enough parliamentary support from regional parties. However, after over two months of negotiations he succeeded in hammering out a deal with three of them; the tiny Canary Islands Alliance, the Basque PNV and, crucially, the Catalan CiU, which had previously maintained the Socialists in power [2.3.4]. The PP's long march to power was finally over.

2.4.4 The PP in office

Aznar's first cabinet represented living proof of the PP's dual nature. Some ministers were drawn from the old AP [2.4.1], others had roots in the more centrist UCD [2.2.2]. Its two most experienced figures illustrated the point. The new Foreign Minister was Abel Matutes (see Table 4.2), an AP stalwart. His colleague at Interior was Jaime Mayor Oreja, the nephew of the UCD grandee who had been one of the PP's founders [2.4.2]. More generally, the PP's policies during much of its first term displayed a similar duality, sometimes evoking comparisons with the Francoist past, sometimes indicating an openness and moderation previously alien to the Spanish Right.

Among the latter could be counted, first, a surprisingly successful relationship with the trade unions that contrasted sharply with the confrontation typical of the Socialists' later years in power [5.2.1.2]. As well as improving the PP's image among floating voters, this approach produced concrete benefits in terms of social security funding [9.1.2] and employment creation [6.2.4.2]. The PP also made no significant attempt to reverse social or legal reforms undertaken since 1978; in particular it dropped demands for a return of the death penalty and for convicted ETA terrorists to be deprived of the right to remission of their sentences.

It also unequivocally accepted the new, devolved structure of government, something the old AP had always regarded with suspicion, and even introduced reforms aimed – in theory at least – at diminishing the role of central administration still further [1.5.2]. Aznar managed the tricky task of cooperating with the Catalan regionalists of CiU surprisingly well, and did not hesitate to impose discipline on his own followers in the region when they threatened to upset the relationship [3.2.1.3]. And he made significant concessions over fiscal policy to both the CiU and the Basque PNV [3.3.3] whose demands the Spanish Right had traditionally regarded as little better than treason, albeit here Aznar was clearly influenced by his need to keep the regionalists' parliamentary support. The positive political impact of these various steps was evident at the regional elections held in the Basque Country in 1998 and in Catalonia a year later, in both of which the PP made significant advances (see Tables 3.2 and 3.1).

On the other hand, in some of its dealings with regionalism and the related issues, the PP's approach was more reminiscent of the traditional Spanish Right. This was especially true in the Basque Country. That it took a very hard line against ETA was understandable, given that the party had itself become the main target of terrorism [3.2.2.3] and certainly enjoyed widespread public support; it made Home Secretary Mayor Oreja, himself a Basque, Spain's most popular politician. Moreover, Aznar's failure to make any substantive response to the ETA ceasefire of 1998/99, while criticized by many at the time, was arguably vindicated by the subsequent resumption of violence.

However, even though the PP had been happy to exploit allegations about the GAL's 'dirty war' against ETA as an election tactic, once in power it showed no more enthusiasm than its Socialist predecessors for uncovering the whole truth [10.4.2]. And Aznar also insisted on treating the region's largest party, the nationalist PNV [3.2.2.2], as if it were directly allied with terrorism, an allegation that, for all the PNV's ambivalence about violence, was patently absurd. The PP's hope that this confrontational attitude would pay electoral dividends was dashed at the 2001 regional election, the results of which greatly strengthened the PNV. Much more importantly, its attitude was likely to hinder attempts to heal the wounds in Basque society, not help them.

More generally, the PP government tended to display signs of a reactionary Spanish nationalism for which notions of the country's diversity were anathema. The crassest example came in 1997 when the then Education Minister Esperanza Aguirre attempted to impose a standard history curriculum throughout the country. Its strong emphasis on Spain's supposed historical unity was both contrary to most academic opinion, and unhappily reminiscent of Francoist ideas. It was also utterly unacceptable to regionalists, with whom it provoked a bitter dispute (*conflicto de humanidades*). The outcome was highly embarrassing for the government, which was forced to drop both its proposals and, shortly after, the minister herself.

A similarly combative approach, but of a very different nature, was apparent in the government's health policy, which displayed a dogmatic preference for the private sector over the public [9.2.2], reflecting the PP's conversion to a neoliberal view of economics that was also apparent in the enthusiasm for deregulation and privatization displayed by the Economics and Finance Minister Rodrigo Rato. It was a line that caused disquiet to some party traditionalists, notably the Christian Democrat Miguel Herrero de Miñón [2.4.2].

Others on the PP's right wing were more unhappy with the way Aznar had quietly accepted so many of the changes made since 1975, in particular his concessions to the regions. His ally, the Catalan leader Pujol [3.2.1.2], was frequently the target of their spleen. But, far from heeding their concerns, their leader returned to his theme that the PP was a party of the centre [2.4.3] – indeed he started to use the term alone, not in the form 'centre-right' previously favoured. To back up the notion, in 1999 he replaced party chairman Francisco Alvarez Cascos, who was associated with the adversarial politics of the early 1990s, with the less flamboyant Javier Arenas, and also sacked his notoriously aggressive press spokesman, Miguel Angel Rodríguez.

2.4.5 Aznar ascendant

The payoff for Aznar and his party came on 12 March 2000 (*12-M*). Against all expectations, the PP was not only re-elected but secured a comfortable overall majority in both Houses of Parliament. By consolidating its gains in the Basque Country and Catalonia it also established itself, at last, as a truly national party. The triumph, quite unprecedented for a Spanish conservative, owed not a little to the steady growth in Aznar's personal standing, once such a handicap for the party [2.4.3]. And it, in turn, strengthened his position still further, confirming him as the PP's unchallengeable leader.

Moderation of the PP's image may have been one factor behind its spectacular victory in the 2000 general election. But more important were the Socialist opposition's utter disarray [2.3.6] and, above all, the country's good economic performance. The reasons for that can be debated. Some would give the credit to the PP's slightly more liberal approach; others would argue that the groundwork was laid by the previous government, whose policies the PP largely took over unchanged.

Whatever the reasons, the results were undeniable. Not only did Spain comfortably meet the strict criteria for entry into Economic and Monetary Union [4.2.2]. The benefits were felt in the form of rapid growth and falling unemployment. Aznar's repeated assertion that 'Spain's doing well' (*España va bien*) was derided by his opponents, but it struck a chord with much of the electorate.

The cabinet he subsequently appointed reflected Aznar's greatly enhanced personal position. The most prominent minister, Rodrigo Rato, saw his power-base curtailed with the separation of the finance and economics portfolios

[1.4.5]. Moreover, unlike that of four years earlier the government was now dominated by figures who had made their careers inside the PP itself, under Aznar. The most important of these was Mariano Rajoy, initially in charge of the Prime Minister's Office [1.4.5], but moved in 2001 to Interior when Mayor Oreja [2.4.4] stood down to run, unsuccessfully, for Basque regional PM. The consequent reshuffle underlined the extent of Aznar's control, Rajoy's successor in his former post being Juan José Lucas, a long-time associate of the PM from his home base of Castile-Leon.

The margin of his 2000 victory also freed Aznar from his dependence on outside parliamentary support, a circumstance that some expected to see reflected in more distinctively right-wing policies. In the field of immigration these expectations were borne out in a tougher new Aliens Act [0.4.3]. Generally, though, the policy mixture seems to be much as before. A broadly neoliberal economic policy was tempered by a willingness to reach negotiated agreements with the unions, for example on pension reform. The desire for consensus extended also to the Socialist opposition, with whom the government entered agreements (*pactos de Estado*) on the approach to ETA terrorism [3.2.2.4] and reform of the legal system [10.1.4].

On the other hand, Aznar's second term also saw the continuation of another, less positive trend. Having made much of its predecessors' alleged abuse of power while in office, the PP's record in that regard has not been noticeably better than the PSOE's. Thus in a number of cases state enterprises privatized by it have finished up in the hands of individuals and interests closely linked to the party, the most notorious example being the appointment of Aznar's schoolfriend Juan Villalonga to head the telecommunications giant *Telefónica* [6.4.1]. In turn, *Telefónica* was heavily involved in blatant attempts to control private television news reporting [5.3.2]. Given that manipulation of state television continued more or less unabated [5.3.1], coverage of the 2000 election was just as heavily weighted as ever in favour of the government of the day.

Corruption scandals also continued to emerge, albeit not with the frequency of the early 1990s [2.3.4]. One of the most serious involved Josep Piqué, a Catalan businessman first brought into government as Government Spokesperson and subsequently appointed Foreign Minister. Another, centred on a Madrid financial services firm *Gescartera*, was especially significant because it indirectly implicated Rato, who had been widely seen as Aznar's heir apparent (*delfín*). Almost immediately voices within the PP were raised suggesting the PM should consider his publicly stated intention not to seek a third term. Whatever his decision on the timing, replacing him will undoubtedly prove a difficult task for the PP.

2.5 United Left

Spain's third largest political force – in terms of members and votes, although no longer parliamentary seats – is United Left (*Izquierda Unida/IU*).

IU is in fact an alliance involving both parties and individual members. By far its largest component, however, is the Spanish Communist Party (*Partido Comunista de España/PCE*). Indeed, it is fair to say that until recently IU was a mere vehicle for the PCE, its existence a reflection of the latter's failure to make a significant impact on Spanish politics in its own right.

2.5.1 IU's origins

That failure contrasts with expectations at the time of Franco's death. Both the PCE and outside observers believed that the party would emerge as a major political force – that was why its legalization by the Suárez government before the 1977 election was such a delicate moment in the transition [0.3.2]. The PCE had been the only force to undertake significant opposition activity throughout Spain and had close links to the Workers' Commissions, the strongest trade union federation [5.2.1.1]. Many younger educated Spaniards outside its traditional working-class base had been attracted by its activism.

However, these advantages proved illusory, for a variety of reasons. The emergence of so-called Euro-communism in the 1970s caused turmoil in Western Communist parties. At the very time of Spain's transition to democracy the PCE was hit by deep internal divisions. Furthermore, it had been portrayed for 40 years by regime propaganda as the incarnation of evil and chiefly to blame for the Civil War; even many on the left had bitter memories of its behaviour then. Alone of the major party leaders, the PCE's Santiago Carrillo was old enough to have participated in that conflict.

The desire felt by most Spaniards to bury the memory of the Civil War was a lesson read by many into the results of the 1977 election (see Table 2.1). Both then and in 1979 the PCE performed poorly. In 1982 it suffered a further catastrophic defeat; many former supporters, especially those who had seen the PCE essentially as a means of opposing Franco, now opted to cast a tactical vote (*voto útil*) for the Socialists in order to ensure a government of the left. After this debacle Carrillo resigned and was replaced as general secretary by the much younger Gerardo Iglesias. But he proved unable to turn the party's fortunes around, at a time when the euphoria of the PSOE's arrival in power rendered a left-wing opposition seemingly superfluous. The party was racked by internal dissent, and suffered several splits [2.6].

The 1986 NATO referendum offered a fresh opportunity to the PCE, since it was the only major party to oppose the government outright, and was strongly represented on the Citizens' Platform (*Plataforma Ciudadana*) which coordinated the 'no' campaign. Although this campaign was ultimately unsuccessful [2.3.2], it did attract considerably more support than the PCE had proved able to do at elections. The party's leadership attempted to capitalize on this, by forming a broad grouping of those involved in the Platform to fight the general election held three months later.

The new alliance was christened United Left (*Izquierda Unida/IU*), and succeeded in marginally improving on the Communists' vote four years before.

Later in 1986 IU was given a more formal structure. Originally seven parties formed part of it, but, other than the PCE, only one proved of any lasting importance: the Socialist Action Party (*Partido de Acción Socialista/Pasoc*), made up of PSOE dissidents.

During the late 1980s the collapse of Communist regimes in Eastern Europe made it difficult for IU to make electoral headway, given its domination by the PCE. On the other hand, it received a fresh impulse from the same direction in the shape of a new, more dynamic leader. This was Julio Anguita, the Mayor of Cordoba and known as the 'Red Caliph' because of his success in turning the city into a Communist electoral bastion. Elected PCE general secretary in 1988, the following year he took over as IU's 'general coordinator', or effective leader.

Along with the unpopularity of the government, Anguita's high standing among voters helped IU to double its share of the vote at the 1989 election. Given the Socialist government's abandonment of left-wing policies [2.3.2], this result was actually not particularly impressive. But with the government in ever deeper political trouble [2.3.4], IU's hopes were high in the early 1990s.

2.5.2 Isolation, division, decline

In fact, though, IU's breakthrough never came. Its disappointing showing at the 1993 election, when it made only an insignificant advance, was ascribed at the time to the heart attack suffered during the campaign by its leader, Julio Anguita [2.5.1]. However, Anguita's return to the helm after a rapid recovery revealed that his leadership was more problem than solution, owing to his extreme intransigence in three respects.

First, Anguita refused to allow dissolution of the PCE into IU, a step that would have allowed the latter to become a party in its own right with a simpler organizational structure. It would also have got rid of the Communist name, at a time when it was even less helpful than ever. Second, he was extremely critical of the direction of European integration [4.1.2], and the government's determination to keep Spain at the forefront of the process [4.2.2]. While his criticisms may well have been justified, they – and their harsh tone – were simply not in tune with public sentiment.

Finally, Anguita pursued an unrelentingly hard line against the PSOE, refusing absolutely to cooperate with the Socialists unless they radically changed their economic policies. He was especially loud in condemning the various corruption scandals which affected the Socialists in the 1990s [2.3.4]. In Andalusia IU went so far as to join with the conservative PP in forcing the Socialist regional government to resign. The move gave substance to damaging accusations from the PSOE, who claimed that IU was involved in a 'pincer movement' (*pinza*) on the party, an unholy alliance of left and right that favoured only the latter.

Inside IU too many were unhappy with Anguita's strategy and aloof style. The main focus of dissent was a faction known as the Democratic New Left

Party (*Partido Democrático de Nueva Izquierda/PDNI*), whose main leaders were Cristina Almeida, a combative and popular Madrid lawyer, and Diego López Garrido. These modernizers (*renovadores*) wished to see IU take a more flexible attitude to possible alliances with the PSOE, and to place more stress on new issues, such as feminist and environmentalist ones.

Ranged against the modernizers were those loyal to the Anguita leadership (*oficialistas*). Most of these belonged to the PCE, the only group within IU with a well-established organization. Moreover, like other Communist parties it was used to operating in a highly centralized manner. IU's own structure, by contrast, was weak and ill-defined, which not only presented problems at election times but also made it more difficult for the modernizers to bring about change.

Anguita might have won the internal battle but he had lost the external war, as became crystal clear at the 1996 general election. Despite securing the support of environmentalists in some areas [2.6], IU failed almost entirely to profit from the Socialists' defeat. In theory, the election results brought IU tantalizingly close to power, as they made a coalition government with the PSOE possible. But in practice the deep antagonism which had built up between the two parties – admittedly by no means all Anguita's fault [2.3.6] – ruled that option out. And to rub salt in the wound, at the Andalusian regional election held on the same day the PSOE was re-elected with an increased majority, while IU actually lost ground.

In 1997 IU's already parlous situation was worsened still further when Anguita made a futile attempt to assert his authority. Relations with IU's sections in several regions were severely disrupted, and its semi-independent Catalan organization, Initiative for Catalonia (*Iniciativa per Catalunya/IC*), was prompted to break away entirely. Anguita also expelled the PDNI, whose leadership subsequently opted to link up with the PSOE. Meanwhile the Communists who provided his sole remaining prop were further weakened by the progressive breakdown of their relationship with the trade union federation Workers' Commissions [5.2.1.2].

Finally, in 1999, Anguita stood down as PCE leader, to be replaced by his former deputy Francisco Frutos. In an astonishing reversal of his strategy, Frutos opted to fight the 2000 general election in a loose alliance with the PSOE [2.3.6]. The move cost IU much of its remaining credibility and half of its support; thanks to the vagaries of the electoral system [1.3.1] IU even lost its place as third largest parliamentary party, being overtaken by the Catalan CiU in terms of seats.

Later the same year IU held a special conference to elect a new 'coordinator'. In a very close vote Frutos was defeated by Gaspar Llamazares, a virtual political unknown, who thus became IU's first non-Communist leader. That change in itself removed a major handicap for IU, and Llamazares has enjoyed some success in rebuilding bridges to IC, the Workers' Commissions and some sections of PDNI. He has also attempted to strengthen IU's links with leftist regionalist parties, especially in Galicia, Aragon and Catalonia, while in the Basque Country IU has joined mainstream, centre-right nationalists in a coalition government. Whether these moves, and the Socialists' continuing disarray, will enable a recovery from the disasters of the last decade must be doubted, however.

2.6 MINOR PARTIES

The last twenty years have seen an extraordinary flowering of small parties in Spain. However, almost without exception, these operate at regional level [3.2.3]. Since the demise of the centrist CDS [2.2.3], no Spain-wide party other then the PSOE, PP and IU has come even close to being represented in Parliament.

The absence of a substantial environmentalist party even comparable to the UK Greens reflects a general lack of awareness about environmental issues in Spain [7.3.2]. As well as being weak the country's Greens have also been divided, with no less than five different groups contesting elections in the 1980s. Ecologist groups in some regions have stood jointly with United Left, an ally which has done little to help their cause [2.5.2]. Only in Catalonia, where Greens have taken part in a more wide-reaching realignment of the left [11.10], is their situation slightly more hopeful. At the most recent general election, in 2000, various ecologist groupings again stood, the largest of them obtaining a mere 0.3 per cent of the votes.

That was still more than any party of the extreme right or left could manage, both of which have been perpetually divided into numerous tiny groupings (*grupúsculos*), many ephemeral. This has been particularly true on the left. Immediately following the legalization of parties in 1976 an enormous number of small revolutionary groups professing Trotskyist, Maoist and other revolutionary ideas sprang up. In total these received some 3 per cent of the votes cast at the 1979 general election. Subsequently they have all sunk into insignificance or disappeared altogether.

So too have two parties which in the 1980s split off from the Communist Party (PCE), and which were briefly of minor importance. The Communist Party of the Peoples of Spain (*Partido Comunista de los Pueblos de España/ PCPE*), led by Ignacio Gallego, left the PCE in disagreement with its abandonment of strict Communist orthodoxy. The PCPE later joined United Left [2.5.1], before falling into oblivion. The second such party was formed by the former Communist leader Santiago Carrillo, after he too left the PCE. The ironically titled Spanish Workers' Party–Communist Unity (*Partido de los Trabajadores de España-Unidad Comunista/PTE-UC*) was eventually dissolved by its founder, who advised his few remaining followers to join the PSOE.

In the early years after Franco's death the far right enjoyed a modicum of success under the leadership of Blas Piñar, a devoted follower of Franco. In 1979 National Union (*Unión Nacional/UN*) won one seat in Congress. Subsequently he was associated with the groupings New Force (*Fuerza Nueva*) and National Front (*Frente Nacional/FN*), the latter modelled on Jean Marie Le Pen's party of the same name in France. Neither achieved any significant support, however, and in 1986 they effectively withdrew from electoral politics. Instead, the far right's influence has been apparent in the worrying problem of quasi-organized youth violence, associated especially with skinhead gangs [9.4.2].

The only two smaller parties to have made any impact at all are both maverick formations serving essentially as vehicles for the egos and interests of their leaders – who are also similar in being shady right-wing business figures. Both the Grouping (*Agrupación*), set up by José María Ruiz Mateos, and Jesús Gil y Gil's Independent Liberal Group (*Grupo Independiente Liberal/GIL*) succeeded in winning seats at the 1994 European election (see Table 4.3). Subsequently Ruiz Mateos faded from the political scene. Gil, however, remains a highly controversial mayor of Marbella, while his party has also established a strong presence in Melilla by agitating against immigration into the enclave from Morocco [11.18].

2.7 GLOSSARY

28-O m	28 October 1982 (first PSOE general election victory)
3-M m	3 March 1996 (first PP general election victory)
6-J m	6 June 1993 (fourth and final PSOE general election victory)
abstencionismo m	tendency to/practice of abstaining; abstention rate
afiliación f	membership
agrupación local f	local (party) branch
alternativa de poder f	alternative government
barón m	party baron, powerful faction leader
base electoral f	electoral support (of a party)
bases fpl	rank and file members
binomio m	partnership
bipartidismo m	two-party system
cacique m	(corrupt) local party boss
campaña electoral f	election campaign
cargo m	post, office; office-holder
caso m	affair, scandal
centro-centro m	pure (political) centre
chaqueteo m	party-hopping
coalición electoral f	electoral alliance
Comisión Ejecutiva f	National Executive (of party)
conflicto de humanidades m	dispute over proposed new history syllabus in 1997/98
Congreso Federal m	National Conference (of party)
consenso m	consensus, spirit of compromise
cristiano-demócrata m	Christian Democrat
cuota de afiliación f	membership fee
cúpula f	upper echelons (of party)
delfín m	heir apparent (to political post)

democristiano m	Christian Democrat
desgaste m	loss of popularity (as a result of holding office)
elecciones anticipadas fpl	early election
elecciones generales/legislativas fpl	general election
elecciones primarias fpl	primary election (to select party's candidate for PM)
electorado m	electorate, voters
federación f	regional section of PSOE
felipismo m	personalized leadership style of Felipe González
Ferraz	PSOE headquarters (from Madrid street where it is located)
fichaje m	signing; prominent personality incorporated onto party's slate of candidates
financiación f	funding
fontaneros mpl	'plumbers', Adolfo Suárez's group of political advisers
Génova	PP headquarters (from Madrid street where it is located)
gobierno de coalición m	coalition government
gran derecha f	broad party of the right
grupo parlamentario m	parliamentary party
grupúsculo m	microparty
guerrista m	supporter of Alfonso Guerra in PSOE internal disputes
independiente m	non-party member brought onto party slate or appointed to political office
Juventudes Socialistas fpl	Young Socialists (PSOE youth wing)
mayoría natural f	natural party of government
militante mf	(party) member, activist
Movimiento m	Franco regime's state-party
Nuevas Generaciones fpl	New Generation (PP youth wing)
obrerismo m	traditional working-class socialism
oficialista mf	supporter of party leadership in internal dispute (especially of J. Anguita within IU)
pacto de Estado m	formal agreement between government and opposition on major issues
pacto municipal m	mutual support pact in local government
participación electoral f	(election) turnout
partido de cargos m	party largely made up of office-holders
partitocracia f	state dominated by parties
pinza f	pincer movement; tacit alliance of IU and PP to attack PSOE
presidente fundador m	founding chairman (of PP), honorary title given to Manuel Fraga
programa electoral m	election manifesto
referéndum de la OTAN m	1986 NATO referendum
renovación total f	complete overhaul (of a party, or other organization)

renovador m	modernizer (in PSOE or IU)
siete magníficos mpl	'magnificent seven', founders of AP
sopa de siglas f	'alphabet soup', myriad small parties which appeared after legalization in 1976
tasa de abstención f	abstention rate
techo electoral m	electoral ceiling, level of support that a party is unable to break through
tendencia f	current of opinion, faction (in party)
transfuguismo m	practice of crossing the parliamentary floor, i.e. switching parties
voto útil m	tactical vote/voting

3

REGIONALIZATION AND REGIONALISM

Spain is a famously diverse land, partly because of topography and climate. Yet diversity is also the result of the country's belated and partial economic development which, in the late nineteenth century, led to political regionalism, in the form of demands for self-rule in the Basque Country and Catalonia. These soon became an important issue in Spanish politics, and Franco's brutal attempt to resolve it only increased its salience. This chapter begins by examining the very different response of the democratic regime installed after his death. It then looks at how this has interacted with feelings of regional identity to bring about new tensions, before finally considering the further institutional changes to which these, in turn, have contributed.

First, however, a point of terminology: throughout, the term 'region' is used in a purely geographical sense, to mean a part of Spain. It is in no sense contrasted with 'nation', which is understood to be a political and social concept. 'Regionalism' is used to describe political activity based on the notion that the people of a particular area have shared interests and a right to some form of self-rule. It includes some movements or parties that consider the inhabitants of their particular region to form a nation, and are therefore often termed – and term themselves – 'nationalist'.

3.1 THE INITIAL ROUND OF DEVOLUTION

Arguably the most sweeping of all the changes which Spain underwent following Franco's death was the rapid devolution of power to the country's regions. Within eight years the dictatorship's highly centralized power structures had been replaced by the regionalized form of state known as the *Estado de las Autonomías*. The change is widely regarded, inside and outside Spain, as perhaps the major achievement of the 1978 Constitution. That is a misleading view, however – and not only because it is by no means clear that devolution has been an unequivocal success [3.3.1]. Quite simply, the Constitution's architects did not set out to establish a new form of state but to solve a specific political problem. And the form which emerged was as much a reflection of political manoeuvring as of the framework laid down by the Constitution.

3.1.1 Regions in the Constitution

It is no exaggeration to say that the single most important challenge facing the Constitution's framers was the pressure for self-rule in Catalonia and the Basque Country. A major issue in its own right, this pressure was also closely linked to the danger of military insurrection, since the army was highly sensitive about Spanish national unity and because the security forces were bearing the brunt of terrorism in the Basque Country [3.2.2.1]. The purpose of the Constitution's provisions for the regions was accordingly to strike a delicate balance between satisfying Basque and Catalan demands, on the one hand, and provoking the army, on the other.

These provisions were contained in the lengthy Title VIII, and it is little wonder that they gave anything but a precise blueprint for nation-wide devolution. In fact they did none of the things that would normally be expected from such a blueprint. They did not define clearly the powers to be wielded by regional authorities; they did not specify how these were to be funded; they did not even establish a set of regional boundaries.

What the Constitution did do was to stipulate that regions might accede to a degree of limited self-rule if they chose to do so. Any province or group of provinces which could demonstrate the existence of popular demand for devolution would have the right to become an autonomous region (*Comunidad Autónoma/CA*). The mechanism for achieving such status was defined as a Statute of Autonomy. A region's Statute would serve as a sort of mini-constitution, establishing institutions of regional government and defining the policy fields in which they could exercise powers, either legislative or executive.

Title VIII also defined upper and lower limits to the extent of such powers. Article 148 listed subject areas in which powers would be assumed by any region becoming autonomous, while Article 149 defined those in which powers were to be reserved to the central government. Since the lists were far from exhaustive, this arrangement left open the possibility of regions acquiring powers in areas appearing on neither. There was also provision for central government to devolve its own powers to particular regions by decree.

Within this framework, two different procedures were established by which a region could become autonomous. The simpler, specified in Article 143, required only the approval of a sufficient proportion of the region's municipalities. However, regions going down this track would accede only to the powers set out in Article 148. Before taking on any others – up to the limit set by Article 149 – it would have to wait for five years. Moreover, it would then have to get parliamentary approval for amending its Statute of Autonomy, a potentially difficult process since Statutes have entrenched status [1.3.3]. Because of this time lapse, the procedure established in Article 143 is known, rather confusingly, as the slow route (*vía lenta*) to autonomy.

If a region wished to follow the fast route (*vía rápida*) to more extensive powers it was required to satisfy much more complex and demanding conditions. Set out in Article 151, these included holding a referendum, in which the proposed Statute must be approved not just in the region as a whole but also in each of its provinces. However, in three cases this requirement was waived by the Constitution's second Transitional Disposition [1.1.2].

That was devoted to regions which had previously 'approved by referendum a draft Statute of Autonomy', giving them the status of 'historic nationalities' – an invented term which avoided the use of either nation or region. Along with Galicia, this formula conveniently singled out Catalonia and the Basque Country. The particular complexity of the latter case was reflected in a further Transitional Disposition, the fourth, which explicitly allowed for Navarre's eventual incorporation into a Basque autonomous region.

3.1.2 Devolution in practice

Thus, in constitutional terms, devolution could perfectly well have affected only the 'historic nationalities' [3.1.1], plus perhaps a few more regions with clear historical claims to be considered distinctive. Indeed, that may well have been the intention of those who framed the Constitution. If so their plans went dramatically awry; within five years devolution had extended to the whole of Spain.

Ironically, the reasons why the process went so far so fast were to a large extent of their own making. For, by singling out some regions for privileged treatment they laid the basis for feelings of resentment and discrimination elsewhere (*agravio comparativo*). And, by placing such complex obstacles in the way of other regions who wished to catch up, they not only aggravated such feelings but also ensured that resolving any resultant disputes would be a messy and conflictual process.

The political reality that devolution was essentially meant to pacify Basque and Catalan pressure was emphasized by the fact that it was under way even before the Constitution itself was approved. In the three 'historic nationalities', bodies were set up to prepare for forthcoming autonomy (*órganos preautonómicos*) – specifically, to negotiate with the central government over the details of their Statutes [3.1.1]. By the autumn of 1979 drafts including wide-ranging powers had been agreed in the crucial Basque and Catalan cases and, on 25 October of that year, both received overwhelming popular approval in their respective regions. In Galicia the process took rather longer, reflecting the lack of political and popular pressure there [11.12], but by the end of 1980 it too had achieved autonomy, albeit with significantly fewer powers.

By then, however, the focus of attention had moved elsewhere, to Andalusia. Politicians in Spain's largest region were acutely concerned that their region's grave economic backwardness [11.1] would be aggravated still further if it were left behind politically as well. They therefore took the initiative in drawing up proposals for an Andalusian Statute that went well beyond the basic level of autonomy specified in Article 143 of the Constitution. Having been agreed with representatives of the central authorities, on 28 February 1980 these were submitted to a referendum and obtained a clear majority in the region as a whole.

However, a narrow 'no' vote in one province (Almería) prevented the Statute from coming into force [3.1.1]. Whatever the Constitution might say, this result was politically intolerable. Recognizing as much, the government defied explicit constitutional restrictions and allowed a second referendum on a slightly revised text. Held on 20 October 1981, it resulted in a favourable majority in all eight Andalusian provinces.

These convoluted and highly publicized developments were largely responsible for triggering off so-called devolution fever (*fiebre autonómica*) in the rest of Spain. Even in regions where there was little sense of a distinct identity, and where self-rule had never previously been an issue, demands grew loud for a measure of autonomy – for coffee all round (*café para todos*) in the phrase of the day. They were viewed with alarm by the centrist government and the main opposition party, the Socialists. Especially after the 1981 attempted coup [0.3.3], both were concerned that the army might use Spain's alleged disintegration as an excuse for further interventions. In the summer of 1981 they therefore reached a pact on the regions (*pacto autonómico*) intended to keep devolution within bounds.

Specifically they agreed that they would block any attempts by other regions to follow Andalusia down the fast route to autonomy [3.1.1]. They also agreed on a Devolution Standardization Act (*Ley Orgánica del Armonización del Proceso Autonómico/LOAPA*), bulldozed through Parliament with their joint support. The LOAPA laid down that, in the numerous policy areas where both the Madrid government and the regions enjoyed legislative powers, central laws would always take precedence. It also asserted Madrid's right to pass 'coordinating' laws to constrain regional legislation, even in fields where regions' Statutes had given them exclusive legislative powers.

The main effect of the LOAPA was, once again, far removed from what had been intended. In Catalonia and, especially, the Basque Country, it was widely seen as an attempt to snatch back much of what had only just been granted. Regionalists mounted ferocious campaigns against the Act that undoubtedly greatly strengthened them politically. They also challenged its provisions in the Constitutional Court [1.1.3]. To the government's considerable embarrassment, the Court found almost entirely in their favour and in 1983 all the LOAPA's key provisions were struck from the statute book.

The other main point of the 1981 pact proved largely irrelevant. No more regions made any real attempt to follow the fast route. On the other hand, devolution itself proved unstoppable; the question was no longer whether it would extend to the whole of Spain but how the country would be divided up. The main issues in that regard arose in and around the two Castiles, Old and New, and were resolved by giving autonomous status to the Castilian provinces of Madrid, Cantabria and the Rioja, while denying it to the historically separate region of Leon (*León*).

Overall, these decisions served to increase markedly the disparities between the new autonomous regions in terms of population and resources, and in doing so stored up certain problems for the future [3.3.4]. But in the short term they enabled much more speedy and complete devolution than had seemed likely in 1978. By the end of 1983 only the two North African enclaves of Ceuta and Melilla had still to have their status regulated; not until 1994 did they finally become 'autonomous cities' [11.18]. The remainder of the country – mainland Spain (*España peninsular*) and the two island groups (*archipiélagos*) of the Balearics and Canaries – had been divided into autonomous regions, 17 in total.

3.1.3 Regional institutions and powers

The maps which soon appeared showing Spain neatly divided into regions gave the impression that these constituted a homogeneous tier of government. Another Spanish neologism, *autonómico*, was coined to refer to it, once again to avoid hurting Basque and Catalan sensibilities. The impression of homogeneity was misleading, but it was reinforced by the remarkable similarity in the institutional structures of the new regions.

In effect, all of them adopted the model prescribed by the Constitution for those following the fast route to autonomy [3.1.1], itself largely a copy of that applying at national level. Thus, each of the regions has a High Court of Justice [10.1.3]. A regional prime minister (*presidente*) leads the regional government, the official designation of which often reflects historical or linguistic factors (see Chapter 11). It is made up of regional ministers (*consejeros*), who head the various departments (*consejerías*) into which the regional administration is divided.

Every region also has a single-chamber parliament elected for a four-year term, using electoral systems which, with minor differences, are copies of that used for general elections [1.3.1]. In the Balearics and Canaries each island elects its own regional MPs, while in Murcia special regional electoral divisions have been created. Otherwise the provinces serve as constituencies, the more rural ones being generally over-represented as for general elections. This effect is especially marked in the Basque autonomous community, whose three provinces are equally represented in the regional parliament despite their widely differing populations [11.5].

Another area of difference is in the timing of elections. The four regions which achieved more extensive autonomy following a regional referendum (Andalusia, the Basque Country, Catalonia and Galicia) [3.1.2] have their own electoral calendars, both because their initial polls were held on individual dates and because in all four the government has exercised its right to call an early election. In the remaining 13 regions, those which followed the slow route to autonomy [3.1.1], elections are held on a single day, coinciding with the nation-wide municipal elections. These polling days have acquired importance as indicators of the national political situation; the next is due in 2003.

However, by far the most significant differences among the regions at the end of the initial devolution process lay in the extent of their powers (*competencias*) or, more precisely, of the fields in which they could legislate independently. In the case of the four fast-route regions these were wide, and in many fields virtually untrammelled once the central government's right to impose 'coordinating' legislation had been limited by the Constitutional Court [3.1.2]. The precise extent of these regions' autonomy varied according to provisions of their Statutes. All had education powers, for instance, whereas only the Basques and Catalans had the capacity to establish their own police forces [10.2.2].

The remaining regions' powers were limited to the fields specified in the Constitution's Article 148 [3.1.1], which exclude all major economic functions as well as education and policing. In other fields these regions had powers to legislate only if authorized to do so by the Spanish Parliament, and then only within the guidelines of framework laws passed by it [1.3.3]. Otherwise they were restricted to carrying out administrative tasks delegated by the central government.

In all cases, the speed with which powers were assumed in practice was inevitably conditioned by logistical considerations, such as the availability of suitable premises in the regional capitals, as well as by the enthusiasm and competence of the new regional administrations. Clearly these could not assume all powers accorded to them overnight. Instead there was a gradual process of handing over individual areas of responsibility (*transferencias*), the course of which was negotiated between the central authorities and those of the region concerned, in joint committees.

The situation was further complicated by the special arrangements made for three regions where, for various reasons, there was significant pressure for extended powers [3.2.3]. In the cases of the Canary Islands and Valencia, the government made use of the constitutional provision to devolve legislative responsibility by decree in a number of fields excluded from the minimum list [3.1.1]. In Navarre, however, this solution was rejected by regional representatives. Instead they insisted that autonomy be treated as a reaffirmation of the historical rights (*fueros*) which Navarre, alone of all the new regions, had retained through even the Franco era [11.15]. In practice, though, the effect was identical, placing Navarre too among a group of seven regions all with slightly different powers in excess of the minimal level enjoyed by the remaining ten.

3.1.4 Funding

Crucial to any system of decentralized government are the arrangements for funding (*financiación*) of the various sub-state units. In the Spanish case this, too, is an area of differences between the various regions. Here, though, the reasons were less political than historical, and the outcome was that the Basque Country – along with Navarre – was placed on a separate footing from all the other regions, this time including Catalonia.

These 15 regions are covered by a common funding scheme (*régimen común*), the basis of which was set out in the Autonomous Regions' Funding Act (*Ley Orgánica de Financiación de las Comunidades Autónomas/LOFCA*). Under this measure they received a block grant, dependent on the cost of carrying out the responsibilities transferred to them. They were also allowed to retain the revenues from certain, relatively unimportant taxes, and from other sources such as fines, once authorized to do so by the central government. Within this common scheme certain special arrangements apply to the Canary Islands [11.6], and also to Ceuta and Melilla [11.18], because of their geographical distinctiveness.

In practice, this system meant that much depended on political negotiations. Officially they took place in a body established by the LOFCA, the Joint Fiscal Policy Council (*Consejo de Política Fiscal y Financiera de las Comunidades Autónomas*). This Council was made up of the central government Ministers of Finance and Public Administration, and the various regional finance ministers (*consejeros de Hacienda*). Unofficially, deals were inevitably struck behind the scenes, between and within parties.

That gave a double advantage to the regions with the greatest autonomy – and therefore the largest block grants – which were almost by definition those with most political clout. Moreover, in a number of cases, specifically that of Catalonia, they were also already among the wealthiest. The system thus threatened to widen the already considerable economic disparities between regions [6.3.5].

This effect acquired particular significance once the Socialist Party (PSOE) came to dominate Spanish politics in the mid-1980s [2.3.2], since it relied heavily on support from the country's three poorest regions (Andalusia, Castile-La Mancha and Extremadura). In 1985 the PSOE introduced various reforms designed to reduce the system's imbalances. The most important was to activate an instrument provided for in the Constitution but previously unutilized: the Inter-regional Compensation Fund (*Fondo de Compensación Interterritorial/FCI*). Drawn from central resources, the FCI is distributed on the basis of regions' needs and so provides a mechanism, albeit relatively limited, for redressing the disparities between them.

Two regions, the Basque Country and Navarre, are not covered by these arrangements. Instead, they have their own funding system (*régimen foral*) which, like other special features of their autonomy, derives from their historical rights (*fueros*) [11.5]. Under it most taxes, in particular income and corporation tax, in the two regions are collected by the provincial authorities. These then pay a certain sum – a reverse block grant (*cupo* in the Basque case, or *aportación* for Navarre) – to the central government in respect of the services it provides. Along with the precise range of taxes covered, the amount of the reverse grant is laid down in a special financial agreement (*concierto económico* or *convenio económico*). The original agreements were limited to a period of twenty years, with the details – including the amount of the reverse block grant – to be renegotiated every five.

This system places the two regions in a much stronger position than those covered by the common scheme. First, they negotiate directly with the central government and do not have to face up to the competing demands of other regions. Secondly, their tax collecting role means that any delay in reaching a decision prejudices not them but the central government, so that any pressure to reach a rapid agreement falls on Madrid. Given that the two regions are also among the country's more prosperous, their special treatment has added weight to the argument that devolution aggravates regional differences.

3.2 THE REGIONALIST REACTION

The uneven outcome of the initial round of devolution, and the fact that it was to a large extent the result of overt political pressure, meant that it could only be the first stage in a continuing process. On the one hand, it posed considerable administrative problems [3.3.1]. On the other, far from neutralizing regionalism as a political force, it gave rise to new regionalist pressures. Admittedly the immediate aim of containing the situation in the Basque Country and Catalonia was achieved. But in both areas demands for greater self-rule continued, and in some ways even became more radical. And at the same time, parties claiming to represent distinctive local interests sprang up in virtually every one of the newly created autonomous regions, in some cases gaining sufficient strength to become a force not just in regional but in Spanish politics.

(NB. This section concentrates on developments of significance at the Spanish level. For further information on those internal to a particular region, readers should refer to the appropriate section(s) of Chapter 11.)

3.2.1 Catalonia

Of the two regionalist movements to which devolution was in large measure a response, historically much the stronger was that in Catalonia. On the other hand, Catalan regionalism (*catalanismo*) was also noted for its moderation and flexibility. The result was that, after the dictator's death, devolution of powers to the region took place in an atmosphere of consensus. Subsequently, however, the very fact of autonomy, combined with political developments across Spain as a whole, has led to significant changes in the nature of regionalism and in its relationship with the central authorities.

3.2.1.1 The 1970s regionalist consensus

The notion that Catalonia's distinctive character should be reflected in some form of self-government has long been shared by much of the region's industrial elite and the broad mass of its population. Yet generally regionalists have wanted no more than extensive self-government within Spain, and were disposed to reach agreements with the Spanish authorities on this and other issues (*pactisme*). They were thus satisfied by the establishment of a devolved regional government (*Generalitat*) under the Second Republic [0.1].

That was subsequently abolished by Franco, as part of his efforts to stamp out regionalism [0.2]. While these backfired spectacularly and only succeeded in greatly reinforcing it, they did not alter its rational and peaceable nature. For regionalist opposition to his rule centred on cultural issues, and on building a broad consensus on the need for wide-ranging self-government once democracy was restored, both inside Catalonia and with opposition forces throughout Spain. These efforts were so successful that Catalan regionalism and its demands were closely integrated into the transition process of the late 1970s.

Thus the 'fathers' of the 1978 Constitution [1.1.1] included a regionalist, while Catalonia produced a massive 'yes' vote in the referendum on the final text. And a Catalan Statute of Autonomy was relatively easily agreed between the region's representatives and the central government, before it too was overwhelmingly approved by popular vote [3.1.1]. This was hardly surprising since, with the exception of the right-wing People's Alliance [2.4.1], whose presence in Catalonia was minimal, all significant political forces in the region backed devolution.

Support was particularly strong among the two main left-wing parties, both of which themselves enjoyed a considerable degree of autonomy from their Spanish counterparts. Indeed the Catalan Communist Party (*Partit Socialista Unificat de Catalunya/PSUC*) was formally independent of the Spanish PCE [2.5.1], although in practice the two cooperated closely. The PSUC had been a major force in the 1930s and ran a strong third in Catalonia at the first elections after Franco's death. From 1982, however, its fortunes declined dramatically. Eventually it split over the decision to dissolve itself into Initiative for Catalonia (IC), the autonomous Catalan wing of United Left [2.5.2]. Although IC has managed a modest recovery it remains a minor force even in regional politics.

By contrast, the Catalan Socialist Party (*Partit dels Socialistes de Catalunya/ PSC*) has topped the poll in Catalonia at every general election since 1975. It also has a strong presence in local government, especially in the regional capital Barcelona; Pasqual Maragall, the city's mayor for almost twenty years from 1979, is the party's leading figure. Technically the PSC, which was set up as recently as 1978, is the Catalan regional section of the Spanish Socialist Party (PSOE). However, it was created largely outside the PSOE, which had virtually no roots in Catalonia before the Franco era. It also continues to enjoy a uniquely wide degree of autonomy within the PSOE [2.3.3], whose leadership it has frequently defied. In particular, the PSC has consistently advocated Spain's conversion into a fully-fledged federation.

In that respect the PSC's position, like that of the PSUC, is indistinguishable from that of traditional regionalists. Prior to the Franco era the largest such force was Catalan Republican Left (*Esquerra Republicana de Catalunya/ ERC*), which dominated the region's politics during the 1930s. Both then and since 1975 ERC has occasionally voiced demands for outright independence, but has always returned to backing devolution eventually. In any case, since 1975 it has been only a minor player in regional politics, with no real impact on the Spanish level at all.

Indeed as early as the inaugural general election of 1977 ERC was replaced as the leading Catalan political force by the newly formed Convergence and Union (CiU) [3.2.1.2]. Even it came only fourth in the region, behind not only the PSC and PSUC but also the local section of the centrist UCD [2.2.2], a performance it repeated in 1979. It was therefore a major surprise when CiU, which fully backed devolution as the best option for Catalonia, topped the poll at the first regional election held in 1980. Although it fell well short of an overall majority, the degree of consensus prevailing in the region meant that it was able to form a government alone. Over the next few years, too, it could usually rely on broad cross-party support for its legislation, which was concerned mainly with organizing the new regional institutions and with promoting the regional economy.

3.2.1.2 The rise of Pujolism

Since 1980 the main feature of Catalan politics has been the extraordinary success of the young regionalist party Convergence and Union. While at general elections it has been regularly outpolled by the Socialist PSC [3.2.1.1], it has won most seats at every single regional election, and from 1984 to 1995 held an overall majority in the regional parliament. And ever since 1980 it has run the regional government (*Generalitat*) alone, without once having to rely on coalition partners.

Convergence and Union (*Convergència i Unió/CiU*) is actually an alliance of two separate parties. One, the Catalan Democratic Union (*Unió Democràtica de Catalunya/UDC*), is a Christian Democrat formation set up in the 1930s. The other partner is Catalan Democratic Convergence (*Convergència Democràtica de Catalunya/CDC*), a party set up only in 1976. CDC, which was and is much the more important component of CiU, originally defined itself as centrist, even centre-left, in socio-economic terms. Its founder was Jordi Pujol, a leading figure in opposition to Franco, whose prestige was a major factor in CiU's initial success and who has been regional PM (*president de la Generalitat*) since 1980.

CiU's dominance of the new Catalan institutions had a profound effect on it as an organization. Like other governing parties in Spain it was able to exploit the resultant powers of patronage and, on occasion, the opportunities for illicit financing [2.1.3] to consolidate its position. Like them, too, it tended to become highly centralized [2.1.2]. CiU also strengthened its links with business, especially the powerful banking sector, and was even involved in setting up a new bank, *Banca Catalana*. Indeed, while never fully abandoning the rhetoric of social solidarity among Catalans, it has become increasingly aligned with business interests.

Above all, CiU's success allowed it to project itself as the champion of regional interests, especially *vis-à-vis* Madrid. In the 1980s the regional government repeatedly clashed with the central authorities over aspects of the devolution process, such as the speed at which powers were transferred or attempts by Madrid to constrain their use [3.1.2]. Catalonia accounted for more cases of this nature referred to the Constitutional Court than any other region at this time, even the Basque Country [3.2.2.2]. At the same time, CiU took to attacking Spanish parties operating in Catalonia, especially its main rival, the PSC, as mere 'subsidiaries' of their Madrid headquarters with no real loyalty to the region. This gross distortion of the PSC's position in particular [3.2.1.1] was a clear attempt to claim the sole right to speak for Catalonia as a whole, something quite new in Catalan regionalism.

Also foreign to traditional regionalism was the sense of hostility towards things Spanish. It went hand in hand with Pujol's tendency to hint at a desire for more than mere autonomy, most notoriously following the Baltic states' achievement of independence. The CiU leader was extremely active in promoting Catalan interests internationally, especially once Spain joined the European Community in 1986 [4.2.1], within which the region was economically well-placed to go it alone if necessary [6.3.5]. Linked to these implications that Spain was more a part of Europe than of Spain was a growing tendency to assert Catalonia's status as a nation and not a mere region.

Pujol's importance to CiU is impossible to exaggerate. He was and is its major electoral asset and its unchallengeable leader, his standing in Catalonia enhanced by his extraordinary stint in office. Not for nothing did CiU's new, more assertive brand of regionalism become known as Pujolism (*pujolisme*). But, rather like the *felipismo* associated with long-serving Spanish premier Felipe González [2.3.3], Pujolism is less a philosophy than a political style. In Pujol's case that meant a hard-headed concern to squeeze the maximum benefits for Catalonia from the Spanish state, often with little apparent regard for the effects on the rest of the country.

In that respect, too, his approach was at odds with Catalan regionalism, for which a prosperous Catalonia required Spain as a whole to prosper. That was also the position of Pujol's long-serving deputy Miquel Roca, who served first as Catalonia's representative among the 1978 Constitution's 'fathers' [3.2.1.1], and later as leader of CiU's MPs in the Spanish Parliament. When, in 1993, the Socialist government there turned to CiU for support [2.3.4], Roca favoured accepting its offer to enter a formal coalition – as Catalan leaders had done in similar crises before. But by now he was marginalized within CiU, whose leader agreed only to provide parliamentary support (*pacto legislativo*).

Over the next seven years this arrangement allowed Pujol to exert enormous pressure on successive Madrid administrations, while keeping to a minimum the constraints on his own freedom of manoeuvre. Thus he made sure that the Socialists never strayed from the tough economic line required to join European Monetary Union [4.1.3], a strategy strongly favoured by his own business backers but painful for many Socialist voters [6.1.3]. Yet he pursued policies at odds with those of the central government in several policy areas, notably health [9.2.2], a sort of *de facto* extension of Catalonia's already wide autonomy.

Meanwhile, however, the formal basis of the region's privileged position was coming under threat. For the second round of devolution, begun in the early 1990s [3.3.2], undermined the special status enjoyed by it along with the other 'historic nationalities' [3.1.1]. Pujol responded by demanding for Catalonia the exceptional funding arrangements enjoyed by the Basque Country and Navarre, which had proved to give those regions significant practical advantages [3.1.4]. There was no real ground for this claim, which was essentially a negotiating device and in the end Pujol settled for lesser changes [3.3.3] that were nonetheless seen as highly beneficial for his region.

The extent of Pujol's influence at this time was graphically illustrated by the way he avoided being dragged down along with the increasingly unpopular Socialist government. First, late in 1995, he abandoned his hitherto ally on the thinnest of excuses [2.3.4] and called an early regional election on even more spurious grounds. This allowed him to exploit the weakness of CiU's main rival, the Socialist PSC [3.2.1.1], before the conservative People's Party, a growing force in Catalonia [3.2.1.3], could profit from its inevitable general election victory.

When the PP duly won the Spanish poll held early the following year Pujol was able to exploit its lack of an overall majority to re-assume his powerbroker position with a different ally [2.4.3]. Part of the price was a further major concession on the question of regional finance [3.3.3]. The whole episode reinforced the popular impression of Pujol as the most powerful politician, not just in Catalonia but in Spain.

3.2.1.3 Pujolism at bay

During the PP's first term of office Pujol's position remained strong. Yet, at the same time, cracks began to appear in his power edifice. For one thing, the financial settlement he imposed on the new government further aggravated the growing ill-feeling that his aggressive style of regionalism had already aroused in the rest of Spain. It was particularly prevalent on the right-wing of the PP, which remains strongly (Spanish) nationalist and suspicious of regionalism in any form. To add insult to injury, Pujol had propped up the right's biggest bogey, the Socialists. On the night of its 1996 election triumph, some of the PP's younger supporters in Madrid notoriously celebrated by chanting personal insults against the CiU leader, interspersed by calls on him to 'speak Castilian'.

These latter were a reference to the language dispute then going on in Catalonia. Unsatisfied with the results of its earlier legislation to 'normalize' (effectively promote) Catalan, CiU had taken steps which further downgraded the status of (Castilian) Spanish in several respects. The PP's Catalan section, much of whose leadership was strongly anti-regionalist, responded by setting itself up as the champion of the region's Spanish speakers, alleging that they now faced discrimination. Whether or not as a result, it then made significant gains at the 1995 regional election. Its rise represented a new and very real threat to Pujolism since, unlike its previous main challenger the

Socialist PSC [3.2.1.1], the PP competes directly with the CiU for middle-class, centre-right votes.

For the moment the danger was blunted by the PP's need for Pujol's support in Madrid. Before long the new Prime Minister, José María Aznar, purged his party's Catalan leadership and imposed a new, much more moderate one. Moreover, he made clear that the PP now accepted autonomy as a fact, renouncing the Right's earlier pledge to revoke or at least curtail it. But, at the same time, he was also keen to tidy up the devolution process by standardizing the level of autonomy exercised by regions [3.3.2]. And that ran directly counter to the thrust of Pujolism.

Pujol's response was not long delayed. Soon he began placing renewed emphasis on ensuring that Catalonia would have its own voice in the European Union. He reacted suspiciously to the attempt at administrative reform contained in the measure known as the LOFAGE [1.5.2]. He explicitly rejected any idea of converting Spain into a federation – precisely the solution traditionally advanced by Catalan regionalists! In 1998 he even put his name to a joint declaration with Basque and Galician regionalists [3.2.2.3] proclaiming the 'sovereignty' of the three 'historic nationalities' [3.1.1].

Subsequently, though, Pujol distanced himself somewhat from a type of rhetoric more usually associated with Basque nationalism in general, and ETA in particular [3.2.2.1]. He also went along with steps – admittedly minimal – to move the Spanish Senate in the direction of a federal upper house [3.3.4]. His radicalism had definite limits, it seemed, so long as he retained his strong influence in Madrid. That, however, came to an abrupt end with the PP's unexpectedly decisive victory at the 2000 general election [2.4.5].

Indeed, due to the results of the Catalan poll held the previous year the relationship between Pujol's CiU and the PP was now reversed. Admittedly the PP had itself lost ground in 1999, but it was also now Pujol's essential ally in a regional parliament where, for the first time, CiU faced a strong and coherent opposition. Indeed it was only able to form a government at all thanks to the electoral system's bias towards more rural areas [3.1.4]: in terms of votes it had been outpolled by a broad left-wing slate put together by the PSC.

Thereafter the sense of realignment in Catalan politics was heightened when the small regionalist party ERC [3.2.1.1] agreed that its representative in the Senate would join with those from the PSC in a new grouping to be known as Catalan Unity (*Entesa Català*). In the early 1980s ERC had sided with CiU on most issues. Its change of line now challenged the notion, central to Pujolism, that politics is essentially a struggle between Spaniards and Catalans [3.2.1.2]. As if recognizing that an era had come to an end, in 2001 Pujol announced his intention to step down as regional PM and CiU leader before the next regional election.

A future without him (*pospujolismo*) holds several problems for the movement he has done so much to shape over the last two decades. Most obviously CiU's electoral appeal will be reduced; for many Catalans Pujol retains enormous prestige. In particular, this has been crucial in holding together the two, rather different parties that together make up CiU [3.2.1.2]. Under the

Table 3.1 General and regional election results in Catalonia, 1977–2000

		General elections								Regional elections					
		1977	1979	1982	1986	1989	1993	1996	2000	1980	1984	1988	1992	1995	1999
Convergence and Union (CiU)	P	17	16	22	32	33	32	30	29	28	47	46	46	41	38
	S									43	72	69	70	60	56
Catalan Republican Left (ERC)	P	5	4	4	3	3	5	4	6	9	4	4	8	10	12
	S									14	5	6	11	13	12
Catalan Socialists (PSC)[a]	P	28	29	45	41	36	35	39	34	22	30	30	28	25	38
	S									33	41	42	40	34	52
Initiative for Catalonia (IC)[b]	P	18	17	5	4	7	7	8	4	19	6	8	7	10	3
	S									25	6	9	7	11	3
People's Party (PP)[c]	P	26	23	16	16	15	18	18	23	13	8	9	7	15	10
	S									18	11	9	7	17	12

Notes: [a] In 1999 headed joint candidature including IC and Citizens for Change (CPC) [11.10].
[b] Prior to 1986, Catalan Communist Party (PSUC). Since 1996 allied with Catalan Greens (EV). In 1999 stood separately in Barcelona province only.
[c] Prior to 1989, People's Alliance (AP) plus other Spanish centre-right parties (UCD, CDS).
P = per cent poll; S = seats.

arrangements for Pujol's succession, CiU is to be converted into a party in its own right, a move that smacks a little of desperation.

The new party's leader is to be Antonio Durán i Lleida, head of the smaller but more established UDC, who in the past has frequently displayed unhappiness at CiU's moves away from traditional regionalism [3.2.1.2]. Meanwhile Artur Mas will run for regional PM in 2003. He comes from Pujol's own CDC, among whose followers Pujol's combative rhetoric has had its effects. Most of CDC's younger members now claim to favour outright independence rather than devolution. It remains to be seen how they will react now that CiU has lost its hold over central government, not to mention if it were to lose control of the regional institutions.

3.2.2 The Basque Country

Apart from the fact that it also emerged in Spain in the late nineteenth century, Basque regionalism has virtually nothing in common with its Catalan counterpart. By 1900 the Basque language (*euskera*) had disappeared from most of the region without giving rise to any significant literature; Spanish was the native language of most Basques, including early regionalists. The movement they created was long politically weak, with limited popular support and very little from the region's economic elite. Yet when Spain returned to democracy after the death of Franco 'the Basque problem' had become probably the country's most important. It has remained so ever since.

3.2.2.1 The ETA factor

The intractability of the 'Basque problem' is mainly due to the activities of the armed group known as ETA. The initials stand for *Euskadi ta Askatasuna*, or 'Basque Homeland and Liberty' in the Basque language. ETA was set up in 1959, to resist Franco's attempts to stamp out Basque culture and national consciousness, and was initially linked to the traditional vehicle of Basque regionalism, the PNV [3.2.2.2]. However, from the outset ETA differed from the PNV in three crucial respects: it espoused revolutionary left-wing ideas; it demanded nothing less than outright independence for the Basque Country; and it was prepared to use violence, to which it first turned in 1968.

ETA's active resistance to the dictatorship, at considerable cost to its own activists (*militantes*), brought it widespread popular sympathy by no means confined to the Basque Country. In particular, its assassination of Franco's designated successor [0.2] enjoyed much unspoken approval. Moreover, its success in establishing links with the region's well-established workers' movement gave regionalism there the broad base it had previously lacked. It is no exaggeration to say that the wide-ranging provisions of the Basque Statute of Autonomy, and the massive 'yes' vote it received at the referendum held in 1979 [3.1.1], were largely attributable to ETA's activities.

Equally, it was the group's reaction to devolution that effectively scuppered hopes of a quick solution to the 'Basque problem'. For ETA maintained that, despite the return of democracy and the granting of autonomy, essentially nothing had changed. In its eyes, the Basque Country continued to be occupied by a foreign power – the 'Spanish state', as ETA always refers to Spain – just as repressive as the Franco regime. And, instead of desisting from violence, it actually stepped up its 'armed struggle', the death toll from which rose to a peak in 1980 and declined only slowly thereafter.

The range of its victims also widened. Initially these had been confined almost entirely to the security forces. Then, during the transition period, representatives of Madrid-based political parties, as well as businessmen, became regular targets. Once the Basque Autonomous Community (CAV) was set up, its employees, particularly officers of the regional police force or *Ertzaintza*, came into the firing-line. So too did those ETA activists who took advantage of the government's arrangements for early release [10.3]. Members of the public also died as ETA turned increasingly to random bombings.

As a result of these developments public sympathy for ETA's activities fell sharply, even in the Basque Country, where it was increasingly concentrated among the region's large pool of disaffected and disoriented young people [9.4.2]. At the same time, however, the continued use against ETA of methods inappropriate in a democracy, such as arbitrary arrest, torture or harassment, were almost equally offensive to many people in its home region as terrorism itself. Above all, the 'dirty war' of the mid-1980s [10.4.2] was always believed by many in the Basque Country, by no means all of them extremists, to be government-orchestrated. For these reasons ETA continued to enjoy both a small but steady stream of recruits and a lingering basis of sympathy in Basque society.

At various times such sympathy was expressed in support for two political organizations. The older was Basque Left (*Euskadiko Ezkerra/EE*), created in 1977 under the auspices of ETA's then 'politico-military' branch, ETA-pm. It soon rejected violence, and in 1981 persuaded the *poli-milis* to do so too. Thereafter EE aspired to act as a bridge between nationalists and their opponents. And, although it had rejected the 1978 Constitution for failing to recognize Basques' right to self-determination, EE enthusiastically backed devolution and opposed any suggestion that it be widened in the short term. Indeed, it became an outspoken opponent of ETA, and was instrumental in the drawing up and approval of the 1988 Ajuria Enea Pact, a cross-party agreement designed to isolate the organization and its supporters.

By then, sympathy for ETA and its aims was expressed exclusively through another grouping. People's Unity (*Herri Batasuna/HB*) was set up in 1979 by ETA-m, the 'military' branch that was to persist with the 'armed struggle', and which since 1981 has been the sole ETA. Throughout, HB has acted as its political wing (*brazo político*), subservient to its wishes, with the purpose of justifying violence and generating conditions propitious to its continuation. Thus HB's supposed programme is set out in the so-called 'KAS alternative', which demands that the Spanish government should negotiate independence for the Basque Country – to include Navarre – directly with ETA. The point of these extreme demands, and others made periodically by HB, is precisely that no Spanish government could ever concede them.

In the 1978 constitutional referendum HB campaigned for a 'no' vote. Subsequently it has asserted that the ambiguous outcome in the Basque Country [1.1.1] means that 'Basques rejected the Constitution'. It denounced devolution, not just as an inadequate response to Basque aspirations but as the product of an illegitimate regime. For long it boycotted both the Spanish and regional parliaments, refusing to take up the seats to which it was entitled.

It also ran numerous campaigns centred on the alleged denial of Basques' right to self-determination (*autodeterminación*), and the situation of imprisoned ETA activists, particularly the government's policy of holding them far from their homes. But in classic populist style HB exploited other issues as they arose. Examples were the proposals for a nuclear power station at Lemoniz and a motorway through the Leizarán valley, which were abandoned and amended respectively as a result of campaigns orchestrated by HB.

From its formation HB succeeded in attracting 15 per cent and more of the vote at elections in the Basque Country; it became particularly strong at local government level, where it has always taken up its seats. Unlike most regionalist parties it performed no better in regional than Spanish elections. And that was wholly logical, for from the mid-1980s at the latest its support had little to do with political issues; instead it was based largely on support for, and identification with, ETA's violence.

3.2.2.2 The PNV; from crisis to renewal

Notwithstanding the electoral success of HB [3.2.2.1], Basque regionalism's largest political force was and is the Basque Nationalist Party (*Partido Nacionalista Vasco/PNV*). The PNV is one of Spain's oldest parties, having been founded in 1895 by Sabino Arana. Prior to the Franco era it was effectively regionalism's sole vehicle, and tended to regard its supporters as the only true Basques. The PNV's demands lacked a clear cultural basis, due to the early decline of the Basque language, and it failed to attract the backing of the region's industrial elite. But in much of the countryside its supporters formed a substantial and tight-knit 'nationalist community' focused on the PNV's local clubs (*batzokis*), giving the party a popular base unrivalled in Spain [2.1.1].

It was these deep roots in Basque society that enabled the PNV to survive the Franco era, although it took no great part in popular opposition to the regime. Thereafter, despite the intervention of ETA's political wing, HB [3.2.2.1], it emerged as the region's largest political force. As a result it had the largest representation in the body set up to prepare the ground for devolution there [3.1.1], and in effect negotiated directly with the central government the terms of Basque autonomy. Above all because the PNV insisted that this should reflect traditional Basque rights (*fueros*) [1.1.1] this proved a tortuous process, during which the party was able to pose as the Basques' champion against the central government.

Once the PNV won the inaugural regional election held in February 1980 and formed the regional government it cultivated this role further. Repeatedly the PNV administration engaged in disputes with Madrid over the implementation of devolution in practice, many of which ended up in the Constitutional Court; the most serious was that over legislation designed to place limits on the devolution process [3.1.3]. Not only that, it also began to criticize as inadequate the extensive autonomy overwhelmingly approved at the 1979 referendum [3.1.1] – an arrangement it had itself negotiated.

This adversarial attitude gave spurious credibility to ETA's contention that Basques were locked in a continuing conflict with the 'Spanish state'. Even more dangerously, the PNV echoed HB's claims that the Constitution – which it had played no part in drafting and subsequently refused to endorse – had no validity in the Basque Country [3.2.2.1]. Moreover while never condoning violence, the party habitually linked it to the government's refusal to consider even greater self-government, thus appearing to justify it. And the PNV's contacts with both ETA and HB, whose parliamentary boycott alone allowed it to govern alone, were an open secret.

The PNV's ambivalence greatly aggravated the already high level of tension in the region. But, initially at least, it proved highly successful for the party. At the 1984 regional election it increased its vote still further, having extended its hold on local government the year before. Subsequently, though, signs of a backlash began to emerge. One cause was that, like parties elsewhere in Spain in similarly dominant positions, the PNV had indulged in various practices verging on corruption [2.1.3]. More importantly its links – real and perceived – with ETA were becoming a liability, especially once its own members and supporters in the regional institutions came under terrorist attack [3.2.2.1].

The PNV was also hit by disputes between its party apparatus and its representatives in the regional government, two groups which in the PNV – unlike other parties in Spain [2.1.2] – are kept strictly separate. The latter, who tended to favour a more flexible approach, were led by the first regional PM (*lehendakari*) Carlos Garaikoetxea. In late 1984 he was forced by hardline party boss Xabier Arzalluz to resign. Two years later Garaikoetxea left the PNV and formed a new party, Basque Solidarity (*Eusko Alkartasuna/EA*). The split forced the PNV to call an early election, at which it suffered severe losses.

The election results added a hopelessly fragmented political system to the Basque Country's woes, which as well as violence included a grave economic crisis and severe social disruption. The negotiations to form a new government were long and tortuous. Eventually, however, the PNV agreed to form a coalition with the Socialists, previously its bitterest opponent [3.2.2.3]. The decision had profound effects. It effectively forced the PNV to distance itself from ETA/HB by joining the Ajuria Enea Pact [3.2.2.1]. Indeed, largely owing to his close identification with the agreement the new regional PM José Antonio Ardanza, originally a rather grey figure, became the region's most popular politician.

The coalition also made the PNV tone down its rhetoric, especially its demands for independence. Pressure came also from the Basque business community, to which the PNV is now much closer, and which was keenly aware that entry to the EC had if anything increased the region's need for economic ties to Spain [6.3.5]. Happily for the party the vogue for a 'Europe of the Regions', given substance in 1991 by the EU's creation of a Committee of the Regions [4.1.3], allowed it to argue that inside the Union devolution was indistinguishable from independence.

Finally, the PNV began to show interest in using the powers devolution had provided [3.1.4]. During its first years in power it had introduced virtually no legislation other than to regulate the regional institutions themselves. Towards the end of the 1980s, however, it became much more active, especially on the economic front. In 1992 a new party programme talked of replacing 'nationalism of the heart' by a more pragmatic 'welfare nationalism', to be implemented by the regional authorities. In 1993 the PNV even showed an unaccustomed concern for Spanish politics when it agreed to help prop up a minority government in Madrid [2.3.4].

In parallel with these various changes in the PNV's attitudes went a strong recovery from the electoral disaster of 1986. By the mid-1990s, although unable to dispense with coalition partners, it was again clearly in command of the regional government. Of the other regionalist parties, its bitter critic EE had disappeared as a separate force [3.2.2.3] and EA was reduced to the status of permanent junior coalition partner. In this situation, the PNV's hardliners scented the opportunity of a 'nationalist front' with the other Basque force, ETA/HB.

3.2.2.3 The sovereignty issue

The more moderate course taken by the PNV [3.2.2.2] was one reason to believe that the 'Basque problem' might finally be on the verge of solution. The feeling was strengthened by a number of successful security force operations against ETA. One, carried out at Bidart, in the French Basque Country, in 1992 led to the arrest of its then leadership and the capture of much useful information on its activities. There were also signs of movement in ETA's political wing HB [3.2.2.1], which from 1990 attended not only the Basque but also the Spanish Parliament. Some leading figures even questioned HB's complete subjugation to ETA, and were expelled from its ranks as a result.

Meanwhile major changes were taking place in the region's second party, the Socialists, which had traditionally enjoyed strong support among the region's industrial workers. Many of these were either incomers or their descendants, and understandably suspicious of the PNV. In the early 1980s the PSOE had aggravated their fears by portraying devolution as a threat to a supposed immigrant 'community'. But thereafter a younger generation of Basque Socialists actively enthusiastic about autonomy took control of the party's regional section, the Basque Socialist Party (*Partido Socialista de Euskadi/PSE*). In 1993 the PSE absorbed the majority faction of Basque Left (EE) [3.2.2.1] and became known as the PSE-EE.

At the same time the conservative People's Party (PP) dropped its opposition to devolution in general and Basque autonomy in particular. The change was helped by the nature of the language issue in the region. Given that so many Basques, even nationalists, cannot speak Basque, there was no question of the aggressive 'normalization' undertaken in Catalonia [3.2.1.3] – and thus less to worry the PP's centralists.

Unfortunately, however, the 1990s also brought virtual proof that the 'dirty war' of the previous decade had been organized by the Madrid government [10.4.2], as well as revelations of continuing security force malpractice. Regionalists in general were resentful and, once again, ETA was given fresh life. In 1995 it launched a new campaign of killings. This time the victims were mainly individually chosen, and included several local representatives of the PP. Public revulsion was widespread; in 1997 the particularly callous killing of Miguel Angel Blanco, a young councillor in Ermua, sparked off massive demonstrations inside and outside the region.

Another factor in generating renewed tensions was the central government's moves to standardize the level of autonomy across the country [3.3.2]. These were anathema to the PNV, which boycotted the minimal attempts made to reform the Senate along federal lines [3.3.4]. Relations with Madrid temporarily improved with the election of a minority PP government in 1996 which badly needed support [2.4.3]; the PNV used the opportunity to negotiate a favourable renewal of the Basque Country's special financial arrangements [3.1.4]. But with the PP determined to press ahead with standardization – and understandably bitter about its assassinated Basque colleagues – relations between the two parties soon deteriorated again.

It was against that background that the PNV proclaimed the doctrine that the three 'historic nationalities' [3.1.1] enjoy sovereignty (*soberanismo*). By that it meant that they have the right to decide their own futures, without reference to the rest of Spain. In 1998 this idea formed the basis of the 'Barcelona Declaration' issued jointly by the PNV, the Catalan CiU [3.2.2.1] and the Galician BNG [3.2.3.2]. But the joint approach was disingenuous at best. For, whereas there is no dispute as to the boundaries of Catalonia or Galicia, the PNV and other Basque regionalists claim as their 'sovereign' homeland not just the present autonomous region but also Navarre and the French Basque Country (the 'seven historic territories'). And only in the Basque case has the claim been backed up by violence.

There is no doubt that the PNV's moves followed contacts with ETA, under severe pressure at the time. Its renewed violence had cost the group any residual popular sympathy; at the 1996 general election HB's vote fell significantly for the first time ever. In 1997 the party's mouthpiece, the newspaper *Egin*, was raided by the police and closed down (a replacement, *Gara*, soon appeared), and its entire leadership jailed for inciting terrorism (it was released two years later by a Supreme Court decision).

HB's new leadership, headed by Arnaldo Otegi, was disposed to seek new options. First, it founded a new front organization to be known as Alliance for the Basque People (*Euskal Herritarrok/EH*). Then, in September 1998, EH signed a joint declaration with the PNV and various smaller associations. Named after the Navarrese town where it was signed, the Pact of Lizarra (Spanish: *Estella*) asserted the 'sovereignty' of the Basque Country defined as the seven territories. Four days later ETA declared a ceasefire (*tregua*).

3.2.2.4 New millennium, same problem

The PNV's decision to join the Pact of Lizarra brought down the regional government, which the Socialists abandoned in protest. The results of the resultant election reflected the enormous optimism unleashed by the ceasefire [3.2.2.3], particularly among left-wing nationalists opposed to violence. Under the EH banner HB's vote rose to a new high, while the PNV held its own. It immediately formed a new coalition with its offshoot EA [3.2.2.2] under a new regional PM with a more hardline reputation, Juan José Ibarretxe. Crucially its majority depended on the agreed parliamentary support from EH/HB.

This tacit alliance was furiously denounced by the Spanish parties. The PP, which had overtaken the Socialists to become the PNV's main challenger in the region, took a particularly tough line. It made little attempt to open talks on a permanent end to violence, citing ETA's demand that they should also address political issues. In early 2000 ETA began killing again, with critical journalists now joining local Spanish politicians among its chief targets. At the same time HB withdrew its backing for the regional government, and refused to present candidates at the 2000 general election.

That poll brought the Basque PP further gains. Seeing their intransigent strategy vindicated, the conservatives stepped up their attacks on the PNV, accusing it more or less directly of backing terrorism and claiming that it no longer had a mandate to run the region. In December 2000 the PP attracted Socialist backing for its hard line, when the two parties signed an anti-terrorism pact which, among other things, debarred any agreements with the PNV so long as it held to the notion of sovereignty [3.2.2.3]. The two main Spanish parties now formed a 'constitutionalist' front, with the PSOE making clear that it would back a conservative-led Basque government should the PP win the regional election scheduled for May 2001.

The campaign for this poll reached depths of bitterness not seen since the 1980s, whipped up by fervid denunciations of the PNV in the Madrid-based media. In the event the PP, although it again increased its support, fell well short of victory. To ETA and its allies Basque voters delivered a more decisive defeat – EH's vote was 50 per cent down on 1998. The big winner was the PNV, whose support rose strongly. Yet its euphoria was tempered by the fact that the total backing for regionalist parties had reached an all-time low. The result thus had salutary lessons for all, and brought welcome moves back towards sanity.

Thus the 'constitutionalists' toned down their anti-PNV rhetoric, and accepted without question the party's right to form a new coalition with EA. It was subsequently joined in a very junior role by the Basque section of United Left, so that – at least symbolically – it now straddles the Basque–Spanish

Table 3.2 General and regional election results in the Basque Country, 1977–2000

		General elections								Regional elections						
		1977	1979	1982	1986	1989	1993	1996	2000	1980	1984	1986	1990	1994	1998	2001
Basque Nationalist Party (PNV)ᵃ	P	29	28	32	28	23	24	25	30	38	42	24	29	30	28	43
	S									25	32	17	22	22	21	33
Basque Left (EE)	P	6	8	8	9	9				10	8	11	8			
	S									6	6	9	6			
People's Unity (HB)ᵇ	P		15	15	18	17	15	12		17	15	18	18	16	18	10
	S									11	11	13	13	11	14	7
Basque Solidarity (EA)ᶜ	P				11	11	10	8	8			16	11	10	9	
	S											13	9	8	6	
Alavese Unity (UA)	P												1	3	1	
	S												3	5	2	
Basque Socialists (PSE-EE)ᵈ	P	28	19	29	26	21	24	23	23	14	23	22	20	17	18	18
	S									9	19	19	16	12	14	13
Basque United Left (EB)ᵉ	P	5	5	2	1	3	6	9	5	19	4	1	1	10	6	6
	S									1	0	0	0	6	2	3
People's Party (PP)ᶠ	P	20	20	13	16	13	15	18	28	13	9	8	9	14	20	23
	S									8	7	4	6	11	16	19

Notes: ᵃ In 2001 headed joint candidature with EA.
ᵇ Did not stand in 2000. In 1998 and 2001 stood under the initials EH [3.2.2.3]. In 2001, name changed to Unity [3.2.2.4].
ᶜ In 2001 stood jointly with PNV.
ᵈ Prior to 1993, PSE-PSOE.
ᵉ Prior to 1986, Basque Communists (EPK).
ᶠ Prior to 1989, People's Alliance (AP) plus other Spanish centre-right parties (UCD, CDS).
P = per cent poll; S = seats.

divide. While relations between Vitoria and Madrid remained strained, there were at least signs that both sides were disposed to talk.

One especially positive one was the resolution, ultimately amicable, of a dispute over the region's special funding arrangements in early 2002 [3.3.3]. Ibarretxe himself has shown a growing capacity for negotiation and compromise. Much will depend on whether his new-found moderation will prevail within the PNV after the departure of its long-time leader, Xabier Arzalluz [3.2.2.2], whose own chosen successor Joseba Egibar is a noted hardliner.

And, of course, there remains the question of ETA's continuing violence. Recently the group has again come under pressure following a number of successful police operations. As its actions produce ever greater revulsion – and with the 'dirty war' finally fading into history – its supporters seem to be becoming ever fewer and more isolated. They are now led by a new generation, young veterans of the street violence (*kale borroka*) orchestrated by HB's youth wing *Segi* (formerly *Jarrai*) [10.4.2]. These new leaders seem to have rejected any idea of a political solution. In 2001 they were behind the re-foundation of HB as a party under the name of Unity (*Batasuna*), whose subservience to ETA is explicit.

3.2.3 New regionalist movements

When Spain returned to democracy, only in the Basque Country and Catalonia were Spaniards' undoubted feelings of association with a particular area expressed politically to any significant degree. At the time conservatives feared that the prospect of devolution would unleash their latent force, causing the country to fragment into numerous small units (*cantonalismo*) [0.1]. Their concerns proved utterly unjustified. But the following decades did see the appearance, virtually across Spain, of new regionalist movements (*regionalismos*) whose emergence was indeed closely linked to the devolution process.

3.2.3.1 Andalusia, Valencia, Navarre and the Canaries

The process began in historic regions with a distinct sense of identity. Yet such feelings were not in themselves enough; witness the distinctly muted reaction to the disappearance of Leon, one of Spain's most venerable units [11.9]. What Leon lacked was any distinct political tradition, something present in all the regions were new movements first appeared. These also had another factor in common. They were triggered off by the advantage given to the three 'historic nationalities' under the Constitution's complex provisions for devolution [3.1.1], and their subsequent fortunes were often heavily conditioned by developments outside the region concerned.

The point is well illustrated by the region where devolution ceased to be a constitutional issue and became a political one: Andalusia [3.1.2]. Beyond doubt it can lay claim to a distinctive character (*hecho diferencial*). It also has a tradition, albeit a weak one, of regionalist activity, out of which emerged the

Andalusian Socialist Party (*Partido Socialista Andaluz/PSA*) during the campaign to obtain more extensive autonomy for the region. Yet the very success of those efforts meant that by 1981 Andalusia had achieved its aims in that respect.

Thereafter, as a poor region, its interests tended to lie in holding the devolution process as a whole in check, while attempting to extract the maximum of central government support. And that role has been effectively monopolized by the PSOE's local section, which has controlled the regional government since its creation. It also exercises huge clout within its own party, heavily dependent on Andalusian votes as it now is [2.3.5]. By contrast, the PSA – which is now known as the Andalusian Regionalist Party (PA) – has received only modest support.

At least it is still represented in its regional parliament, which is more than can be said for its Valencian counterpart, Valencian Union (*Unió Valenciana/ UV*). Yet during the 1980s UV enjoyed considerable support and influence. For a while it even became an essential coalition partner in the government of a region which also had a low-key regionalist tradition of its own, and which had to wait longer than Andalusia to have its autonomy upgraded to the level of the 'nationalities' [3.1.2].

That was a particularly thorny issue in Valencia, where some conservatives purported to believe that it was threatened with incorporation into a Greater Catalonia (*Països Catalans*). This idea, essentially a cover for reactionary Spanish nationalism, underlay UV's rise, which also coincided with a time of chronic weakness for the mainstream Spanish Right [2.4.1]. With the more recent success of the PP – and in the complete absence of any signs of Catalan expansionism – UV's support has evaporated.

To some extent a similar phenomenon was observable in Navarre, which was also briefly in danger of being left behind in the first devolution round. There, too, there were fears of possible annexation by one of the 'nationalities', in its case the Basque Country, while the Spanish Right's weakness left conservative voters feeling unprotected. And in Navarre, too, the result was the emergence of a new party, the Navarrese People's Union (*Unión del Pueblo Navarro/UPN*), which also entered the regional government.

There the similarities end, however, for UPN not only became Navarre's largest party, it remains so today. It also continues to provide the regional PM and has forced the PP to give it a free run in regional elections, in return for its support at general ones. The reasons for its continuing strength lie both outside and inside the region. Unlike their Catalan counterparts, Basque regionalists – some of them violent – explicitly claim Navarre as part of their homeland, so that the threat of incorporation cannot be dismissed. On the other hand, Navarre has its own peculiar conservative tradition in the form of Carlism [0.1] and is in several respects itself a special case among the regions.

That is also true, on purely geographical grounds, of the final region to receive special treatment in the first devolution round: the Canary Islands [3.1.2]. And indeed the Canaries had produced a number of small regionalist groups in the 1970s. However, not until 1986 did these come together to form a single coherent force, Canary Islands Alliance (*Coalición Canaria/CC*). Its creation was prompted by an event not just in Spanish but in European politics, Spain's accession to the EU, which potentially placed the Canaries as a whole in a position of dangerous isolation. Subsequently CC has been able to establish itself as the islands' strongest political force. Unlike UPN, it also sends MPs to the Spanish Parliament, and from 1993 to 2000, during the period of minority governments in Madrid, its small representation there gave it an additional measure of bargaining power.

3.2.3.2 Aragon, Galicia, other regions

By 1983 autonomy was a reality throughout Spain. Yet, far from removing the basis for regionalism, this provided fertile ground for its further development. By the end of the 1980s regionalist parties had been formed in virtually every region, and were represented in the parliaments of most. Their emergence was one reason for the start of a second devolution round in the 1990s [3.3.2], the course of which has in turn conditioned their own development along with other factors, both regional and national.

One reason why autonomy actually stimulated regionalism was that the new regions provided a fresh, and powerful, focus of identity and action. At the most basic level, every region now had its own flag, ubiquitously and prominently displayed. Interest groups of all types began to organize on a regional basis. Regional politics, above all regional election campaigns, tended to suggest that a region's people had common interests, perhaps even a common character, implicitly distinct from those of other parts of Spain. Typically this was expressed in terms of some disadvantage allegedly suffered by a region. And, crucially, the uneven result of the first devolution round [3.1.2] meant that most regions had cause to feel a sense of discrimination specifically in terms of autonomy.

Such feelings surfaced most dramatically in Aragon. This region, which has an undoubted sense of identity, had remained quiescent during the first devolution round, perhaps because its only distinctive political tradition, anarchism, provided no basis for action in Spain's new democracy. However, its relegation to the group of slow route regions [3.1.1] provoked a dramatic upsurge of popular opinion which included the formation of the Aragonese Regionalist Party (Par). Like Valencia's UV and Navarre's UPN a basically conservative grouping, the Par profited from the weakness of the Spanish Right [2.4.1], even heading the regional government for a number of years.

Similarly, the Par too has subsequently lost ground in the face of the PP's rise. But, in contrast to UV, it remains an important player in regional politics. That is partly because, once aroused, Aragonese feeling has proved powerful. During the 1990s the region's Statute of Autonomy had to be amended twice, as a result of which Aragon now has the status of a 'nationality' (although not a historic one).

Additionally, the question of whether water should be transferred away from the region to provide irrigation elsewhere [7.3.2] has been a running controversy, and one in which specifically Aragonese interests are manifestly at stake. Indeed, another grouping explicitly pledged to defend them recently entered the regional parliament. Interestingly, at a time when the PSOE is in eclipse at Spanish level [2.3.5], it is a party of the Left.

The same is true of the most successful new regionalist party of recent years, the Galician National Alliance (*Bloque Nacional Galega/BNG*), currently the region's second largest political force. As an avowedly leftist formation the BNG has only loose connections with traditional Galician regionalism, which was mostly conservative and generally weak. Culturally distinctive but socially and economically backward, Galicia long remained the fief of corrupt party bosses controlled by their Madrid masters [2.1.1]. Its privileged treatment in the constitutional provisions for devolution bore no relation to demands from the region itself, but was a by-product of the over-riding need to satisfy Basque and Catalan feeling [3.1.1]. In the 1981 referendum on its Statute of Autonomy a mere 30 per cent of the electorate bothered to vote.

Nonetheless, the Statute was approved and Galicia acceded to the extensive autonomy to which it was entitled as a 'historic nationality' [3.1.1]. The fact that in the 1990s successive central governments seemed intent on undermining this special status may have been one reason for the belated emergence of Galician regionalism. Certainly the BNG enthusiastically joined a Basque initiative to protest against these developments [3.2.2.3]. But probably rather more important was another, very different factor; the attempts by the region's own government to revive and foster Galician culture.

Ironically these have been the work of Manuel Fraga [2.4.1], who in 1989 returned to lead the PP in his native region and has subsequently won four successive regional election victories, each time with an overall majority. Since his return, the former arch-centralist has displayed an unexpected enthusiasm for Galician distinctiveness and for the idea of devolution in general [3.3.4]. At times, he has shown open sympathy with the aspirations of Catalan regionalists and has pursued a policy of language 'normalization' along roughly Catalan lines, provoking some of the same tensions [3.2.1.3]. More generally, he has backed numerous cultural projects, losing scarcely an opportunity to stress Galicia's distinctive character.

It is not only in Galicia that a Spanish party has taken up regionalist causes. The Aragonese PP and PSOE both openly espoused calls for greater autonomy in defiance of their Madrid leaderships. Indeed, regional sections of the main country-wide parties now typically seek to portray themselves as defenders of local interests; in a sense, all parties are regionalists now. That may be one reason why the growth of specifically regionalist groupings seems to have slowed down recently, and in some cases been reversed.

Another is the fact that some such parties have been essentially vehicles for the personal ambitions of individual local politicians; such is the case of URAS in Asturias and, to some extent, the Basque Country's EA [3.2.2.2], as well as the now defunct Galician Alliance (*Coalición Galega/CG*) and Cantabrian UPCA. In addition, insofar as devolution has become more standardized, some of the grounds for regional grievance have been removed – at least outside the 'historic nationalities'. But in several regions and for various reasons new regionalist parties appear to be so well established that they will remain a part of the political scene for the foreseeable future.

3.3 A NEVER-ENDING STORY?

Barely had the initial devolution round been completed in 1983 than pressure began for autonomy to be extended, both from the Basque Country [3.2.2.2] and from some of the regions who had fared least well so far [3.2.3.2]. Understandably, the central authorities and Spanish politicians generally were reluctant to touch the much-lauded edifice so recently created. But they were also becoming aware that the *Estado de las Autonomías* had brought problems as well as solutions for them and the country as a whole. At the start of the 1990s they therefore embarked on a new round of changes. It, in turn, triggered off new pressures, and has since been followed by two more. As yet there is no end to the process in sight.

3.3.1 The problems of regionalization

The regionalized system of government created by the initial devolution round was a complex and, in some regards, ill-defined one. These features were not accidental: they were the inevitable result of the approach adopted back in 1978 [3.1.1]. Quite probably devolution, or at least rapid devolution, would have been impossible without them. But they also implied substantial costs, in both administrative and political terms.

Initially attention focused on the handing over of powers in specific areas to the new regions (*transferencias*), while these were simultaneously creating their own institutional and administrative structures, in most cases from scratch. As there were few clear rules as to how this process was to be carried out, it tended to involve painstaking negotiation. In the Basque Country and Catalonia, in particular, it caused significant friction with the central government – indeed, it was exploited for that very purpose [3.2.2.2, 3.2.1.2]. From 1985 on, however, such tensions eased and in the early 1990s the flow of disputes being referred to the Constitutional Court slowed to a trickle.

By then a more pressing administrative issue had become apparent; a seemingly unstoppable increase in the number of public servants. In part this reflected the wider range of tasks undertaken by the state since the country's return to democracy, notably in the fields of education and social services [8.2, 8.3, 9.3]. But devolution had also made a significant contribution. As most posts in the new regional administrations were taking on responsibilities previously discharged by central government, in theory their creation should have been matched by a loss of posts in Madrid or the centre's outlying administration [1.5.2]. In practice this was by no means always so.

In any case regional governments, most of whom did not have to raise the taxes to pay their new employees [3.3.3], often lacked restraint in expanding their wage bills. They also displayed a tendency to their own form of centralization, taking on functions already carried out by the municipalities and provinces [1.6]. The resultant overlap and duplication were aggravated still further in 1986 when Spain joined the EU, thereby adding yet another tier of administration. For all these reasons devolution pushed government spending sharply upwards. Undesirable in itself, this became especially problematic after 1992, as the government strove to fulfil the stringent criteria for European Monetary Union [4.2.2].

Another important issue for central government was the sheer complexity of a system involving eight distinct grades of autonomy – the minimal level in the ten slow route regions, and one each for the remaining seven [3.1.3]. As a result the latter, particularly the richer among them, were sometimes able to offer higher levels of service in particular fields. That not only increased resentment elsewhere. Coming in such key areas of state activity as health it raised questions about Spain's fundamental unity.

Moreover, in many areas responsibility was shared between the regional and central tiers, leading to severe problems of coordination. The government attempted to resolve them by setting up joint sectoral working groups (*conferencias sectoriales*), each dealing with a single subject area and bringing together representatives of all the regions and of the central government. Nevertheless, the costs in terms of administrators' time remained high. Similar problems resulted from the existence of two separate funding schemes, themselves including various exceptions and involving regular lengthy negotiations [3.1.4].

These difficulties highlighted another problem of the regionalized system. It lacked a formalized structure through which regions could have an input into the workings of the state – or, after 1986, into those of the EU. Of course, that may have suited Madrid well enough in one sense. But it also meant that there were no clearly defined mechanisms for resolving conflicts between the central government and the regions, or between different regions. And, as such conflicts showed no sign of vanishing, that implied not just administrative costs but also persistent political turmoil.

3.3.2 Extension of regional powers

By the end of the 1990s the governing Socialist Party was seriously concerned about the administrative and other costs of devolution [3.3.1]. It accordingly resolved to try and remove some of the inconsistencies of the existing system. To be politically feasible such a move would have to involve an increase in regional powers, and not just because of the pressure for this in Aragon and elsewhere [3.2.3.2]. Any move in the other direction would inevitably antagonize Basque and Catalan regionalists, and thus undermine devolution's original purpose [3.1.1].

In order to proceed with its plans, the government would have to amend some or all of the various regional Statutes of Autonomy [3.1.1]. That implied a hurdle, part constitutional, part political. For Statutes have the status of entrenched legislation [1.3.3], and so require to be approved by an overall parliamentary majority. And that, as well as political prudence given the delicate nature of the issue, meant that the PSOE would need the support of the conservative People's Party.

Happily for the government the PP, having shed much of its earlier suspicions about devolution [2.4.2], was anxious to counter the electoral threat of the right-wing groupings that had emerged in several regions under regionalist banners [3.2.3.1]. It was accordingly disposed to reach agreement, and in 1992 a second pact on the regions (*pacto autonómico*) was signed. Like the first [3.1.3], it involved only the two largest Spanish parties and excluded all the regional ones, even those from Catalonia and the Basque Country.

In the pact, the PSOE and PP agreed to hand over more powers to the ten regions which had received only minimum autonomy in the first round (all of which they governed, either alone or in coalition). This was achieved partly by the government's delegating powers as allowed by the Constitution [3.1.1], and partly by amendment of the relevant Statutes of Autonomy, which took place in 1994. The powers that were thus transferred to regional control concerned issues related to education (by far the most important), social services and a number of other areas. Deliberately excluded was the health service, responsibility for which most regions were reluctant to assume because of the complexity and cost.

The 1992 pact also covered steps to counterbalance this further loss of central government control. As well as extending the role of the various joint working groups [3.3.1], it hoped to set a definitive ceiling (*techo*) on devolved powers. But the hope proved illusory. Before the changes agreed by the main Spanish parties had even been implemented, regionalists in the 'historic nationalities' [3.1.1] began demanding further changes to restore the differential between their regions and the rest. During 1993 and early 1994 their governments issued a series of demands for powers in the grey areas which the Constitution did not explicitly reserve to the central government [3.1.1]. Although the Basques and Catalans were particularly vociferous, their claims acquired extra weight from the unexpected backing of Galician premier Manuel Fraga [3.2.3.2].

Moreover, with the Socialist government having lost its overall majority in 1993, the Basques and Catalans were in a strong position to force concessions. The price of their parliamentary support was apparent in Felipe González's investiture speech, where he spoke of giving new momentum to the process of devolution (*impulso autonómico*). His government began efforts to agree exactly which areas of responsibility could, under the Constitution, be devolved to regional control (*competencias transferibles*). In parallel, discussions were opened on the handover of specific powers, even in the previously taboo area of social security administration.

In the event little progress was made on this front over the next four years, during which the Basque and Catalan governments focused more on funding issues [3.3.3]. Once the PP came to power in 1996, again with Basque and Catalan support [2.4.3], progress resumed however. The next year the PP reached a third pact with the PSOE on transfer of a further tranche of powers, including control over active measures to fight unemployment (*políticas activas de la Seguridad Social*), and the ten slow route Statutes were amended for a second time.

While the Basque and Catalan governments were happy enough to see their own powers extended, they were also worried by the further erosion of their privileged position. Relations deteriorated, especially with the Basques, who took the lead in asserting the 'sovereignty' of the 'historic nationalities' [3.2.2.3]. They also stepped up their demands for powers over social security benefits (*políticas passivas de la Seguridad Social*), the uniform level of which is generally seen as one of the fundamental features of a modern state.

Not surprisingly, this twofold challenge to Spain's basic unity was utterly rejected by the PP government. Yet it remained anxious to resolve the devolution issue once and for all. Once re-elected with an overall majority [2.4.5] it therefore introduced plans to standardize the level of autonomy throughout the country. As a sop to the 'nationalities' the plan included a further extension of their competences.

But the main aspect was devolution of powers over health, the one remaining major area of difference between the fast and slow route regions [3.1.1]. Several of these latter, including conservative-controlled Cantabria and the Rioja, were unhappy about taking on the very high costs involved, especially as they felt the central government was deliberately underestimating the amounts concerned [9.2.2]. Eventually, however, the government used financial pressure [3.3.3] to force them to concede, and now health too has joined the list of subjects for which all regions are responsible.

3.3.3 Reform of regional funding

In parallel with the gradual extension of regional powers during the 1990s, a related but separate set of changes was taking place. These other reforms concerned the mechanism by which the regions were funded. As in the first case they reflected partly the concerns of central government, and partly pressure from some regions to remove perceived disadvantages. With regard to funding, however, such differences were not between the fast and slow route regions, but between the two regions governed by special arrangements – the Basque Country and Navarre – and the remainder. And the main pressure for change came from the most powerful of the second group, Catalonia.

Concern in Madrid centred on the view that, financially, the regions were having their cake and eating it. On the one hand, they now enjoyed a high profile as providers of public infrastructure and services. On the other, under the block grant arrangements that applied to most of them [3.1.4], they reaped none of the opprobrium attached to collecting the corresponding taxes.

Nor was it merely a question of political profile. By the 1990s regional spending accounted for a major part of the total public budget, and failure to control it might threaten Spain's efforts to meet the criteria for European

Monetary Union [4.2.2]. As a result the central authorities were increasingly anxious to introduce a measure of shared fiscal responsibility (*corresponsabilidad fiscal*), that is, to link regional budgets more directly to taxes.

At the same time, Catalan premier Jordi Pujol had been eyeing with increasing interest the alternative arrangements operated by the Basques and Navarrese. Under these the regions actually collected most taxes and negotiated their contribution to state finances directly with Madrid [3.1.4]. Aware that he could not realistically expect to achieve the same situation, in 1992 Pujol began to push the idea of a mixed scheme; tax raising would remain a central government responsibility, but regions would have an automatic right to 15 per cent of income tax receipts within their territory. Implementation of this proposal was Pujol's main demand in return for supporting the minority Socialist government elected in 1993.

It was vociferously attacked by the opposition People's Party as a threat to Spain's essential unity. Yet, since Pujol's assumption that the system would greatly favour the richer regions – in particular Catalonia – was widely shared, the subsequent debate brought divisions not just along party lines but also along those of economic geography. The most vociferous opposition came from the Socialist Juan Carlos Rodríguez Ibarra, premier of Extremadura, but he was backed by the heads of government of other poor regions, irrespective of party allegiance. Conversely, their counterparts in better-off parts of Spain tended to support Pujol, as did the PSOE's own Catalan section.

When the scheme was finally introduced on a trial basis in 1994 it accordingly contained various provisions to cushion the effects on the poorer regions. Even so, three of them – conservative-run Castile-Leon and Galicia, along with Extremadura – refused to join it and remained covered by the old block grant arrangements. Galicia's refusal was particularly interesting. Evidently Manuel Fraga's awareness of his region's economic weakness remained stronger than his enthusiasm for wider autonomy [3.2.3.2].

His party's narrow victory in the 1996 general election left it even more dependent than its Socialist predecessor on Pujol's CiU [2.4.3]. To secure his support the PP was forced to abandon its resistance to fiscal decentralization; indeed it made a further concession, increasing the proportion of income tax revenue retained by regions to 30 per cent. This time it was the three southern regions of Andalusia, Castile-La Mancha and Extremadura, which were both poor and Socialist-run, that refused to accept the amended scheme and appealed to the Constitutional Court [1.1.3]. Pending its decision they continued to be funded entirely by block grants whose level was essentially set by the central government, a situation that represented the worst of all worlds for them.

Accordingly the PSOE was prepared to negotiate with the government. In 2001, while the three regions' appeal was still awaiting the Court's decision, agreement was reached on further changes, which also enjoyed the backing of Catalan and other regionalists. They were based on bringing regions' revenue more into line with the taxes actually collected there. Thus, as well as increasing to 33 per cent the proportion of income tax receipts they retain, the new system also allots regions 35 per cent of VAT receipts from their territory and 40 per cent of those from certain other taxes, in particular that on hydrocarbons (mainly petrol). In addition, the powers they had been given in 1996 to set the rates of certain taxes (*capacidad normativa*) within strict limits were extended.

At the end of 2001 these changes were put in jeopardy. The government insisted that they be linked to its plans for a general levelling off of autonomy [3.3.4], and in particular that they would only apply to regions which accepted responsibility for health care. Yet eventually all agreed to this transfer, thus clearing the way for the new system. This is intended to be permanent, and contains no mechanism for adjusting the complex formula used to calculate how much additional funding regions are to receive, over and above their entitlement to taxes raised in their territory.

These additional payments are theoretically meant to ensure that the poorer regions do not lose out unfairly; in reality, their size and distribution was the outcome of lengthy horse trading and political negotiation. As economic circumstances and the political landscape change in the future, pressure to adjust the formula is highly likely, if not inevitable. Another problem is that regions' tax-setting powers continue to be very limited, so that they are still effectively sheltered from the political discipline such competences would impose. Indeed, up to now they have shown little inclination to use the limited powers they possess.

Moreover, the new formula only applies to the fifteen regions covered by the common funding scheme. Navarre and, most importantly, the Basque Country continue to have their own separate arrangements, with all the potential for grievance that implies [3.1.4]. In 1996/97 the Basque government exploited the PP's need for its parliamentary support to renegotiate its agreement with the government on favourable terms. Five years later the agreement as a whole came up for renewal, and once again the Basques were successful in obtaining concessions; in particular the new agreement is indefinite in duration.

3.3.4 Towards federalism?

The various reforms of the 1990s did much to reshape the *Estado de las Autonomías*, but did not resolve several fundamental problems. For one thing, the distribution of functions between regions and centre remained ill-defined, so that problems of overlap and duplication persisted [3.3.1]. One proposal for dealing with these came from a rather surprising source: the veteran conservative politician Manuel Fraga.

Once installed as regional premier of Galicia [3.2.3.2], Fraga suggested the creation of a single administrative structure (*administración única*) along German lines. This would mean the regions carrying out all administrative tasks within their territories, irrespective of whether the tasks related to central or regional legislation. To some extent this idea has been taken up in government by Fraga's party, the PP [1.5.2]. However, quite apart from the difficulty of implementing such a solution in practice, it is concerned only with administering the existing situation not with redefining it. Nor does it provide any means of resolving disputes between the central and regional governments and among the latter, another current lack [3.1.1].

As part of its efforts to introduce greater standardization in 2001 [3.3.2], the PP government proposed legislation to regulate centre–region and inter-regional relations (*cooperación autonómica*). Thus the various joint sectoral working groups [3.3.1] would be given an enhanced role, and a new Committee of Regional Prime Ministers (*Conferencia de Presidentes Autonómicos*) established. But the tone of government pronouncements suggested that the main aim was to reinforce the central authority's role in the existing system, for instance by upgrading the role of its regional representatives [1.5.2] or by establishing a financial reserve that would allow it to ensure a uniform country-wide response to situations such as the BSE threat.

This emphasis was apparent in the government's handling of another issue: regional relations with the European Union. These are important not least because of the regions' role in allocation and distribution of resources provided by the EU's Structural Funds [4.1.1]. More generally, regions are affected by many EU decisions and have understandably clamoured for an input into the processes by which they are made.

The government had already attempted to meet their demands by setting up a special joint working group on EU-related affairs (*Conferencia para los Asuntos Relacionados con la Comunidad Europea/CARCE*), and had also been forced to allow the regions to maintain official representative offices in Brussels [4.3.3]. By 2001 the debate had come to focus on the question of regional representation in Spain's delegations to the heart of Union decision-making, the Council of Ministers [4.1.3]. Having initially suggested the possibility of this, Prime Minister José María Aznar later rejected it out of hand.

He also set his face firmly against any meaningful reform of the Upper House of Spain's Parliament, the Senate, defined by the Constitution as a 'chamber of territorial [by implication, regional] representation'. In theory it should provide an arena in which centre–region and inter-regional disputes can be settled [3.3.1]. In practice, however, the Senate's current method of election renders this impossible, since only a fifth of its members are regional representatives [1.3.1]. Changing this model is therefore regarded by most experts as an essential step towards improving the operation of Spain's system of government.

In 1993 a first attempt was made at reform, when the Socialist government reached agreement with the PP and CiU on setting up within the Senate a General Committee on the Regions (*Comisión General de las CC AA*). In addition, an annual debate was to be held in the House as a whole, devoted to the situation and further development of the *Estado de las Autonomías*, to be attended by the Spanish prime minister and his regional counterparts. A motion was even adopted that the Senate be converted into a genuinely regional chamber, possibly along the line of the German *Bundesrat*. The changes were bitterly opposed by the Basque PNV [3.2.2.2], whose representative boycotted the annual debates. In the event only two of these ever took place, and overall the changes had no discernible effects.

The essential problem lay in the reluctance of both major parties to consider any amendment to the Constitution (*reforma constitucional*), for fear that such a move would open the door to other, more drastic changes. Particularly after winning an overall majority in 2000 the PP remained unbending on this point, and its plans of the following year contained only the most bland of proposals with regard to the Senate: provision for the Upper House to consider bills with regional implications, and for regional PMs to attend the Senate without voting powers. The timidity of his party's proposals was attacked by Manuel Fraga, one of the Constitution's architects [1.1.1], who publicly rejected the idea that amending it was unthinkable.

The main attacks, though, came from the PSOE, which had shifted its stance considerably in opposition. Having explicitly accepted the idea of federalism [2.3.6], it now proposes amending those parts of the Constitution relating specifically to the Senate, to allow half of its members to be elected on a regional franchise. In addition the sectoral working groups, far from being strengthened, would be abolished; instead, central and regional governments would be given a statutory duty to cooperate, as in Germany. And there would be a further – supposedly final – extension of regional powers, designed to clarify the division between central and regional responsibilities once and for all. Faced also with rejection from the main regionalist parties, the PP climbed down and agreed to set up a Senate Comittee including regional representatives to examine the issue.

The PSOE's proposals undoubtedly have a certain coherence lacking in the present system, but they also gloss over a number of questions. For one thing, genuine federalism would pose obvious practical problems. The problems faced by the smaller regions in taking on the same responsibilities as the larger and more powerful ones have already been apparent in the case of health [3.3.2]. Indeed, the PSOE's Catalan section, the PSC [3.2.1.1], which largely determined the party's new line, talks openly of 'asymmetric' federalism – essentially a contradiction in terms. For no less than pure Catalan regionalists [3.2.1.3], not to mention their Basque counterparts, the PSC is not prepared to accept that all Spain's regions are equal.

As long as that idea receives strong support in two such important regions, the tensions and inequalities so apparent within the current regionalized system will almost certainly continue whatever name it is given. For some, especially on the Right, that is a major drawback, and even a danger. However, it is also possible to take a less gloomy view – and not merely because the *Estado de las Autonomías*, with all its faults, has on balance worked fairly well. Most observers would agree that even by the standards of other contemporary democracies, power within the Spanish state is concentrated [1.4.1] and political debate constrained. Against that background, the diversity and conflict generated by the country's territorial structure can be seen as welcome if not downright necessary.

3.4 GLOSSARY

abertzale mf	(militant) supporter of Basque regionalism; Basque nationalist
administración única f	(system of) single administrative structure
Ajuria Enea	residence of Basque PM
Amejoramiento Foral m	Restoration of Navarre's Historic Rights
aportación f	reverse block grant (paid by Navarre to central government)
autonomía f	autonomy; autonomous region
autonómico adj	relating to the regionalized Spanish state, or to the regions themselves
batzoki m	PNV local branch premises
brazo político m	political wing
cacique m	(corrupt) local party boss
café para todos m	(see *fiebre autonómica*)
cantonalismo m	cantonalism, demands for local self-rule
capacidad normativa f	power to legislate (especially to set tax rates)
catalanismo m	Catalan regionalism
comisión mixta f	joint committee
competencias fpl	powers, responsibilities (of government)
competencias transferibles fpl	areas of responsibility susceptible to being handed over to the regions under the 1978 Constitution
Comunidad Autónoma f	autonomous region
concierto económico m	financial agreement (between Basque Provinces and central government)
conferencias sectoriales fpl	joint sectoral working groups
consejería f	regional ministry
consejero m	regional minister
consejo de gobierno m	(regional) cabinet
Consejo de Política Fiscal y Financiera de las CC AA m	Joint Fiscal Policy Council
constitucionalista m	(in Basque Country) opponent of *soberanismo*
convenio económico m	financial agreement (between Navarre and central government)
cooperación autonómica f	centre–region and inter-regional cooperation
corresponsabilidad fiscal f	shared fiscal responsibility
cupo m	reverse block grant (paid by Basque Provinces to central government)
elecciones autonómicas fpl	regional election(s)
Ertzaintza f	Basque police force
Estado de las Autonomías m	present regionalized form of Spanish state
Estatuto de Autonomía m	Statute of Autonomy
Euskadi m	Basque homeland; Basque Country
euskera m	Basque language
fiebre autonómica f	'devolution fever', outbreak of demands for devolution in 1980–82
financiación autonómica f	regional funding

Fondo de Compensación Interterritorial m	Inter-regional Compensation Fund
fueros mpl	historic rights (esp. of Basque Provinces and Navarre)
Generalitat f	Catalan regional government/Valencian regional government
gobierno autonómico m	regional government
ikastola f	Basque-language school
impulso autonómico m	fresh momentum given to process of evolution
Junta f	name of government of various regions, esp. Andalusia
lehendakari m	Basque prime minister
mapa autonómico m	division of Spain into regions
Mossos d'Esquadre (Cat.) mpl	Catalan police force
nacionalidad histórica f	'historic nationality', region granted autonomy under Second Republic
órganos preautonómicos mpl	bodies set up specifically to prepare for devolution
pactisme (Cat.) m	(Catalan) traditional readiness to reach negotiated agreements
pacto autonómico m	pact on the regions (1981; 1992)
Països Catalans (Cat.) mpl	Greater Catalonia (incl. Valencia and Balearics)
parlamento autonómico m	regional parliament
parlamento unicameral m	single-chamber parliament
políticas activas de la SS fpl	active measures to fight unemployment
políticas passivas de la SS fpl	social security benefits
pospujolismo m	Catalan politics and regionalism after the retirement of Jordi Pujol
presidente autonómico m	regional prime minister
proceso autonómico m	(process of) devolution
pujolisme (Cat.)/*pujolismo* m	contemporary Catalan regionalism, associated with Jordi Pujol
régimen común m	funding scheme applicable to most regions
régimen foral m	traditional system (esp. of funding) applicable to Basque Provinces and Navarre
regionalismo m	regionalism; regionalist movement
soberanismo m	doctrine that a region (especially the Basque Country) has the untrammelled right to decide its own future
sucursal f	branch party, regional party subordinate to Madrid leadership
techo m	ceiling, upper limit (on devolved powers)
transferencias fpl	handover of powers to regional governments
tregua f	ceasefire
vasquismo m	Basque regionalism
vía lenta f	slow route (to autonomy)
vía rápida f	fast route (to autonomy)

4

THE EUROPEAN TIER OF GOVERNMENT

Until recently government in Spain, as in other developed Western countries, was essentially a domestic matter. Today, however, considerable areas of government activity are wholly or partially subject to the direction of the European Union. Conversely, structures exist to permit Spanish citizens to participate, either directly or indirectly, in EU decisions that affect them. This situation is the result of the process known as European integration. Like the UK, Spain initially stood on the sidelines. But subsequently it became an enthusiastic participant, with the result that the emerging European tier of government is of particular importance there. This chapter will examine Spain's involvement in the continuing process of integration, and the principal mechanisms which currently bind it into the EU's supranational government structure. First, however, it will give a brief overview of integration and the EU's machinery, for those unfamiliar with one or the other.

4.1 EUROPEAN INTEGRATION AND THE EU

The idea that Europe forms a natural unit and should be governed as such is an old one, and down the centuries various attempts were made to realize it by conquest. However, the first moves towards bringing the peoples of the continent together on a peaceful, democratic basis were taken in the aftermath of the Second World War. They were motivated by the need for economic reconstruction, by the desire to prevent further conflicts and by the perceived threat from the Soviet Union, and they set in train a process that became known as European integration (*unión europea*). By the end of the millennium its main product, the European Union (*Unión Europea/UE*), had assumed a wide range of governmental responsibilities over almost the entire western half of the continent, and stood poised to expand to the borders of the former Soviet Union.

4.1.1 The beginnings of integration

The first postwar moves towards integration involved a number of organizations in various fields. In 1948 the Organization for European Economic Cooperation (OEEC) (*Organización para la Cooperación Económica Europea/ OCEE*) – later to become the OECD (*Organización para la Cooperación y el Desarrollo Económico/OCDE*) – was founded to administer the American aid provided under the Marshall Plan. The following year saw the formation of the Council of Europe (*Consejo de Europa*), which was concerned mainly with fostering educational and cultural contacts on a voluntary basis. And in 1954 the Western European Union (*Unión Europea Occidental/UEO*) was set up to coordinate European defence policy, although in practice it was strictly subordinated to NATO – dominated, then as now, by the USA.

The origins of integration as it was later to develop lay in a fourth organization. In 1951, a group of OEEC members (France, West Germany, Belgium, the Netherlands, Luxembourg and Italy) formed the European Coal and Steel Community (ECSC) (*Comunidad Europea del Carbón y del Acero/CECA*). Crucially 'the six', as they became known, ceded powers of decision over their own affairs to the ECSC institutions. In 1957, they set up two more organizations on a similar basis: the European Atomic Energy Community, or Euratom, and the European Economic Community (*Comunidad Económica Europea/CEE*). The latter was to form the nucleus of subsequent integration.

The Treaty of Rome which established the EEC included a statement of its members' intention to proceed towards 'ever closer union', implicitly political in nature. But, as its name implied, the Community was essentially economic and had two main aspects. First, it was a common market (*mercado común*). In other words, its members established a free trade area (*zona de libre comercio*) by abolishing all internal tariff barriers (*barreras arancelarias*) to trade in goods, and also agreed to impose a common external tariff (*arancel aduanero común*) on imports from outside, or 'third countries'. Secondly, the six established a Common Agricultural Policy (*Política Agrícola Común/PAC*) designed to ensure stability of food supplies and farm incomes by a system of guaranteed prices. These measures were an immediate success, providing a massive boost to trade and prosperity among the member states (*estados miembros*).

The UK, at the time still Europe's leading power, initially considered forming part of the Community but then held back because of the potential effects on trade with its former colonies. In 1960 it set up another, looser grouping, known as EFTA (*Asociación de Libre Comercio Europea/ALCE*). But this produced much more modest results, and the UK soon recognized its effective failure by belatedly applying to join the EEC.

In 1973 it was finally admitted, along with two fellow EFTA members, Denmark and Ireland (the voters of a third, Norway, rejected the proposed terms of accession in a referendum). This first enlargement (*ampliación*) was followed by two more in the next decade, Greece being admitted in 1981 and Spain, together with Portugal, five years later [4.2.1]. Together these moves represented a major step towards one of the main aims of integration, the creation of a genuinely pan-European organization.

Meanwhile steps were also taken towards the other, known as deepening (*profundización*); that is, extending the scope and intensity of cooperation between the Community's members. In 1965 the three existing Communities merged to become the European Community (*Comunidad Europea/CE*). The accession of Britain prompted the EC to extend its arrangements to help poorer regions within the Community through various Structural Funds (*Fondos Estructurales*). And the late 1970s saw the creation of a European Monetary System, as part of which most – but not all – members agreed to peg their currencies' values against each other by means of an Exchange Rate Mechanism (*mecanismo de cambios*). But overall there was relatively little advance on this second dimension of integration up to the mid-1980s.

Then, however, the pace of deepening too began to pick up. Once more, the entry of new, relatively poor members prompted an upgrading of regional policy and the Structural Funds, a change enshrined in the 1986 Single European Act (*Acta Única*). The Act's main purpose, however, was to streamline the Community's decision-making procedures, in particular by limiting member states' ability to block proposals to which they objected [4.1.3].

This, in turn, was intended to enable a massive programme of legislation to complete the Community's single, or internal market (*mercado interior*) by removing a multitude of non-tariff barriers (*barreras no tarifarias*) to trade, and to the free movement between the members of persons and services as well as goods. The target date for the massive legislative programme this involved was set at 1992, and on 1 January 1993 the single market was declared complete, although a number of measures were still to be finalized. In their original, trading terms the aims of economic integration had now been achieved, at least on paper.

4.1.2 The development of the EU

By then, however, the member states had signalled their intention of going further. In February 1992 they had signed the Treaty on European Union (*Tratado de la Unión Europea/TUE*), at Maastricht in the Netherlands. A complex and unwieldy document, it marked the first attempt to move from economic to political integration. To signal this decisive step it formally converted the EC into the European Union.

The TEU established two new fields, or 'pillars', of Union activity in the political sphere. These were concerned with developing a Common Foreign and Security Policy (*Política Exterior y de Seguridad Común/PESC*) and cooperation in justice and home affairs (*Justicia y Asuntos de Interior*), and were to function intergovernmentally, that is, by separate agreement of the member states rather than through the Union's decision-making structures and institutions. The Treaty also included a Social Chapter (*Acuerdo Social*) establishing certain – rather unambitious – minimum standards of social provision and economic justice.

But the key aspect of the Maastricht agreement was once again economic: its plans for Economic and Monetary Union (*Unión Económica y Monetaria/UEM*). Under these a single currency (*moneda única*) was to be adopted in 1999, with national currencies disappearing three years later. Originally termed the ecu, it was subsequently renamed as the euro. At the same time, a European Central Bank (*Banco Central Europeo/BCE*) would be created to manage the new currency's exchange rate, and monetary policy in general. In order to qualify for EMU, member states would have to meet five convergence criteria relating to their economic performance. These greatly restricted their autonomy to set their own budgets (Table 4.1).

This selective approach tacitly recognized the existence of a two-speed Europe (*Europa de distintas velocidades*), in which not all Union members would proceed towards integration at the same pace. It reflected both the concerns of some, especially the UK, at the gradual loss of their own sovereignty involved in integration, and the frustration of those anxious to push ahead. Such divergences had already led to the 1985 Schengen Agreement, under which some countries had agreed on the gradual abolition of controls at their common borders. Both the new pillars introduced at Maastricht also effectively involved a two-speed approach, while the opt-out (*cláusula de exclusión*) negotiated by the UK from the Social Chapter represented a further example. Yet another was the decision later in 1992 to create a Eurocorps (*Euroejército*) made up of military contingents from several countries.

The 1990s also brought a revival of activity on the second dimension of integration. Accession negotiations were begun with Austria, Finland, Norway and Sweden; in 1995 all joined the Union bar Norway, which for a second time voted to remain outside [4.1.1]. This fourth enlargement brought the number of EU members to 15 (*Unión de los Quince*). When the qualification date for EMU came in 1997 all but Greece were deemed to have met the convergence criteria, although Denmark, Sweden and the UK declined to join the single currency, at least initially. With the subsequent admission

Table 4.1 The Maastricht convergence criteria

Indicator	Condition
1 Exchange rate	Currency must remain within narrow band of European Monetary System for two years prior to adoption of single currency.
2 Inflation rate	Inflation must be no more than 1.5 per cent higher than average of three member states with lowest rates.
3 Interest rates	Long-term rates must be no more than 2 per cent higher than average of three member states with lowest inflation rates.
4 Public debt	Total debt must be less than 60 per cent of country's GDP.
5 Public sector deficit	Annual deficit must be less than 3 per cent of country's GDP.

of Greece, the number of members of Euroland (*zona euro*) currently stands at 12.

Despite the progress on EMU, integration in general hit a number of problems in the 1990s. Completion of the single market failed to provide the expected economic boost. The inadequacies of the Common Foreign and Security Policy were repeatedly shown up in the weakness of European responses to crises in ex-Yugoslavia and elsewhere. Germany, still struggling to cope with the immense task of incorporating its formerly Communist eastern part, was increasingly unhappy at providing the lion's share of the Union budget, and pressed for a reform of its finances. And there was increasing evidence that many of its citizens regarded the EU with indifference at best, a situation known in Union jargon as a 'democratic deficit'.

The 1997 Treaty of Amsterdam attempted to address this issue by tinkering with the Union's institutional structure. More concretely, the Euroland members agreed on a Stability and Growth Pact (*Pacto para la Estabilidad y el Crecimiento*), which committed them to maintain the budgetary discipline imposed by the Maastricht criteria once the single currency was introduced. The new Treaty also effectively institutionalized two-speed Europe by providing for subgroups of members to engage in enhanced cooperation (*cooperación reforzada*) under certain conditions.

None of these steps did much to relieve the Union's problems, however, and 1999 brought further setbacks. First, there was the embarrassing spectacle of the central Union institution being forced to resign [4.1.3]. And then, after the euphoria surrounding its launch at the start of the year, the euro slumped in value against both the dollar and the pound, the main European currency to have remained outside EMU.

Yet, despite these travails, the Union continued to press ahead with its most ambitious project yet. This was a further enlargement, designed eventually to incorporate up to twelve Central and Eastern European countries (*países de Europa central y oriental/pecos*), most of them from the ex-Communist bloc. By the Treaty of Nice signed in December 2000, the EU states reconfirmed their determination to press ahead with this project, which presents enormous challenges for two reasons. On the one hand, the candidates for membership (*aspirantes*) are without exception considerably poorer than the existing members, in some cases massively so. Their accession will therefore place enormous strains on the Union's finances, above all the Common Agricultural Policy and the Structural Funds. And, on the other, they will stretch its equally creaky institutional arrangements to breaking point.

4.1.3 The EU machinery

At the apex of the EU's institutional machinery stands its supreme decision-making body, the European Council (*Consejo Europeo*). It is composed of the various member states' heads of government, and by heads of state with executive powers (the presidents of Finland and France). It meets between two and four times a year. In between these summits (*cumbres*) there are regular meetings of the government ministers responsible for particular subject areas; originally known as the Council of Ministers (*Consejo de Ministros*), these forums are now officially designated the Council of the European Union (*Consejo de la Unión Europea*).

At any one time all the various Council meetings are chaired by the representatives of a particular member state. This function is known as the Presidency (*Presidencia*) and rotates on a six-monthly basis. During its term, the country holding the Presidency is also responsible for representing the Council of Ministers *vis-à-vis* other EU institutions, and the Union as a whole *vis-à-vis* the outside world. It also hosts a summit held at the end of each presidential term. A Presidency acquires particular significance if it coincides with the preparation or holding of a so-called Intergovernmental Conference (*Conferencia Intergubernamental/CIG*), the process of consulting all member governments before carrying out a change to the EU's fundamental treaties.

Some Council decisions, including all those on the new pillars introduced by the Maastricht Treaty, must be taken unanimously, effectively giving each state a veto. However, as a result of the same treaty, and of the Single Act [4.1.1], those on a growing range of issues are put to a ballot. For these purposes each member has a certain number of votes; of the 87 in total, 62 constitute the qualified majority (*mayoría cualificada*) needed for a proposal to be approved.

The allocation of votes is weighted towards the smaller states; currently the Union's 'big four' (France, Germany, Italy and the UK) have ten votes, and tiny Luxembourg two. Under the arrangements agreed at Nice to cater for the forthcoming eastern enlargement [4.1.2] the total votes will rise to 345, with 255 needed for a qualified majority. In addition, the relative disadvantage of the larger states will be reduced, but not removed. Finally it should be noted that Council votes have a second significance, in that they define the EU's pecking order; that is, members' Council voting strengths tend to determine their status for a number of other Union-internal purposes as well.

Powerful as it is within the EU machinery, by its nature the Council's position cannot be compared to that of the cabinet in a single state. Apart from anything else, it lacks the requisite administrative support. The bulk of the Union bureaucracy – which, contrary to popular myth, is not all that large in total – works for the European Commission (*Comisión Europea*). The Commission is the most distinctive Union institution and in many ways its driving force. It combines some of the traditional features of an (elected) cabinet with those of a permanent civil service, being responsible both for the Union's day-to-day operation and for initiating new legislation or projects.

The Commission is headed by a President, appointed by the European Council for a five-year term. In consultation with national governments he – as yet there has been no female president – selects the 20 Commissioners (*Comisarios*) who make up his governmental team. He also assigns them responsibility for particular policy areas and chooses two to act as his deputies, or vice-presidents. The largest member states currently nominate two Commissioners and the remainder one, but under the Nice arrangements they will lose this privilege. In its broader sense the Commission also includes a considerable underlying administrative apparatus, divided up into 23 Directorates-General (*Direcciones Generales*).

The third major Union institution is the European Parliament (*Parlamento Europeo*). The EP is markedly less powerful than either the Council or the Commission, although its ability to influence decisions was increased by the Single Act and the Maastricht Treaty [4.1.2]. In 1999 it caused something of a sensation by sacking the entire Commission after its investigations suggested that several Commissioners had engaged in irregularities or malpractice. Originally its members, or MEPs (*eurodiputados*), were appointed by national governments, but since 1979 they have been elected at EU-wide polls held every five years, for which each country is free to choose its own electoral system.

Currently the total number of MEPs is 626. As in the Council, although less dramatically, the allocation of seats favours the smaller members, ranging from 81 for the 'big four' down to six for Luxembourg. Here too the Nice post-enlargement arrangements will somewhat redress the imbalance. Under them all existing member states will lose some seats to prevent the Parliament becoming too large, but even so the number of MEPs will rise to 732.

The Parliament's sessions are chaired by the President or by one of the deputies, or vice-presidents. Together these make up its bureau, or presiding council. The vast majority of members opt to join one of the Parliament's official 'groups', usually known by their French initials (Table 4.4), around which the Parliament's work revolves. In particular, representation on the committees (*comisiones*), where most substantive work is done, is allocated to the groups on the basis of their relative strength, while the influential committee chairpersons (*presidentes*) are appointed on a similar basis.

In addition to these three, the EU has a number of other institutions and bodies of which four can be singled out here.

- The Court of Justice (*Tribunal Europeo de Justicia/TEJ*) is the final arbiter on disputes arising from the Treaties or legislation based on them, having ultimate authority over the various national judicial systems for the matters concerned.
- The Court of Auditors (*Tribunal Europeo de Cuentas/TEC*) is responsible for control of Union expenditure.
- The Economic and Social Council (*Consejo Económico y Social/CES*) is an advisory body bringing together representatives of European civil society – in practice, chiefly those of the social partners (*agentes sociales*), in other words employers and trade unions.
- The Committee of the Regions (*Comité de las Regiones*) also has advisory status; set up by the Maastricht Treaty it is made up of representatives of regional and local authorities.

In all of these, as in the three main institutions, each EU country is guaranteed a certain degree of representation; one member on each of the Courts and a number roughly proportional to population on the other two bodies.

The system of guaranteed representation is a tacit admission that the politicians and administrators who staff the Union's institutions are in an ambiguous situation. For, while their responsibilities are, in theory, to their electors or to the Union as a whole, in practice they are almost certain to retain a degree of allegiance to their country. Similarly the Union Presidency offers an excellent chance for the holder to promote its own agenda – or to antagonize its fellow members – as well as serving common interests. This ambiguity is part and parcel of a larger one. For, while the Union is ostensibly a framework for the members to cooperate, it is also an arena in which they attempt to advance their individual, and sometimes competing interests.

In that arena there are several well-tried strategies for success. One is precisely that of filling as many influential EU posts as possible with a country's nationals. Ideally these should be well-versed in the Union's ways but retain a sense of allegiance to their country – and to its current government. Conversely, a country that succeeds in increasing its influence within the Union can hope for more such posts, and so to cement its influence further. A second principle of intra-Union politics, particularly for smaller members, is to cultivate the friendship of the bigger, more influential countries, above all Germany. And thirdly, a country keen to increase its influence should display active commitment to integration, or at least express rhetorical support for the process even – or especially – when it is acting exclusively in its own national interests.

From the Union's origins in the old EEC [4.1.1] France has applied these strategies, especially the last, with consistent success. On the other hand, the former British Prime Minister Margaret Thatcher virtually ignored the rules of the European game. She made no secret of her contempt for the integration process, or of her fundamental dislike for her continental partners, especially Germany, and tended to regard EU postings as a form of punishment for awkward colleagues. By persistent belligerence she was able to obtain very considerable concessions on specific issues. But they came at the cost of marginalizing the UK within the Union – even in the eyes of some of its own representatives within the EU machinery.

4.2 SPAIN AND INTEGRATION

Marginalization from the rest of Europe was Spain's experience for much of its modern history. Moreover, Spaniards seemed to have internalized their isolation, showing a tendency – like that of the British – to refer to 'Europe' as an alien place. The 'disaster' of 1898 [0.1] prompted some reaction against such attitudes; most famously the philosopher Ortega y Gasset became one of the first proponents of a federal Europe, which he saw as the remedy for Spain's many problems. By a sad irony, though, when his vision finally started to take real form Spain found itself more marginalized than ever. Yet events were soon to change the situation radically, creating both a tremendous enthusiasm within Spain for the idea of Europe (*europeísmo*) and the conditions for its fulfilment.

(NB. Throughout this section reference is made to the general description of the integration process in sections 4.1.1 and 4.1.2.)

4.2.1 From pariah to partner

When the integration process began Spain was ruled by the Franco dictatorship, whose support for the Fascist powers during the Second World War had made it an international outcast [0.2]. In return, the regime purported to regard its democratic neighbours as corrupt and unjust, so that there was no question of Spain's forming part of the various international organizations formed between 1948 and 1957. However, shortly thereafter the regime was forced into a radical change of economic course, which in 1962 led it to apply to join the European Economic Community.

The application was a disaster for Franco. Not only was it rejected outright, but it provoked the EEC into making his regime's pariah status explicit. Spanish membership, it stated, was out of the question so long as the country remained a dictatorship, although in 1970 it did agree to sign an Association Agreement with Spain.

By this time, Europe had already acquired very positive connotations for Spaniards, especially among the many who had experienced at first- or second-hand the higher living standards and greater political freedom enjoyed by their northern neighbours. Among those who already wished for a return to democracy, the EEC's stance reinforced that appeal. It also helped swing key parts of the business community, who were keen to join the Community for economic reasons, firmly behind the process of democratization after Franco's death. Indeed generally, the idea of becoming more like the rest of Europe (*europeización*) became closely linked to the transition process, and so profited further from its success [0.3].

Not surprisingly, then, popular and political opinion was massively behind the renewed application submitted, to what was now the EC, by the first democratically elected government of Adolfo Suárez, in 1977. In principle the Community's existing members, too, were well-disposed to it; that same year they welcomed Spain into the Council of Europe. As well as a sense of guilt that Spain had been abandoned to its Francoist fate after 1945, there was also a clear feeling that a Europe without Spain (and Portugal) would always be incomplete. In the case of the EC, economic considerations also played a crucial role. By now the initial boost to growth in its founder members had begun to slacken, and the six – above all Germany, the Community's economic powerhouse – saw in the large and relatively unexploited Spanish market the potential for renewed momentum.

In practice, though, economics also rendered the subsequent negotiations long and tortuous. One major problem was that of integrating Spain's fishing fleet, considerably larger than those of existing members, into the EC's arrangements. Even more serious were France's concerns about its agricultural sector; much Spanish farm produce, especially fruit and vegetables, was in direct competition with French, and once inside the EC's common market would be able to undercut it considerably. Moreover, from 1979 both Suárez and his successor were assailed by massive political problems at home [0.3.3]. As a result, they had little energy left over for European matters, and less credibility.

The arrival in power of the Socialists under Felipe González in 1982 marked a turning point. Not only did the new government enjoy a clear mandate. Unlike most of their predecessors, Spain's new rulers had impeccable democratic credentials, and enjoyed contacts with politicians in the EC countries built up during the twilight of Francoism and the transition. The two men who now took charge of the negotiations, Foreign Minister Fernando Morán [4.3.2] and Manuel Marín (see Table 4.2), were both cases in point. Indeed Marín, who was responsible for the details of the talks, was already a senior figure in the Party of European Socialists [4.3.1]. Together they drove the talks on with new vigour and tenacity and, despite several crises caused by French misgivings, Spain's Treaty of Accession (*Tratado de Adhesión*) was finally signed in mid-1985.

When it came into force on 1 January 1986, the country became a full EC member state, with all the attendant rights in terms of representation in its institutions [4.1.3]. However, Spain was forced to wait for some of the economic gains it expected from joining the common market. While her duties on imports from her new partners were to be removed at once, their tariffs on some Spanish agricultural products would be phased out only gradually, over a seven-year transitional period (*período transitorio*). Spain obtained no reciprocal concessions for its vulnerable dairy sector [6.3.1], while the treaty terms arguably failed to provide adequate protection for its fishing industry. In addition, in order to prepare for the inevitable shock to its economy, the country was already engaged on a painful process of industrial restructuring [6.1.2]. All in all, accession did not come cheap.

On the other hand, Spain succeeded in ensuring that the forthcoming European Single Act would include a major increase in the EC's Structural Funds, from which it would be by far the greatest beneficiary [6.1.2]. Even here there was a price to be paid, in that the country effectively surrendered the ability to set its own priorities for regional assistance. Yet very few doubts indeed were expressed about the terms that had been negotiated, and they were swamped in the general euphoria surrounding what was widely seen as the end of Spain's isolation. Significantly, the option of holding a referendum on the terms of entry, taken up in several other prospective members before and since, was never seriously considered. It would have been a pointless exercise, as no one, euphoric or not, was in any doubt as to the outcome.

4.2.2 In the vanguard

The situation regarding Spain's membership of another international organization could not have been more different. Spain had become a member of NATO in 1982, almost certainly in defiance of public opinion. The decision had been bitterly contested by the Socialists in opposition, and they came to power pledged to reverse it. However, it soon became clear to Prime Minister Felipe González at least that his EC counterparts were deeply unhappy at the prospect of having a new, and important partner which was not integrated into the Western world's common defence system. Although never explicit, staying in NATO became a sort of unspoken condition for EC accession.

González had no doubt where his priorities lay, and seems to have persuaded EC leaders to accept his ability to impose them on Spanish voters. Their trust proved well-placed. González first convinced his party to drop its demand for immediate withdrawal and concede that, on this point, the Spanish people should decide. Then he managed to hold off the promised referendum until March 1986, when he was basking in the glory of recent EC accession [4.2.1]. And finally, in a highly personal campaign, he managed to reverse the opinion poll findings and obtain what was eventually a clear majority in favour of remaining in NATO's political – although not its defence – structure. In a postscript to these dramatic events, Spain was admitted to the Western European Union in 1988.

At the time, the NATO referendum was bitterly divisive. Opposition to membership reflected anti-American feeling spread right across society [0.4.1], but the organizers of the 'no' campaign were mainly on the political left. They provided the seed of a new party, United Left (IU), which over the next few years became increasingly hostile towards European integration in general, and the EC in particular. This might have been expected to strike a chord with several groups of voters: the victims of restructuring in the early 1980s [6.1.2]; those who failed to benefit from the post-accession boom; and the many who were badly hit in the subsequent slump [6.1.3]. Yet IU was dismally unsuccessful [2.5.2]. Its performance was in line with the surveys which consistently showed Spaniards to be very positively disposed towards the EU, more so than almost all their fellow Europeans.

Several reasons can be suggested for their enthusiasm. On balance, Europe had brought some benefits to most Spaniards, and very substantial ones to some. The role of the Structural Funds in a range of major infrastructure projects was highly visible. In some regions, including the Basque Country, Europe provided a means of side-stepping the conflicts caused by regionalism [3.2.2.2]. And the fact that many Spaniards had, under Francoism, been deeply alienated by the Spanish state meant that surrendering some of that state's sovereignty caused few of the fears felt elsewhere, especially in Britain. But the key factor was probably the absence of any equivalent to the UK's large – and well-resourced – eurosceptic lobby. Apart from IU, the political class was united in its europhilia (*europeísmo*), and the same was true of the vast majority of other key opinion formers in business and the media.

As a result, once inside the EC Spain showed practically none of the suspicion towards further integration that surfaced in other member states. The government signed the European Single Act without hesitation. Then, in 1989 it took the peseta into the Exchange Rate Mechanism of the European Monetary System, despite the fact that, for one of the Community's less developed economies, that was likely to prove problematic – as indeed it later did [6.2.2]. Nor did Spain show any of the reservations about the Maastricht Treaty displayed by some of its partners, adopting the Social Chapter and participating actively in the first moves to develop a Common Foreign and Security Policy. In 1992 it was one of the founder members of the Eurocorps, and three years later it signed the Schengen Agreement.

Above all, the González government immediately pledged Spain to join Economic and Monetary Union. The decision to try and meet the convergence criteria set for prospective EMU members was brave, even foolhardy. It was bound to bring significant economic hardship for Spain in the short term and, in any case, seemed likely to end in embarrassing failure. The government's Convergence Plan did indeed prove painful for many [6.1.3], at a time when González was under massive political pressure at home [2.3.4]. Yet EMU was one area in which the opposition steered clear of political point-scoring. And when the conservatives finally came to power in 1996 they maintained intact the commitment to joining EMU. In the event, the criteria were achieved with some comfort and Spain had made good its aspiration to be in the vanguard of integration.

This strong commitment to integration undoubtedly helped Spain to become, surprisingly quickly, an important player in internal Union politics. And if some suggested that its excellent record on incorporating EU legislation into its own national code was not necessarily accompanied by the requisite enforcement – for instance on environmental matters [7.3.1] – that only underlined how well it had learnt the rules of internal Union politics [4.1.3].

In addition, Prime Minister González was careful to fill the EU posts to which Spain was entitled with close and trusted colleagues, who had a good knowledge of the EU's complex workings [4.3.1]. And he also cultivated close relations with other major EU leaders, especially his German counterpart Helmut Kohl. As a result, although Spain acquired a reputation for defending its interests as tenaciously as the French, or even more so, it attracted none of the opprobrium reserved for Margaret Thatcher's Britain [4.1.3].

On one occasion, González did act in a manner distinctly reminiscent of Thatcher. It came at the 1992 Edinburgh Summit and concerned the Cohesion Fund (*Fondo de Cohesión*) which had been agreed at Maastricht earlier in the year. This was designed to alleviate the problems that joining Economic and Monetary Union would place on the Union's weaker economies and – as with the Structural Funds [4.1.1] – its main beneficiary by far would be Spain. At Edinburgh the majority of members wanted to drop the Fund because of its high costs. González threatened to block further progress on EMU and brought the Summit to the point of breakdown, until they finally relented.

Significantly, his obduracy seemed to have little effect on Spain's standing, or his own; thereafter he continued to be quoted as a possible Commission President [4.1.3]. His appointment, had it come about, would have been merely the last in a string of influential Union posts which Spain's partners awarded it during its first decade of membership [4.3.2]. All in all, life in Europe was turning out to be something of an extended honeymoon.

4.2.3 End of the honeymoon?

González's successor, José María Aznar, has never questioned Spain's commitment to integration as such, and indeed oversaw his country's completion of the difficult journey to EMU [4.2.2]. However, while still in opposition and keen to attack the Socialists on every front, he had tended to seize on any minor concessions made to Spain's partners – inevitable in any working partnership – as proof that González was failing adequately to stand up for Spanish interests. To avoid charges of back-pedalling once elected, he has found himself forced to maintain the rhetoric of 'national interests'.

Partly as a result, his premiership has also been marked by poor personal relations with a number of EU leaders, especially his German counterpart Gerhard Schröder, and a growing tendency for Spain to be seen by its fellow members as a ruthless and even unreasonable negotiator. Of course, this cannot all be put down to Aznar, who has shown himself in domestic politics to be a good learner of political skills. Other factors have also been at work, one being the differences between the two men's party bases.

The relative youth and peculiar origins of Aznar's People's Party [2.4.1] mean that it has nothing like the extensive connections with counterparts in other countries enjoyed by the Socialists; indeed only since 1989 has it been integrated in one of the main EU party groupings [4.3.1]. Additionally, while the Socialists' move to the right under González [2.3.3] placed them in the ideological mainstream of the continental EU, especially France and Germany, the PP remains somewhat of an ideological outsider. For, in its move away from authoritarian conservatism, it has tended towards the sort of market-based ideology associated with Margaret Thatcher. It is no coincidence that in several internal EU battles Aznar has found himself allied with the UK, still – despite Thatcher's departure – very much the EU's odd-man-out.

The crucial point, though, is that integration has lost some of its attraction for Spain. For one thing, the Union's Common Foreign and Security Policy, apart from its overall weakness, has proved to be of little relevance for the country's two main foreign policy concerns outside the EU itself, Latin America [0.4.2] and North Africa [0.4.3]. As yet CFSP has focused almost exclusively on the Eastern Mediterranean and, above all, Eastern Europe, partly for security reasons but above all because of prospective enlargement. Not surprisingly, Spain's enthusiasm for it has slackened.

However, it is enlargement itself that is Spain's main concern. For the EU as a whole, and especially Germany, this represents a massive economic opportunity. For Spain, by contrast, it implies considerable dangers. One is that enlargement to the East shifts the EU's economic centre of gravity, and brings in new members whose interests are mostly different from those of the Mediterranean countries in general, and Spain in particular. Such considerations lay behind the unease displayed by the González administration about the 1995 enlargement. But the countries admitted then were too small to greatly affect the EU's economic geography, and all were richer than the

Union average so that their accession actually reduced common budgetary costs for the existing members.

Current plans for a second eastern enlargement are a very different matter. If they are fulfilled the Iberian Peninsula will become a peripheral area, remote from the Union's economic core. Almost all of the candidate countries are non-Mediterranean in character and some, notably Poland, are large enough to wield significant influence in their own right. Most important of all, given their relative poverty the admission of these countries will undoubtedly mean an end to the Structural and Cohesion Funds [4.2.2] in anything like their present form, and to the massive financial support Spain has received under them.

That represents a very considerable threat indeed, which Aznar has had no option but to resist. He has been shrewd enough not to question the principle of enlargement. But in practice his battle to preserve Spain's current receipts for as long as possible is one of the main reasons why financially viable arrangements for an enlarged Union have proved so hard to devise. Nor has he been helped in presenting his case by Spain's very economic success since joining the Union [6.1.3] and its determination to be at the forefront of integration [4.2.2], both of which sit ill with pleading poverty.

The result has been to exasperate most of Spain's fellow EU members, a situation Aznar himself has occasionally aggravated. In particular, a threat to veto Germany's proposal for a transitional period on free movement of workers from the East – a delicate political issue in Germany but of no immediate concern to Spain – backfired badly. True, Aznar succeeded in preserving Spain's funding virtually intact up to 2006. Yet already there have been some indications that relations with its partners and the Union authorities themselves may be suffering [4.3.2]. That must be worrying for what is still a much weaker economic power than the UK. For Spain, renewed marginalization, in terms not just of economic geography but also of ability to influence the EU's overall direction, is a far from attractive prospect.

4.3 SPAIN IN THE EU MACHINERY

As a result of its involvement in the integration process, Spain has handed over to the EU responsibility for wide areas of its own affairs, above all in the economic field. In return, it has acquired access to the Union's decision-making machinery, in three ways. One is through the representation in the EU's various institutions to which it is entitled under the Union's various defining treaties and the terms of its accession. The second is through Spanish politicians and public servants appointed to other senior EU posts. And third, a range of public bodies exist in Brussels and within Spain itself to act as links between the country and the Union machinery.

(NB. Throughout this section reference is made to the general description of the EU machinery in [4.1.3].)

4.3.1 Spain's assured representation

Spain's representation in the most senior of EU institutions is identical to that of its fellows: through the Prime Minister in the European Council and the responsible government ministers in the Council of Ministers. For the purposes of qualified majority voting in the Councils Spain currently has eight votes, giving it a status clearly closer to that of the 'big four' (10 votes each) than to any of its other partners, none of whom has more than five.

Under the reallocation agreed at the Nice summit, Spain will be the main beneficiary of re-weighting in favour of larger countries. Its voting strength will rise to 27 after enlargement, compared with 29 for the big four and a maximum of 14 for the smaller members. On the other hand, as and when Poland joins it will also have 27 votes. Spain fought hard to prevent this, on the grounds that Spain's population is slightly higher. Its motive was not so much that one or two votes are likely to have any real effect on Council decisions, but rather to maintain a higher status in the EU's internal pecking order than the newcomer. Failure to get its way represented a small but significant setback, perhaps reflecting the recent deterioration in its standing within the EU [4.2.3].

Spain has so far taken on the role of Union President three times, its terms falling in the first half of 1989, the second of 1995 and the first of 2002. On the first two occasions the customary end-of-term summit was held in Madrid; in 2002 the venue was Seville. As a relatively new and less developed member, in 1989 Spain was content merely to show that it could meet its obligations in an efficient manner, an aim generally agreed to have been achieved. By 1995 it was rather more ambitious, but the efforts of the then Socialist government to promote Spanish interests were hampered by its domestic political troubles [2.3.4].

In the event, its only major success was to organize the first Euro-Mediterranean Conference in Barcelona, an initiative that has had few long-term effects [0.4.3]. The second Madrid summit is remembered for christening the euro, but little else. In 2002, finally, the conservative administration was in an awkward position, since its main concern was to block, or at least slow down, progress on expansion to the East, the EU's major project [4.2.3]. Not surprisingly, it took a rather low-key approach to its responsibilities.

One important success achieved by Spain under the terms of its accession was the right to nominate two Commissioners, a privilege previously enjoyed only by the 'big four'. Like them, however, it will lose this right after enlargement under the terms agreed at Nice. In nominating its Commissioners Spain has followed the same practice as the UK, putting forward one from each of the two largest political parties irrespective of which is in power. This arrangement has enabled Spain to avoid the political horse-trading nomination causes in some countries and send a succession of well qualified Commissioners (Table 4.2); four are or were domestic political heavyweights, while the other had unrivalled knowledge of EU–Spanish relations.

On accession Spain was allocated 60 seats in the European Parliament, raised to 64 in 1994 and due to fall to 50 after enlargements. Its first MEPs

Table 4.2 Spain's European Commissioners

Manuel Marín	1986–99	PSOE	Former Secretary of State for EC Relations Senior official in Party of European Socialists Key figure in negotiations for Spanish accession [4.2.1]
Abel Matutes	1986–94	AP/PP	Leading businessman and politician in the Balearics Foreign Minister (1996–2000)
Marcelino Oreja	1994–99	PP	Foreign Minister (1976–80) Secretary-General of Council of Europe [4.1.1] (1984–89) Key figure in foundation of PP [3.4.2] MEP 1989–94
Loyola de Palacio	1999–	PP	Senior figure in the PP Minister of Agriculture (1996–2000)
Pedro Solbes	1999–	PSOE	Former Secretary of State for EC Relations Finance Minister (1993–96)

were appointed by the King pending a special election in 1987, since when Spain has taken part in the five-yearly Europe-wide elections for the Parliament (see Table 4.3). For these, like several other Union members, Spain uses a single, country-wide constituency (*circunscripción única*), for which the parties present lists as in domestic elections [1.3.1].

Theoretically, this arrangement should make it easier for smaller, country-wide parties to obtain seats. However, only in 1989 was such an effect apparent, and then purely because the mainstream right was then so weak [2.4.1]. In particular, no Spanish Greens have yet been elected to the EP. On the other hand, the system makes it harder for regionalist parties to gain representation than in general elections [1.3.1]. In order to counteract this effect and ensure some level of representation, a number of such parties have joined together in alliances (*coaliciones*) with their fellows in other regions to fight European elections.

Public interest is also strictly limited. As elsewhere in the EU, turnout is consistently lower than in domestic elections, even when these are held on the same day, as was done with some local and regional polls in 1987 and 1999. On the other hand, Spanish parties seem to place a relatively high value on European representation. The candidates they present, or at least those with realistic chances of election, tend to carry some political weight; there are few of the mavericks or marginal figures common among British MEPs. Four former or future Spanish Foreign Ministers have served as MEPs: Fernando Morán [4.2.1] and Carlos Westendorp [4.3.2] in the Socialist ranks and Marcelino Oreja and Abel Matutes – both also Commissioners in their time – on the right.

Table 4.3 Results of principal parties in European elections, 1987–99

		1987	1989	1994	1999
Social and Democratic	P	10.4	7.1		
Centre (CDS)	S	7	5		
Spanish Socialist Party (PSOE)	P	39.4	39.6	30.8	35.3
	S	28	27	22	24
People's Party (PP)	P	24.9	21.4	40.1	39.7
	S	17	15	28	27
United Left (IU)	P	5.3	6.1	13.4	5.8
	S	3	4	9	4
Convergence and Union (CiU)[a]	P	4.5	4.2	4.7	4.4
	S	3	2	3	3
Nationalist Alliance (CN)[b]	P	1.7	1.9	2.8	2.9
	S	1	1	2	2
European Alliance (CE)[c]	P				3.2
	S				2
Others	P	13.8	19.4	8.2	8.7
	S	1	6	0	2

Notes: [a] Leading Catalan regionalist party.
[b] Includes Basque Nationalist Party (PNV), Basque Solidarity (EA) [3.2.2.2, 4],
Catalan Republican Left (ERC) [3.2.1.1] and Majorcan Union (UM) [11.4].
[c] Includes Canary Islands Alliance, Andalusian Regionalist Party (PA), Valencian Union
[3.2.3.1] and Aragonese Regionalist Party (Par) [3.2.3.2].
V = votes (in thousands); P = per cent poll; S = seats.
Source: Interior Ministry

Almost all the Spanish parties represented in the EP have opted to join one or other of its trans-national groups (see Table 4.4). Four points are worthy of additional note here. First, all groups have agreed to cold shoulder Herri Batasuna, ETA's political wing, because of its attitude to violence. Its single MEP therefore sits among the non-attached members (*no inscritos*). Second, while most of Spain's regionalist parties represented in the EP choose to sit with their fellows from other countries, those from the Canary Islands as well as the Catalan CiU have joined other groups based on ideological affiliation. Third, members of regionalist electoral alliances may sit in different groups once elected.

Finally the position of Spain's current ruling party, the conservative People's Party (PP), is of interest. From 1987 to 1989 its forerunner, People's Alliance [2.4.1], formed part of a minor right-wing group whose only other significant component was the British Conservatives. However, as part of the operation that led to the creation of the PP, its MEPs joined the European People's Party, the Christian Democrat umbrella organization, even though hardly any were previously known for such views. Their admission to the EPP prompted the Basque Nationalist Party, a long-standing member of the organization, to resign in protest.

Table 4.4 Party groups in the European Parliament

Group[a]	Spanish name	Spanish representatives
Party of European Socialists (PSE)	*Partido de los Socialistas Europeos*	Spanish Socialist Party (PSOE)
European People's Party[b] (PPE)	*Partido Popular Europeo*	People's Party (PP) Convergence and Union (UDC)[d]
European Liberals, Democrats and Reformists (ELDR)	*Partido Europeo de los Liberales, Demócratas y Reformistas*	Convergence and Union (CDC)[d] Canary Islands Alliance
European United Left (GUE)	*Izquierda Unida Europea*	IU [2.5]
Greens-European Free Alliance[c] (Verts-ALE)	*Verdes-Alianza Libre Europea*	Basque Nationalist Party[e] Catalan Republican Left Galician National Alliance Andalusian Regionalist Party

Notes: [a] In most cases the French initials/abbreviation are generally used.
[b] Christian Democrats.
[c] Greens and regionalists.
[d] The leading Catalan regionalist grouping is made up of the parties CDC and UDC [3.2.1.2].
[e] Previously formed part of PPE but withdrew following PP's admission.

In addition, Spain has assured representation on various other EU institutions and bodies. It nominates one judge to the Court of Justice and one representative to the Court of Auditors, while the governor of its central bank, the Bank of Spain, sits on the Governing Council (*Consejo de Gobierno*) of the European Central Bank. It also has 21 representatives on the Economic and Social Council.

Spain also appoints 21 members to the Committee of the Regions (*Comité de las Regiones*). Here again the practice of nominating relative political heavyweights contrasts sharply with the UK's. Spain's seats are occupied by the prime ministers of the country's 17 regions, and the mayors of Madrid, Barcelona and two other major cities. Catalans have been particularly assiduous in using the Committee to lobby for their region's interests; former Barcelona mayor Pasqual Maragall has served as its Vice-President, and regional prime minister Jordi Pujol [3.2.2.2] is one of its most active members.

4.3.2 Spaniards in appointed posts

As well as its assured representation in Union institutions, a member state can also hope to improve its situation in EU internal politics by having its nationals appointed to a wide range of posts that are not reserved for any particular country. In a sense this applies to its nominees on the European Commission since, unlike their number, their responsibilities are not fixed.

Instead, commissioners are appointed to portfolios by the Commission President, and it is clearly in a member state's interests for these to be as broad and as influential as possible.

In this respect Spain's policy of nominating Commissioners with good knowledge of Union matters paid dividends immediately, when Manuel Marín [4.2.1] was appointed a Commission Vice-President, a considerable coup for a new member. Marín went on to become one of the longest-serving commissioners ever, retaining his position for thirteen years. During that time he held a number of important portfolios and became an influential figure in internal EU politics. Latterly, however, he rather fell from grace, being the subject of serious allegations about irregularities in the administration of development aid under his authority in the 1999 affair that led to the entire Commission's removal [4.1.3].

While none has been as prominent as Marín, Spain's other Commissioners (see Table 4.2) have also tended to be given fairly significant portfolios, which could be seen as either a recognition of their calibre, or a pay-off for Spain's commitment to integration, or both. Between 1994 and 1999 Marcelino Oreja, a highly experienced international administrator, had a broad portfolio including responsibility for the crucial telecommunications sector. In the present Commission, Loyola de Palacio has succeeded Marín as a Vice-President while also controlling a weighty portfolio that includes transport and energy, and Pedro Solbes has responsibility for the key area of Economic and Monetary Affairs. In the top rank of the Commission administration, two directors-general (out of 23) are from Spain.

Spaniards have also tended to hold more than their fair share of important posts in the European Parliament. Two have served as the chamber's president; Enrique Barón Crespo (1989–92) and José-María Gil-Robles Gil-Delgado (1997–99), while since 1994 three of the fourteen vice-presidents have also been Spanish. Currently Spain also provides the chairs of three of its 17 standing committees. This proportion was even higher in the previous parliament, when there were 20 committees and four Spanish chairs. Finally, Barón Crespo currently chairs the Parliament's second-largest political group, the Party of European Socialists.

The expansion of Union activity following the Treaty of Maastricht created a new range of appointed posts within the ambit of the European Council, a number of which went to Spaniards. One who has emerged as an archetypal Union figure is Carlos Westendorp who, like several of Spain's representatives and appointees, was responsible for European policy in the Foreign Ministry before becoming Foreign Minister. Among other jobs, Westendorp headed the group which prepared the ground for the 1996 Intergovernmental Conference and was thereafter the Union's High Representative to Bosnia; currently he chairs the Parliament's Industry Committee. Another senior Spanish appointee is Miguel Angel Moratinos, currently the EU's envoy to the Middle East peace process.

But the highest ranking Spanish appointment within the Union came in 1999, when the European Council decided to name a High Representative

(*Alto Representante*) for the Union's Common Foreign and Security Policy [4.1.2]. This position, which incorporates that of Secretary-General of the Council of Ministers, is arguably the second most influential post within the entire Union structure. The man chosen to fill the role of *Mister PESC*, as it is often called, was Javier Solana, Spanish Foreign Minister from 1992 to 1995. Shortly after his appointment he was also named as Secretary-General of the Western European Union [4.1.1], further increasing his already substantial influence.

Solana unquestionably had impressive credentials for his new job. A cabinet minister for thirteen years in total, he was Secretary-General of NATO from 1995 to 1999. Yet his appointment to such a sensitive post would have been unthinkable without Spain's ostentatious commitment to the CFSP under the Socialist governments in which he served [4.2.2], and represented a further dividend from their strategy of establishing Spain as a 'good European'. It is too soon to say whether such benefits will be affected by the deterioration of Spain–EU relations evident under the present government [4.2.3]. The small decline in Spain's share of Parliamentary Committee chairs, like the setback it suffered over the allocation of Council votes after enlargement [4.3.1], might be a straw in the wind. Certainly it seems unlikely that the EU's top post, Commission President, for which former Prime Minister Felipe González was often quoted as a candidate in the early 1990s, will go to a Spaniard in the foreseeable future.

4.3.3 Communication with the EU

The Union's role in running Spanish affairs, and the need to defend Spanish interests within its structures, have led to the creation of various mechanisms designed to facilitate communication between the EU, national and regional levels of government. The first of these is Spain's 'permanent representation' in Brussels. Intended to assist the country's representatives in the Council of Ministers [4.3.1], it is headed by an ambassador and composed of senior diplomats and civil servants seconded from ministries in Madrid. It also represents Spain on the two so-called Coreper committees (*Comités de Representantes Permanentes*) in which Council business is prepared.

Regular contact with the Brussels representation is maintained by a special division within the Ministry of Foreign Affairs, which is responsible for all EU matters and is headed by a Secretary of State [1.5.2]. Its task is to coordinate the stances taken by all those ministers and civil servants who, in one forum and another, represent Spanish interests within the EU. It is assisted in this task by the Interministerial Working Group on Community Affairs (*Conferencia Interministerial para Asuntos Comunitarios/CIAC*), on which all the ministries are represented. Any disputes that cannot be settled there are referred to the cabinet committee on economic affairs.

In addition, other ministries which have to deal with Brussels on a regular basis – the great majority – have set up special units to do so, usually under a Director-General [1.5.2]. That in the Ministry of Finance and Economics is especially important, as it coordinates all initiatives connected with the Structural Funds [4.1.1]. It also administers the receipts from several, including

- the European Regional Development Fund (*Fondo Europeo de Desarrollo Regional/FEDER*), which is much the largest and deals mainly with infrastructure projects;
- RECHAR, concerned with declining coal mining areas in Asturias, Catalonia, Leon and Teruel;
- STRIDE, the Union's programme to promote innovation;
- ENVIREG, which supports environment-friendly coastal development; and
- PRISMA, which provides infrastructure and services for small businesses.

The Ministry of Agriculture, Fishing and Food also plays an important role, since it administers the European Agricultural Guidance and Guarantee Fund (*Fondo Europeo de Orientación y Garantía Agrícolas/FEOGA*). The guidance section, which constitutes the second structural fund, is managed by the National Land Reform and Agricultural Development Agency (*Instituto Nacional de Reforma y Desarrollo Agrario/IRYDA*). The guarantee section, on the other hand, supports prices under the arrangements of the Common Agricultural Policy [4.1.1]. It is managed by the Farm Products and Prices Regulatory Fund (*Fondo de Ordenación y Regulación de Productos y Precios Agrarios/FORPPA*). The third structural fund, the European Social Fund (*Fondo Europeo Social/FSE*), is administered by the Ministry of Labour and Social Affairs, while those of Education and Culture handle the SOCRATES (academic education) and LEONARDO (vocational training) programmes respectively.

The Spanish Parliament, too, has made arrangements for coordination by creating a Joint Committee of both its Houses [1.3.4] to deal with EU affairs. First, this Committee deals directly with the European Parliament, having the right to comment on any EP proposals. Secondly, it seeks to exercise parliamentary control over the Spanish government's policy towards the Union. And finally, it cooperates with the national parliaments of the other member states on matters of mutual concern.

Links with the EU are also of prime importance for Spain's autonomous regions. On the one hand, they are now responsible for a major part of the country's government [3.3.2], making the need for coordination almost as great as at Spanish level. Not surprisingly, all seventeen now have a department for EU affairs; most have a special unit to administer Structural Funds money; and nearly all of them have set up offices in Brussels whose job is to lobby the Union institutions concerned. A number of regions have been vocal in demanding that regional representatives should attend the Council of Ministers on Spain's behalf when it deals with certain issues, as is the case of the German *Länder*, but so far their demands have been resisted by the central government [3.3.4].

In addition to these arrangements made by Spanish authorities, the EU has established a number of bodies in Spain, as in other member states. These are intended to allow Spanish society and business access to the Union and its institutions, the largest being the offices of the European Commission and Parliament in Madrid. European Documentation Centres (*Centros de Documentación Europea/CDE*) are scattered throughout the country, while several of the main cities host European Business Information Centres (*Centros de Información Empresarial*), commonly known as *Euroventanillas*. There is also a more extensive Business Cooperation Network (*BC Net*) intended to provide support for small and medium enterprises. The locations of all these types of office vary widely: a few have their own premises; some are located in regional government offices, universities or business associations [5.2.2]; others – especially among the last group – are hosted by private firms.

Finally, two EU specialist agencies are located in Spain: that concerned with health and safety at work (*Agencia Europea para la Seguridad y la Salud en el Trabajo*) in Bilbao, and the Internal Market Harmonization Office (*Oficina de Armonización del Mercado Interior/OAMI*) in Alicante. This latter is the largest of all such bodies in terms of the staff employed, and Spain is so far the only country apart from Ireland to have attracted two such bodies. That can certainly be seen as another fruit of its government's determination to establish Spain as an important player in Union affairs. Whether it, or indeed the various European offices, do much to reduce the democratic deficit [4.1.2] by making Spaniards feel more involved in the Union, is less clear.

4.4 GLOSSARY

Acta Unica f	(European) Single Act
Acuerdo Social m	Social Chapter (of the Maastricht Treaty)
adhesión m	accession (to the EU)
agentes sociales mpl	social partners
ampliación f	enlargement (of the EU)
arancel aduanero común m	common external tariff
aspirante m	candidate (for admission to EU)
asuntos de Interior mpl	home affairs
barreras arancelarias fpl	tariff barriers
barreras no tarifarias fpl	non-tariff barriers
circunscripción única f	single, country-wide constituency (for European elections)
cláusula de exclusión f	opt-out
Comisario m	(European) Commissioner
comisión (del Parlamento) f	(parliamentary) committee
Comisión Europea f	European Commission
Consejo de Gobierno m	Governing Council (of European Central Bank)
Consejo de Ministros m	Council of Ministers
Consejo Europeo m	European Council
cooperación reforzada f	enhanced cooperation
cumbre m	summit
Dirección General f	Directorate General (within the Commission)
estados miembros mpl	(EU) member states
eurodiputado m	MEP

Euroejército m	Eurocorps
Europa de distintas velocidades f	two-speed Europe
europeísmo m	enthusiasm for (the idea of) the EU, europhilia
europeización f	process of (Spain's) becoming more like the rest of Europe
integración f	entry (into the EU)
mayoría cualificada f	qualified majority
mecanismo de cambios m	Exchange Rate Mechanism
mercado común m	common market
mercado interior m	internal market
moneda única f	single currency
no inscrito m	MEP who is not a member of any of the European Parliament's groups
pecos mpl	Central and Eastern European countries
período transitorio m	transitional period
presidencia f	presidency
President del Parlamento Europeo m	President (Speaker) of the European Parliament
presidente (de una comisión) m	(committee) chair
Presidente de la Comisión m	President of the (European) Commission
profundización f	deepening (of the EU)
Unión de los Quince f	existing 15-member EU
unión europea f	European integration
Unión Europea f	European Union
zona de libre comercio f	free trade area
zona euro f	euro zone, Euroland

INTERESTS AND LOBBIES

Modern democratic societies are characterized by a complex relationship between the apparatus of government and the rest of society. The interests of civil society – that is, those areas of national life outside the state's ambit – are channelled not just by political parties but a host of other organizations. In doing so they attempt to influence public policy but, like parties, they can act also as reverse channels, assisting the state to manipulate civil society. In Spain the nature of the Franco regime meant that certain of these organizations acquired a particular importance, and this chapter will begin by examining them. It will then go on to consider the representatives in Spain of the main interests and lobbies in contemporary Western societies: economic interest groups, the media and non-institutional pressure groups.

5.1 FRANCOISM'S DE FACTO AUTHORITIES

Under the Franco regime, so powerful was the influence of certain interests outside what would normally be understood as the structure of the state that it was habitual to speak of them as the country's de facto authorities (*poderes fácticos*). By its very nature the term is a vague one, and deliberately so. Yet there was never any doubt about the identity of the two main powers behind the throne: the military and the Catholic Church. Although retaining a degree of influence since 1975, both have seen their role greatly diminished, especially since the end of the transition. In the case of a third pillar of Francoism, the major banks, that is far from true; more important in their case has been a change in the nature of the influence they wield.

5.1.1 The military

Franco had been brought to power by the military [0.1], and throughout his rule it remained a major prop of his regime. Its personnel were by and large fiercely loyal to him, and many vehemently opposed the moves to democracy after his death. Furthermore, the Spanish military had a long history of intervening in politics going back over 150 years. Little wonder, then, that well into the 1980s it continued to be seen as a significant threat to the country's stability.

5.1.1.1 Transition and the army

Throughout the transition to democracy [0.3] the question of how to keep the three armed forces (*fuerzas armadas/FFAA*) out of politics was perhaps the most important one facing Spain's new rulers. In fact, their concern was focused almost exclusively on the army (*Ejército de Tierra*). Not only was it by far the largest of the three services (*ejércitos*); in 1975 it numbered 220,000 men, the navy (*Marina*) only 46,000 and the air force (*Ejército del Aire*) a mere 35,000. It was also the army that had been particularly closely involved in the former regime and was most heavily impregnated with Francoist beliefs.

Not only that; the army had also been involved in running the country to an extraordinary degree. Serving officers habitually held ministerial posts unconnected with military affairs; they exercised administrative responsibilities of many types and at various levels; they helped run the economy's huge public sector; they were even involved in private business, being invited on to the boards of a number of important companies.

These activities were clearly different from those normally expected of the army in a democracy. The same was true of its operational role during the Franco era. Rather than defending Spain against external threats, the army acted essentially as an internal occupation force, defending the regime against its own people. It was accordingly deployed on a territorial basis, in military regions each under the command of a captain-general. In each province a military authority (*Gobierno Militar*) worked alongside the civilian one [1.5.2], and the army was frequently called in to maintain public order.

Finally, the army had an important ideological role, exercised through the system of compulsory military service. As well as providing the army with the necessary manpower, this was seen by many officers as a means of inculcating into the country's young men the fundamental principles of the regime: unquestioning respect for authority, represented above all in the person of Franco, fervent Spanish nationalism and contempt for any vaguely socialist, or even liberal ideas.

Against this background it is scarcely surprising that, after the death of its former leader, the army should have been the main centre of extreme reactionary thinking and activity (*involucionismo*). Between 1976 and 1980 a succession of coup plots was uncovered, the most serious being the Galaxia affair named after the Madrid café where it was planned. In 1981 a coup attempt was actually launched [0.3.3]. The wholly negative reaction it evoked, which ranged from the monarch to the mass of ordinary Spaniards, was a salutary lesson for the reactionaries. But as late as 1985 it would seem that a plot to assassinate King Juan Carlos, involving senior army officers, reached an advanced stage of planning before it was thwarted.

The centrist governments of 1976–82 were keenly aware of the dangers posed by the army's predisposition to plotting coups (*golpismo*). After the inaugural 1977 election a senior army figure convinced of the need for change, Lieutenant-General Manuel Gutiérrez Mellado, was brought into the cabinet as Deputy to Prime Minister Adolfo Suárez. Given special responsibility for defence matters, his task was to ensure that the army's opportunities to intervene in politics were removed.

The 1977 cabinet changes also ended the practice of according ministerial rank to the heads of the three armed forces. Instead, a Ministry of Defence was set up, to whose political authority the service chiefs were subordinate. Military direction was placed in the hands of a new Joint Chiefs-of-Staff Council (*Junta de Jefes de Estado Mayor/JUJEM*). The following year the Constitution distinguished the role of the armed forces in defending Spain against external threats from that of the civilian security forces (*cuerpos de seguridad*) [10.2].

The Constitution's characteristic ambiguity was evident in other key aspects of the military's role. On the one hand, its mission to defend Spain's sovereignty and territorial unity was given the status of a fundamental principle [1.1.2]. On the other, much less prominence was given to a specification that all the military's actions, including any related to national unity, are carried out under the supreme command of the monarch, itself subject to endorsement by democratically elected authorities [1.2]. It has sometimes been argued that this left the door dangerously open for the army to take unilateral action supposedly in the national interest. Yet in practice what mattered was not the Constitution's wording but the army's readiness and effective capacity to act unconstitutionally.

Sensibly, the government moved to limit both these factors. Before standing down as Defence Minister in 1979 to make way for a civilian, Gutiérrez Mellado took steps to reform pay scales and so reduce the risk of discontent. Under Suárez's successor, Leopoldo Calvo Sotelo, legislation was introduced to allow the dismissal of officers for alleged incompetence. This second measure was, in effect, a recognition that the government's real control over the army remained dangerously limited. Gutiérrez Mellado had been publicly insulted on several occasions by officers opposed to his reforms. And a number of the instigators of the 1981 coup attempt had previously been convicted of involvement in the Galaxia plot but had received only laughable sentences.

5.1.1.2 Modernization and reform

This situation changed in 1982, with the arrival in office of a Socialist administration with a massive popular mandate and a clear parliamentary majority [2.3.1]. From this much stronger position the new government effectively called the army's bluff, invariably taking quick and decisive action against recalcitrant officers in marked contrast to its predecessor. Crucially, however, it also recognized that the army's tendency to intervene in politics was due not only to political conviction but also to officers' grievances over pay, conditions of service and professional satisfaction. Accordingly Narcis Serra, Defence Minister from 1982 to 1991, set out to address these concerns, which in some respects had been aggravated under the former regime.

That was largely because Franco's maintenance of a large officer corps constantly replenished from the military academies had left the country with a top-heavy army – of the 1975 strength of 220,000, over 24,000 were officers (*oficiales*). As a result, even though individual officers' pay was poor, the overall wages bill was high and represented a major constraint on purchase of modern equipment. At the same time, promotion remained strictly based on length of service (*ascenso por antigüedad*). This ensured that mediocre officers reached senior positions while more able colleagues languished lower down the scale, with ample time to channel their frustration into political plotting.

The promotion issue was traditionally a sensitive one, and Serra shrewdly chose to finesse it. Merit criteria for promotion, introduced by the previous government at the levels of major and brigadier, became general. However, they applied only to active commands, the number of which was greatly reduced. Those who failed to meet the new standards continued to receive pay and even promotion, just as they would have done under the old system, but were transferred to a bizarrely named 'active reserve'. These measures improved officer quality and provided a means of sidelining potential troublemakers. In the longer term they also cut the real wages bill: more immediately they allowed financial juggling to free up funds for spending on hardware.

That in turn was essential for the second front of Serra's strategy, which was to involve the army in new, strictly defence tasks. It was a route on which Calvo Sotelo had already embarked by taking Spain into NATO. The PSOE had opposed that move when in opposition, but reversed its position once in office [2.3.2]. Well before 1996, when the country became fully integrated into NATO [0.4.1], its forces were regularly involved in joint exercises with those of its democratically run neighbours. Once a joint European Union corps was established, Spain was quick to join it. Participation in UN peace-keeping missions has been another means to the same end. In 1989, in Angola, seven Spanish officers became the first to take part in such a mission. Within three years Spain had become the largest single contributor to UN forces.

At home the PSOE governments redeployed the army along lines more in accord with an external defence role, a process begun by the plan known as META (*Modernización del Ejército de Tierra*). The posts of captain-general and, later, provincial military governor were abolished. In 1984 the JUJEM [5.1.1.1] was reorganized and its head renamed Chief of the Defence Staff (*Jefe del Estado Mayor de la Defensa*). A second major plan approved in 1994, and known as Norte (*Nueva Organización del Ejército de Tierra*), provided for closure of many installations no longer needed and a slimmer, restructured army.

These moves, together with the effects of time, have brought a gradual change in military attitudes. In 1989, when Serra again addressed the promotions issue by introducing fast and slow tracks for promotion as low down the scale as major, his move provoked some immediate controversy but no lasting problems.

Admittedly, the army today still contains some extreme reactionaries with the will to intervene in politics. But happily they no longer have the capacity to do so, their links to powerful political and economic interests now being as limited as their public support. Far-right parties have enjoyed negligible success since 1975 [2.6], while the newspaper *El Alcázar*, which openly backed a return to authoritarianism and was closely linked to various military plots, was forced to close in 1988 due to its pitiful sales.

Within the forces themselves debate has switched away from political issues to the technical question of their ability to carry out their new external defence role. In part it has focused on Spain's level of defence spending – at 1.26 per cent of GDP the lowest in NATO outside Luxembourg – and the severe logistic problems to which this gives rise. But during most of the 1990s the main topic of discussion was possible professionalization of the military.

One reason for this was the increasing rejection of military service among the young [9.4.2]. But in the new, less political climate some army opinion too began to favour scrapping it, on efficiency grounds. The Socialist governments in power up to 1996 showed great caution in responding to such suggestions, despite the potential electoral benefits. One reason was their awareness that abandoning conscription altogether would be costly. However, the PSOE also remained wary of the traditionalist feelings of army officers, many of whom remained suspicious of democracy into the 1990s.

The decision to professionalize was thus not taken until after the election of a conservative government, which could afford to take such feelings more lightly. In 1999 the Armed Forces Personnel Act (*Ley de Régimen del Personal de las Fuerzas Armadas*) was passed, introducing the principle of full professionalization, and the following year the final intake of conscripts was taken on. One problem with this solution appears to be that young Spaniards are little more attracted by a professional military career than they were by compulsory service.

The 1999 Act also sealed another important change. Since 1989 women had been allowed to serve in the Spanish forces, but with certain restrictions as to the activities they might undertake. These restrictions were removed by the Act, which accords both sexes equal status within the services. Perhaps even more than the end of conscription this step shows how much the military has changed since Franco's death.

5.1.2 The Church

Like the military, the Church was a pillar of the Franco regime, and indeed provided it with its main ideological foundation. Yet latterly important elements within it had begun to distance themselves from the dictatorship, or even overtly oppose it [0.2]. Understandably, then, the religious question was a much less thorny aspect of the transition than the military one. On the other hand, unlike the military, the Church has retained both a concern with wider issues and links to other social forces, and thus also a certain political significance.

5.1.2.1 Transition and the Church

The fact that the Church featured prominently in the minds of those who guided Spain's transition to democracy after 1975 was due above all to historical reasons. For almost two centuries the Church hierarchy had been closely allied with the country's most reactionary political forces. And there was a keen awareness that its last experiment in democracy, the Second Republic, had been fatally wounded by the anticlerical provisions included in its constitution. Much more than in the case of the army, therefore, the prospective new constitution was seen as crucial to resolving the Church's position.

The Church's role during the Franco era, like that of the military, went far beyond the norm in most Western societies. School education was largely under its control [8.1.2], as well as most of what passed for a health and welfare system [9.2.1]; it played a major part in censorship of the arts and media; its youth organizations helped to inculcate the regime's values. It also owned a number of newspapers – most notably the national daily *Ya* – and the chain of radio stations known as COPE (*Cadena de Ondas Populares Españolas*). At the same time, it received extremely generous state funding that effectively met the costs not only of its social service provision but also of its own ministry.

In return for these extensive privileges, the Concordat signed by Franco and the Vatican in 1953 gave his regime the right to appoint Spain's bishops. That gave him a considerable degree of control over them. Latterly, however, it proved inadequate to insulate the Spanish Church from the changes taking place in Catholicism as a whole, changes that were given especial impetus by the Second Vatican Council (*Concilio Vaticano II*) held between 1962 and 1965. Their influence was particularly apparent after 1971, when Cardinal Enrique y Tarancón became chairman of the Conference of Spanish Bishops (*Conferencia Episcopal Española/CEE*).

Under Tarancón, support for liberalization of the regime was increasingly apparent within the Church. At the same time, priests and bishops in the Basque Country and Catalonia became more vociferous in their backing, never completely hidden, for regionalist feeling in the two regions. Such attitudes were by no means universal in the Church, large parts of which remained deeply traditionalist in their social and political views. But they were sufficiently widespread to prevent it from providing concerted opposition to democracy.

Certainly it tended to back the most conservative of the new, legalized political parties – in 1979 Church leaders explicitly called on the faithful to vote for People's Alliance [2.4.1]. Aware of the danger of reopening old wounds, however, they refrained from backing the formation of a specifically Christian Democrat party. They also urged voters to support the 1976

Political Reform Act, which effectively destroyed the political structure of the old regime [0.3.2], and the 1978 Constitution which defined the new democratic one.

The Constitution implicitly acknowledged the Church as an objective feature of Spanish society (*hecho sociológico*) – Catholicism remains Spain's largest faith, indeed virtually its only one since membership even of other Christian Churches is negligible. Yet the acknowledgement was minor and grudging. It required a parliamentary amendment to the draft text to insert the only specific reference to the Catholic Church. Even that was bracketed with mention of the 'remaining confessions', with whom the state must also 'maintain cooperative relations'. In general, although not going as far as that of 1933 by explicitly barring the Church from fields such as the education system, the Constitution made virtually no concessions to it. Article 14 establishes equality of all religions and outlaws discrimination against any, while Article 16 declares that the state shall have no official religion.

5.1.2.2 Church and state under democracy

Beyond doubt, the 1978 Constitution has finally placed relations between Church and state in Spain on a basis compatible with normal democratic development. This normalization was symbolized by the Church's acceptance of the Socialists' election to power in 1982, and by the presence of practising Catholics (*practicantes*) in governments formed by the traditionally anticlerical PSOE. Nevertheless, significant friction remained; in particular, the Church vehemently opposed several of the Socialists' social reforms.

The Church's sensibility over social issues – and its growing remoteness from most public opinion – was apparent even before the Socialists came to power, in the heated debate provoked by the legalization of divorce [2.2.2]. It increased markedly once the conservative Angel Suquía was elected chairman of the Bishops' Conference in 1987, in succession to Cardinal Tarancón [5.1.2.1]. In particular, limited legalization of abortion in 1985 met strong Church opposition.

The main area of contention, however, was education. Initially, it related to the government's measures to impose greater control over private schools through the 1984 Act known as the LODE [8.2.2]. Subsequently, however, the Church's concern came to focus on the downgrading of religious instruction in schools, first in the LODE, and then under the 1990 LOGSE [8.1.2]. In neither case did it succeed in getting the government to back down.

Meantime, the Socialists had made what they could justifiably regard as a major concession to the Church. It concerned state funding for the Church's own ministry, which had continued unchanged up to 1982. Given that Spanish Catholics had no recent tradition of donation, the removal of funding traditionally advocated by the PSOE was potentially disastrous for the Church. Rather than force the issue, the Socialists introduced a measure allowing individual taxpayers to designate a small percentage (around 0.5 per cent) of their income tax payments for the Church's use.

The payment was immediately labelled a 'Church tax' (*impuesto religioso*). In fact that was not strictly accurate; the government had also agreed that, whatever the sum raised in this way, it would continue to maintain the Church's overall subsidy in real terms. In other words, all taxpayers continued to support the Church whether they opted to or not. For that very reason the measure was widely regarded as infringing the Constitution's provisions on religious equality [5.1.2.1]. To blur the point, the arrangement was originally announced as transitional, to be phased out over a six-year period. However, the government did not apply this condition, and the measure remained in force.

The Socialists' relative generosity on the financial issue, and the Church's view that the solution was insufficient for its needs, both reflected the fact that the latter's influence on society was declining. Although the percentage of Spaniards who claim to be Catholics has remained fairly static in recent years, the number of practising ones is falling steadily; it is now reckoned to stand at around 30 per cent of adults. The number of persons entering Holy Orders (*vocaciones*) has dropped more rapidly. As with church-going there are marked regional variations, but in some areas there is now a severe shortage of personnel to carry out the Church's social functions and even its own ministry. Moreover, opinion polls show that the great majority of Spaniards, Catholics or not, oppose Church intervention in politics. In 1993 the CEE tacitly recognized as much when it elected as its new chairman Elías Yanes, a much more conciliatory figure than Suquía.

Nevertheless, the Church remains an important institution in Spain. It still runs around one-sixth of the country's schools, albeit under much tighter government control than before; in some the level of education is sufficiently good to persuade even non-Catholic parents to opt for them. Despite the loss of its press interests, the COPE radio station remains under Church control [5.1.2.1], and enjoys a very considerable audience. And it still has important links to business and political elites, most controversially through the Catholic lay organization Opus Dei.

The 'Opus', as it is widely known, is notorious for the important role it played during the latter stages of the Franco era. In particular, many of the regime's expert advisers were members [0.2]. Conversely, it was the dictator who permitted Opus Dei to set up the University of Navarre, in Pamplona, and its business school offshoot, the Barcelona-based IESE, both of which have reputations for producing high-quality graduates. Opus members also control the Banco Popular, which is still a significant player in the country's financial sector [6.3.3]. Most significant of all, several leading figures in the conservative People's Party, in power since 1996, allegedly belong to its ranks.

Not only for that reason the PP's election aroused considerable expectations in the Church of renewed influence. After all the party's very name, adopted only in 1989, was an explicit affirmation of Christian Democrat tendencies [2.4.2]. Thus encouraged, in the later 1990s the Church hierarchy became noticeably more assertive again. It publicly questioned the state's right to legislate on certain issues, specifically abortion, and brought forward plans for new universities under its control.

Yet these proposals were rejected by the Council of State [1.4.4] in their original form; while the PP government, furthermore, persistently declined to satisfy the hierarchy's demands on Church funding or religious education, despite considerable pressure from the hierarchy. Unofficially, but unmistakably, the country's conservative rulers have let it be known that they are not prepared to jeopardize their hard-won centrist image [2.4.5] by reopening issues which, for the mass of the public, remain associated with the reactionary right. When, in 2002, Yanes' successor as CEE chairman Antonio Rouco Valera declined to sign up to a government-sponsored anti-terrorist pact [3.2.2.2], the Church found itself in the novel position of being vilified by leading conservatives – and having to rely on their Socialist counterparts for expressions of understanding.

5.1.3 The banks

In recent decades the financial sector has come to play a crucial role in Western economies, with a commensurate increase in its political influence. Perhaps surprisingly given the country's relative economic backwardness, Spain's large banks (*gran banca*) were already a powerful interest group prior to 1975, albeit less prominent than either the military or Church.

The banks' importance during the Franco era derived essentially from the regime's extensive intervention in the country's economy [6.1.1], which made control over the sources of credit vital. To a certain extent that was achieved by direct intervention. The country's central bank, the Bank of Spain, was nationalized in 1962 and the government was a major supplier of business credit. By and large, however, Franco left the large private banks (*banca privada*) untouched, confident in the unquestioning support of the deeply conservative families which controlled them, and which acquired considerable power as a result.

Their influence was, if anything, enhanced by the delicate process of transition after 1975, to which a functioning banking system was essential in order to avoid complete economic collapse. As a result all the leading political players were at pains not to alienate the sector, including those on the left who might normally have hoped to curtail bank influence. Consequently the banks continued to control large swathes of Spanish industry through their shareholdings and their role as credit-provider. When large-scale investment funds appeared in the country they too did so largely under the banks' aegis. Moreover, the coming of democracy allowed them to extend their influence in several ways.

Thus with the opening up of the media to private capital, the banks inevitably acquired a considerable degree of control in that vital sector. At the same time, they acquired a new, formalized role in the formulation of government economic policy. Since government control over the Bank of Spain was loosened in 1980, the larger banks have been assured representation on its Supervisory Board (*Consejo General*). Similarly, they are represented on the

National Banking Authority (*Consejo Superior Bancario*), which has a statutory right to be consulted on interest-rate policy decisions.

The banks' influence has also been reinforced by their important role in financing the political parties [2.1.3]. It was reflected in the strenuous efforts made by the Socialist PSOE to cultivate contacts with them, before and after the party came to power in 1982. The key intermediary was its first Finance Minister Miguel Boyer, who himself later returned to a senior post in the sector. Under Boyer's successor, Carlos Solchaga, even closer links were established between the banks and the Finance Ministry, which itself operated semi-independently from the cabinet as a whole [1.4.5]. Both then and under the more recent conservative governments, economic policy has tended to reflect closely the desires of bankers.

Perhaps as a result there has been little or no evidence that Spanish banks have used their control over credit to favour the Socialists' main opponents, as has often been the case in the UK. The only time they have overtly attempted to influence party fortunes came in 1986, when they denied credits to the new centrist party founded by Adolfo Suárez [2.2.3]. The attempt was a failure, not least because it gave the outspoken attacks on the big banks for which Suárez was already noted a new credibility. In that sense the outcome showed how democracy had limited the banks' power as well as consolidating it, by opening it up to public scrutiny.

However, it is not democracy as such that has most affected the banks' political influence, but rather the altered business environment it has brought about. Under the Franco regime the private banking sector operated in a way that had very little to do with modern business practice. Internally, decisions were taken by a bank's chairman, often a virtually hereditary post, with little regard for the opinions of other shareholders. The 'big seven' banks, as they then were, operated as a cartel, preferring cooperation to competition in business as well as in lobbying government.

Since 1975 this situation has been radically altered, as Spain's economy has been opened up to the forces of free-market capitalism and international competition. One result was a succession of mergers which have reduced the number of leading banks to two [6.3.3]. Such concentration may have increased the commercial power of the survivors, but not necessarily their collective political influence. For one thing, the Spanish banking system is now subject to a considerable degree of foreign control.

By 1995 almost 30 per cent of its shares were held by foreign investors, mainly themselves banks. Neither these nor their Spanish counterparts now play the game by the same rules as their predecessors. An early illustration came when the *Banco Central*'s attempt to take over *Banesto* was thwarted by two major shareholders opposed to the chairman's plans. A more spectacular one was provided by the rise and fall of the controversial businessman Mario Conde [10.4.1], who first acquired *Banesto* and then effectively destroyed it by his speculative – and fraudulent – activities.

These changes do not mean that the banks can no longer significantly influence government policy. Quite the contrary; as elsewhere in the West their interests are of considerable importance in that regard, and the Association of Spanish Banks (*Asociación Española de Banca Privada/AEB*) remains one of the country's most powerful lobbies. However, those interests are now more purely economic than in the past. In so far as they are political, they are essentially those of international finance capital, not of a particular social group within Spain itself.

5.2 ECONOMIC INTERESTS

In modern capitalist democracies typically the most prominent of the lobbies which attempt to sway government policy are economically based. Specifically, they relate to the interests of the main factors of production: on the one hand, labour or the workforce, or on the other, capital and its owners, the employers. For various reasons neither is particularly powerful in Spain, which is one reason for a continuing tendency to institutionalize their influence.

5.2.1 Trade unions

Despite the country's belated industrialization, the Spanish labour movement dates from the late nineteenth century. Nonetheless, like the parties of the left to which the labour movement was allied, the country's trade unions long suffered from a lack of potential recruits and, latterly, from Francoist repression. Under the particular circumstances of the transition the unions acquired an enhanced status, but subsequently their influence has once again been eroded by a variety of factors.

5.2.1.1 Organization and status

The main Spanish trade unions (*sindicatos*) are actually 'confederations' of individual unions covering a particular industry or industries. In that sense they are more akin to the TUC than to individual British trade unions. Rather than in the professions they represent, they differ in their political orientation – or, more precisely, in the political tendencies with which they were originally connected.

Of these the most important of all was anarchism. Indeed in the 1930s the anarchist-linked National Labour Confederation (*Confederación Nacional de Trabajo/CNT*) was the country's largest political association. However, the loosely-organized CNT was virtually destroyed by the Franco regime, although it retains some following in certain industries.

The CNT's long-standing rival, the General Workers' Union (*Unión General de Trabajadores/UGT*), fared rather better after 1975. Closely linked to the Socialist PSOE since its foundation in the 1880s, the UGT had deep roots not just in several industrial areas (the Basque Country, Asturias, Madrid) but also in the rural south. It also had a well-known and popular leader,

Nicolás Redondo. Its strength was further increased by absorbing much of the Workers' Trade Union (*Unión Sindical Obrera/USO*), a smaller body which had been active in opposition to the Franco regime. The UGT, however, had been reticent in that respect, and had consequently been outstripped in membership by a much younger organization.

Resistance to the dictatorship was the original aim of the Workers' Commissions (*Comisiones Obreras/CCOO*), which from the late 1950s spread to become a country-wide underground movement. In addition, CCOO enjoyed significant success in infiltrating the government-controlled unions, which were the only legal ones at the time [0.2]. Before long it came to be effectively controlled by the Communist Party (PCE), under whose direction its activities became both better organized and more overtly political. Its prominence in opposition, and that of its leader Marcelino Camacho who was imprisoned by the regime, meant that it enjoyed a high standing when the transition began.

At that time, when parties remained illegal, the unions briefly assumed a leading political role and their membership soared. This new importance was soon legally recognized. Many of the social provisions of the 1978 Constitution reflected union concerns. Rather more significantly, unions' right to defend their members' legitimate interests was included among the text's fundamental principles [1.1.2]. This and other constitutional provisions were given concrete form in the 1980 Workers' Charter (*Estatuto de los Trabajadores*) and the 1984 Trade Union Freedom Act (*Ley Orgánica de Libertad Sindical/LOLS*).

In particular, the LOLS consolidated the system of workplace elections (*elecciones sindicales*) established by the Charter. They operate on a list system similar to that used for parliamentary contests [1.3.1], the lists being presented by unions or other groupings of workers. In companies with over 50 employees the elected representatives (*delegados*) make up a workforce committee (*comité de empresa*) with the statutory right to be informed and consulted by the employer. In EU parlance these committees are often described as works' councils, so it is important to stress that, unlike the latter, they are representatives of the workforce, not forums for debate with the employer.

Unions' status in the new Spain was underlined between 1979 and 1985 by their involvement in a series of pacts on aspects of economic policy with government and employers. Yet, in most cases these brought only minor, or intangible gains for union members, at the cost of considerable concessions [5.2.3]. Union participation in them indicated not strength but weakness, traceable in part to Spain's persistent unemployment problem but also to certain features of the trade union movement itself.

First, after the brief surge experienced during the transition, the density of union membership – that is, the proportion of the workforce which is affiliated to a union – has sunk steadily. By the mid-1990s it was among the lowest in Europe, standing at around 15 per cent according to most estimates. This, in turn, is attributable to a number of causes.

The first cause is Spain's industrial structure, which is dominated by small and medium-sized firms [6.4.2], which everywhere have a low level of union membership. Secondly, there is no requirement to be a union member in order to vote in workplace elections. Thirdly, unions' incentive to recruit is further reduced by the fact that non-members must pay a contribution towards union funds (*canon sindical*). Finally, like parties, unions receive public funding (*financiación estatal*) – and that is based on the results of workplace elections, not membership figures.

The second feature of the union movement is that it is fragmented, with a number of smaller unions enjoying significant support in particular regions and industries. Thus the largest union in the Basque Country is Basque Workers' Solidarity (*Eusko Langileak Alkartasuna/ELA-STV*), which has links to the nationalist PNV [3.2.2.2]. Other important regional unions are Basque Workers' Commissions (*Langile Abertzale Batzordeak/LAB*), which despite its name is linked to ETA rather than CCOO, and the Galician Interunion Confederation (*Confederación Intersindical Gallega/CIG*).

Sectoral unions include a number of highly disparate groups. Some represent workers in the expanding white collar occupations, the best established being the Confederation of Independent Public Servants' Unions (*Confederación de Sindicatos Independientes de Funcionarios/CSIF*). At the opposite end of the occupational spectrum is the Landworkers' Union (*Sindicato de Obreros del Campo/SOC*). The SOC is the heir to Andalusia's tradition of rural anarchism, and during the 1980s it organized direct action in favour of land reform [6.3.1]. Its ideological opposite is to be found in the company-sponsored employee associations established by some large firms. Despised by the rest of the movement as 'bosses' unions' (*sindicatos amarillos*), these are of particular significance in the retail sector, notably in the *Corte Inglés* chain of department stores and hypermarkets.

The wide differences between these smaller employees' representatives have inevitably led to disagreement on aims and strategy. Yet even despite the existence of these other organizations, UGT and CCOO dominate the union movement, regularly filling between 70 and 80 per cent of places on workforce committees. For that very reason their failure to agree a common strategy during the critical period of the 1980s was especially damaging to the unions' cause.

5.2.1.2 In search of a strategy

The roots of disunity between the two largest unions were to be found in the transition. At that time the communist-dominated CCOO [5.2.1.1] saw itself as an instrument to win political concessions from government as much as economic ones from employers, which implied the use of militant methods. It was thus the prime mover behind the high level of industrial unrest (*conflictividad laboral*) during the early part of the transition, frequently backing strikes in individual firms or calling them to support wider political demands.

Meanwhile the UGT [5.2.1.1] tended to take a more cautious line. It concentrated on workplace issues, specifically pay and conditions, and was much more disposed to pursue demands through negotiation, either with individual employers or with the government. That moderate approach proved more successful in winning concrete concessions, and by 1982 the UGT had overtaken CCOO in support at workplace elections [5.2.1.1]. When its sister party (*partido hermano*), the Socialist PSOE, came to power that year, the UGT leadership confidently expected to consolidate its position through privileged links to government.

As regards the UGT's interests as an organization, these hopes were largely fulfilled. In particular, the 1984 Trade Union Freedom Act [5.2.1.1] contained two provisions for which UGT had lobbied. It increased the period between workplace elections from two years to four, and gave the main role in collective negotiations not to company committees [5.2.1.1], but to union sections representing a whole industry (*sección sindical*). In both cases these measures favoured UGT at the expense of CCOO, which tended to be better established at workplace level.

However, UGT's expectations on behalf of its members were disappointed; from an early stage the government pursued economic policies which hit them hard [6.1.2]. In 1985 reform of the pension system, to the actual or potential disbenefit of many union members, led UGT leader Nicolás Redondo [5.2.1.1] to threaten resignation as a Socialist MP; two years later he carried out his threat in response to proposals for further cuts in social spending. Thereafter relations between the industrial and political wings of the socialist movement (*familia socialista*) deteriorated progressively, with the UGT increasingly joining CCOO in demanding that the government pay less attention to purely economic considerations and more to social ones (*giro social*).

It also adopted the more militant methods to which CCOO had clung, three times joining it to organize general strikes against government policy. The biggest of these stoppages was the first, called on 14 December 1988 (*14-D*) against government plans for special low-wage contracts for the young. The enormous turnout brought virtually the whole country to a standstill and demonstrated the unions' ability to command support well beyond their membership on particular issues. Some four years later a government decree cutting unemployment benefit provoked a second general strike. This stoppage, held on 27 May 1992 (*27-M*), commanded less popular support. The downward trend continued when UGT and CCOO issued their third joint strike call, in January 1994, directed as in 1988 against proposed labour market reforms [5.2.3].

Declining public support for such militancy, despite considerable sympathy with its motives, both mirrored the unions' relative impotence and further aggravated it. Although the youth employment plan was withdrawn in 1988 and minor concessions were made in 1992, in neither case did the unions' show of strength force a change in the general direction of government policy. Admittedly, unions' lobbying bore some fruit in the relatively favourable provisions of the 1994 Strikes Act (*Ley de Huelga*). But in general their influence remained low in the later years of Socialist rule.

The Spanish unions' plight was not unique. Throughout the West such organizations have had little success in preventing deregulation of economies, which in turn has further weakened their position. However, in Spain their position was particularly difficult in the 1980s. Time and again unions were in the impossible position of opposing the attempts of a Socialist government to repeal measures originally introduced under Franco. Once most such measures were gone their situation was, in a sense eased. And, at the same time, the unions themselves have shown greater awareness of the need to escape the legacy of their past.

In both cases this has involved a-change of leader, UGT's Redondo being replaced by Cándido Méndez, and CCOO's Camacho by Antonio Gutiérrez. In the latter case the change was accompanied by a lengthy struggle to free CCOO from communist control, a process that was ultimately eased by the Communist Party's virtual collapse [2.5.2]. There has also been a sharp move away from militancy by both unions, the level of strikes declining throughout the 1990s. Instead both main unions have concentrated increasingly on workplace issues, leaving political ones to the parties.

This approach has brought dividends since the coming to power of a conservative party anxious to establish its centrist credentials, and to defuse accusations of being anti-worker. As a result, the PP government has shown a somewhat unexpected willingness to broker and even join deals between employers and unions [5.2.3], something the Socialists had almost completely abandoned after 1985. Equally ironic is the fact that CCOO, which remains the principal employee representative in most of Spain's larger firms, has been the more enthusiastic participant in this process. In 2001 it was the UGT which finally ended 13 years of cooperation between the two main unions by refusing to join the government and CCOO in signing the latest in a series of agreements on the pension system [5.2.3].

5.2.2 Employers' organizations

If the development of Spanish trade unions was held back by the country's peculiar history, the same was even more true of their natural opponents, employers' organizations (*organizaciones empresariales*). Prior to 1975 there was in fact no country-wide organization representing employers (*patronal*), only a few regional associations in the more advanced parts of the country. The most significant of these was the Catalan Development Association (*Fomento de Trabajo Nacional/FTN*), a body dating back to the late nineteenth century when it had provided much of the impetus for Catalan regionalism [3.2.1.1].

When industrialization eventually began on a significant scale, in the 1960s, it did so under very special circumstances. The Franco regime's authoritarian policies ensured that, with occasional exceptions, the labour force remained docile and wage demands muted. At the same time the country's economic isolation effectively protected its businesses from outside competition [0.2]. It is understandable that employers saw little need to organize, even if they had been permitted to do so.

On the other hand, Franco's belief in strict state control led him to impose on the country's developing industries an extraordinary mass of regulations.

They covered virtually all aspects of business activity, including prices as well as the labour market, and were only partially dismantled after the change in economic policy in 1959/60 [0.2]. Their stifling effect on business initiative latterly caused more enterprising employers to press discreetly for moves to bring the country's business environment in line with the much less restricted conditions of its democratic neighbours.

Once Franco had died, such deregulation became the central demand of the body set up in 1977 to represent the interests of employers at national level, the Spanish Employers' Confederation (*Confederación Española de Organizaciones Empresariales/CEOE*). As its title suggests, the CEOE is in fact a relatively loose alliance of organizations which have retained considerable independence. Some 130 of them represent employers in particular industries, including – rather unusually by international standards – agriculture, in the shape of the National Farmers' Confederation (*Confederación Nacional de Agricultores y Ganadores/CNAG*). Others, over 50 in total, are regional and provincial groupings among which the Catalan FTN continues to be prominent. Nevertheless, a number of significant organizations operate outside the CEOE, especially in the agricultural sector.

Individual firms typically belong to several of these affiliated associations. They acquired renewed importance after the mid-1980s, due both to the growing importance of regional government, and to the abandonment of the country-wide union–employer agreements of the previous decade [5.2.3]. In any case, the stress placed by the CEOE's national leadership on deregulation has not always been well received by the small and medium-sized enterprises which form such a large part of the Spanish corporate sector (*sector empresarial*). For the protected conditions of the Franco era left many SMEs (*pequeñas y medianas empresas/pymes*) technically ill-equipped and psychologically ill-prepared for the increased competition implied by deregulation.

These particular interests were reflected during the transition in the creation of a distinct Spanish Confederation of SMEs (*Confederación Española de Pequeñas y Medianas Empresas/CEPYME*). In 1980 CEPYME affiliated to the CEOE, but continues to operate with considerable independence. Moreover, the smaller General SME Confederation (*Confederación General de Pequeñas y Medianas Empresas/COPYME*) remains outside the CEOE, as did a third association representing SMEs set up in the 1990s, the Family Business Institute (*Instituto de la Empresa Familiar/IEF*). And, in any case, many SMEs look to a different type of organization as the most effective channel for their interests.

Spain's Chambers of Commerce, Industry and Navigation (*Cámaras de Comercio, Industria y Navegación*) date from 1911 and are organized on a provincial basis. Like those in most continental countries, the Chambers have considerably greater practical importance than their British counterparts. They exercise statutory responsibilities relating to the general economic well-being of their area and are funded by the dues all local employers are required to pay. This compulsory affiliation naturally provokes some employer resentment. But the tensions frequently evident between the Chambers and the CEOE also reflect the fact that the Chambers represent interests specific to the

CEOE's smaller members which sometimes seem to be neglected by its national leaders.

At the same time, larger firms also sometimes feel the need for alternative means of lobbying. In some cases this is done through the appropriate industry-specific organization, of which the most powerful is that representing the banks [5.1.3]. To represent interests common to all bigger firms, a number have banded together in the Business Circle (*Círculo de Empresarios*), which in some ways resembles the UK Institute of Directors. The management education it provides is in Spain promoted by a separate organization, the Association for Progress in Business (*Asociación para el Progreso Empresarial/APE*).

As well as in this variety of organizations, the differing interests of Spanish employers have been reflected in apparent uncertainty on the CEOE's part about how best to influence public policy. Its first chairman was Carlos Ferrer Salat, of the Catalan FNT. Under his leadership the CEOE entered a series of broad agreements on economic and social policy with unions and government [5.2.3], an approach maintained after the Socialists came to power in 1982. It was radically changed, however, once Ferrer was replaced as chairman by José María Cuevas. Before his election in 1984 Cuevas had been involved in attempts to bring together all the forces of the right and centre-right in a party capable of challenging the Socialist government [2.4.1]. After it, he took a more confrontational attitude both to the PSOE and to the unions, with whom the CEOE signed no new agreements after 1984.

Instead, the CEOE concentrated on building up influence over the conservative opposition party, People's Alliance (AP), to which it gave considerable financial backing. When in 1987 AP switched to a policy line less acceptable to employers Cuevas abruptly withdrew this support [2.4.2]. The move was instrumental in AP's transformation into the People's Party (PP), and a switch back to more employer-friendly policies. Thereafter CEOE's renewed support, public and financial, was an important factor in the PP's rise to power in 1996.

This close link with the new party of government obviously gives the CEOE greatly increased influence, yet it remains limited by other pressures on the PP. During the 1996 general election campaign, Cuevas publicly listed the CEOE's expectations of a conservative administration. The PP's leader, José María Aznar, was quick to deny that these demands were his party's policy. Desperate to portray itself as 'centrist' [2.4.3], it simply could not afford the appearance of being in the employers' pocket. Recognizing this, the CEOE has displayed renewed interest in agreement with unions since 1996 [5.2.3], as an alternative means of influencing events.

5.2.3 Limited corporatism

Corporatist is a term used to describe societies in which key decisions are taken by the government in conjunction with organized interest groups, in particular employers and employees. The Franco regime, with its government-run trade unions [0.2], shared some features of this model, albeit in an authoritarian form. More importantly, the nature of Spain's transition to democracy after Franco's death favoured the growth of corporatism, with the leaderships of all major political forces anxious to prevent events slipping out of control [0.3.3].

The most visible example of corporatism during the first decade of democracy was successive governments' practice of negotiating major policy issues with the national representatives of employers and workers (*concertación social*). It resulted in a series of agreements between these social partners (*agentes/interlocutores sociales*). Some were tripartite, the government being a third signatory; on other occasions it promoted the pacts without actually joining them.

The 1977 Moncloa Pacts between the political parties [0.3.3] represented a forerunner of these agreements, four of which were signed between 1980 and 1984. The subject matter varied, but invariably included a national benchmark for wage increases, along with a number of other economic, industrial relations and social issues (see Table 5.1). The last such pact, the 1984 Economic and Social Agreement, was twice renewed after its initial one-year term, but finally lapsed in 1987.

Thereafter the practice of national tripartite negotiation lapsed. Despite frequent reference to the desirability of a further social contract (*pacto social*), few real attempts were made to conclude one. Those that were, ended in

Table 5.1 Social contracts, 1977–87

Title	Year signed	Signatories	Main issues covered
Moncloa Pacts (*Pactos de la Moncloa*)	1977	Political parties	Wages Taxes and public spending Public security
Union–Employer Framework Agreement (*Acuerdo Marco Interconfederal/AMI*)	1980	CEOE; UGT, USO	Wages and conditions Job creation Industrial relations
National Employment Agreement (*Acuerdo Nacional de Empleo/ANE*)	1981	Government; CEOE; UGT, CCOO	Wages Social security Industrial relations
National Union–Employer Agreement (*Acuerdo Interconfederal/AI*)	1983	CEOE, CEPYME; UGT, CCOO	Wages and conditions Industrial relations
National Economic and Social Agreement (*Acuerdo Económico y Social/AES*)	1984	Government; CEOE, CEPYME; UGT	Wages Job creation and investment Public spending Social security

failure; neither the 1990 Competitiveness Pact (*Pacto para la Competitividad*) nor the 1991 Social Contract for Progress (*Pacto Social para el Progreso*) were ultimately signed. Unions were disillusioned at repeated failure to bring down unemployment levels [6.2.4.1], while employers and government seemed content to allow market forces to determine wage levels and other economic variables.

Another retreat from corporatism was the failure to implement fully an injunction set out in the Constitution. This required the establishment of a body, to include representatives of the social partners, charged with ensuring that economic policy reflect certain social objectives including income redistribution. After lengthy discussion a National Social and Economic Policy Forum (*Consejo Económico y Social/CES*) was finally established in 1992, with equal representation of unions, employers' organizations and consumer groups. However, the CES is purely advisory, and is generally regarded as a mere talking shop.

Even so, a considerable degree of corporatism continues to exist in Spain. Unions and employers enjoy statutory representation on the governing bodies of many administrative entities. Perhaps the most important are the agencies responsible for the Health Service (INSALUD), Social Security (INSS) and Social Services (IMSERSO), as well as the National Employment Agency (INEM). In addition, since union attitudes began to moderate in the 1990s [5.2.1.2], some national union–employer agreements have once again been reached. Unlike the general pacts of the 1980s, however, they related to specific issues such as vocational training [8.3.3] or industrial relations (*relaciones laborales*), Spain's poor record in which had given concern ever since 1975.

One attempt at improving the situation had already been made, in 1979, through the establishment of a government-run Mediation, Arbitration and Conciliation Agency (*Instituto de Mediación, Arbitraje y Conciliación/IMAC*). However, the IMAC, whose approach was based on time-consuming and expensive recourse to the courts, proved ineffectual and was wound up in 1985.

The 1996 Agreement on Out-of-Court Settlement of Industrial Disputes (*Acuerdo sobre Solución Extrajudicial de Conflictos Laborales/ASEC*) aimed to avoid such problems. Thus, although it commits employers and unions to submit disputes to mediation, under the ASEC conciliation services are entrusted to independent individuals appointed by a Bipartite Mediation and Arbitration Service (*Servicio Interconfederal de Mediación y Arbitraje/SIMA*). The government's role is restricted to funding the SIMA.

This return to a limited corporatist approach well suited the conservative government elected in 1996, which was anxious to establish its moderate, centrist credentials. Later that year it succeeded in persuading both the major union federations to join it in signing an 'Agreement on Consolidation and Rationalization of the Social Security System', which laid the basis for restructuring of social security finance [9.1.2].

The following year it encouraged unions and employers to conclude three formal pacts on employment and industrial relations, the most important being the Bipartite Agreement on Employment Stability (*Acuerdo Inter-confederal para la Estabilidad del Empleo*), which opened the way to significant job market reforms [6.2.4.2]. A year later these were followed by a further agreement on part-time employment, this time with the government as an active partner. Even after being re-elected with an overall majority the conservatives have continued to conclude agreements with the social partners, in particular on the thorny topic of pensions [9.1.2].

Finally, union federations and employers' organizations are represented on a host of administrative bodies at the regional tier of government established in the 1980s. Andalusia is a particular stronghold of regional corporatism. On the other hand, as at national level, participation remains restricted essentially to employers and unions. Beyond the social partners, Spanish interest groups are too weak to sustain a more broad-based type of corporatism [5.4].

5.3 THE MEDIA

As in other developed societies Spain's mass media (*medios de comunicación de masas*) today play an important part in the country's power structure. Indeed the news media (*medios informativos*) – traditionally the press but now also its audiovisual cousins radio and, above all, television – are seen by some as a fourth estate (*cuarto poder*), alongside parliament, government and the judiciary. Elsewhere this has given rise to concern about the influence of privately controlled media interests on public policy. In Spain, however, concern has tended to centre on the opposite problem: excessive state control over the media.

5.3.1 Media and the state

The Spanish media, like so many of the country's institutions, are heavily influenced by the experience of the Franco regime. Like many dictatorships, it censored media output, a situation that continued to exist even after the more liberal legislation introduced in 1966 by Manuel Fraga [2.4.1] and commonly known as the Fraga Act (*Ley Fraga*). But, in addition, the regime controlled vast swathes of the media, either directly or through its close ally, the Church [5.1.2.1]. Along with the official news agency Efe, this media empire included a chain of newspapers and the entire radio and television networks.

Indeed, television in Spain was a creation of the Franco regime, the Spanish Television Authority (*Televisión Española/TVE*) being set up as a state monopoly in 1952. A first channel (*canal*) began broadcasting four years later, followed in 1963 by a second. In 1973 TVE was merged with the state's radio stations (*emisoras*), principally Spanish National Radio (*Radio Nacional de España/RNE*), to create the public corporation (*ente público*) known as the Spanish Broadcasting Authority (*Radiotelevisión Española/RTVE*). Like the state's other media interests its prime task was the dissemination of propaganda.

With the coming of democracy, this concentration of media power was diluted. By 1984 the last of the state's own chain of newspapers had been sold off. In the late 1970s and again a decade later hundreds of new radio broadcasting licences were issued, although in both cases the government of the day allocated licences to sympathetic business interests and, in the latter one, local authorities controlled by its party. Furthermore Efe, by far the largest Spanish-language news agency and among the world's biggest, remains under central government control. This position is unique among Western democracies and of particular significance in Spain, given the dependence of the country's many regional newspapers [5.3.3] on agency reports for national and international news.

But by far the most obvious, and controversial, area of continuing state control was the television service, which successive governments seemed determined to retain as an instrument of party propaganda. The first elected PM after 1975, Adolfo Suárez, had served as head of the Francoist state television service, and during his term of office he drew heavily on that experience. Admittedly he used the powerful influence of television news programmes (*espacios informativos*) to help implant democratic attitudes among Spaniards. But it was also a key element in the 1977 and 1979 election campaigns of Suárez's own party, UCD, which was given massively wider – and more positive – coverage than all its opponents.

Understandably, these protested vociferously and demanded that democratization be extended to RTVE. As a result, in 1980 the corporation was given a charter (*estatuto*). This set up a Board of Governors (*Consejo de Administración*) whose twelve members are appointed by Parliament. It is on the Board's advice that the government appoints RTVE's executive head, the director-general, whose independence is theoretically protected in that he or she may be dismissed only on professional grounds.

Like a number of aspects of Spain's new democracy, these arrangements were posited on the assumption of minority or coalition governments [1.4.1]. Even without an overall majority, UCD was able to persuade the governors three times in two years of successive director-generals' 'incompetence'. The PSOE's sweeping 1982 election victory allowed it unbridled control over the appointment of governors and the director-general, and its abuse of news coverage became the stuff of legend.

The nadir was reached in 1986 during the campaigns for the NATO referendum [4.2.2] and the subsequent general election; in the latter case the government actually created a special team within RTVE to 'coordinate' coverage. Public and political pressure subsequently forced some reduction in interference, which nevertheless has continued to the present. The People's Party government elected in 1996 appointed and dismissed three governors in its first two and a half years in office, and has also exercised a clear control over the tone and content of news reporting.

The PP's time in power has brought further developments. In the late 1990s the government carried on a very public vendetta against the PRISA media group [5.3.4], whose organs are generally supportive of the PP's Socialist opponents. At the same time it encouraged the growing media interests of the *Telefónica* group [5.3.4], which it had previously – and controversially – sold off to an associate of Prime Minister José María Aznar [2.4.5]. The rabid backing subsequently offered to Aznar by the group's organs, notably the *Antena 3* television station [5.3.2], gave a new and worrying twist to the tortuous relations between state and media.

5.3.2 Broadcasting

Probably more than elsewhere, television is today the most important of the mass media in Spain. Almost all households have a set, and Spaniards rival the British as Europe's most enthusiastic viewers. Even if news plays a relatively minor role in contemporary schedules (*programaciones*), TV's potential influence is enormous. With the manifest failure of attempts to bring government abuse under control through legislation [5.3.1], pressure to introduce competition from private stations became overwhelming.

Indeed by 1986 all parties were promising to do just that. However, the Socialist government re-elected that year immediately began to trumpet the potential dangers of such a step and the virtues of public broadcasting. As a result, the first move to increase the range of TV channels came from a different quarter, through the establishment of TV stations run by the country's new regional authorities.

The first of these, Basque Television (*Euskal Telebista/ETB*), began broadcasting at the end of 1983; the following year *TV-3*, run by the Catalan Broadcasting Corporation (*Corporació Catalana de Ràdio i Televisió/CC/RTV*), came on the air. In both cases the original justification was promotion of the respective regional languages, as it was later to be in Galicia. Yet before long ETB, in defiance of previous agreements and legislation, opened a purely Spanish-language channel. In 1989 the PSOE government granted licences to three more regions, two of whom had no regional language but all of which were under its political control. By 2002, a total of ten regional channels were in operation in the Basque Country, Catalonia, Galicia, Andalusia, Valencia, Madrid and the Canary Islands (see Chapter 11).

Meantime, private stations too had long since come on the air, as the result of legislation the government was finally obliged to introduce in 1989. This abolished RTVE's monopoly on the right to broadcast, and set up a company, known as *Retevisión*, to manage the network. In addition it provided for the creation of three private TV stations (*televisiones privadas*), and set conditions for the concession of licences and their subsequent operation.

The following year the three successful bidders (*Antena 3*, *Canal Plus* and *Tele 5*) went on the air. They brought about a revolution in the habits of Spain's viewers (*televidentes*). *Antena 3* and *Tele 5* now dispute the largest viewing figures (*audiencia*) with the first public channel, *TVE-1*. *Canal Plus*, reception of which requires the viewer to buy a decoder (*descodificador*), has a share that is considerably lower, but still above that of the second public channel, renamed *La2*. Several of the regional channels also claim significant audience shares, especially in Catalonia and Madrid. As yet cable networks have only very small numbers of viewers.

The state's control over news broadcasting has thus been radically reduced. Whether the objectivity of coverage has been correspondingly increased is debatable. For one thing, all the regional channels are run on lines similar to RTVE, and so subject to a considerable degree of control from the respective regional governments. In other words, rather than political influence being removed, its direction has been changed – at least in those regions governed by parties different from that in power nationally.

With the private stations the situation is rather more complex. At the time these were granted their licences, it was widely assumed that the allocation would involve some sort of political carve-up, with the two largest parties each receiving their 'own' station. This view proved to be wrong, but in its underlying acceptance of television's continuing politicization it has been borne out to some degree.

One of the new licensees, *Canal Plus*, was a consortium headed with the French station of the same name and the PRISA group [5.3.4]. Predictably in view of that, its coverage has been of relatively high quality and, in news terms, broadly sympathetic to the Socialists. But given its small audience, the impact of any bias is strictly limited.

The same is broadly true of *Tele 5*, but for very different reasons. The station's main shareholder was, and is, the Italian media magnate and now Prime Minister Silvio Berlusconi; other major stakes are held by the German media mogul Leo Kirch, currently in severe financial straits, and the Correo group [5.3.4]. The extent of Berlusconi's financial involvement remains something of a mystery, and indeed has given rise to judicial investigations. But in any case *Tele* 5 is essentially a commercial operation, and gives correspondingly little weight to news.

The case of *Antena 3* is considerably more complex. The channel was originally allocated to a consortium headed by the Catalan Godó group [5.3.4], but in 1992 Godó was ousted by its rival Zeta [5.3.4], which assumed effective control over the station. At this time *Antena 3*'s relatively extensive news coverage took a strongly anti-Socialist line while keeping within the limits of journalistic licence. In a sense it could be seen as a desirable counterweight to RTVE, and once the conservative PP came to power in 1996 there were some signs that Zeta intended *Antena 3* to maintain this role.

In 1998, however, Zeta sold its holding in *Antena 3* to the media arm of the former state telecommunications monopoly *Telefónica*, which at the time was controlled by a close associate of Prime Minister José María Aznar [2.4.5]. *Antena 3*'s news coverage soon took on a blatantly pro-government tone. Indeed, its coverage of the 2000 election recalled for many the worst excesses of RTVE in the 1980s [5.3.1]. The wave of criticism that followed seems to have forced some moderation of bias but not its removal, and as a result the supposedly pluralist TV news landscape remains strongly favourable to the ruling conservatives.

That may be one reason why many Spaniards rely on radio for news reporting; certainly the country has a very high number of radio listeners (*oyentes*) for its population, with over three-quarters of households owning a receiver. Successive issues of new licences [5.3.1] have given rise to 'battles of the airwaves', with not only the broadcasters but also the government showing scant regard for national and international regulations limiting the number of stations, most of which are local. The audience is correspondingly fragmented, but the major country-wide stations are *Cadena Ser*, part of the PRISA group [5.3.4], and the Church-controlled COPE [5.1.2.1].

5.3.3 The press

Although Spanish news dailies (*diarios informativos*) have a low readership (*audiencia*) by international standards, they nonetheless have a considerable significance. For, as elsewhere, in terms of news coverage the broadcast media to some extent live off the press, which consequently has an important agenda-setting role. At the Spanish level this is played by an even smaller number of actors than in the case of TV, but this apparent concentration conceals a rich variety of local and regional papers.

Bald statements about Spanish newspaper readership require first to be put in context. Certainly sales (*difusión*) are not high – according to one recent survey, only one young person in seven is a newspaper reader – and are markedly lower in the south than the north of the country. But comparisons can be misleading; in particular journalistic standards in Spain are generally high and its readership figures are not inflated by any direct equivalent of the British tabloids. Instead their market is covered, at least in part, by two distinct types of publication, one being the weekly gossip magazines (*prensa del corazón*) of which the best-known is *Hola*. The other is specialist sports dailies, of which there are a number. The most successful are *Mundo Deportivo*, *As* and above all *Marca*, which is read by more Spaniards than any individual news daily.

The biggest-selling of those, *El País*, has a circulation (*tirada*) of only around 400,000 copies, although as with other papers this doubles in the case of the weekend edition (*dominical*) bought usually on a Saturday. Owned by the PRISA group [5.3.4] it first appeared in 1976, and soon established itself as Spain's newspaper of record with an international reputation for quality reporting. It has tended to be broadly sympathetic to the Socialist Party, and when the PSOE government fell into discredit in the early 1990s the paper's sales suffered accordingly. Subsequently, however, it has re-established a clear lead over all its rivals.

The nearest of these, in terms of readership but not sales, is *Abc*. Acquired in 2001 by the Correo group [5.3.4], it was previously published by *Editorial Española*, a company mainly owned by the big banks. *Abc* is a long-established publication which survived, indeed thrived under the Franco dictatorship. It remains deeply conservative in both layout and editorial line.

Indeed, as its then editor Luis María Ansón later revealed, in the early 1990s it was involved in a concerted media campaign to oust the Socialist government of the time by just about any means, fair or foul.

Along with the Church-controlled radio station COPE [5.1.2.2], the other main participant in this campaign was *El Mundo*, the country's third daily in terms of sales and second in terms of readers. The paper was founded in 1989 by a prominent journalist, Pedro J. Ramírez, who became its editor. Its meteoric rise was achieved by virulent editorial attacks on the Socialist government, backed up by aggressive investigative journalism that uncovered a number of the scandals of the period [2.3.4].

Even at the time this caused concern. Some of the revelations, most notoriously a story about alleged nepotism by Prime Minister Felipe González, proved to be false. And Ramírez's financial backing seemed to come mainly from anti-Socialist businessmen, including the subsequently disgraced Mario Conde [10.4.1]. Later Ramírez was himself the victim of what appears to have been a revenge plot, when a video showing him engaging in unusual sexual practices acquired widespread notoriety. Nonetheless he continues to edit the paper, whose position in the conservative camp was underlined when partial control over it was acquired by the *Telefónica* group [5.3.4].

Currently these three dailies, which together account for barely a quarter of readership, effectively constitute Spain's national press. Apart from *Abc* all those which survived the Franco era disappeared soon after 1975, while a number of new papers have come and gone. These included *Claro*, the only attempt to establish a British-style tabloid. Brought out in 1989 by *Editorial Española* and the German Springer group, publisher of Europe's best-selling sensationalist daily, *Bild*, it survived for only three months. The most recent venture, entitled *La Razón*, was launched in 2000 by Ansón after he was removed from *Abc*; as yet it has failed to take off.

The remaining 75 per cent of daily news readership is made up by regional and local papers. The two largest are both based in Catalonia. Much the older is *La Vanguardia*, the flagship of the Godó group [5.3.4]. The traditional paper of the Catalan middle-classes, it was sufficiently conservative to remain independent under Franco, after whose death it was briefly the top-selling daily in the whole of Spain. However, its sympathy for Catalan regionalism has subsequently limited its appeal to its home region. Even there it has now been overtaken by *El Periódico*, which forms part of the Zeta group [5.3.4], and is now the country's fourth-selling news daily. However, its wider ambitions have also been thwarted; outside Catalonia it sells significantly only in Aragon.

In fact, the press market as a whole is highly regionalized. Outside Madrid, which is obviously a special case, there is only one region – Castile-La Mancha – with no paper of its own apart from purely local dailies. Elsewhere regional dailies in total comfortably outsell national ones. And, apart from in Andalusia where *Abc* is the most widely read individual paper, the best-selling daily is invariably a regional title. Indeed, in Asturias, the Canaries, Galicia and Valencia such papers fill the top three places, and in the Basque Country the top four.

As with television, only a small part of the appeal of regional papers can be attributed to language differences [5.3.2]. By far the most popular daily printed wholly in a language other than Spanish is the Catalan *Avui* [11.10], which shares with *El País* the distinction of being the first newspaper to appear after Franco's death; it sells a little over 30,000 copies. The Basque Country's *Gara* and *Deia* both have rather higher readerships, but only part of their copy appears in Basque – and in both cases its presence is essentially a token of nationalist allegiance [11.5].

5.3.4 Media groups

Control of the media in Spain, at least that exercised by private interests, was traditionally highly dispersed. With the newspaper market unattractive, the sector held little attraction for investors so long as the state retained its television monopoly. The advent of private television, and the intervention of foreign interests it attracted, was therefore crucial to the most significant recent development on the Spanish media scene; the establishment of domestic media groups (*grupos mediáticos*) with interests ranging across the various media and beyond.

The best known of these is the concern known as PRISA (*Promotor de Informaciones SA*), whose chairman is Jesús de Polanco. Polanco was the leading figure among a group of intellectuals who jointly founded PRISA in 1972. The immediate result was *El País*, which soon became Spain's leading news daily [5.3.3]. Thereafter, PRISA brought out or acquired various other magazines and newspapers, including specialist business and sports dailies (*Cinco Días* and *As*), each currently ranked second in its segment. It also set up its own publishing house, *Editorial El País*, which produces analyses of topical issues by top journalists, and later acquired a major holding in another, *Santillana*.

PRISA's first move into broadcasting was a radio station under the *El País* name, but this failed. However, in 1984 it became market leader in the segment by taking over Spain's oldest and most popular station *Cadena Ser* [5.3.2] from the Catholic lay organization Opus Dei [5.1.2.2]; subsequently it acquired holdings in a number of other stations. PRISA moved into television in 1989 through its holding in *Canal Plus*, one of the three initial private channels [5.3.2]. More recently it set up the pay-TV company *Sogecable*, while its current interests also include advertising, music, and film production, as well as an internet arm. Outside Spain, it has holdings in M40, a French music radio station, along with Britain's *Independent* and the Mexican daily *La Prensa*.

These various holdings give PRISA considerable potential influence. By and large this has been exercised in line with the objectives of its founders: to provide an independent information source and forum for public debate, and so promote Spain's democratization and also modernization. Perhaps inevitably, that has tended to translate into fairly consistent – although not uncritical – support for the Socialist Party, and when the conservative People's Party came to power in 1996 it seemed bent on cutting PRISA down to size. Thus the PP openly backed PRISA's rival Zeta in the infamous dispute over the rights to screen top Spanish League football games, known as the 'football war', and attempted to prevent *Sogecable* from operating. The latter move gave rise to a protracted legal dispute, which the Supreme Court eventually decided in PRISA's favour.

In the 1980s, PRISA had two main domestic rivals for the title of Spain's premier media group. One, *Grupo16*, was based on the weekly news magazine *Cambio16*, which established a justified reputation during the transition. Later it acquired a daily stablemate, *Diario16*. Aimed at a less highbrow market than *El País*, it became Spain's fifth most popular paper in the 1980s. However, at the end of the decade a dispute within the group led to the departure of its editor, Pedro J. Ramírez [5.3.3]. Thereafter the group lost its way – *Diario16* in particular steadily lost readers before eventually closing in 1999 – and it is no longer a significant media force.

The Godó group has fared rather better. Controlled by the family of the same name, its core was and remains the venerable Barcelona-based daily *La Vanguardia* [5.3.3], whose editorial line reflects its owners' moderate Catalan regionalism. When the first FM radio licences were issued in 1979, Godó set up the station *Antena 3*. A decade later it became the main shareholder in the private television station of the same name [5.3.2]. However, in 1992 the group's head was ousted as chairman of *Antena 3* television, from which it has subsequently withdrawn altogether. But Godó retains various other broadcasting interests, as well as owning *Mundo Deportivo*, number three in the lucrative sports daily market [5.3.3], and a number of magazines.

Godó's replacement as the lead shareholder in *Antena 3* was a younger media combine which subsequently overtook it to become Spain's second largest. The Zeta group's rise began with the success during the transition of the weekly magazine *Interviú*, which was based on a highly personalized approach to news reporting liberally dashed with soft pornography. More recently this has proved a less popular mix, but it had already enabled Zeta's founder, Antonio Asensio, to extend the Barcelona-based group's interests.

As well as other, less sensationalist weeklies – the best-known is *Tiempo* – these include the news daily *El Periódico* [5.3.2], the Catalan sports daily *Sport*, and a string of regional magazines and dailies. Zeta differs from PRISA, and Godó, in that it is fundamentally a business operation. Thus in order to compete with the nationalist *La Vanguardia*, *El Periódico* has tended to back the Catalan Socialists, although under its control *Antena 3* was generally very critical of the then Socialist central government [5.3.2].

Zeta's interest in the television station came to an end in 1998, when it sold its stake to the newest and most controversial power on the media scene. *Telefónica* is the former state telecommunications monopoly, the privatization of which was completed by the conservative government elected in 1996. The move itself attracted considerable comment, since it resulted in control over Spain's largest company passing to a close associate of the Prime Minister José María Aznar [2.4.5]. But the disquiet was greatly increased when its media arm, now known as *Admira*, used its enormous financial muscle to build up a major empire.

Thus, as well as *Antena 3* television, *Admira* acquired the *Onda Cero* radio station set up and owned by the blind organization ONCE [9.4.4]. It has a stake in the publisher *Recoletos*, whose stable includes Spain's top business and sports dailies (*Actualidad Económica* and *Marca*, respectively). And it is also involved in *Unión Editorial*, the fervidly anti-Socialist publisher of Spain's number two selling daily *El Mundo* [5.3.3]. The pro-government bias subsequently apparent in the news coverage of its organs, especially *Antena 3* [5.3.2], gave rise to such uproar that it was toned down. Moreover, following a management upheaval in the parent company there are signs that *Telefónica* may be reviewing its loss-making media involvement as a whole.

The other main development of recent years has been the rapid rise of the combine headed by the Bilbao-based daily *El Correo Español* (previously known as *El Correo Español-El Pueblo Vasco*). Controlled by conservative Basque business interests the Correo group now sells more dailies than any other proprietor in Spain. On the one hand it has built up a large string of regional dailies by taking over a number of titles and launching several more. On the other, in 2001 it acquired one of the three major country-wide titles in the shape of *Abc* [5.3.3]. It is currently developing a network of local papers in Latin America, and has also moved into broadcasting by acquiring the 25 per cent share in the television station *Tele 5* [5.3.2] formerly held by ONCE [9.4.4]. With that move, and the sale of *Onda Cero*, ONCE itself has effectively abandoned its own previous pretensions to becoming a media power in its own right.

5.4 PRESSURE GROUPS

In Spain pressure groups (*grupos de presión*), other than those connected with either the state or any of the major economic or media interests, are of only minimal importance. Such groups are a phenomenon of developed societies, and up to 1936 Spain provided barren ground for their development. Under the Franco regime any attempt to mobilize outside the regime's own aegis was, of course, strictly prohibited.

It is true that the Franco era did see the emergence of neighbourhood associations (*asociaciones de vecinos*). In some areas these were an important local focus of opposition during the regime's latter stages. However, like the much more powerful trade unions, the associations were marginalized during the transition period. Today Spaniards remain statistically much less likely than most of their Western counterparts to be members of voluntary associations of any sort, in particular so-called non-governmental organizations (*Organizaciones No Gubernamentales/ONGs*). The most influential pressure groups are professional bodies, such as the Medical and Lawyers Associations (*Colegio de Médicos, Colegio de Abogados*).

Opinion polls consistently show that Spaniards overwhelmingly look to the state to solve social problems. Their attitude was reflected in the 1978 Constitution, which is pervaded by the ethos that social problems are best addressed communally. In practice, that essentially altruistic approach has allowed government and the parties to channel pressure through organizations they themselves control. Thus to a considerable extent development of a genuine Spanish women's movement was pre-empted by the creation of an official National Women's Bureau (*Instituto de la Mujer*) [9.4.3]. Similarly, the country's various voluntary consumer groups have been sidelined by the government's own National Consumer Bureau (*Instituto Nacional de Consumo*).

In one part of Spain the picture is very different. The Basque Country has a considerable and very active network of pressure groups. In recent years it has witnessed the most impressive example of such activity in Spain: the growth of genuinely popular protest against the violent activities of ETA [3.2.2.1]. This movement, whose members display not just commitment but often considerable courage in the face of intimidation, is centred on the group Gesture for Peace (*Gesto por la Paz*).

Other aspects of pressure group activity in the Basque Country are less positively connected with violence. In effect most such associations are controlled by ETA itself, either directly or through the groups of its sympathizers who campaign for the release of convicted ETA members (*Gestoras Pro-Amnistía*). Examples were the supposedly environmentalist campaigns against the proposed Lemoniz nuclear power plant and, more recently, the new motorway link between Navarre and the French border. Neither campaign, in reality, had much to do with the environment; both were backed by ETA intimidation and, in the first case, murder.

The motorway episode also had another strange aspect. It later transpired that opposition to the original route through the Leizarán valley was also linked to corruption in the Socialist-run Navarre regional government. The revelations provided bizarre confirmation of the extent to which pressure group activity in Spain is manipulated by other powerful interests linked to the state.

5.5 GLOSSARY

The military

ascenso m	promotion
ascenso por antigüedad m	promotion based on length of service
búnker m	diehard (military) supporters of Francoism
cascos azules mpl	blue helmets/berets, UN peace-keeping forces
cuerpos de seguridad mpl	(civilian) security forces
Ejército del Aire m	Air Force
Ejército de Tierra m	Army
ejércitos mpl	armed forces
fuerzas armadas fpl	armed forces

golpe m	(military) coup
golpismo m	predisposition of military to stage coups
intentona (golpista) f	(failed) coup attempt (especially that of 23 Feb. 1981)
involucionismo m	extreme reactionary beliefs and activity
Jefe del Estado Mayor de la Defensa m	Chief of the Defence Staff
Junta de Jefes de Estado Mayor (JUJEM) f	Joint Chiefs-of-Staff Council
Marina f	Navy
mili f	(see *servicio militar*)
nostálgico m	reactionary
oficial m	(military) officer
problema militar m	problem of the military
pronunciamiento m	(nineteenth-century) military coup
reserva activa f	'active reserve', status of promoted officers denied an active command on grounds of merit
servicio militar (obligatorio) m	(compulsory) military service

The Church

aconfesionalidad f	absence of an official religion/Church
(Concilio) Vaticano II m	Second Vatican Council
hecho sociológico m	objective feature of society
impuesto religioso m	Church tax
practicante mf	practising Catholic
Santa Sede f	Holy See, Vatican
vocación f	entry into holy orders

Economic interests

14-D m	14 December 1988 (first post-1978 general strike)
27-M m	27 May 1992 (second post-1978 general strike)
agentes sociales mpl	(see *interlocutores sociales*)
banca privada f	the private banks
Cámara de Comercio f	Chamber of Commerce
canon sindical m	compulsory union levy
central (sindical) f	trade union (confederation)
comité de empresa m	workforce committee
concertación social f	system of national agreements between (government) employers and unions
conflictividad laboral f	industrial unrest
conflicto laboral m	industrial dispute
Consejo Económico y Social m	National Economic and Social Policy Forum
Consejo General m	Supervisory Board (of Bank of Spain)
Consejo Superior Bancario m	National Banking Authority
delegado m	(workforce) representative
desregulación f	deregulation

elecciones sindicales fpl	workplace elections
familia socialista f	socialist movement
financiación estatal f	public funding
frentes sociales mpl	(see *interlocutores sociales* – now outdated)
giro social m	greater emphasis (in government policy) on social issues
gran banca f	the big banks
interlocutores sociales mpl	social partners, employers and unions
liberalización f	deregulation
pacto social m	'social contract', national agreements between (government,) employers and unions
partido hermano m	sister party
patronal f	employers
pymes pequeñas y medianas empresas fpl	SMEs (small and medium-sized enterprises)
relaciones laborales fpl	industrial relations
sección sindical f	industry section (of trade union confederation)
sector crítico m	dissident faction (of union)
siete grandes mpl	'big seven', seven largest banks during 1980s
sindicalismo m	trade union movement
sindicato m	trade union
sindicato amarillo m	bosses' union (i.e. controlled by employer)
sindicato vertical m	government-controlled union

The media

audiencia f	audience share/quota
canal m	(TV) channel/station
Consejo de Administración m	Board of Governors (of Spanish Television Authority)
cuarto poder m	'fourth estate', press/media
difusión f	(newspaper) readership, sales
dominical m	weekend supplement/edition
emisora f	(radio) broadcasting station
ente público m	public corporation
espacio informativo m	news programme
estatuto m	charter (of public corporation)
guerra de las ondas f	'battle of the airwaves' (proliferation of competing radio stations)
medios (de comunicación de masas) mpl	(mass) media
medios informativos mpl	news media
oferta radiofónica/televisiva f	range/choice of radio/TV stations
oyentes mpl	(radio) listeners
prensa amarilla f	(see *prensa sensacionalista*)
prensa del corazón f	gossip magazines
prensa sensacionalista f	sensationalist press (cf. UK tabloids)
presencia f	degree of control (over firm/market sector)
programación f	TV/radio schedule
público m	audience; readership

revista f	magazine; journal
semanal m	weekly (magazine, etc.)
telediario m	TV news programme
televidentes mfpl	(television) viewers
televisiones autonómicas fpl	TV stations run by regional governments
televisiones privadas fpl	private TV stations
tirada f	circulation (of paper)

Pressure groups

asociación de vecinos f	neighbourhood association
colegio m	professional association
grupo de presión m	pressure group
lobby m	lobby, interest group
organización no gubernamental (ONG) f	non-governmental organization (NGO)

6

THE SPANISH ECONOMY

For all the enormous political transformation Spain has undergone since Franco died, perhaps the greatest changes to affect the country in recent decades have been economic. In the 1950s it was still regarded by the United Nations as part of the developing world: now it has the planet's seventh largest GDP. The first section of this chapter traces the course of economic change since 1975, highlighting two major themes. The second then considers four areas of imbalance in the economy that have clouded Spain's success story, and to some extent still do so. The third section then describes briefly the major sectors of economic activity in Spain, and its distribution between regions, while the last looks at the main features of Spanish companies.

6.1 APERTURA AND AJUSTE

In 1975 the Spanish economy remained largely isolated from the outside world. By far the most important factor in its development since then has been a gradual process of exposure to international and especially to European markets (*apertura*). That process has been fundamental in promoting the country's development; almost universally it is seen as positive. Yet, especially coming at a time of unprecedented economic change in the world as a whole, it has given Spain enormous problems. Even more than its neighbours the country has been repeatedly obliged by economic circumstances to undertake policy changes, usually painful for some, or many, Spaniards (*ajustes*).

6.1.1 Prelude; boom and bust

In today's rapidly globalizing world it is hard to comprehend just how cut off the Spanish economy was in 1975. Even if the Franco regime had long since abandoned its pretensions to self-sufficiency [0.2], the country's trade and investment flows remained very low. Indeed, it was only this isolation that had enabled Spain's belated but rapid economic modernization under the dictatorship. But even before Franco died the limitations of this approach were being cruelly exposed.

Spain's economic boom of the 1960s and early 1970s was based largely on heavy industries such as mining, shipbuilding, metalworking of various sorts, and basic chemicals. The firms involved were severely lacking in modern equipment. Instead they relied on relatively primitive technology and an abundant supply of poorly paid labour. Many, whether or not state-owned, received substantial government subsidies. Virtually none were in a position to compete with their better-equipped counterparts in other countries.

Consequently Spanish industrial exports were minimal, while the country's manufacturing firms relied heavily on the protection of their own domestic market from foreign imports. Most obviously Spain imposed unusually high tariffs on many incoming goods. It also operated an elaborate system of quotas (*contingentes*) on particular products, as well as other forms of non-tariff barriers. By these various means the availability and prices of imported goods were regulated in such a way as to prevent them forcing Spanish ones off the market.

Yet, ironically, restrictions on foreign trade could not prevent Spain from falling prey to the development which brought growth in Western Europe as a whole to an abrupt end. Lacking significant energy reserves of its own, Spain had become even more highly dependent than other Western countries on cheap oil imports, above all from the Middle East. It was thus especially hard hit when, in 1973, OPEC (*Organización de los Países Exportadores del Petróleo/OPEP*) imposed a massive rise in oil prices. The effects on the economy were devastating. Unemployment started to rise, the balance of payments suffered severely, and inflation rose sharply – even though the government ill-advisedly kept energy costs artificially low by subsidizing them.

The impact was magnified further by the political situation following Franco's death. For almost a decade the attention of Spain's leaders was focused almost exclusively on the problems of building a democratic state. Economic issues were pushed into the background. Meantime many workers were understandably concerned for their living standards in the face of rising prices, and vigorously demanded wage rises to match. Even after trade union leaders agreed to moderate their claims in the 1977 Moncloa Pacts [0.3.3], wage rises continued to fuel price inflation for some years.

Consequently, during the early 1980s Spain's inflation rate ran consistently well above the average for the European Community. The difference was of particular significance because, after 1975, all the major political parties were convinced that the country must join the EC. Doing so would, by definition, involve free trade with other member states. Unless inflation were brought down to EC levels, the country's products would be unable to compete in the Common Market.

6.1.2 Into Europe

When the Socialists came to power in 1982 intent on joining the EC [4.2.1], inflation was accordingly a major priority for them. The government's response was to promote a series of agreements with employers and unions [5.2.3], all of which set national benchmarks for wage increases designed to bring inflation down. The resultant wage moderation (*moderación salarial*) played a big part in bringing inflation under control. But it was also the first of a number of painful 'adjustments' for many.

The new government's second priority was to overhaul the antiquated industries bequeathed by the Franco regime [6.1.1], to give them a chance of competing inside the EC. Some attempts had already been made to tackle this task, but they were sporadic and ineffectual. As a result the Socialists had little option but to undertake a massive programme of industrial restructuring (*reconversión industrial*), the second key element of 'adjustment'.

The programme involved changing the structure of Spanish manufacturing industry at two levels. First, the intention was to shift its basis from outdated industries to those with good future prospects. Secondly, within individual industries or branches, the government aimed to create firms of a scale large enough to compete with their European competitors. Restructuring thus implied a managed run-down of older industries which were in decline not just in Spain but throughout the developed world.

A prime example was shipbuilding. During the 1960s, Spain had become the industry's world leader, essentially because its shipyards paid lower wages than those elsewhere in the West. By the 1980s, however, it had been undercut in wage terms by new competitors, above all the Newly Industrialized Countries of South-east Asia. Similar considerations applied to a range of older industries, including iron and steel manufacture and the chemical industry. In all of them there was a need to eliminate loss-making firms (*empresas deficitarias*). Previously these had been kept alive by state financial support, much of which was now phased out to prepare for conditions within the EC.

For many companies the result was closure. The healthier ones were concentrated into potentially viable units through mergers and takeovers. The survivors of this process were subject to tough measures designed to rationalize them, that is, put them on a sound financial footing (*saneamiento*). In essence that meant a stringent reduction in costs, typically through radical downsizing (*ajustes de plantilla*) – in plain English, job cuts.

Many workers were required to take early retirement (*jubilación anticipada*). Their younger colleagues were offered, at least in theory, retraining in new skills (*reciclaje*) as preparation for redeployment in the second stage of restructuring – re-industrialization, or the establishment of new industries. This policy, however, proved less easy to implement than the first. For many, 'adjustment' turned out to mean long-term unemployment.

In terms of their overall objective the policies pursued by the Socialists proved remarkably successful. Not only did Spain's economy survive entry to the EC, it actually flourished. Between 1985 and 1989 GDP grew at an annual rate only marginally short of 5 per cent, the highest in the Community and, indeed, among the major developed countries. This 'second economic miracle', as it became known, was partly due to internal factors. Restructuring had put parts of the country's economy on a much sounder footing. Political stability seemed assured and the country had a government with the will to act and the parliamentary majority to allow it to do so [2.3.2]. However, the main cause was precisely Spain's entry into Europe.

As an EC member, Spain was in a position to benefit from the expansion enjoyed in the late 1980s by the Community, and by the Western world as a whole. Foreign investment, the great majority now from its new partners, flowed into the country [6.2.1]. And, as one of the poorer members, Spain was also a major recipient of grants from the Community's Structural Funds [4.1.1] designed to reduce imbalances between different parts of the EC (*desequilibrios territoriales*). Such support was fundamental to the sharp increase in public spending, especially on education and infrastructure, which in turn was one of the principal driving forces behind rapid growth.

6.1.3 The impact of EMU

Throughout Western Europe the brief boom of the late 1980s was followed by the deepest recession (*crisis*) for 60 years. Spain was particularly hard hit. By the middle of the 1990s the ratio of its per capita GDP to the EU average had fallen back to around three-quarters, barely different from the level in 1975. There were various reasons for this setback.

One was the rise in government spending at the end of the previous decade [6.1.2]; although badly-needed, it was simply too fast for the country's economy to bear, particularly in regard to social welfare. Another was the partial nature of restructuring [6.1.2]. A third cause was the fact that growth had been concentrated heavily in the services sector, and financed to a dangerous degree by short-term foreign capital which could be – and was – withdrawn when the international economic climate changed.

As a member of the EC club, Spain was no longer cushioned from such unpleasant developments. Moreover, their impact was aggravated by the Spanish government's slowness to react. By 1989 it was already clear that the economy had reached the stage of overheating (*calentamiento*). Yet the government failed for some time to take the steps necessary to produce a gradual cooling-down (*enfriamiento*). Instead, partly because of the impending prestige events of 1992 [0.4], it continued to spend heavily well into the 1990s. The results were very severe indeed. Inflation rose again and in 1993 economic growth went into reverse, that is, the economy contracted.

Because Spain had waited too long to adjust to the changing economic climate, the necessary deflationary measures were all the more severe when they finally came. By then wage moderation by agreement had been ruled out by the split between government and unions [5.2.1.2]. Instead, the emphasis fell on public spending cuts (*ajustes presupuestarios*). Infrastructure projects came to an abrupt halt, and in 1992 the government introduced a package of measures slashing entitlements to unemployment and other forms of benefit. Issued initially by a surprise decree, they became infamous under the name of *decretazo*.

These austerity measures eventually proved successful in getting recovery under way, albeit rather more slowly than elsewhere in the EU, as it now was.

In the meantime, however, the government had committed itself to meeting the conditions set in 1991 for Economic and Monetary Union (EMU) (see Table 4.1). It was clear that meeting these convergence criteria would be a hard task for Spain, even with the help of the Cohesion Fund (*Fondo de Cohesión*) set up at her insistence [4.2.2]. To meet the challenge, Economics Minister Pedro Solbes drew up a Convergence Plan (*Plan de Convergencia*) which brought further restrictions on government spending and monetary policy.

Over the next few years convergence placed considerable strains on even the healthiest European economies. In Spain the situation was aggravated by the further opening up brought about by the European Single Act in 1993 [4.1.1]. Within a year the government had been forced to alter radically the forecasts on which its Convergence Plan was based. Nevertheless, it persisted with its restrictive policies. By the time it was defeated at the polls in 1996 Spain had been set firmly on the road to convergence, which was pursued with equal determination by the new conservative government. In 1997 these efforts were crowned with success when Spain was officially given the go-ahead for EMU [4.2.2].

By then, too, the country's economic fortunes were once more rising sharply, and continued to do so over the next few years. In the late 1990s Spain once again outstripped most other Western nations in terms of growth. As a result it began to close the gap between it and the EU once more; in 2000 its per capita GDP reached 83 per cent of the Union average, the highest figure ever. Admission to EMU was not a fundamental cause of these developments, but it did act as a psychological boost to public and business morale.

One clear sign of this was that, for the first time, Spain's economy began to open up in a much more active sense. A growing number of Spanish firms began to penetrate foreign markets and to invest abroad [6.2.1], above all in Latin America. This active participation in globalization is usually seen as positive. Nonetheless, the massive losses suffered by Spanish companies when the Argentinean economy imploded in 2001/02 was a reminder of the possible dangers.

6.2 IMBALANCES

Spain's impressive progress over the last two decades was far from a smooth process; in fact it was more like a roller-coaster ride. By the same token, the advances achieved were by no means uniform across all aspects of its economy. At various times, four areas of imbalance have caused particular concern. One is that aspect most obviously affected by the process of integration into the world economy – the balance of payments. Two more – the value of money and the state of public finances – relate directly to the criteria laid down for entry into Economic and Monetary Union. The fourth is unemployment, which did not figure in the convergence criteria, but which was gravely affected by the efforts made to meet them.

6.2.1 Balance of payments

Spain's balance of payments was a problem as long ago as the 1950s. Indeed, the country's inability to earn sufficient foreign currency (*divisas*) in order to pay for its purchases abroad was one of the factors that forced the Franco regime into a radical change of economic policy at the end of the decade. Yet Spain's foreign trade (*comercio exterior*) remained so limited that in absolute terms the balance of payments deficit (*déficit exterior*) was small.

In fact, the mild liberalization measures undertaken in 1959/60 [0.2] considerably increased the trade gap (*déficit comercial*). However, for the next 15 years it was covered by two non-trade items. One was the remittances (*remesas*) of money sent home to their families by emigrant workers. The other was revenue from the burgeoning tourist industry. As a result, Spain's overall balance of payments with the outside world was reasonably healthy; at the beginning of the 1970s it actually moved into surplus. This success was soon wiped out by the effects of the 1973 oil crisis of 1973 [6.1.1]. But thanks to the substantial decline in real world oil prices over the next decade, the balance gradually improved again.

From 1986, however, the situation was again reversed by the dismantling of customs barriers (*desarme arancelario*) on EC entry [4.2.1]. As a result the Spanish market was invaded by goods from other EC countries, above all France and Germany. Indeed, the influx was actively encouraged by the government, which was conscious that, in order to build up new industries, Spain must import capital goods (*bienes de equipo*). Although Spanish exports also rose, it was at nothing like the same rate. The result was that the trade deficit increased fourfold between 1985 and 1989.

The opening up of trade in services in 1993 which resulted from of the Single European Act [4.1.1] was another severe blow for the country's balance. Spain's own service sector was small and inefficient, and the country offered a tempting new market for European firms. Nor was it any longer feasible to cover the deficit by non-trade earnings.

Remittances have long ceased to play any significant role. Tourism, it is true, continues to represent a major source of income for the country. Unfortunately though, the steady increase in its volume was reversed in the early 1990s, worsening the situation still further. In any case, with the trade in goods and other services having grown so much in real terms, tourism can no longer single-handedly balance the country's books, as it did in the 1970s.

Nonetheless, the balance's strong recovery later in the 1990s was greatly assisted by an upturn in tourist numbers and receipts [6.3.4]. More important for the long term was the fact that, for the first time in the country's history, recovery from recession was export-driven; in other words, firms' export earnings were the first means by which new demand was injected into the economy. In addition, the composition of exports started to shift away from traditional agricultural products to higher-value manufactured goods. Another factor was Spain's growing attractiveness to foreign investment (*inversión extranjera*), which rose rapidly in the decade after 1986.

Thanks to these various effects, by 1997 Spain's current account was actually back in the black; the following year it recorded the highest surplus ever. Ironically, by then, inward investment had not only slowed but been overtaken by the investment of Spanish firms abroad (*inversiones en el extranjero*), which rose by a factor of ten between 1995 and 1999. The great majority of the large outflow was destined for Latin America, where the country's two major banks (BSCH and BBVA) [6.3.3] became major investors along with the privatized state monopolies *Telefónica* (telecommunications), *Repsol* (hydrocarbons) and *Endesa* (energy).

However, the renewed deficit recorded in 2000 was more the result of a worsening in the terms of trade for Spain, notably rising oil prices. The country's dependence on foreign energy is one reason why, despite the real progress made, its balance of payments remains vulnerable. And, with the coming of EMU, it can longer use devaluation of its currency to boost exports, as happened in the 1990s.

6.2.2 Monetary aspects

Spain's former currency, the peseta, was traditionally weak. That is, it tended to lose value against other currencies, a fact which made imports expensive. Thus, when the government was keen to facilitate the import of capital goods in the late 1980s [6.2.1], its exchange-rate policy (*política cambiaria*) was aimed at maintaining a strong peseta. In an attempt to underpin its value, in 1989 the then Finance Minister, Carlos Solchaga, took the peseta into the European Monetary System [4.1.1], effectively pegging it against the other main European currencies at a relatively high level.

As the country's economy deteriorated over the next few years [6.1.3], the peseta came under increasing pressure. This the government resisted, determined to meet the criteria for EMU (see Table 4.1). Even when the pressure became irresistible, the Spanish government was reluctant to acknowledge the extent of the peseta's overvaluation. The result was that on 13 May 1993 Spain was forced to devalue by a full 13 per cent, far more than allowed by the criteria. The date became known as Black Thursday (*jueves negro*).

This setback was a humiliation for the government but by no means disastrous for the economy; in fact it helped the balance of payments by improving export performance. In any case, only a few months later the EMS itself effectively collapsed. When a new, more flexible system was cobbled together in late 1993 the Spanish government re-joined, even though it seemed likely that the peseta was still too high for comfort.

This time, however, the gamble paid off. Rapid economic recovery, along with a weakening of the German mark, enabled the Spanish currency to maintain its value until, with the onset of EMU in 1999, it found shelter beneath the protective umbrella of the new European Central Bank [4.1.2]. Three years later, at the start of 2002, the peseta was replaced as Spain's currency by the euro, at a rate of 1 euro to 166.386 pesetas.

Spanish participation in EMU was only possible because of a dramatic reduction in inflation. Conversely, one reason why successive governments were so keen to join first the EMS and then EMU was that the discipline they imposed was seen as a means of maintaining the peseta's internal value, its purchasing power (*poder adquisitivo*), by slowing down the rise in prices. For, although inflation had been brought down from the dramatic levels of the late 1970s [6.1.1], it remained significantly above the EU average into the 1990s.

Cutting it further was the main aim of the austerity measures adopted from 1991 on [6.1.3]. They had the desired effect, and by 1998 the rate was at a record low of 1.4 per cent, one of the best figures in the EU. This situation could not be maintained, however, and strong growth pushed inflation back up to around 4 per cent early in the new century. Even so, this represents a considerable improvement on past performance.

Keeping the peseta high and inflation low long required Spanish interest rates to be held well above the EU average. Not only did that infringe a third convergence criterion (see Table 4.1). It also held back the investment needed to ensure recovery after the recession of the early 1990s [6.1.3]. However, as inflation fell and confidence grew that Spain would indeed qualify for EMU, it proved possible to ease monetary policy as well. In 1998 base rates fell to their lowest ever level of 3 per cent. And the advent of EMU the following year meant that, in this respect too, the differentials between Spain and the other euro countries were effectively removed.

6.2.3 Public finances

One ironic advantage of its belated economic development was that Spain has had less opportunity to build up the national, or public debt (*endeudamiento público*) typically associated with the process. As a result, that particular aspect of the criteria for EMU was of relatively little concern for it. This was far from true, however, of the final criterion, that relating to the annual public sector deficit (*déficit público*), which had been causing concern since the Franco era and was still doing so in the 1990s.

Several reasons underlay Spain's swelling public deficit. One was the high cost of building a modern welfare state [9.1.1], another the state's involvement in a number of unprofitable economic activities [6.4.1]. While some of these were sold off as part of industrial restructuring in the 1980s [6.1.2], that process added new burdens on the public purse in the shape of redundancy payments, early pensions and unemployment benefit [6.2.4]. Moreover, even after the massive expenditure of the 1980s, Spain continued to need costly investment in infrastructure and technology, much of which had to come from the state. A further pressure on state spending was high interest rates [6.2.2], which pushed up the interest payments on government bonds or debt (*deuda del estado*).

Yet, despite all these pressures on expenditure, the deficit's main cause lay on the income side, in the tax system of the Francoist era. Not only was the overall tax burden (*presión fiscal*) then extraordinarily low by the standards of the developed world. It was also very oddly distributed. Direct taxes (*fiscalidad directa*) were levied almost exclusively on those whose wages were easily monitored, which, in practice, meant employees (*trabajadores por cuenta ajena*) who figured on the payroll of a large firm. Little attempt was made even to establish the tax liability of workers in the small firms which dominate the country's economy [6.4.2], or of the self-employed (*autónomos*). More than half of all tax revenues came from indirect taxation (*fiscalidad indirecta*), the rates of which were higher on basic than luxury items.

Reform of this bizarre system began in the late 1970s. The then Finance Minister, Francisco Fernández Ordóñez, launched a series of publicity campaigns to promote public awareness of the essential nature of taxation in a democracy. He also instituted the first effective system for checking tax returns and so eliminating some tax evasion (*fraude fiscal*). Under the Socialist governments of the following years, efforts to increase revenue continued.

By 1989, the rates of both personal income tax (*impuesto sobre la renta de las personas físicas/IRPF*) and corporation tax (*impuesto de sociedades*) had increased substantially. In addition, Spain's entry into the EC brought the introduction of value added tax (*impuesto sobre el valor añadido/IVA*). Even so, the system had become much more progressive, in the sense that more tax income now came from direct taxes, the rates of which rise with income levels. As a result, growing prosperity in the late 1980s and again a decade later brought proportionately more into the government's coffers (*arcas del estado*).

The state's growing demands, and its increasing effectiveness in tax collection (*recaudación*), caused considerable public resentment, especially among those unused to the role of taxpayer (*contribuyente*). This was especially true of firms. Previously little bothered by the tax authorities (*Hacienda*), they now had to face not only a growing burden of corporation tax but also successive rises in their social security contributions. In this situation, the acceptability of tax evasion has remained high; a senior employers' representative went so far as to suggest that it was 'essential for firms' survival'. Such attitudes inevitably constrain further increases in tax revenue.

They are also reflected in the growth of a large informal economy (*economía sumergida*). By that is meant all those economic activities carried on outside the state's knowledge and so omitted from official statistics. By its very nature the extent of a country's informal sector is hard to measure, but in Spain's case studies have suggested it may account for as much as 20 per cent of GDP. Industries believed to be particularly affected are construction and footwear. What is beyond doubt is that the informal economy, as well as its negative implications for workers' health, safety, social security protection and job security, also causes a substantial leakage of government revenue.

That did not prevent reduction of the deficit to the 3 per cent required for EMU entry in 1997, however. Indeed, by the turn of the century it was down to around 1 per cent, and that despite the government having reduced tax rates in 1998. For the present, Spain is comfortably within the limits on fiscal policy (*política fiscal y financiera*) set by the Stability Pact adopted in conjunction with EMU [4.1.2]. Two worries remain, however. The more immediate concerns how to keep regional spending, which now makes up 45 per cent of all public expenditure, under control. The other, more long-term, is the effect on Spain's budget of a rapidly ageing population, with the consequent increase in pension and other welfare payments.

6.2.4 Labour market

If inflation and the deficit were the main concerns of Spain's rulers over much of the last two decades, for the country's people another problem tended to take priority, unemployment. And indeed joblessness is the one indicator on which Spain remains radically out of line with the rest of the developed world, at least according to official figures. Attempts at resolving the problem have focused mainly on making the country's job market (*mercado laboral*) work more efficiently, and in recent years have finally begun to show some positive effects.

6.2.4.1 Unemployment

Mass unemployment came as a particular shock to Spain because it was a new experience; during the depression of the 1930s the country was still overwhelmingly rural. In the Franco era it exported joblessness through emigration [0.2], so that into the early 1970s the jobless rate never exceeded 3 per cent. Subsequently, however, it rose sharply and has remained well above those in other EU countries.

For lengthy periods in the 1980s and 1990s, over three million Spaniards were officially recorded as out of work by the government-run National Employment Agency (*Instituto Nacional de Empleo/INEM*). Using the rather higher figures of the Official Labour-force Survey (*Encuesta de Población Activa/EPA*), unemployment peaked in 1994 at 24 per cent, and thereafter declined only slowly. It should be noted, however, that these figures are almost certainly inflated due to the existence of a large informal economy [6.2.3].

Unemployment hits women especially hard, among whom it is generally over 10 percentage points higher than that for men. On the other hand, men are disproportionately represented among the long-term unemployed (*parados de larga duración*), i.e. those out of work for over a year, which in turn make up around half of the total. The most worrying aspect of all is the extremely high rate of youth unemployment (*paro juvenil*), which affects both sexes. In the mid-1990s it rose over 40 per cent, and in some areas reached 75 per cent.

Joblessness was a major issue as far back as 1982, when a Socialist government arrived in power promising to create 800,000 jobs. The fact that unemployment not only persisted but rose steeply during its term of office was often quoted to show that this pledge had been broken. Such accusations betrayed misunderstanding of unemployment's causes. In fact, over the next decade the number of people in work rose by well over a million. The problem was that the labour force (*población activa*) – the number of Spaniards working or seeking work – grew even more.

There were several reasons for this. Few Spaniards now work outside the country, and the high birth rates of the Franco era have worked through into the numbers of working age. Most important of all, relatively more adults are now seeking jobs than before. Since 1970 Spain's participation rate, or economic activity rate (*tasa de actividad*), has increased steadily. The rise would have been even greater had not many men made redundant in older industries ceased to seek work. By contrast, the female participation rate – previously very low indeed – rose dramatically. The trend is set to continue, since the Spanish participation rate is still below the EU average, substantially so in the case of women.

Especially after 1986 there was also a severe mismatch between the skills of the unemployed and the jobs becoming available. Thus most job losses (*destrucción de empleo*) have been in traditional heavy industries or agriculture, whereas most new employment has been created in light industries and, above all, in the service sector. Successive governments have attempted to counteract this problem by improving training provision in general [8.3.3], and providing specific retraining (*reciclaje*) for those thrown out of work. The impact of these and other 'active' employment policies has been limited.

The direction of 'passive' policies, that is those designed to cushion the effects of unemployment, has varied. On the one hand, pressure on public finances [6.2.3] has several times brought cutbacks in the level and coverage of unemployment benefit. On the other, general welfare provision has been greatly expanded since 1980. That is usually seen as a major reason why Spaniards now show little inclination to move in search of work; internal migration, previously high, has almost dried up. And, since new jobs are mainly outside the areas worst hit by unemployment [6.3.5], this has posed another barrier to reducing it.

One particular welfare measure, introduced by the Socialists, became notorious for its negative aspects. The Rural Employment Plan (*Plan de Empleo Rural/PER*) provided benefit for casual farm labourers, and a programme of public works designed to compensate for the chronic lack of agricultural employment in regions such as Andalusia. The PER gave rise to numerous accusations of corruption because of the control exercised over its operation by local authorities, which in the rural south are overwhelmingly controlled by the Socialist Party. But its worst drawback was that it effectively removed any incentive for the unemployed to seek work, or for others to provide it.

6.2.4.2 Flexibility

The PER was just one example, albeit an extreme one, of a problem which, according to most economists, is at the root of the Spanish labour market's problems. These are various forms of inflexibility, or rigidity (*rigideces*); that is, features which constrain the market's ability to meet rapidly changing economic conditions. In large measure they result from the complex system of employment regulation instituted by the Franco regime.

One aspect was the standard minimum wage (*salario mínimo interprofesional/ SMI*) introduced in 1963 and set annually by the Ministry of Employment after consultation with unions and employers' organizations. In fact, employers have shown little concern over the SMI, as its effect on wage levels is negligible. Even in theory only 5 per cent of the workforce are affected by it: in practice, high unemployment means that workers are willing to collude with employers in working for lower rates in the informal economy [6.2.3]. Altogether more important in holding back job creation are employers' social security contributions (*cuotas empresariales*). Appreciably higher than in other EU countries, they are often referred to as a jobs tax (*impuesto sobre el empleo*).

However, the principal causes of labour market rigidity derive from the legal conditions on employing workers, which were updated in the 1980 Workers' Charter (*Estatuto de los Trabajadores*) [5.2.1.1]. The Charter made collective agreements (*convenios colectivos*) between unions and employer representatives binding, thus restricting individual firms' ability to respond to their circumstances. It also consolidated the existing strict regulations on terms and conditions of service, and on the nature of employees' contracts, almost all of which were automatically permanent. Any changes to them required an official authorization (*expediente*), and were subject to appeal to an employment court [10.1.3]. In particular, it was both difficult and costly for employers to reduce the size of their workforce.

During the 1980s this situation increasingly worried not only employers but also the government. In 1984 it introduced reforms, including legalization of fixed-term contracts (*contratos temporales*). The aim was to encourage employers to take on new workers in the knowledge that they were not saddled with the related costs indefinitely. Although fixed-term contracts soon became the norm, their net impact on job creation was marginal. Moreover, they reduced job security, and thus the consumer confidence essential in a modern economy. Nor did the 1984 changes satisfy employers, who remained subject to restrictions in various respects.

Accordingly, in 1994 the government introduced a further, and much broader set of changes. For the first time since the 1940s employers were permitted to issue part-time contracts (*contratos a tiempo parcial*), thus regularizing a situation already common in the informal economy. More significantly in terms of employment policy, two new contract types – work placements (*contratos en prácticas*) and apprenticeships (*contratos de aprendizaje*) – were introduced, allowing for greater flexibility in terms of wages and conditions.

The 1994 reforms also included several other measures. They abolished the monopoly position of the INEM [6.2.4.1] as an employment broker by lifting the ban on private employment agencies (*agencias de contratación*). They relaxed the obligations on employers to respect national or sectoral agreements. Also significantly eased were the restrictions applying to dismissals (*despidos*). Even so, there was no question of an unrestricted right to fire at will (*despido libre*), which was and remains an extremely hot political potato in Spain.

While not worthless, these new reforms proved inadequate either to bring down unemployment or to satisfy employers. They also had the unforeseen effect of greatly reducing job security; in 1996, only 4 per cent of new contracts were permanent. As a result, the conservative government elected in 1996 was able to persuade unions and employers to reach an agreement the following year [5.2.3] as the basis for a further round of changes.

These 1997 reforms restricted the use of temporary contracts while introducing a new type of permanent one to which much less onerous conditions on severance pay (*indemnización*) apply. These new contracts were available only to certain groups of employees – basically, younger and older workers, the long-term unemployed and the disabled. In addition, employers' social service contributions were reduced. Combined with the general economic upswing [6.1.3], these measures finally brought some concrete success. In 1998, 450,000 new jobs were created, 80 per cent of them permanent. And by 2001 unemployment had fallen to 13 per cent (on the higher, EPA measure [6.2.4.1]), still well above the EU average but a major improvement nonetheless.

6.3 SECTORAL AND GEOGRAPHICAL STRUCTURE

The continuing existence of imbalances, particularly unemployment, is a reminder that Spain's recent economic history has not been an unbridled success story. And, in terms of the rate of advance, progress has been very uneven, with periods of rapid growth followed by stagnation or even recession. But in other respects change has been enormous and irreversible, especially when one looks beyond the features of the economy as a whole to its constituent parts: the different sectors of economic activity and the country's various regions.

6.3.1 Primary sector

Spain's primary sector has been shrinking for decades. In 1960 it accounted for over 20 per cent of GDP; by the 1990s the figure had fallen to around 6 per cent. As in other countries it is made up of various subsectors. Of these both forestry (*sector forestal*) and the mining industry (*sector minero*), although of significance in particular local areas and especially in environmental terms, play purely minor roles in the economy as a whole.

Spain's fishing industry (*sector pesquero*) is by far the largest in the EU, although for obvious reasons its significance is restricted to certain areas. It also faces a number of problems. Inshore fishing (*pesca costera*) has declined due to severe overfishing (*sobreexplotación*). More generally, EU conservation measures have forced reductions in the size of the fleet, especially in the main centres of Galicia and the Basque Country. Fishermen from these regions have led the way in seeking new fishing grounds (*caladeros*) on the high seas. Their often aggressive methods have led to confrontations with the authorities of several countries, including Ireland, Morocco and Canada.

The great bulk of the primary sector is made up of agriculture (*sector agropecuario*). In proportional terms too it still accounts for considerably more employment in Spain than in the EU as a whole. Indeed, into the 1990s it provided over a fifth of jobs in 19 provinces; in two (Lugo and Ourense) around half the employed population still works in farming a decade later. Nevertheless, since 1960 Spain has experienced a massive drift of population from the land (*éxodo rural*), a process begun by the low priority placed by the Franco regime on agriculture. The results of its neglect were clearly apparent in 1975, when Spanish agriculture was extremely backward and unproductive.

One pressing issue was the structure of agricultural landholding (*estructura agraria*), which in the south was linked to the question of ownership. In much of Spain farmers, whether owners or tenants, have traditionally enjoyed rea-sonable security of tenure. In wide areas of Andalusia and Extremadura, how-ever, the countryside was dominated by large estates (*latifundios*). The bulk of the rural population consisted of day-labourers (*jornaleros*), employed at low wages and on extremely poor conditions. During the Second Republic their parlous situation had inspired attempts at land reform (*reforma agraria*), that is changes in the structure of land ownership. But little was achieved in terms of breaking up the estates, while under the Franco regime virtually all were returned to their former owners.

The question of land ownership overlapped with another, that of the size and nature of farm units (*explotaciones*), for the large southern estates were often notoriously ill-managed. In other parts of the country, on the other hand, many holdings were uneconomically small. To make matters worse, tiny smallholdings (*minifundios*) were often split up into plots (*parcelas*), sometimes widely separated. The first attempt at combating these intercon-nected problems was made during the transition, when a Landholdings Rationalization Service (*Servicio de Concentración Parcelaria*) was established to encourage the creation of larger, unified holdings through the exchange and sale of plots between smallholders. Government grants were provided to help the process along.

When the Socialists came to power in 1982 attention was extended to the question of the big estates, and the Service absorbed into a new Land Reform Agency (*Instituto de Reforma Agraria*). Working in conjunction with regional governments, and spurred on by the protests of the Landworkers Union [5.2.1.1], the Agency has enjoyed some success in transferring previously unused land to new owners, although the pressure to do so was to some extent relaxed by the extension of unemployment support to landworkers [6.2.4.1].

Instead, the focus of attention has shifted to the more general issue of agri-culture's efficiency. In that sense the small scale of most farms continues to be a problem, because it makes the use of modern machinery difficult for both technical and financial reasons. Only recently have tractors been widely introduced into some areas; Galicia is especially notorious in this regard. Small farm size also militates against the establishment of effective distribu-tion and marketing networks. One response to this problem has been to set up cooperatives.

Small farmers are also disproportionately affected by lack of knowledge about new techniques and alternative crops. As a result, attempts to increase productivity by these means have often created fresh problems. By and large they have involved bringing more land under irrigation (*riego*), a practice which is not only often harmful to the environment but also of doubtful utility in the longer term [7.2.2].

Provision of information on crops and techniques, and incentives to apply it, is one purpose of the EU's Common Agricultural Policy [4.1.1], from which Spanish farmers have benefited since 1986. Unfortunately for them, however, the bulk of its resources are devoted to the system of guaranteed farm prices, while under the CAP most resources are still focused on farmers in the original, more northerly EC member states.

The impact of EU membership on Spanish agriculture varies dramatically between different types of farming. Especially hard hit has been the dairy industry (*sector lácteo*). Concentrated on small, hilly farms in the northern coastal regions, it is poorly placed to compete with the much larger and more easily worked holdings common elsewhere in Europe.

Cereal farming, traditionally the backbone of the Castilian economy, has been another victim. On the other hand, new opportunities have opened up for some farmers, especially in the south and east where the climate is truly Mediterranean. There intensive techniques, using greenhouses (*invernaderos*) and extensive irrigation, have allowed profitable specialization in fruit and vegetables (*productos hortifrutícolas*). The southerly location gives a particular advantage in early season products (*primicias*).

6.3.2 Industry

In contrast to the situation in other advanced countries, industry (*sector secundario*) was only briefly the largest and most important sector of the Spanish economy. Dwarfed by the primary sector until the 1960s, it was overtaken by services when the economy finally modernized thereafter. The share of GDP and employment for which it accounts has changed little since the 1970s.

The main feature of industry's development over that period has been restructuring [6.1.2], a process that remains unfinished. Spanish industry still displays many of the same problems as before, albeit to a lesser degree. It lacks adequate technology and know-how. It suffers from fragmentation into a large number of small, often very small firms (*atomización*); some of the larger indigenous ones remain within a public sector of dubious efficiency [6.4.1].

These conditions are probably both cause and consequence of an oft-remarked lack of enterpreneurial spirit (*mentalidad empresarial*) in Spanish society (here Spanish should be read as excluding Basque and Catalan, but not Galician). It has been ascribed to a number of factors, including an alleged Castilian disdain for manual work and the negligible influence of Protestantism. Coming nearer to the present, enterprise was stifled by the Franco regime's policies of state intervention and protectionism [0.2]. Observers point also to the slow speed at which vocational training has adapted to changing economic circumstances [8.3.3].

The effects are hard to identify precisely, but are thought to be serious. They may well provide one reason for the poor results of restructuring in terms of generating new industrial activity [6.1.3]. Historically they seem to underlie Spain's reliance on the export of primary products rather than higher value finished goods (*productos elaborados*); only in the 1990s did this situation, typical of the Third World rather than the First, begin to change [6.2.1].

The food and drink industry (*sector alimenticio*) – actually one of Spain's most buoyant – provides a good illustration of these sorts of problems. Domestic firms within it were often slow to grasp the opportunities offered by the country's wealth of produce, much of it high quality and well adapted to consumer tastes in the developed world. Yet rather than being processed in Spain, olives are exported to Italy. Traditional meat products, such as cured ham, have not always been marketed adequately. The establishment of a promotional initiative in 1995 was, significantly, driven by public authorities, in this case the Andalusian regional government.

Lack of private initiative and investment has been a long-standing problem. Instead Spain has tended to rely on the state, or on foreign capital. In the nineteenth century foreign firms virtually monopolized the only two industrial activities of any significance outside the Basque and Catalan regions – railways and mining. Indeed, the protectionist policies pursued by successive governments up to and including the Franco regime were in large part a reaction to this situation.

With the opening up of Spain's economy after Franco's death, and especially after EC entry in 1986 [6.1.2], penetration of foreign capital greatly increased. Such investment has brought Spain many benefits, generating industrial development where none existed and preserving firms and industries that would otherwise have disappeared. On the other hand, it has involved loss of control over decisions in many of the country's largest firms.

These various aspects can all be seen in Spain's automobile industry (*sector automovilístico*), the third largest in Europe. The only major Spanish car producer, SEAT (*Sociedad Española de Automóviles de Turismo*), was founded in 1950 and long produced models under licence from the Italian manufacturer Fiat. Gravely affected by the post-1973 recession [6.1.1], SEAT was baled out by a 1982 cooperation agreement with the German Volkswagen company, which now has a controlling share. Similarly, the production of Pegaso trucks, begun by the state-owned firm ENASA (*Empresa Nacional de Autocamiones SA*), is now in Italian hands.

All other vehicle production in Spain is the result of inward investment. The longest established foreign manufacturer is the French FASA-Renault, which began production in 1951. Subsequently it has been joined by its compatriot Peugeot-Citroën, and by leading firms from the USA (Ford, General Motors) and Japan (Toyota, Suzuki). Many dependent component manufacturers (*industria auxiliar*) are also wholly or partly foreign-owned.

In conjunction these various operations are a major source of employment. However, it is a source which is highly vulnerable to changing business conditions. When economic times are hard the first to be hit are often subsidiaries based outside the home country of the parent company (*casa matriz*). The results can be traumatic. Thus in 1993 Suzuki announced its intention to close the Santana jeep factory on which the town of Linares was almost entirely dependent.

Their importance as job providers gives multinationals enormous bargaining power *vis-à-vis* public authorities. Also in 1993, Volkswagen invested heavily in a new hi-tech SEAT plant at Martorell in Catalonia. Yet almost immediately VW announced its intention to pull out of the existing factory in the Barcelona Enterprise Area (*Zona Franca*) to which it had been lured by tax breaks and other incentives. The plans were only altered after further financial concessions from regional and national governments desperate to preserve jobs.

6.3.3 Financial sector

Lack of investment in Spanish industry is closely linked to another aspect of the country's late modernization: the relative underdevelopment of mechanisms for the supply of business finance. Spain's stock exchanges (*bolsas*) were, until recently, minuscule operations by international standards. Even though trading on them has increased substantially in recent years, Spanish companies remain heavily dependent on credit to finance their operations.

Here too, the state stepped in during the Franco era, when state agencies were set up to provide businesses with loans. They included an Overseas Trade Bank (*Banco Exterior de España*), as well as a number of institutions designed to channel credit to specific industries. In 1971 these were brought together as the Official Credit Agency (*Instituto de Crédito Oficial/ICO*). Nevertheless, the principal source of credit remained the banking system.

Traditionally this was divided into two parts. The first – slightly the smaller – consisted of the savings banks (*cajas de ahorros*). Locally based and managed, they served a particular city or province; many were originally pawnbrokers (*montes de piedad*). Today the savings banks still supply important amounts of credit for particular types of business, especially farmers. They also continue to provide much useful documentation on the economy of their area and to carry out non-lucrative tasks (*obra social*), e.g. cultural and recreational projects, even though they are no longer required by law to devote stipulated proportions of the loans they provide to such projects of public interest.

The effective elimination of this requirement, and of other measures giving the savings banks protected status, means that there is now little practical distinction between them and the remainder of the banking system. In order to compete in this new environment, most savings banks have come together in larger entities covering several provinces or even the whole country. The sector is now dominated by just two institutions: the Barcelona-based *Caixa*, originally a mutual pension fund, and *Caja Madrid*. While it has enabled the savings banks to survive in name, this concentration has prevented their conversion into semi-public regional banks on the German model, specifically charged with industrial promotion in their area.

Concentration has also been the main feature of developments among the commercial banks. A first round of mergers and takeovers was triggered off by the failure of a number of smaller banks during and immediately after the transition. It resulted in the emergence of a group of major banks, known as the 'big seven': the *Bilbao, Vizcaya, Central, Hispanoamericano, Banesto, Santander,* and *Popular*. In 1987 a second period of upheaval began. It began with the crisis experienced by *Banca Catalana*, closely linked to Catalan prime minister Jordi Pujol and his regionalist supporters [3.2.1.2]. Soon, however, it spread to the big banks themselves.

The causes lay in the outdated practices characteristic of Spanish banks and in the 1987 Single European Act [4.1.1], under which there would be open competition between banks across the EC from 1993. Faced with the prospect of competing with more efficient foreign banks, whose advantages derived partly from sheer size, the more dynamic of the 'big seven' opted to break the gentleman's agreement that had previously governed relations between them [5.1.3]. The result was an outbreak of forced mergers and takeover bids, often tacitly encouraged by the government.

The first two bids, by the *Bilbao* and then the *Central* for *Banesto*, failed. In 1989, however, the two great Basque banks came together to form the *Banco Bilbao Vizcaya* (BBV). Two years later the ailing *Hispanoamericano* was absorbed by the *Central* to form the *Banco Central Hispano* (BCH). Then, in 1994, after a severe crisis which led the government to exercise its emergency powers to intervene, *Banesto* was effectively acquired by the *Santander*, although technically the two remained separate. Meantime, a further major player was added by the merger and privatization of the state's banking interests under the name of *Argentaria* [6.4.1]. It was then acquired by the *Bilbao Vizcaya*, now known as BBVA, and finally – at least to date – the *Santander* and BCH merged to form BSCH.

The 'big seven' have thus been reduced to just two, the *Popular* having been relegated to the second rank. Having seemingly secured their domestic position, BBVA and BSCH have been at the forefront of Spanish penetration into Latin America [0.4.2], but even so it remains uncertain if they are big enough to compete successfully on the international stage. They still suffer from the problem of having too many branches, twice as many relative to population as in the EU as a whole, which obviously undermines their efficiency. On the other hand, the extreme concentration of the bank sector can hardly be seen as positive for consumers.

6.3.4 Services

The service or tertiary sector (*sector terciario*) has come to dominate Western economies in recent decades. The same is true of Spain, albeit to a slightly lesser degree, with services now providing around 60 per cent of employment. This situation represents a remarkable change for the country; in 1960 services accounted for little over a quarter of the economy. As in other countries it is difficult to generalize about the service sector, composed as it is of a wide range of highly diverse activities. Of these, two are especially important in terms of the employment they provide.

The first is wholesale and retail trade (*comercio mayorista y minorista*), which accounts for around a quarter of all service jobs in Spain. In recent years this share has been declining steadily as small shops (*pequeños comercios*) are driven out of business by the less labour-intensive large-scale outlets (*grandes superficies*), such as super- and hypermarkets. Their supremacy was reinforced by the 1995 Trading Act (*Ley de Comercio*), which among other measures partially deregulated shops' permitted opening hours (*horario comercial*). Unlike the case in most EU countries, in Spain the larger outlets are mainly in foreign ownership; French chains are particularly important.

The second major subsector in employment terms is that of public administration and other services provided by public authorities (principally education, health and social services). All these activities expanded rapidly in the 1980s, at both central and regional level. Combined, they now account for almost as many jobs as wholesaling and retailing.

The most rapidly growing subsector in recent years has been that of business services. As well as banking [6.3.3], this includes insurance and the remainder of the financial services industry. Like the banks, they remained heavily protected up to the coming into effect of the EU's single market in 1993. Largely as a result the financial sector as a whole remained underdeveloped and inefficient by international standards, and offered a tempting target to foreign investors.

In terms of overall economic significance, a fourth service subsector stands out. Now, as for many years, Spain's ability to pay for its imports depends crucially on the tourist industry (*sector turístico*) [6.2.1]. After tailing off from the late 1980s, the tourist trade rose sharply again in the mid-1990s, when Spain benefited from the troubles suffered by several of its Mediterranean competitors. The authorities have also invested heavily in campaigns designed to distribute tourism more evenly over the country and the calendar year.

A major problem continues to be the low average amount injected into the Spanish economy by each tourist who visits the country. In part this is a reflection of the continuing emphasis on mass tourism (*turismo de masas*). But it also derives from the dominant role played by foreign tour operators (*tour operadores*) in managing the trade. As in the case of industry [6.3.2], here is evidence of inability on the part of Spanish business to exploit fully the country's natural resources.

6.3.5 Regional differences

As well as the massive sectoral shifts it has undergone in recent decades the Spanish economy has also experienced another sort of structural change. The geographical distribution of economic activity and wealth is markedly different now from what it was in 1960, or even 1975. The causes of change lie in the decline of certain established economic activities – traditional agriculture, heavy industry – and the rise of new ones, whose location is determined not by the presence of raw materials but by other factors, especially proximity to markets.

Up to the 1960s the two wealthiest and most developed parts of Spain were Catalonia and the Basque Country or, more precisely, the metropolitan areas of Barcelona and Bilbao. Otherwise industrial development was limited to a few smaller outposts, mainly along the northern Atlantic coast (*Cornisa Cantábrica*). Madrid, almost entirely because of its role as the centre of administration, was the single enclave of prosperity in a vast area covering both Castiles, and the entire south.

In the 1990s, however, this pattern was replaced by another in which wealth and development is concentrated in two connected strips. The more important extends down the Mediterranean coast from Catalonia, through Valencia and Murcia and into the easternmost Andalusian province of Almería. The other runs up the valley of the Ebro from Tarragona in Catalonia, through Saragossa, into Navarre before petering out in the inland Basque province of Alava. Together with the y-shaped area formed by these two strips, Madrid and the two island regions (Balearics and Canaries) now make up 'rich Spain'.

The reasons why these areas have prospered vary. In the case of Madrid, success is mainly attributable to the expansion of government and the growing attractiveness of capital cities in general as business locations. In the islands tourism has obviously played the leading role. It has also been vital to the rise of the Mediterranean coastal strip (*eje mediterráneo*).

This last area, however, also displays a number of features common to economically successful regions in developed countries. Thus it has little heritage of industrial blight, in terms of outdated plant and environmental damage. Its workforce is young and unwedded to the skills and practices of traditional heavy industry. It has a number of medium-sized centres, which provide an attractive working and living environment for incoming executives, as well as a major financial and business centre in Barcelona. Since the 1980s it has enjoyed an excellent system of internal communications. And it is also directly linked with one of the EU's main growth areas, the Mediterranean coastal area of southern France and northern Italy.

In all these respects conditions are very different along the northern Atlantic coast, the part of Spain which has lost most ground in the last few decades. From being among the country's most prosperous regions the Basque Country, and above all Asturias, have fallen down the regional league table. In the former case, a strong business tradition and a series of initiatives by a determined regional government have helped to alleviate the problems of industrial decline. Yet the peripheral position of the area as a whole relative to the main centre of the European economy means that its prospects are far from rosy.

That also applies to the southern regions of Andalusia, Extremadura and Castile-La Mancha. These continue to be the country's poorest, although the western part of Castile-Leon also contains pockets of extreme relative poverty. As such, they have been major recipients of EU regional aid. Rather more hopefully, there are signs that, as in the Basque Country, devolution is producing positive effects. There is some evidence that regional governments are more sensitive to the needs of regional economies, and quicker and more innovative in responding to them than Madrid. In a reversal of previous experience, the poorer regions were less badly hit by the recession of the early 1990s than the country as a whole. And, albeit slowly, the gap between them and their richer neighbours is narrowing.

6.4 SPANISH COMPANIES

The basic building blocks of a country's economy are its individual companies. These can and do vary enormously in size, management structure and ownership within countries as well as between them. In Spain's case the last of these three features has been and remains of particular importance. Compared with the Anglo-Saxon countries in particular, in Spain the state's role as entrepreneur has been, and to some extent still is, an important one.

6.4.1 Public sector

The public sector of the economy embraces a number of activities that relate to the country's people as a whole. In most of the developed world, as well as administration itself they include responsibility for education, health and social services. In Spain too the state is a major employer in this capacity [6.3.4]. There, however, its role in the economy goes much further. For it has also owned, in whole or in part, a considerable number of firms operating in industries that elsewhere in the West are usually in private hands.

The Spanish state's first major venture into business was CAMPSA (*Compañía Arrendataria del Monopolio de Petróleos SA*), the oil and petrol monopoly created in 1927 by the then dictator, Primo de Rivera. However, it was under Spain's second twentieth-century dictatorship that the government became a major economic player. Partly from the same desire as that of Primo to prevent the penetration of foreign companies, partly because the state was the only significant source of capital after the Civil War, the Franco regime became involved in many diverse industries.

In 1941 Franco set up a state holding company, the National Industry Agency (*Instituto Nacional de Industria/INI*), to oversee the government's rapidly burgeoning interests. Some of these, however, he assigned to an expanded Directorate-General of State Assets (*Dirección General del Patrimonio del Estado/ DGPE*), which dated from the previous century. By the time of his death these two bodies had a considerable presence in many sectors of the economy.

Thereafter the public sector grew further as a result of industrial restructuring in the 1980s [6.1.2]. In a number of industries acquisition by the state was the only way of preserving either jobs or a Spanish presence, or both. By 1988 the INI had become Spain's largest industrial conglomerate. More than 150,000 workers were employed in the widely diverse companies – over 50 in total – in which it had holdings.

In fact, along with the illogical division between the INI and DGPE, excessive diversity was one of the public sector's main problems. Another was the unproductive, loss-making character of many of the companies it had acquired. These considerations led the government to implement major changes. In 1981 the National Hydrocarbons Agency (*Instituto Nacional de Hidrocarburos/INH*) was created, bringing together the INI's various petroleum and petrochemical interests in a separate unit. In a number of other cases, companies in the same or related fields were merged in order to create more viable entities.

The Socialist governments of the 1980s also took steps to rationalize the overall structure of the public sector by clarifying the roles of the INI and DGPE. The latter, subsequently renamed as the State Assets Group (*Grupo Patrimonio*), became the holding company for a diverse range of operations, mainly related to some sort of government or monopoly service. A new holding company, *Teneo*, was set up within the INI, to oversee companies capable of showing a profit, and hence with potential for privatization.

The INI was left with direct responsibility for those firms which, for various reasons, were incapable of surviving unsupported in the marketplace, mainly in declining traditional industries. The division was by no means clear, however. The notoriously inefficient national airline, *Iberia*, was assigned to *Teneo* – indeed, the firms within the new group generally failed to show the desired profitability. On the other hand, the highly profitable telecommunications monopoly, *Telefónica*, was assigned to the State Assets Group.

From the late 1980s onwards the Socialist government began to privatize various state-owned companies. Some were sold off directly to private sector firms while several of the largest were floated on the stock market, including *Telefónica*, the electricity company *Endesa*, and the oil firm *Repsol* set up within INH in 1981. In the last two, as in most of the larger companies affected, the government retained 50 per cent of the stock, and thus a decisive voice in company policy.

Also partially privatized was *Argentaria*, the state banking corporation. This was created in 1991 by bringing together in a single federated entity a number of public financial institutions, including the Post Office Savings Bank (*Caja Postal de Ahorros*) as well as the Overseas Trade Bank and the Official Credit Agency [6.3.3]. By 1996 three-quarters of *Argentaria*'s shares had been sold through the stock market; shortly thereafter it was acquired by the *Banco Bilbao Vizcaya*, one of the leading private banks [6.3.3].

This whole process was subject to virtually no public scrutiny; it was never debated in Parliament, and the key decisions seem to have been taken by the powerful Finance and Economics Ministry [1.4.5] in consultation with the banks. In line with this approach, one of the Socialists' last acts before they left office in 1996 was to dissolve the INI. Its functions were assumed by two new entities more independent of public oversight: the State Industrial Holding Company (*Sociedad Estatal de Participaciones Industriales/SEPI*) and the Spanish Industry Agency (*Agencia Industrial Española/AIE*).

Under the new conservative government, privatization was taken a step further. The remaining state holdings in a number of companies, including *Repsol*, *Argentaria* and *Telefónica*, were sold off. Many observers felt that in most cases the effect was merely to create private rather than public monopolies, or situations of extreme market dominance. Nevertheless, none of the cases were referred by the government to the Competition Commission (*Tribunal de Defensa de la Competencia/TDC*). There were also more serious allegations that businessmen close to the ruling People's Party were given favourable treatment in the sales. *Telefónica*, Spain's second largest company, came under the control of Juan Villalonga, a close associate of Prime Minister José María Aznar.

6.4.2 Private sector

The most obvious characteristic of Spanish private sector firms is their small size. Numerically both industry and the service sector are dominated by SMEs, that is small and medium-sized enterprises (*pequeñas y medianas empresas/ pymes*). Over 90 per cent of firms employ less than 100 people. In fact, the most common form of business operation in Spain continues to be the sole trader (*comerciante*).

Of course, larger firms provide a disproportionate share of both employment and output. Yet even Spain's largest companies are relatively small by international standards. In 1999, only five figured among the world's top 500 by earnings; of these, three were former state-owned monopolies – *Repsol* (122nd), *Telefónica* (164th) and *Endesa* (330th) [6.4.1] – and two banks – BSCH (148th) and BBVA (326th) [6.3.3]. Moreover, many of the largest firms in Spain are owned by foreign interests (see Table 6.1).

The problems posed by small scale have led to the formation of cooperatives in certain areas and sectors (e.g. wine production). The best-known example is the group founded in Mondragón, in the Basque province of Guipúzcoa, in the 1950s. Its activities have since expanded throughout the region and beyond, and now encompass a wide range of activities including a domestic appliance manufacturer (*Fagor*) and a supermarket chain (*Eroski*).

Other than cooperatives, firms are of four main types. The first corresponds roughly to the British concept of the partnership (*sociedad colectiva*); in such firms the partners (*socios*) are personally liable in the event of bankruptcy (*insolvencia*). By contrast, in a limited partnership (*sociedad en comandita*) some or all of the partners have liabilities limited to their initial capital participation. Companies of these types are identified by the suffixes *y Compañía* (*y Cía*) and *Sociedad en Comandita* (SC) respectively. Neither is common in Spain.

The remaining two types of business association are forms of limited company, corresponding broadly – but not exactly – to UK private and public companies. Under the 1990 Companies Act (*Ley de Sociedades*) the conditions governing their structure and operation were substantially revised. One result was to save from extinction the Spanish equivalent of the private

Table 6.1 Spain's largest companies, 1999 (excludes financial sector)

Company	Business
Repsol (S)	Energy (hydrocarbons, gas)
Telefónica (S)	Telecommunications
Endesa (S)	Energy (electricity)
TI Telefónica Internacional España	Telecommunications
El Corte Inglés	Retail distribution (department stores, hypermarkets)
Altadis (S)	Cigarettes and tobacco; distribution (formerly Tabacalera)
CEPSA	Energy (hydrocarbons, gas)
FASA-Renault España (F)	Cars and components
Centros Comerciales Carrefour (F)	Retail distribution (hypermarkets)
Iberdrola	Energy (electricity)
Seat (F)	Cars and components
Opel España (F)	Cars and components
Citroën Hispania (F)	Cars and components
Ford España (F)	Cars and components
Eroski	Retail distribution (hypermarkets)
Fomento de Construcción y Contratos	Construction and property
Volkswagen Audi España (F)	Vehicle dealers
Iberia (S)	Air travel
Telefónica Moviles España	Telecommunications
Grupos Dragados	Construction and property
Aceralia (S)	Steelmaking
Gas Natural (S)	Energy (gas)
Peugeot España (F)	Cars and components
BP Oil España (F)	Energy (hydrocarbons)
Cepsa Estaciones de Servicios	Energy retailing
RENFE (S)	Railways and bus services
Mercadona	Retail distribution (hypermarkets)
Unión Fenosa	Energy (electricity)
Mercedes Benz España (F)	Cars and components
ACS	Construction and property

Notes: F = Foreign (non-Spanish) controlling interest. S = Current or former state holding.

limited company (*Sociedad de Responsabilidad Limitada/SL*). For this type of enterprise there is no longer any upper limit on the company's capital (*capital social*) as recorded in the Register of Companies (*Registro Mercantil*); the minimum required is 3005 (previously 500,000 pesetas). The capital is held in the form of shares; as and when they are offered for sale the existing owners and the company itself have the right of first refusal. These and other stipulations ensure that the typical Spanish private limited company is a family firm (*empresa familiar*).

The reason why the 1990 Act resulted in a revival of the private company was that, for the first time, it set a minimum on the capital required to form a public company (*Sociedad Anónima/SA*). Currently this stands at 60,101 (10 million pesetas). Public companies are also distinguished from private ones by the fact that their shares can be freely traded. In some, but not all cases, trade occurs through the mechanism of a stock exchange listing (*cotización*). Changes of share ownership do not have to be recorded in the Register of Companies, as is the case for private limited companies – hence the Spanish name.

By law, a public company is required to hold an annual general meeting of shareholders (*Junta de Accionistas*), which must approve the annual report and set a dividend. Between such meetings the company's affairs are run by the board (*Consejo de Administración*), made up of directors (*consejeros*) elected by the AGM. The board has the power to appoint one of its members as managing director (*consejero delegado*), who then exercises in the board's name the powers bestowed on it by law, and by the AGM.

6.5 GLOSSARY

adquisición f	purchase; takeover
agencia de contratación f	employment agency
agricultor m	(arable) farmer
agrios mpl	citrus fruits
agro m	agriculture
ajuste m	adjustment; reduction
ajuste de plantilla m	job losses, redundancies
ajuste presupuestario m	cut in (government) spending
ajuste salarial m	wage cut
aparcero m	sharecropper
apertura f	opening-up (of economy to outside world/competition)
arcas del estado fpl	government coffers, the Treasury
arrendatorio m	leaseholder
atomización f	fragmentation (of economy), existence of many small firms
autónomo m	self-employed person
autoridad laboral f	employment authority
ayuda f	grant
banda ancha/estrecha f	broad/narrow band (of EMS)
barreras aduaneras fpl	customs barriers
barreras no tarifarias fpl	non-tariff barriers
bienes de equipo mpl	capital goods
bolsa f	stock exchange
caja de ahorros f	savings bank
caladero m	fishing ground
calentamiento m	overheating (of the economy)
casa matriz f	parent company

cierre m	(factory) closure
comerciante m	(sole) trader
comercio m	trade; shop
comercio exterior m	foreign trade
concentración parcelaria f	rationalization of landholding structure
congelación salarial f	wage freeze
consejero m	company director
consejero delegado m	managing director
Consejo de Administración m	Board of Directors
contingente m	(import) quota
contratación f	hiring (of labour)
contrato a tiempo completo/parcial m	full/part-time contract
contrato de aprendizaje m	apprenticeship
contrato de duración indefinida m	permanent contract
contrato en prácticas m	work placement
contrato temporal m	temporary/fixed-term contract
contribuyente mf	taxpayer
convenio colectivo m	collective agreement
cosecha f	crop; harvest
cotización f	share price; exchange rate; social security contribution
crisis f	crisis; recession
crudos mpl	(crude) oil
cuota empresarial f	employer's social security contribution
déficit exterior m	foreign deficit
déficit público m	public sector deficit
demanda laboral f	demand for labour
desarme arancelario m	removal of customs barriers
desequilibrio m	imbalance; problem
desequilibrios territoriales mpl	regional imbalances
desmantelamiento m	removal (of trade barriers)
despido m	dismissal, sacking
despido colectivo m	dismissal of a number of employees
despido libre m	employer's right to (hire and) fire
destrucción de empleo(s) f	job losses
deuda del estado f	government debt/bonds
devaluación f	devaluation; fall (in value of currency)
divisas fpl	foreign currency
economía sumergida f	informal/black economy
eje mediterráneo/atlántico m	Mediterranean/Atlantic coastal strip
empleo m	employment; job
empresa deficitaria f	loss-making firm
empresa familiar f	family firm
empresa nacional f	Spanish firm; domestic firm
Encuesta de Población Activa f	Official Labour-force Survey
endeudamiento público m	public/national debt
enfriamiento m	cooling-down
estacionalidad f	seasonal nature
estanflación f	stagflation (simultaneous stagnation and inflation)

Estatuto de los Trabajadores m	Workers' Charter
estructura agraria f	structure of land-ownership
excedente m	surplus
éxodo rural m	rural depopulation, flight from the land
expediente m	authorization
explotación f	farm, (land)holding
extinción f	termination (of a contract)
filial f	subsidiary
fiscalidad f	taxation; tax rate
flexibilización f	making the labour market more flexible/less rigid
formación continua f	in-service training
fraude fiscal m	tax evasion/fraud
fusión f	merger
ganadero m	livestock farmer
grandes superficies fpl	large-scale retail outlet
grupo m	group (of companies), conglomerate
holding m	holding company
horario comercial m	permitted shop opening hours
horario laboral m	working hours
horas extra(ordinarias) fpl	overtime
hostelería f	hotel and restaurant trade
impuesto de sociedades m	corporation tax
impuesto sobre el trabajo m	'jobs tax'
impuesto sobre el valor añadido (IVA) m	value added tax (VAT)
impuesto sobre la renta de las personas físicas (IRPF) m	income tax
indemnización f	compensation; severance pay
industria f	industry; firm
industria auxiliar f	component industry/firm
insolvencia f	bankruptcy
Instituto Nacional de Empleo (INEM) m	National Employment Agency
invernadero m	greenhouse
inversión en cartera f	portfolio investment
inversión en el extranjero f	investment abroad, outward investment
inversión extranjera f	foreign investment, inward investment
jornada laboral f	total working time/hours (usually weekly)
jornalero m	day labourer
jubilación anticipada f	early retirement
Junta de Accionistas f	Annual General Meeting (AGM)
latifundio m	large estate
medidas deflacionistas fpl	anti-inflation measures/policies
mentalidad empresarial f	entrepreneurial spirit
mercado laboral/de trabajo m	labour/jobs market
mercado nacional m	domestic market
minifundio m	very small farm/holding
minifundismo m	predominance of excessively small farms
minifundismo empresarial m	(see *atomización*)

minorista m	retailer
moderación salarial f	wage moderation
monte de piedad m	pawnbrokers
nómina f	payroll
obra social f	non-lucrative work (of savings banks)
oferta de trabajo f	job offer
oferta laboral f	labour supply
oferta pública de adquisición (OPA) f	takeover bid
Organización de los Países Exportadores de Petróleo (OPEP) f	OPEC
parcela f	plot (of land)
paro de larga duración m	long-term unemployment
paro femenino/juvenil/ masculino m	female/youth/male unemployment
persona en edad de trabajar f	person of working age
pesca f	fishing (industry)
pesca costera f	inshore fishing
pesca de altura f	high-seas fishing
política cambiaria f	exchange rate policy
política monetaria f	monetary policy; exchange rate policy (loose usage)
presión fiscal f	tax burden
primicias fpl	early-season produce
productos mpl	products; (agricultural) produce
productos elaborados mpl	finished products
pyme f	SME (small/medium-sized firm)
rama f	branch; industry
recaudación f	tax receipts; tax collection
reciclaje m	retraining; recycling
reconversión (industrial) f	industrial restructuring
recuperación f	recovery
reforma agraria f	land reform
Registro Mercantil m	Register of Companies
remesas fpl	remittances
revaluación f	rise (in value of currency)
riego m	irrigation
rigidez f	(source of) rigidity (in the labour market)
salario m	wage; earnings
Salario Mínimo Interprofesional (SMI) m	standard minimum wage
saneamiento m	rationalization; streamlining; setting on sound financial footing
sector m	sector; industry
sector agropecuario m	agriculture
sector alimenticio m	food and drink industry
sector automovilístico m	vehicle/car industry
sector hortifrutícola m	fruit and vegetable growing
sector lácteo m	dairy industry

sector naval m	ship-building industry
sector pesquero m	fishing industry
sector productivo m	manufacturing industry
sector siderúrgico m	(iron and) steel industry
sector turístico m	tourist industry
sobreexplotación f	over-exploitation; overfishing
sociedad anónima f	public limited company
sociedad colectiva f	partnership
sociedad de responsabilidad limitada f	private limited company
sociedad en comandita f	limited partnership
socio m	partner
subvención f	subsidy
tasa de actividad f	participation rate, economic activity rate
tasa de desempleo/paro f	unemployment rate
tipo central m	central rate (of currency in EMS)
trabajador cualificado/sin cualificar m	skilled / unskilled worker
trabajador por cuenta ajena m	employee
trabajador por cuenta propia m	self-employed person
turno m	shift

7

THE ENVIRONMENT

Throughout the Western world, concern for the environment has grown with the realization that economic development has negative as well as positive effects. Given that Spain long missed out on the advantages of growth, it is scarcely surprising that, as yet, it has paid relatively little attention to the drawbacks. The result is that a country which naturally is one of the most favoured in Europe now faces increasing environmental problems. This chapter begins by looking at those caused directly by pollution. It then goes on to examine underlying changes to the country's landscape and their effects in both ecological and economic terms. Finally it considers the response to these issues in terms of attempts to protect Spain's environment.

7.1 POLLUTION

Precisely because of its nature as a single system, it is hard to classify into distinct categories the impact of human activities on the environment. In Spain as elsewhere, the changes they produce in one aspect inevitably have knock-on effects in others, often apparently unrelated. Perhaps the best starting point is to examine the process known as pollution (*contaminación*), that is the changes produced in the chemical make-up of the elements essential for human, and other life: air, water and the earth itself.

7.1.1 Air pollution

One aspect of the environment in which Spain has, as yet, experienced few problems is that of air quality. In that sense, at least, the belated development of industry was advantageous. Only in small areas of the country did economic development follow the 'classic' pattern common in the UK and northern Europe and based on heavy industry. In addition, Spain's location at the western end of the European continent brings the further advantage that the prevailing winds carry relatively few airborne pollutants. Nevertheless, this positive picture must be severely qualified in two respects.

First, air pollution (*contaminación atmosférica*) is a significant problem in a number of centres which industrialized relatively early. Particularly badly affected is the Greater Bilbao area, the country's main industrial centre up to the early 1980s, which now reputedly has the poorest air quality in the EU. On over 100 days per year the exposure level (*nivel de inmisión*) of its inhabitants to a range of airborne pollutants exceeds official health guidelines. The result is a very high incidence of respiratory illness. Similar, if less grave, effects are observable in the Avilés area of Asturias.

Air pollution also reaches severe proportions in and around centres where industrial development was promoted by the Franco regime. These include Huelva on the southern Atlantic coast; the eastern Mediterranean ports of Cartagena and Tarragona; and Puertollano, in the province of Ciudad Real. The activities principally to blame are the chemical industry, oil refining and petrochemical manufacture, and the generation of electricity in fossil-fuel-fired power stations (*centrales térmicas*).

The second important exception to Spain's generally low level of air pollution comes in the country's two main metropolitan areas, centred on Madrid and Barcelona. Especially in the latter the presence of older industry is a factor here too, but only one among several. In both cities, road traffic has reached extremely high densities, to which the government has reacted only recently and as yet without great success. It was also slow to encourage the use of unleaded petrol (*gasolina sin plomo*), which only became cheaper than leaded varieties in 1990. Emissions from domestic heating systems are a further burden on air quality, especially in Madrid. The capital's geographical position in a shallow, elevated basin, along with the climatic phenomenon of temperature inversion, gives rise in winter to the characteristic 'beret' of visibly polluted air hanging over the city.

Another environmental problem affecting the air in Spain's urban areas, although not strictly speaking pollution, is regarded as such in semi-technical language: noise pollution (*contaminación acústica*). It is a field where international comparisons are fraught with difficulties, due to differences in measurement techniques; so figures suggesting that Spain rivals Japan as the world's noisiest country must be treated with caution, particularly as they have been contested by Spanish official bodies.

Nevertheless, even these authorities' own data make clear that noise levels in central Madrid regularly exceed international guidelines. Moreover, those figures relate to background noise levels and do not take into consideration the situation of workers involved in particularly noisy activities. In such cases, the effects on individuals depend on the observance of prescribed safety precautions, often lax in Spain.

7.1.2 Water pollution and dumping of wastes

In the case of water quality any advantages accruing to Spain from its late economic development have been more than neutralized. Indeed, the problems the country faces in this area are some of the most severe of all. They derive from emissions of various sorts, as well as from the dumping of waste products, a practice which also has other damaging effects.

As elsewhere, a major cause of water pollution (*contaminación del agua*) is industrial emissions. Their severity in Spain can be traced largely to the very special conditions of industrial development during the Franco era. Many of the industries which grew up then used technically outdated processes whose viability depended partly on low labour costs, but partly on the absence of regulations requiring firms to bear the costs of reprocessing harmful wastes (*residuos*). Two especially important examples were the chemical industry and paper manufacture; in the Basque Country in particular emissions from paper mills (*papelerías*) produced very high levels of river pollution.

By the 1970s many towns and villages depended for employment on highly polluting activities, and the absence of controls was taken for granted. In this situation the further wave of industrialization in the 1980s had catastrophic effects. Between 1983 and 1988 production of toxic wastes increased by 300 per cent, and even the government ministry responsible admitted that less than a third of the total was being monitored. Inevitably a significant proportion found its way into water courses.

Mining activities of various sorts are another notorious source of pollution. In 1998 the collapse of a retaining dam at an operation near Aznalcóllar, in Seville province, released millions of cubic metres of toxic water and mud into the River Guadiamar. Much good agricultural land was severely damaged as a result, although mercifully it proved possible to minimize the impact on the Doñana wetland area [7.2.3].

Just over a decade earlier, in 1987, 20,000 water birds died in Doñana when their habitat suffered contamination (*intoxicación*), the cause on that occasion being pesticides used by rice farmers. In general, agriculture is another major source of pollutants entering Spain's supplies of surface and ground water (*aguas superficiales y subterráneas*), since newer, more intensive practices employ considerable amounts of pesticides and artificial fertilizers (*abonos químicos*). These are widely used in greenhouse production of early fruit and vegetables along the Mediterranean coast, especially in Huelva and Almería provinces.

Spain's households also contribute significantly to water pollution because of low levels of sewage treatment. Despite the construction of new treatment plants (*depuradoras*), significant amounts of raw sewage continue to be pumped directly into water courses; less than half of all domestic sewage is adequately treated. The problems are particularly grave in areas of rapid population growth, and in some coastal areas. Along the Mediterranean coast, for example, as much as 30 per cent of sewage passes untreated into the sea.

Spain's coastal waters (*aguas litorales*) are also affected by dumping of solid wastes. Particularly important in this regard are the mining operations carried out at Portman, east of Cartagena on the Murcia coast. Lead and zinc have been mined there for centuries, but it was under the Franco regime that a massive open-cast operation got under way. One of the largest of its kind in the world, this involved washing earth directly into the bay using a mixture of sea water and highly toxic chemicals, including cyanide and sulphur. The bay is now silted up and badly contaminated; a large area on the landward side has been turned into a veritable moonscape. In 1988 the EU obliged the authorities to take action as a result of which the impact of the operations was reduced, but they nevertheless continue.

Inevitably a major contributor to pollution of the seas around Spain is the oil industry. There has been only one major incident so far, in the winter of 1992/93. The tanker *Aegean Sea* ran aground off Corunna with considerable damage to marine life, including economically important shellfish stocks. However, spillages from tankers – which may or may not be deliberate – occur on a regular basis.

Deliberate dumping at sea has also been practised in a number of cases with the active encouragement of the Spanish authorities. For 15 years from 1974 they allowed a chemical firm to dump titanium dioxide waste in the ocean 55 km off Cádiz, until protests from local people forced a reassessment of the situation. Up to 1983 foreign nuclear waste (*residuos nucleares*) was dumped at a site 700 km off the Galician coast, making it the world's largest off-shore deposit of such material.

More recently Spain's own mounting stocks of nuclear waste have begun to pose a major problem. By the 1990s over 500 tons of highly radioactive waste were stored at the country's power stations; by the year 2020 the figure is anticipated to rise to some 6000 tons. As in other countries the search for permanent sites has met with understandable resistance from people in the areas potentially affected. At the end of 1992 the first permanent disposal site (*cementerio nuclear*) for low and medium level waste was opened, at El Cabril in Córdoba province.

Finally, the more mundane topic of general household and other non-toxic solid waste is also problematic. Apart from being extremely intrusive visually, the wholly or partially uncontrolled dumping evident around so many Spanish settlements can also be dangerous. In 1996 an official dump at Bens, outside the Galician city of Corunna, collapsed over a cliff, killing one person and causing extensive damage to the surrounding terrain. This particular case did have a positive impact, however. Subsequently Corunna has set in place a coordinated disposal system which includes household waste separation (*recogida selectiva*), and which has achieved international recognition as a model.

7.2 LANDSCAPE CHANGE

Environmental damage does not, of course, begin and end with the question of pollution. As well as the relatively direct effects of waste dumping and other emissions, change in the environment as the result of human actions involves also more complex and longer-term processes. Some operate at continental or world scale; thus Spain too is affected by the thinning of the ozone layer (*capa de ozono*) or the greenhouse effect (*efecto invernadero*). Other such processes, however, are more localized, in the sense that they operate exclusively or with particular intensity within individual countries. In Spain, two are especially important.

7.2.1 Deforestation and reforestation

The story that in ancient times a squirrel could travel from Gibraltar to the Pyrenees without touching the ground may be apocryphal. What is undeniable is that Spain's once vast woods have been severely depleted over the centuries. It is true that deforestation has been partially reversed in recent years but that has brought new problems.

It was the Franco regime, from the 1940s on, that began to reverse the process of deforestation, but not for ecological considerations – nowhere had they reached the political agenda at that time. Instead its massive programme of reforestation was promoted by economic concerns. The species planted were chosen for their rapid growth, many of them imports to Spain such as the Australian eucalyptus. In addition to the implications in terms of habitat change [7.2.3], this policy has also had an unintended side effect which works against its original objective.

For, as well as growing quickly, eucalyptus and the various species of pine introduced also burn easily. And the biggest threat to Spain's woodland (*bosque*) today comes from the forest fires (*incendios forestales*) which became alarmingly frequent in the 1980s and have literally flared up again repeatedly since 1994. Such fires have hit the new species hard, but not exclusively.

Evidently other factors are at work too, some of which are inherent to the Mediterranean climate and vegetation prevalent in much of the country. Summers are long, hot and dry, lightning a frequent occurrence; indigenous woodland also burns relatively easily, and is intermixed with highly inflammable stretches of scrubland (*monte*). Yet these factors do not explain the upsurge of fires, especially as one of the worst hit regions has been Galicia, where the climate is Atlantic in nature.

One cause there and elsewhere in the country is the declining economic value of Spain's woodland, most of which is privately owned. With wood no longer used significantly for heating, there is no incentive to carry out the work of selectively lopping branches, collecting fallen ones and clearing undergrowth. The resultant dense mass of live and dead timber both burns easily and makes extinction difficult; it cannot, however, explain why fires start so frequently.

That can only be the result of human action, which is increasingly impacting on woodland. Population growth and changing leisure patterns are bringing more people into the Spanish countryside; many, unlike their forebears, are completely unacquainted with it. Carelessness of various types undoubtedly causes many fires. Nor are the countryside's own inhabitants blameless in this regard; one recent study in the Valencia region found careless burning of stubble (*rastrojo*) and pasture land (*pastizales*) to be the main cause of fires.

These are not always the result of mere carelessness, however. Rural resentment against re- and afforestation is based on a number of grounds including loss of farming land and damage to it allegedly caused by woodland wildlife. Nor is it restricted to farmers; in some areas it appears to have become part of local tradition, perhaps dating back to the loss of former common lands in the nineteenth century. Sometimes, too, burning of woodland seems to be used as a means of settling private disputes. For all these reasons, some fires – no one can be sure what proportion – are undoubtedly the result of deliberate action by local people.

Finally it is suspected that larger interests are also at work. In some cases logging firms (*industrias madereras*) have been accused of responsibility, their alleged object being to buy up large quantities of fire-damaged, but still usable wood at knock-down prices. However, the most serious allegations have been levelled at property developers (*empresas inmobiliarias*), especially in areas close to the Mediterranean coast where there is a lot of pressure for out-of-town housing developments (*urbanizaciones*).

There prime building land is often wooded, and subject to planning restrictions. Some of the worst fires have removed the woodland such restrictions were designed to protect – and hence also the arguments against development. Economically that can be very attractive not just for the developer but for the local economy as a whole. For that reason suspicion has occasionally been voiced against local councillors; the interests of their municipality, and also the prospect of party or personal rake-offs [2.1.3], provide possible motives for collusion with fire-raisers.

To the extent that such suspicions are justified, it is clear that more than environmental measures will be needed to remove the main contemporary threat to Spain's woodland. However, that is not to say that such measures cannot help, and indeed in a number of areas they are being taken. Both central and regional governments have undertaken campaigns designed to increase environmental awareness [7.3.2]. More directly, Galicia has had particular success with simple measures designed to stop fires spreading once started, for example through the systematic cutting of firebreaks (*cortafuegos*).

7.2.2 Desertification

Deforestation is a particularly serious problem in Spain because it, in turn, is one of the main causes of a second process of long-term landscape change – desertification. Here a terminological point should be clarified. Internationally a distinction is drawn between desertification – the process by which arid land becomes effectively incapable of sustaining life, in other words a desert – and desertization, the abandonment of an area by its human population. The same distinction is also made in official Spanish usage. In Spain, however, the latter phenomenon was already well known as 'depopulation' (*despoblación*). As a result, the less clumsy *desertización* is frequently used, even by experts, when speaking of landscape change in areas of the country which were long since virtually uninhabited.

Such desertification, most commonly associated with Africa, is a threat facing a number of countries in southern Europe. Since the early 1980s Italy and Greece have participated, along with Spain, in a joint Campaign against Desertification in the Mediterranean Region (*Lucha contra la Desertificación en el Mediterráneo/LUCDEME*). However, the scale of the problem is considerably greater in Spain. Already the country has Europe's only genuine desert, an area in Almería province famous – or notorious – as a Western film-set. But desertification is also a real threat in other provinces of Andalusia, in parts of the Extremadura and Valencia regions, and above all in the interior of Murcia.

Deforestation [7.2.1] is clearly an important factor in the erosion which is the prelude to desertification. In Spain this is caused less by wind (*erosión eólica*) than by the action of water (*erosión hídrica*). Here, as with deforestation, the Mediterranean climate plays a key part, with its highly irregular rainfall pattern (*pluviometría*). Lengthy dry spells are typically broken by torrential rainstorms (*trombas de agua*), which in the absence of tree cover wash away large amounts of topsoil.

Agricultural practices (*técnicas agrícolas*) have also contributed to erosion. In Castile, in particular, extensive cereal farming put a premium on bringing as much land as possible under the plough. With the advent of mechanization more marginal land, especially on slopes, was cleared of its natural vegetation and worked with heavy tractors, becoming more vulnerable as a result. Elsewhere overgrazing (*sobrepastoreo*) or other inappropriate land-uses produced similar results. The inefficient methods and general neglect typical of the large estates of the south [6.3.1] may also have played a part.

In recent years such factors have probably become less important; in particular the EU's encouragement of land set-aside (*abandono de tierras*) has taken much marginal agricultural land back out of production. Yet the threat of desertification has not been diminished, and indeed was accentuated by the almost total absence of rainfall throughout much of southern and central Spain during the period 1990–95. The drought (*sequía*), however, may only have served to divert attention from the most serious cause of desertification, which, although water-related, is not climatic but synthetic in origin.

Its cause is excessive use of what is becoming a scarce resource worldwide, particularly in countries where supply is uncertain, such as Spain. There rising water demand comes from various sources. Both domestic and industrial consumption are partly to blame; in some localities, especially on the Andalusian coast, heavy watering of golf courses is also a factor. However, the main cause is the recent large increase in the amount of agricultural land under irrigation.

This technique is used both for intensive fruit and vegetable farming, concentrated along the south-eastern and southern Mediterranean coast, and for other crops, most notably rice, of which the Murcia region is now a major producer. The effect has been a significant reduction in the water table in a number of areas – it appears to be particularly marked on Gran Canaria, where water demand comes mainly from tourism. The consequence is to increase the danger of erosion and thus desertification.

In some coastal areas the drop in the water table has allowed sea water to enter the underground reserves known as aquifers, which in turn affects water used for irrigation. Thus in Almería the presence of salt in irrigation water is thought to be responsible for a reduction in crop yields. More importantly, it gives rise to excessive concentrations of salt in the earth (*salinización*), a further cause of desertification.

Even without sea water contamination it is known that irrigation can produce the same result. High salt concentrations in Extremadura are believed to have been caused in this way when local farmers were encouraged to abandon traditional crops on unirrigated land in favour of others, especially asparagus, which require irrigation. Extremadura has now joined the list of Spanish regions where desertification is a significant danger.

7.2.3 Ecological and economic impact

Both deforestation and desertification are extreme examples of a more general phenomenon. Climate and landscape change results in the loss of natural habitats and so to a decline in biodiversity, that is, of the wealth of plant and animal species. It is an important issue in Spain, which hosts a considerable number of rare, even endangered species. Western Europe's last brown bear colony is perhaps the best-known example, but there are many others, often surprising. The evergreen oakwoods of Extremadura, for instance, are the world's largest, and home to the black vulture and other bird species found nowhere else in Europe.

Alongside the oakwoods themselves, Extremadura also contains large expanses of a habitat effectively unique to Spain, the thinly oak-covered parkland known as *dehesa*. It is, in fact, an artificial landscape, produced by partial deforestation to allow various forms of extensive agriculture (wheat-farming, pig-rearing, cork collection, etc.). The uneconomic nature of such activities in conventional terms has led to pressures for more profitable uses, irrigation and so potential desertification. However, whether or not that drastic stage is reached, upsetting the delicate balance of uses which maintains the *dehesa* in its current condition will inevitably lead to serious losses in terms of biodiversity.

Wetlands (*zonas húmedas*) are by no means unique to Spain but are important there because of the country's location on the migration routes of various species of waterfowl. As well as by direct reclamation for agricultural use, their area is being steadily reduced by increasing irrigation and the consequent fall in the water table [7.2.2]. Three of the most important wetland areas have received some protection through designation as national or regional parks [7.3.1]. Such measures, however, do little to maintain the water table; in the largest wetland area of all, the *Coto Doñana*, it is estimated to be falling by around one metre every year.

Landscape change is detrimental not just in ecological terms but also in the economic ones that dominate official thinking. Especially as the country seeks to diversify its tourist industry away from the Mediterranean coast, it is coming to be recognized that the attractiveness of landscapes – and habitats – is a key asset in maintaining Spain's market leadership. This applies not only to the conservation of hitherto unspoilt areas but also to the improvement of conditions in existing tourist areas whose appearance has suffered particularly from development's visual impact (*impacto paisajístico*).

This comes from a number of sources. One is the massive transport projects undertaken in the 1980s. Another is the common problem of uncontrolled – and sometimes even controlled – dumping of rubbish on the fringe of settlements in full view of the public. Much the most important form of visual impact, however, is tourist accommodation itself, whether in the form of medium- to large-scale holiday villages or as individual second or holiday homes.

For many years such developments were subject to only minimal planning controls; in any case they were frequently constructed without the requisite permission and rarely demolished thereafter. Since the 1988 Coastline Act (*Ley de Costas*) much greater control has been exercised. Unfortunately, however, its approval was preceded by a final orgy of visually intrusive building which blighted new stretches of coast and further worsened conditions on others.

7.3 PROTECTION OF THE ENVIRONMENT

When, in the early 1990s, Spain was a candidate to host the EU's future environmental authority the government was embarrassed by the revelation that none of its ministries included the term environment in its title. Many of the comments passed were unfair. Few governments pay more than lip-service to ecology; for many years the UK had a Ministry of the Environment which in fact had very little to do with the subject. However, it is true that Spain is not well-placed to undertake the task of protecting the environment (*defensa del medio ambiente*), not least because it lacks coherent structures to do so.

7.3.1 Environmental authorities

The oldest Spanish authorities with specifically environmental responsibilities are those which run the country's National Parks. They date back to 1918, when the first two were designated. The first park of all originally encompassed the Covadonga area of Asturias, but was expanded in 1995 to cover a much wider area of the *Picos de Europa* mountain range. The national network (*red estatal*) is currently composed of eleven parks (see Table 7.1).

Five are located in the island regions of the Balearics and Canaries, and in the Pyrenees; one (*Cabañeros*) is intended to protect a rare habitat on Spain's central plateau; and two (*Doñana* and *Daimiel*) are in wetlands areas. In addition a further important wetland in the Ebro Delta, has been created a Regional Park by the Catalan regional government. After protracted debate in the 1990s it was eventually decided to declare the Monfragüe area of Extremadura, which includes some of the country's most valuable habitats [7.2.3], not a National but a Nature Park (*Parque Natural*).

Table 7.1 National Parks

	Area in hectares	Year set up	Province
Ordesa y Monte Perdido	15,608	1918	Huesca
Teide	18,900	1954	Tenerife
La Caldera de Taburiente	4,690	1954	Tenerife (La Palma)
Aigüestortes y Lago San Mauricio[a]	14,119	1955	Lleida
Doñana	50,720	1969	Huelva/Seville
Timanfaya	5,107	1974	Gran Canaria (Lanzarote)
Las Tablas de Daimiel	1,928	1980	Ciudad Real
Garajonay	3,984	1981	Tenerife (La Gomera)
Archipiélago de Cabrera[b]	10,021	1991	Balearics (Mallorca)
Picos de Europa	64,660	1995	Asturias/Cantabria/Leon
Cabañeros	39,000	1995	Ciudad Real/Toledo
Sierra Nevada	86,208	1999	Granada/Almería

Notes: [a] Control transferred to Catalan Regional Government in 1988, but later returned to central authorities.
[b] Officially designated a 'land–sea park' (*parque marítimo-terrestre*).

Each of the National Parks has a Strategic Plan (*Plan Rector*), setting out aims and policies. Yet while they undoubtedly offer a degree of protection to sensitive areas, they also increase pressures on them by attracting visitors. Nor can the parks offer protection against practices carried on outside their boundaries which nevertheless impact strongly within them.

Spain also has various other categories of protected countryside areas (*espacios naturales protegidos/ENP*). Most owe their status essentially to being areas of natural beauty (*parajes pintorescos*), although some are nature reserves (*reservas naturales*) and others are intended to conserve stocks of game. The level of protection offered is, in practice, low.

After the original National Parks, the next public authority with environmental responsibilities to be set up was the National Nature Conservancy Agency (*Instituto Nacional para la Conservación de la Naturaleza/ICONA*). Created in 1971 under the auspices of the Ministry of Agriculture, Fisheries and Food, ICONA had wide and rather ill-defined responsibilities covering a number of aspects of conservation, as well as for fighting forest fires [7.2.1]. It also had the task – a considerable one in Spain – of issuing shooting and angling permits.

A year after ICONA's establishment the importance of environmental considerations for government was recognized, at least formally, with the creation of an Interministerial Environment Committee (*Comisión Interministerial del Medio Ambiente*). This was dissolved in 1987, however, since when coordination has taken place through the Under-secretaries' Committee [1.5.2] and a special cabinet committee. Meanwhile, the 1978 Constitution had included something close to an injunction to set up a government agency specifically to protect the environment. The Environment Directorate-General (*Dirección General del Medio Ambiente/DGMA*) set up the same year inside the then Public Works Ministry fell well short of that. Not till 1990 was the DGMA given its own Secretary of State [1.5.2], and only in 1993 was the term 'environment' included in the Ministry's title.

In 1996, however, a separate Environment Ministry was finally created. Known as MIMAM, it assumed the responsibilities of the old DGMA. It also incorporated ICONA, which became the Nature Conservancy Directorate-General (*Dirección General de Conservación de la Naturaleza*). However, despite the disappearance of a separate Industry and Energy ministry, MIMAM was not given responsibility for energy conservation, which went to the Economics Ministry instead. Urban and rural planning powers were retained by the renamed Development Ministry [1.4.5]. And the Nature Protection Service (*Servicio de Protección de la Naturaleza/SEPRONA*) set up by the Civil Guard [10.2.1] is responsible to the Interior Ministry.

The position is further complicated by the fact that since 1983 autonomous regions have also had environmental responsibilities. Indeed, this is an area in which the division of powers between them and the central government is especially unclear [3.1.3]. Sometimes regions have shown a sense of initiative lacking at the centre. In 1984 Andalusia was the first to set up a distinct Environment Agency (*Agencia del Medio Ambiente/AMA*) in the spirit of the Constitution. Other regions, led by Madrid, Murcia, Asturias and Valencia, subsequently followed suit.

7.3.2 A question of priorities

As well as juggling with administrative structures, from 1982 successive governments have taken a number of legislative and other initiatives to protect the environment. The first major piece of legislation was the 1985 Water Act (*Ley de Aguas*), which established a National Water Board (*Consejo Nacional de Aguas*) to supervise the usage and condition of the country's supplies.

The following year framework legislation [1.3.3] on toxic wastes was introduced, and a decree issued providing for environmental impact analyses of infrastructure and other large-scale projects. There followed the 1988 Coastline Act [7.2.3], and in 1989, the Countryside Conservation Act (*Ley de Conservación de Espacios Naturales*), which brought together and rationalized the various pieces of legislation in that field.

More recently, a series of plans have been drawn up covering topics such as water and air quality, and the disposal of various types of waste. Yet, as with the earlier legislative measures, these seem usually to have been designed to meet EU requirements – on paper. Implementation remains a weak point; the Brussels authorities have several times blocked aid to Spain because it has failed to carry out adequate environmental impact analyses in practice.

Similarly, the 1983 legislation creating the concept of an environmental offence (*delito ecológico*) has had little real effect. It defines such offences solely in terms of waste dumping and emissions, thus omitting other environmentally damaging activities such as illegal building or overuse of scarce resources. The first successful prosecution did not take place until 1988, when emissions from a Catalan power station were held responsible by the courts for damage to 30,000 hectares of woodland and pasture land. However, the station's manager was given only a month's prison sentence; a requirement to reduce future emissions by fitting filters was suspended on 'economic grounds'.

Subsequently the pattern of infrequent prosecutions has been maintained, as has the tendency to show leniency to corporate offenders. On the other hand, an individual fire-raiser found guilty in 1996 of damaging an area of ecological value was given a ten-year sentence. As with the creation of specialist agencies [7.3.1], some regions have led the way in this area too by appointing special environmental prosecution services (*fiscalías de medio ambiente*). Yet, given the slowness with which the Spanish legal system acts [10.1.4], it is questionable whether prosecution can ever provide even minimally effective protection to the environment.

The 1988 Catalan trial served to highlight the underlying problem which afflicts all attempts to protect Spain's environment. It was punctuated by demonstrations from workers at the plant concerned. Fearful of losing their jobs, they were protesting against the environmentalist groups whose pressure had forced the manifestly reluctant authorities to act. In general, and despite the widespread dissatisfaction with traditional parties [2.1.1], environmentalist parties have made very little impact on the Spanish political scene.

Even more significantly, the court which delivered the 1988 judgment was not the only official body to explicitly reject their priorities. When the government announced plans for the building of 15 noxious-waste disposal plants by 1994, one of its declared aims was to avoid placing financial costs on the waste producers. Much more often, the order of priorities is implicit, as in official reluctance to prosecute environmental offenders. At the regional and municipal level it is evident in connivance at the manipulation of bathing water quality figures and evasion of planning restrictions.

More subtly, a belief in the absolute priority of economic growth (*desarrollismo*) is built into administrative structures and government thinking. Despite the creation of an Environment Ministry (MIMAM), several of central government's environment-related responsibilities remain in the hands of ministries principally concerned with promoting economic activity rather than supervising and controlling its unwanted effects [7.3.1]. Moreover, many of MIMAM's staff came originally from ICONA, an organization dominated by foresters (*ingenieros de montes*) whose values were essentially those of traditional engineers. A similar ethos prevails in its waterworks section, which has repeatedly been shown to have the greatest political clout.

The National Water Plan (*Plan Hidrológico Nacional/PHN*), for which MIMAM is responsible, illustrates the point well. It pays lip service to the objectives, set out in the 1985 Water Act, of preventing water pollution and overuse. Yet it fails to address them. Instead, it is mainly concerned with engineering projects, the largest of which is a plan to transfer water on a massive scale from the Ebro to the Segura, for the benefit of farmers in Valencia and Murcia. As well as opposition from environmentalists, it has therefore provoked a major outcry in Aragon and Catalonia, both of which stand to lose considerable amounts of water.

A similar set of priorities was apparent in the 1993 National Reforestation Plan (*Plan Nacional de Reforestación/PNR*), drawn up by MIMAM's predecessor. Among other provisions, it attempts to reverse previous errors by offering four times more financial support for planting indigenous species than non-indigenous ones [7.2.1]. Yet under the PNR, replanting depends on individual farmers' acceptance of grants; inevitably it will be small-scale and uncoordinated. Nor does it affect land outside agricultural use where erosion is already under way. Moreover, although the financial arrangements are clearly beneficial in a sense, they do nothing to ensure that the choice of species is made on the basis of appropriateness to the terrain concerned. In essence, the PNR is not an environmental measure but an agricultural one.

In his 2001 'state of the nation' speech Prime Minister José María Aznar devoted a significant section to environmental issues, which addressed a number of key issues. He indicated that, in future, actions damaging to the environment would be made subject to civil recourse as well as criminal prosecution [7.3.1]. He also announced prospective legislation to protect and regenerate Spain's woodland [7.2.1], as well as a national irrigation plan [7.2.2]. But, even if these initiatives do in fact see the light of day, it remains to be seen whether they will ultimately reflect environmental or other priorities.

7.4 GLOSSARY

abandono de tierras m	set-aside
abono químico m	chemical/artificial fertilizer
aguas litorales fpl	coastal waters
aguas residuales fpl	sewage
aguas subterráneas/superficiales fpl	underground/surface water
bosque m	woodland
cabecera de cuenca f	headwaters
capa de ozono f	ozone layer
cementerio nuclear m	nuclear-waste dumping facility
centrales térmicas fpl	fossil-fuel power station
conciencia (medioambiental) f	(environmental) awareness
Consejo Nacional de Aguas m	National Water Board
contaminación acústica f	noise pollution
contaminación atmosférica f	air pollution
cortafuegos m	firebreak
defensa del medio ambiente f	protection of the environment
deforestación f	deforestation
delito ecológico m	environmental offence
depuradora f	sewage treatment plant

desarrollismo m	belief in absolute priority of economic growth
desertificación f	desertification
desertización f	depopulation; desertification (see 7.2.2)
efecto invernadero m	greenhouse effect
empresa inmobiliaria f	property company/developer
empresa maderera f	logging company
erosión eólica/hídrica f	wind/water erosion
espacio natural m	countryside area
especie autóctona f	native/indigenous species
fiscalía de medio ambiente f	environmental prosecution service
gasolina sin plomo f	unleaded petrol
impacto paisajístico m	visual impact
incendio forestal m	forest fire
industria maderera f	logging company
ingeniero de montes m	forester
intoxicación f	contamination
inundación f	flood
medio ambiente m	environment
medio físico m	natural environment
monte m	scrubland
nivel de inmisión m	exposure level
papelería f	paper mill
paraje pintoresco m	area of natural beauty
pastizales mpl	grazing land
pieza cinegética f	game animal or bird
pluviometría f	rainfall pattern
rastrojo m	stubble
recogida selectiva f	(household) waste separation
reforestación f	reforestation
regadío m	land under irrigation
repoblación forestal f	(see *reforestación*)
reserva natural f	nature reserve
residuos mpl	waste(s)
salinización f	salinization, excessive build-up of salt
secano m	unirrigated land
sequía f	drought
sobrepastoreo m	overgrazing
técnica agrícola f	agricultural practice
terreno inclinado m	slope
tromba de agua f	sudden, tropical downpour
urbanización f	development (i.e. group of houses)
zona húmeda f	wetland area

8

EDUCATION

Contemporary observers have tended to be impressed by the high value placed by Spaniards of all social classes on education. They point to a seemingly insatiable demand for university places, as well as the popularity of various forms of continuing and community education. Yet growing demand has placed additional strains on what, by international standards, has historically been a very poorly resourced system. Nor were resource problems the only ones bequeathed by history; a number of issues of principle also remained unresolved in 1975. This chapter begins by examining these underlying issues, before going on to look at the way governments have addressed them and other, more immediate ones. The final section considers the way in which educational studies are structured as a result of these various reforms.

8.1 EDUCATIONAL PRINCIPLES

As Spain returned to democracy after 1975, three issues underlay the problems of its education system. All have affected most Western countries at some point. In Spain, however, the peculiar nature of the country's social and economic history meant that they had remained unresolved much longer than in its neighbours. The issues concerned could not be more fundamental; they related to the questions of who should receive education, who should provide it, and why.

8.1.1 Elite versus mass education

Compulsory education (*enseñanza obligatoria*) was introduced relatively early in Spain, by the 1867 'Moyano Act' named after the minister responsible for its passage. But, as no public funds were provided to implement it, few children received even the four-years schooling it prescribed. Education accordingly remained the preserve of an elite, geared to producing administrators for the rather small state apparatus.

In the 1930s, under the Second Republic [0.1], attempts were made to bring education to the mass of Spaniards. They included a massive programme of primary school building and corresponding teacher training. Thereafter, however, the Franco regime reverted to the traditional, elite-oriented approach.

Thus, the primary sector was neglected, with the meagre funds available going to provide secondary and tertiary education for the few. Theoretically education was compulsory to age 12; in practice, the level of coverage remained well below 100 per cent even in that age group. Along with a similar reversion to tradition in terms of content, this led to serious problems once the regime switched to an expansive economic policy after 1960 [0.2]. For it now became clear that low general levels of education were holding back the country's economic advance. A modern industrial workforce required more than the minimalist, outdated education which was all most Spaniards had received up to then.

The result of these concerns was the 1970 General Education Act (*Ley General de Educación/LGE*), again often known by the name of the responsible minister. This Villar Palasí Act implicitly shifted the emphasis onto mass education. It lengthened the period of compulsory education, to age 16 in theory, and sought to end selection at age 10. Yet, once again, provisions on paper were not fully translated into reality.

Thus little was done to ease the chronic shortage of school premises in the urban areas to which many families had moved, and no adequate budget was made available to finance the LGE's ambitious plans for vocational education [8.3.3]. In large part as a result, a significant number of children continued to leave education at 14. In addition to this problem of drop-out (*abandono*), adherence to traditional methods and content led to an alarmingly high percentage of pupils failing to complete even their compulsory studies successfully (*fracaso escolar*). In effect, the Francoist attempt to create a mass system had failed.

The return of democracy released the pent-up demand for education among the Spanish public. Anything other than a system catering for the population as a whole was now unthinkable. This inevitably increased the pressure on inadequate facilities, a problem aggravated by the effects of high birth rates in the Franco era. As a result Spain's schools suffered a lengthy period of severe overcrowding (*masificación*) which began to ease only around 1987 as the year cohorts entering the school system began to shrink. By then it had struck in even more severe form at a university sector even less equipped than schools to cope with a mass clientele.

Nevertheless, the mass-versus-elite issue continues to exist in a slightly different form: the question of equality as a value within the new system. It is reflected, for instance, in the ongoing debates about streaming in schools [8.3.1], and about access to higher education [8.2.1.3]. And it also underlies discussion of the role of private universities [8.2.1.2] and, above all, of private schools [8.2.2.2].

8.1.2 Church and state

Historically, most private schools in Spain have been run by the Catholic Church. And, as in several European countries, education was a focal point of the lengthy struggle between the Church and secular liberals there. Liberalism's repeated defeats were reflected not just in the lack of mass education. They also meant that much of what provision there was developed under Church control. Only the university sector remained outside the Church's hands, but even there its influence was felt in deeply traditional teaching. In any case, until recently the universities served only a tiny minority of the Spanish population.

Under the Second Republic, attempts to bring education to the masses [8.1.1] were accompanied by exclusion of the Church from the whole of the education system (a constitutional provision that contributed to the Republic's downfall). Subsequently, during the Franco era, great swathes of the expanded school system were handed back – or over – to the Church, which came to control the bulk of primary education as well as much of the secondary sector. In addition, Franco conceded a long-standing Church demand by granting four of its institutions the right to issue university degrees [8.2.1.2].

The Church's presence in higher education briefly became an issue in the late 1990s when an attempt was made to extend it. This provoked considerable opposition, and was thwarted [5.1.2.2]. The earlier foundations have not proved controversial, however. The same cannot be said of Church involvement in the school system, which was further increased by the actions of the centrist governments in power up to 1982 [2.2.2]. Faced with ever-growing pressure for school places, they were unable or unwilling to find the resources to satisfy this through state provision. Instead they vastly extended the practice instituted by the Franco regime of paying grants (subvenciones) to private schools, most of them Church-run, to do so.

The Church was thus particularly affected when, in 1984, the then Socialist government moved to bring publicly-funded schools under greater public control [8.2.2.1]. As well as by the overall thrust of the legislation, its wrath was aroused by the requirement for all public and publicly-maintained schools to offer classes in ethics as an alternative to the traditional instruction in religion – in practice, in the Catholic faith. As a result, the Church was the driving force behind the substantial campaign of public opposition over the next two years.

In the event, Church fears were assuaged by the fact that take-up of the alternative classes proved to be low. However, the government took this poor attendance as the justification for a further change. As part of its next major reform at the end of the decade [8.3.1], it abolished the requirement to offer alternative classes. Despite intensive lobbying, and the election in 1996 of a conservative government thought to be sympathetic to its claims, the Church has been unable to get this provision reversed [5.1.2.2].

8.1.3 The aims of education

In most Western countries state promotion of education generally reflected a desire to forge a sense of common nationhood and to promote economic development. Indeed, the weakness in Spain of both these phenomena might well be seen as a reflection of the weak impulse given to education by the state there [8.1.1]. On the other hand, in a number of the most advanced countries – Germany and the UK spring to mind – this philosophy provoked a reaction. There educational movements or individual schools sprang up based on the belief that education should centre on the interests of the individual, not on those of the state. In Spain, this reaction too was weak.

Indeed, it was limited essentially to the Free Education Institution (*Institución Libre de Enseñanza/ILE*), set up by Francisco Giner de los Ríos in 1876. Various initiatives between then and the 1930s, especially the students' residence it established in Madrid, meant that the ILE's ideas exerted considerable influence over several generations of Spanish intellectuals. Other than during the brief Second Republic [0.1], however, its effects on the education system in general were strictly limited, and in 1940 it was dissolved by order of the Franco regime.

In a sense the ILE enjoyed a posthumous triumph in 1982, with the arrival in power of the Socialist Party. As has often been pointed out, the PSOE's leaders were the first representatives of the so-called generation of 1968 to reach power. Notions of child-centred schooling – and more generally, of education focused on the needs of the individual – strongly influenced a number of them, notably José María Maravall, Education Minister from 1982 to 1988.

At the same time, the PSOE regarded education as an instrument of social change, as a means both of anchoring democracy in Spain and of improving individuals' lot. This it saw very much in material terms, as an aspect of the country's long overdue modernization, which formed the main focus of its policies [2.3.2]. And that, in turn, meant that education was seen ultimately in a third light, as the servant not just of the individual and society but also, and indeed primarily, of the economy.

This emphasis had been presaged by the 1970 Education Act [8.1.1], which had introduced new provisions for vocational training (*formación profesional/ FP*). However, within a decade it was clear that they were inadequate. FP facilities were few and mostly of poor quality; its content was geared to the needs of the relatively primitive industrial economy of the Franco era [6.1.1]. Especially once industrial restructuring got under way in the 1980s, training was hopelessly out-of-touch with the Spanish economy's rapidly changing needs.

Spain's higher education system was perhaps even worse placed to provide a job-oriented education, above all, but not only, in technical fields. The content of courses had typically remained unchanged for many years. Teaching methods continued to be based on learning by rote in conventional lectures. Once numbers began to increase in the 1970s the problems were multiplied still further. They were compounded by the abysmally low level of research in Spanish universities. Hopelessly neglected for many years, by the early 1980s spending in this area was minimal compared with that of Spain's counterparts – and economic competitors.

The essentially economic focus of Socialist educational policy was apparent in its neglect of one type of institution which, to a considerable extent, embodied the ideal of education centred on the individual. The people's universities (*universidades populares*) had emerged in the 1970s as local, community-based initiatives. Their activities ranged from basic literacy training (*alfabetización*) to advanced level studies, depending on the expressed needs of their students, and the teaching resources available. In fact, they were a practical application of the principles of individual participation and community control. But they were of no obvious economic utility, and benefited hardly at all from the massive growth of government spending on education after 1982.

Subsequently, the primacy of economics has gone largely unchallenged, at least in the education policy of central government. But with the devolution of wide-ranging powers to the country's new regions from 1980 on [3.1.3, 3.3.2], that is no longer the only body in Spain with educational powers. In those regions with a distinct language and, especially, a powerful regionalist movement, the education system has been seen as having more than just an economic function.

The Basque Country and Catalonia, in particular, have not only used it to promote their respective languages. They have also sought to give pupils an alternative view of history to that traditionally imparted in Spain. In 1997/98 this provoked a reaction from the conservative central government, which tried to impose a standardized history syllabus (*plan de humanidades*) for the country as a whole. However, it was forced to back down, not just by the regions but by expert opinion [2.4.4].

8.2 ORGANIZATIONAL REFORM

Perhaps due not least to the strong presence of university and school teachers in the ranks of the Socialist Party, education was a major priority for the government elected in 1982. More than almost any other sector of the economy it benefited from the growth of public spending over the next decade. Between 1985 and 1991 alone the government education budget rose by some 70 per cent in real terms. During this time the organization of virtually the entire education system, at both university and school level, was overhauled. In both cases, however, continuing deficiencies were apparent, while in 1996 the Socialists were replaced by the conservative PP. The result has been still further change.

8.2.1 Higher education

The university system (*universidad*) was more affected than any other sector of education by the advent of mass access [8.1.1]. From about 60,000 in 1962/63 the number of students enrolled rose to 650,000 in 1980 and over one and a half million in 2000, giving Spain a proportionately larger student population than any other Western country. This massive increase resulted in unsatisfactory conditions for university students and teachers alike. It also held back the already urgent modernization of higher education in the areas of syllabus content, teaching methods and research activity, all – but particularly the last – regarded by the PSOE as crucial to the country's economic performance, hence the speed with which the party addressed the university issue on coming to power in 1982.

8.2.1.1 The LRU

The Universities Reform Act (*Ley de Reforma Universitaria/LRU*), the Socialist government's first major education law, was passed in 1983. One of its main aims was to do away with the post of temporary lecturer (*profesor no numerario/PNN*), which had originally been introduced as a stop-gap measure. Because their legal status was anomalous under existing legislation, the PNNs' pay and conditions were far from satisfactory. Yet in the meantime they had come to represent 60 per cent of teaching staff – and a constant source of discontent.

Table 8.1 Spanish universities

Region	University	Notes	Students (1999/2000) (in thousands)
Andalusia	U de Almería	N	15
	U de Cádiz	N	23
	U de Córdoba		21
	U de Granada		61
	U de Huelva	N	14
	U de Jaén	N	16
	U de Málaga		40
	U Pablo de Olavide (Sevilla)	N	5
	U de Sevilla		76
Aragon	U de Zaragoza		43
Asturias	U de Oviedo		42
Balearic Islands	U de las Islas Baleares		14
Basque Country	U de Deusto	C	15
	U de Mondragón	P	3
	U del País Vasco		60
Canary Islands	U de La Laguna		25
	U de Las Palmas de Gran Canaria		25
Cantabria	U de Cantabria		14
Castile-La Mancha	U de Castilla-La Mancha	N	33
Castile-Leon	U de Burgos	N	11
	U Católica de Avila	CN	*
	U de León	N	16

Table 8.1 (*continued*)

Region	University	Notes	Students (1999/2000) (in thousands)
	U Pontificia de Salamanca	C	8
	U de Salamanca		34
	U SEK (Segovia)	N	1
	U de Valladolid		36
Catalonia	U Autónoma de Barcelona		37
	U de Barcelona		62
	U de Girona		13
	U Internacional de Catalunya	P	2
	U de Lleida		11
	U Politécnica de Cataluña		33
	U Pompeu Fabra	N	7
	U Ramón Llull	P	13
	U Rovira y Virgili, Tarragona	N	11
	U de Vic		2
Extremadura	U de Extremadura		27
Galicia	U de A Coruña	N	26
	U de Santiago de Compostela		42
	U de Vigo	N	31
Madrid	U de Alcalá de Henares		20
	U Alfonso X el Sabio	P	8
	U Antonio Nebrija	P	2
	U Autónoma de Madrid		32
	U Carlos III de Madrid	N	13
	U CEU-San Pablo	CN	8
	U Complutense de Madrid		104
	U Europea de Madrid	P	6
	U Politécnica de Madrid		44
	U Pontificia Comillas	C	9
	U Rey Juan Carlos (Móstoles)	N	6
Murcia	U de Murcia		31
	U Politécnica de Cartagena	N	6
Navarre	U de Navarra	C	12
	U Pública de Navarra	N	10
Rioja	U de La Rioja	N	7
Valencia	U de Alicante	N	29
	U Jaume I de Castellón	N	13
	U Miguel Hernández (Elche)	N	7
	U Politécnica de Valencia		34
	U de Valencia		58
Distance learning	UNED		141
	U Oberta de Catalunya	P	12

Notes: C = Church foundation; N = Post-1975 foundation; P = Private foundation;
* = under 500 students.

The LRU therefore abolished the category, which disappeared in 1987. Instead it established a clear distinction between tenured staff, made up of professors (*catedráticos*) and permanent lecturers (*profesores titulares*), and other lecturers. These latter were to make up no more then a fifth of total staff. They included junior lecturers (*ayudantes*) – mainly those completing a higher degree – and teaching associates (*asociados*), part-time teachers who were also practitioners in the relevant field. Unlike those of the PNNs, their teaching loads were supposed to be commensurate with their other duties.

In practice, however, these changes have not worked out as planned, in part due to the difficulty of reallocating resources. Some departments in established but less popular subjects, such as history, are over-staffed. Yet others cannot appoint sufficient tenured staff to meet student demand, so that the new non-tenured posts have become almost as widely abused as the PNNs. Moreover, large as the increase in resources has been, it has not kept pace with rising student numbers. In that regard the large increase in student grants (*becas*), admirable in that it has widened access to higher education, has only served to make the situation worse.

More generally, the LRU focused on a long-standing problem of Spanish higher education, the strict and bureaucratic control traditionally exercised by the central government over the universities. By the 1980s it was felt that this centralist approach had stifled individual institutions' initiative and flexibility, preventing them from finding solutions to the problems they faced. The LRU therefore granted universities a greater degree of freedom to manage their own affairs. Institutions were allowed to elect their own vice-chancellors (*rectores*), while the management boards (*juntas de gobierno*) these headed were given extensive control over internal policy.

Yet autonomy was strictly limited, as universities were subject to considerable outside influence. The least significant channel for it was another creation of the LRU, which required each university to establish a University Court (*Consejo Social*). Sixty per cent of the Court's members are representatives of local trade unions and employers, the intention being to ensure that universities are responsive to the economic needs of their immediate catchment areas. There is little evidence that this has been achieved.

Other forms of outside influence are less institutionalized, but more effective. The election of vice-chancellors is frequently politicized, in that different candidates are closely associated with particular political parties or factions within them. As a result, educational considerations can get entangled with political ones, especially those of the regional governments which now supply much of universities' funding.

At the same time, under the complex arrangements for devolution made in the 1980s [1.3.2], the central government retains powers to 'coordinate' education, and specifically the universities. Under the LRU these powers were exercised through the Universities' Council (*Consejo de Universidades*), attached to the Education Ministry. Despite supposed autonomy, many university decisions still had to be referred to the Council. As a result the delays traditionally typical of Spain's centralized system continued to occur, as for example with the introduction of new undergraduate course structures [8.3.2].

Nor has such real autonomy as was granted had entirely positive results. Appointments and promotions became a purely internal responsibility – previously they had been controlled by the Ministry in Madrid. The change led to a tendency towards academic in-breeding (*endogamia*), in other words, departments appointing their own ex-students and promoting members of existing staff. On the other hand, that could also be seen as a fair reflection of the lack of geographical mobility in Spanish society as a whole [6.2.4.1].

8.2.1.2 Competition

Overall, the results of the LRU were patchy, at best, and discontent among both students and staff remained high. Moreover, the Socialist government became increasingly worried about continuing low standards of teaching and research. Faced with such intractable problems, latterly it latched on to the currently fashionable notions of competition and choice as solutions to the universities' ills.

Probably the least significant step in that marketizing direction has been the establishment of new private universities. It was envisaged in the LRU and its details finally regulated in 1990, with the first new institutions coming into operation in 1993/94. Up to that time the only non-state institutions authorized to award higher degrees were the four given that privilege by the Franco regime. Of these, three were long-standing Church foundations (see Table 8.1); the fourth was the University of Navarre, set up in the 1960s by the Opus Dei [5.1.2.2]. All have small intakes and, in general, high academic reputations.

This is not true of the new private foundations, whose intake consists largely of students who have failed to pass the far from demanding entrance examination for the public universities. The sole exception is the San Pablo University Centre; based on a Church-run former university college [8.3.2], this resembles the four older Church universities. Yet like them its standards are high because its intake is small – and for that reason it does not represent a meaningful competitor to the public universities.

The number of public universities has grown dramatically since 1980. Institutions were founded in those regions which had previously lacked one; in others where population increase or dispersal restricted access to existing universities additional ones were established (see Table 8.1). Within this expanded public sector, choice was encouraged by enabling universities to offer new degree courses of their own design [8.3.2]. The Socialists also began moves to relax the formerly tough rules on universities' catchment areas, and so allow students to attend any university throughout the country [8.2.1.3].

Other measures used by the government to promote competition recalled those taken in the UK. Thus universities were encouraged to seek funding from the private sector, a factor which has been apparent mainly at postgraduate level. In 1993 the government established a national quality assessment plan covering universities' teaching and research (*Plan Nacional de Evaluación de Calidad de las Universidades*). In the latter area a clear trend was established of concentrating university-based research in a small group of leading institutions. The rest, it seems, were to be left to face the problems of mass teaching, with neither a genuine research base nor adequate resources.

8.2.1.3 The LOU

The continuing problems apparent in the university system made further reform inevitable under the conservative government first elected in 1996. Nobody was more aware of that than the institutions themselves. In 2000 the Standing Conference of Spanish Vice-Chancellors (*Conferencia de Rectores de las Universidades Españolas/CRUE*) produced the so-called Bricall Report, named after its chairman, containing its own proposals. But the government took little notice either of this document or of its political opponents, and the following year introduced a measure largely of its own design.

The Universities Act (*Ley Orgánica de Universidades/LOU*) includes reforms in various areas, firstly organizational. Internally, universities' management boards [8.2.1.2] are renamed (*consejos de gobierno*), and student representatives are excluded from them. Meanwhile the university assembly (*claustro*), made up of the representatives of the university community (students, administrative and teaching staff), is reduced to a purely representative body.

In particular, the assembly loses the right to elect the vice-chancellor, which will now be done by the community as a whole, on a weighted franchise in which the teaching staff have 70 per cent of the votes. This change is designed to reduce political influence [8.2.1.2], since assembly members are assumed to be more politically motivated than the mass of staff. But opponents argue it will actually have the opposite effect, with wholesale election campaigns leading to even greater politicization.

The main change affecting students is the abolition of the old, country-wide university entrance examination (*selectividad*), in which pass rates had always been very high. Originally it was intended that universities would assume full responsibility for their own admission requirements. However, that would have undermined previous moves to encourage greater geographic mobility of students [8.2.1.2]; from 2000/01 universities have been required to open at least 20 per cent of places to applicants from outside their own region (*distrito único/abierto*).

It was accordingly decided to introduce a new standardized school-leaving examination [8.3.1], leaving individual universities to conduct such additional tests as they consider necessary. In practice, these will probably be needed for those more popular courses which have an intake limit (*Numerus Clausus*). Special arrangements continue to exist for mature applicants.

Teaching staff are among the most affected by the LOU. All appointees to tenured posts [8.2.1.1] are now required to pass a standard (i.e. Spain-wide) examination of their aptitude for university teaching (*habilitación nacional*), before they are interviewed or tested by individual universities. In addition, two new types of non-tenured posts are created. Lecturers (*ayudantes doctores*) must have completed a higher degree and must not have been attached to the university concerned during the past two years. Senior lecturers (*profesores contratados*) must have at least two years' post-doctoral research experience. Among other goals, these changes were clearly aimed at ending the tendency for 'in-breeding' [8.2.1.1].

Finally, the LOU brings various changes with regard to the university system as a whole. It sets up a Higher Education Quality and Assessment Agency (*Agencia Nacional de Calidad y Evaluación/ANCE*) to oversee teaching and research assessment. The old Universities' Council [8.2.1.1] is replaced by a University Coordination Council (*Consejo de Coordinación Universitaria*), on which private universities [8.2.1.2] are represented with full voting rights. And, in a concession to the Catholic Church, the establishment of Church-run universities is made slightly easier than that of private universities in general.

Given the sensitivity about the Church's educational role [8.1.2], that was one reason for opposition to the LOU, but not the only one. Students were incensed at the lack of any firm provision for an extended system of grants, without which increased mobility seems likely to remain the preserve of the rich. They were also concerned at the continuing possible need to sit separate tests in various universities.

On the other hand, staff felt they were having mobility forced on them, while the vice-chancellors were upset at being required to present themselves for re-election within six months. And, like opposition politicians and the regional governments who are charged with implementing the changes, they complained about the lack of identified resources to carry them through. These various strands came together in a series of demonstrations against the Act, but they could not prevent its approval.

8.2.2 School provision

At school level, the main issue in the 1980s was the status of Spain's private schools, the great majority of them run by the Church. The reason was partly financial. Over the decade to 1982 maintenance grants to private schools had increased by a factor of over 70 [8.1.2]. Yet maintained schools remained largely free of state control. Under measures passed in 1980 they were allowed to select their pupils according to their own criteria; they were even allowed to charge fees (*tasas*), and over half did so. When the Socialists came to power in 1982 they were understandably keen to change this situation.

8.2.2.1 The LODE

The Socialists' second major education reform, the Right to Education Act (*Ley Orgánica del Derecho a la Educación/LODE*), was passed by Parliament in 1984. The LODE addressed the questions of public subsidy and social division, as well as others related to the running of schools. It implicitly recognized that private schools would continue to have considerable importance. But it also redefined the balance of power between them and both the government and parents, in such a way as strictly to limit their educational and social influence.

In order to receive public funds under the LODE, schools must sign an agreement (*concierto*) agreeing to fulfil a number of conditions. Most fundamentally, maintained schools (*centros concertados*) must provide compulsory education free of charge. They are also required to keep proper accounts subject to government scrutiny and to refrain from any supplementary profit-making activities. The LODE also stipulated that government approval was required for maintained schools' statement of educational philosophy (*ideario*).

In addition the LODE barred Church and other private schools from practising selection if they received financial support. Access to maintained schools could be restricted only by the same resource considerations as in the public sector. In other words, where selection was unavoidable due to excessive demand for places it should follow only the criteria laid down by the state; these gave priority to children of poorer families and those living close to the school concerned.

Maintenance agreements under the LODE also required a School Council (*Consejo Escolar*) to be set up. Some 40 per cent of the Council's members are elected by the teaching staff, and the same proportion by parents and pupils. Only the remaining 20 per cent represent the school's operators. Individual School Councils in turn elect the National Schools' Council (*Consejo Escolar del Estado/CEE*). The CEE's 80 members are drawn in specified proportions from representatives of the same three basic interests – staff, pupils and parents, and private school operators – and of the government.

The CEE, first constituted in 1986/87, has only advisory powers and in practice has not proved an effective channel of public input into education policy. The individual Schools Councils, however, have had a major impact, since they considerably reduced the absolute power previously enjoyed by private school operators over internal management. They elect the school's head-teacher (*director*) for a three-year term, and are responsible for appointing and dismissing staff. This latter provision in particular is intended to protect teachers' academic freedom (*libertad de cátedra*), restricting the ability of school operators, and specifically the Church, to influence the way subjects are taught.

The LODE provoked one of the most bitter political confrontations of the 1980s. At a time when the Right was finding it hard to make any real progress in attracting popular support [2.4.2], the Act provided a rallying point for opposition to the government. It brought articulate, better-off parents reluctant to give up the privileges of private education into alliance with the Church and those close to it. Together these interests staged a mass campaign against the proposals. Eventually the case went to the Constitutional Court [1.1.3], which in 1985 found against the objections.

8.2.2.2 Freedom and diversity

Central to the debate over the LODE was the notion of educational freedom. The government held that the Act promoted the freedom not just of teachers but also of children and parents. Subject only to resource constraints, it ensured free access to all state-funded schools, and allowed greater public participation in their operation. The conservative opposition, on the other hand, argued that the LODE restricted freedom by placing constraints on the providers of education. Yet, despite these fundamental differences the Act's provisions are now, by and large, an accepted part of the Spanish education system.

There are a number of reasons for this acceptance. First, selective private schools have continued to function outside the LODE's framework. They receive no public support and continue to cater for a small but significant social group with the resources to pay the fees they charge. They provide not only a high level of education but also entry to a network of contacts in the business and political worlds. The best-known is Madrid's *Colegio del Pilar*, which has been described as Spain's Eton.

Second, it remains possible in practice for maintained schools to erect price barriers to access. For even within the public sector the notion of 'free' education relates only to teaching in the narrowest sense. Schools can and do charge for 'extras' such as sports and recreational facilities, meals and even supervised self-study. As a result, the ability to use income as a selection criterion – the real concern of many of the LODE's most vociferous opponents – has been retained.

Nearly two decades on, private establishments still account for a higher percentage of the Spanish school system than any other in Western Europe. Indeed, their presence has actually increased in recent years. In 2001/02 around a third of both primary and secondary pupils were studying at private schools; in 1992/93 the figures were 30 per cent for primaries and 23 per cent for secondaries. On the other hand, with public control over the bulk of such schools assured by the system of maintenance agreements some of the old divisions have been reduced, if not eliminated.

If that has made schooling more uniform, a new element of diversity was introduced by the devolution of education powers to the regions. Begun in the 1980s, this process was finally completed in 2000 [3.3.2]. By then diversity had come to be seen as desirable in itself, and encouraging it was a major aim of the final major reform carried out by the Socialists: the 1995 Schools' Participation, Assessment and Management Act (*Ley Orgánica de la Participación, la Evaluación y el Gobierno de los Centros Docentes/LOPEG*). The LOPEG introduced an assessment scheme for state and maintained schools, but also encouraged them to develop distinctive educational plans (*proyectos educativos*) which would allow parents to exercise a degree of choice between them.

Like the LODE [8.2.2.1], the LOPEG caused considerable controversy. This time, however, the government received tacit support from maintained-school operators, pleased at the partial return of control over their schools' educational philosophies. On the other hand, the new Act was bitterly opposed by the teaching unions and the Left, who had backed the reforms of the 1980s, as well as by the conservative opposition, the People's Party (PP), which had resisted those. This realignment of forces indicated how the debate on school provision had moved on since the 1980s, but also the extent to which educational issues had become secondary to party political interests.

Once the PP came to power it put considerable emphasis on the notion of choice, in particular parents' supposed right to choose freely their children's school. However, the principal organizational changes included in their first major piece of education legislation ignores this issue, while curtailing parental choice in another regard. Under the provisions of the proposed Education Quality Act [8.3.1] headteachers will no longer be designated by the elected School Council [8.2.2.1], but will be named by the relevant regional ministry.

8.3 THE STRUCTURE OF EDUCATION

The reforms of the 1980s and 1990s did not only affect the principles underlying the education system and its institutional structure. Far-reaching alterations have also taken place in the structure and nature of the studies themselves. Indeed, the situation has been one of almost constant change. For, on the one hand, implementation of structural reforms is inevitably gradual, spread over a period of years; and, on the other, even before one set of modifications was complete another was already under way.

8.3.1 School education

It is in schools that the most complex changes have occurred. For the most part they derive from the third major reform carried out under Socialist rule, the Education System Structure Act (*Ley de Ordenación General del Sistema Educativo/LOGSE*). Passed in 1990, the LOGSE was a massive and ambitious piece of legislation which affected all schooling at secondary level and below, as well as vocational education.

The LOGSE's provisions were introduced on a rolling timetable from 1991/92, replacing those of the 1970 General Education Act [8.1.1] one school year at a time. Following several revisions, by 2002 implementation was complete for all years, except for the final one of vocational education [8.3.3]. In certain pilot schools (*centros piloto*), however, it was completed rather earlier.

The changes introduced by the LOGSE begin with the 0–6 age group, the whole of which is defined by the LOGSE as part of the educative process. As yet, however, there are not even plans for introduction of the first stage (*ciclo*), covering the years 0–2. On the other hand, near 100 per cent provision has now been achieved for the second stage, i.e. for 3- to 5-year-olds.

Under the old system many kindergartens (*jardines de infancia*) and infants' schools (*escuelas de párvulos*) provided children of this age group with little more than supervision. Now, in theory at least, they are receiving education closely linked to that at primary level in nursery schools (*escuelas infantiles*) – hence the abandonment of the old denomination of 'pre-school education' (*educación preescolar*).

At primary level the LOGSE has also brought major changes. Formerly, this was referred to as 'basic' education (*Educación General Básica/EGB*), and covered an unusually long period by international standards, from age 6 to 14. Under the new system primary education (*educación primaria*) runs from ages 6 to 12, in line with international norms, and is divided into three two-year stages (*ciclos*). These arrangements are accompanied by other changes intended to correct many of the faults of the old EGB. In theory, at least, maximum class sizes have been reduced to 25, subject matter has been brought into line with contemporary requirements and more project work introduced.

However, the most far-reaching and controversial changes are in secondary education, which under the old system was both divided and divisive. Only those pupils who obtained the basic-level pass certificate (*graduado escolar*) were allowed to proceed to academic secondary education, modelled on the French Baccalaureate (*Bachillerato Unificado Polivalente/BUP*). Those who failed received a leaving certificate (*certificado de escolaridad*) and were supposed to go on to vocational training [8.3.3]. Successful pupils wishing to go on to higher education took a one-year pre-university course (*Curso de Orientación Universitaria/COU*). Together with BUP and the first level of vocational training, COU made up the secondary sector (*enseñanzas medias/EEMM*). Unlike the situation at primary level, none of its elements was provided free of charge.

The LOGSE's arrangements are very different. They introduced a common programme of compulsory secondary education (*educación secundaria obligatoria/ESO*), covering the 12–16 age group. Since it is attended by all pupils, the stigma of primary school 'failure' [8.1.1] is removed. In addition, ESO is free so that the school-leaving age is now 16 in practice as well as theory. It consists of two two-year stages, the second of which includes a significant vocational element; the aim is to eliminate existing prejudices [8.3.3] and encourage more talented youngsters to follow the vocational path thereafter. On successful completion of ESO pupils receive a secondary pass certificate (*graduado en educación secundaria*), giving an attainment profile. Standards of achievement are monitored by a new Secondary Education Quality and Assessment Agency (*Instituto Nacional de Calidad y Evaluación/INCE*).

Only at age 16 does the new system involve a division into academic and non-academic streams. The first comprises a shortened Baccalaureate (*Bachillerato*), of two years' duration, which will take over the functions of the old COU. A further novelty is that the format is no longer to be standardized. Pupils can now choose between four options (*especialidades*): natural and health sciences, humanities and social sciences, technology, and the arts. One of the LOGSE's achievements, with a view to the country's economic needs, has been the popularity and prestige of the technology option.

More generally, though, the LOGSE reforms have not been seen as particularly positive. Criticism has focused on the new compulsory secondary phase. Levels of achievement are often low, with a considerable proportion of pupils failing to achieve a pass; as a result, the term 'failure' has re-emerged, this time at secondary level. Many secondary schools (*institutos*) are overcrowded, while in rural areas pupils often have to travel considerable distances to reach them. There have also been problems in ensuring that children from minority groups do indeed receive secondary schooling.

Furthermore, teachers' recruitment has proved problematic, as has their quality. That is largely because the move from primary now occurs earlier than before, so that the first two-year stage has been taught mainly by former primary teachers (*maestros*) up to now. Indeed the two stages are typically taught in different buildings, and in many cases have remained effectively separate.

In view of these problems, and given its own political standpoint, the conservative People's Party was highly critical of the LOGSE before it came to power in 1996. It nonetheless allowed implementation to be completed, while preparing its own set of reforms. These are included in the Education Quality Act (*Ley de Calidad de la Educación*), scheduled to be enacted in 2002.

The Act will introduce a country-wide secondary leaving examination (*reválida*) to replace the old university entrance examination [8.2.1.3]. The new test, which seems to have been something of an afterthought, brings Spain into line with other Western countries; it will be called the General Baccalaureate Examination (*Prueba General de Bachillerato/PGB*). Concern has been expressed that pupils' final mark will be an average of the PGB mark and their record of attainment at school (*expediente*). This change was originally introduced by the PP in 1999 for the old entrance examination, and is thought by many to give private school pupils an unfair advantage.

The Act's other main measures, designed to raise standards of achievement, have a distinctly traditionalist air. It reintroduces the option for pupils to repeat a certain number of years' schooling, at both primary and secondary level; under the LOGSE they automatically proceed to the next year irrespective of attainment (*promoción automática*). Much more controversially, the Act introduces streaming (*separación por rendimiento*) in the second stage of ESO. There will be three streams: one destined for the Baccalaureate and one for vocational education [8.3.3], while the third would be expected to leave education at 16. Such covert selection at age 14 is vehemently opposed not only by the left but also by mainstream, centre-right Basque and Catalan regionalists.

8.3.2 Higher education

At higher level, change in the structure of studies was begun by the 1983 Universities Reform Act (LRU) [8.2.1.1]. It has involved the introduction of new qualifications (*títulos*) and degree courses (*carreras*) as well as changes to existing course structures (*planes de estudios*). As in schools, change has been gradual, and at the time of writing some students continue to be affected by old arrangements in the process of being phased out.

The greater part of the higher education system (*enseñanza superior*) is made up of the academic faculties into which each university is divided. Traditionally, these have offered undergraduate courses of five academic years (*cursos*), although these are a less rigid concept than in the UK. At any one time students might be taking subjects (*asignaturas*) from two or more years, and require longer, perhaps considerably longer, than five years to complete.

These old-style undergraduate courses are divided into two parts (*ciclos*). Passing the first, of three years, entitles students to leave with a 'diploma'; most, however, continue to the second in order to obtain a degree (*licenciatura*). The faculties also offer studies at postgraduate level; a programme involving taught classes and a thesis leads to a doctorate qualification (*doctorado*), normally within five years.

In addition to the faculties, universities also incorporate various other types of institution. Some university colleges (*colegios universitarios*) acted in the past as local out-stations, enabling students to take the first part of degrees without travelling to the main university. That function has mainly been superseded by the founding of new universities [8.2.1.1]. Others, in the larger cities, were and are distinguished by being privately run; the best known, the San Pablo college in Madrid, has now acquired full university status [8.2.1.2].

The university schools (*escuelas universitarias*) are also of a hybrid nature. Most of their three-year diploma courses (*diplomaturas*) are vocational or semi-vocational in nature, in specified areas such as nursing and primary teaching. Others, notably those in business studies and engineering, differ little from the early stages of courses offered elsewhere in the system. In general, however, they have enjoyed lower prestige.

This is decidedly not the case with the Advanced Technical Schools (*Escuelas Técnicas Superiores/ETS*). The ETS are broadly comparable to UK engineering faculties, offering a variety of undergraduate courses leading to a qualification as engineer in six years, or architect in five. Entry is subject to strict limits, and demand for places is high. Like the university faculties, the ETS also offer postgraduate studies. In Madrid, Barcelona and Valencia they are grouped together in separate Technical Universities. These have now lost their specialist nature by the addition of faculties where non-technical disciplines are studied.

The high reputation of the ETS is reflected in the fact that they have been left virtually unaffected by recent changes in course structures. In other parts of the system the LRU introduced a rationalization, by distinguishing clearly between diploma and degree courses. The former continue to be of three years' duration (*carreras cortas*), and are offered by the university schools and colleges. They are intended explicitly to allow direct access to the job market.

Following the LRU, undergraduate degrees offered by university faculties are of four years' duration. They continue to consist of two parts, now each of two years, the first being intended to provide foundation knowledge and the second an element of specialization. This is achieved through a system of core subjects (*troncales*), other compulsory subjects (*obligatorias*) and options (*optativas*), some of the latter to be drawn from a specified list and others to be chosen at will by the student (*optativas de libre elección*).

As well as this reform of degree structures, the range of degree subjects has been revised. In Spain official degree titles must, by law, be drawn from a listing established by the government. The age of the list valid in the 1980s was a major reason for the outdated nature of many degrees [8.1.3], and in 1986 the government gave the task of drawing up a new one to the Universities' Council [8.2.1.1]. Yet it was well into the 1990s before many degree titles finally received the Council's approval.

Moreover, despite regional and university autonomy [8.2.1.1], the course structures of new and revised degree courses had to be approved by the Council (now by its successor [8.2.1.3]). That process caused further delays. It also revealed the fact that the legal requirements on course content were far too demanding for the new four-year structure. Consequently in 1997 the government reduced the number of 'credits' required, thus triggering off a further round of changes to course structures. Despite these problems, however, the range of officially recognized degrees offered by universities has been increased from 65 to some 150.

In addition, universities may now offer degrees without the Council's approval, although the corresponding qualifications lack official status. Thus various Catalan universities have pioneered degrees in environmental sciences. Such initiatives, if judged to be successful, may subsequently be incorporated into the government's approved list. Autonomy has also allowed further development of the trend towards shorter, practice-oriented postgraduate qualifications. These are known in Spain as *masters* and, as in the UK, normally involve a taught element followed by a dissertation.

8.3.3 Vocational training

Vocational training (*formación profesional/FP*) has long been a problem area within the Spanish education system. Although its importance was formally recognized by the 1970 General Education Act [8.1.1], vocational provision remained inadequate in terms of both quantity and quality. Although the 1970 Act in theory established a three-level system, in practice only the basic level (FP1), for 14- to 16-year-olds, was developed to any significant extent; the third, advanced level (FP3) was never implemented at all.

The main problem, however, was not paucity of provision but public perception. Because of the selective nature of secondary education [8.3.1], FP1 came to be regarded as a sink for those who had failed to complete primary education successfully. As fewer and fewer able students opted for it voluntarily, FP acquired a poor reputation among employers as well as parents. A similar problem was apparent also at higher level. Despite the poor quality of many university courses, further aggravated by overcrowding [8.1.1], young Spaniards continued to display the traditional obsession with academic qualifications (*titulitis*), irrespective of the job prospects they offered.

By the 1980s these inadequacies were generally accepted, and attempts were made to address them in several of the social contract agreements of 1980–84 [5.2.3]. Thus the 1984 Social and Economic Agreement (AES) set up a Solidarity Fund specifically to promote vocational training. A General Vocational Training Council (*Consejo General de Formación Profesional*) was established, with representatives of government, trade unions and employers. The AES also led to the setting up of training workshops (*escuelas-taller*) and craft training centres (*casas de oficios*).

As a result of these and other *ad hoc* measures, the system began to lose all semblance of an overall structure. Restoration of logic to the vocational sector was an important aim of the 1990 measure known as the LOGSE [8.3.1]. As part of them, basic vocational training (*FP de base*) was integrated into the new, unified secondary stage [8.3.1]. From there pupils may pass to an intermediate stage, designed to last two years and organized in the form of modules (*módulos*). Successful students become qualified technicians (*técnicos*).

The LOGSE also provided for pupils to pass from the revised Baccalaureate [8.3.1] to an advanced level of vocational training; subsequently it has become possible to do so directly from the intermediate level. Access involves an entry test (*prueba de acceso*); it in turn provides an alternative path into higher education.

Despite these changes problems have persisted in the vocational area. Above all, even the more advanced vocational courses still involve little – or no – practical experience (*experiencia laboral*). Increasing this was a major aim of the 2001 Vocational Education Act (*Ley de Formación Profesional*), which establishes a national system of vocational qualifications, some of which may be obtained purely by experience. The success of the scheme depends heavily on getting the private sector much more closely involved in training, an approach that has not proved entirely successful in the UK, for example.

At higher level, both the advanced technical schools and university schools [8.3.2] provide vocationally oriented courses. In particular, training for primary teaching takes place in special university schools, still generally known by their old title *EU de Magisterio*. A number are run privately. Secondary teachers are required to take a five-year degree and then obtain the Certificate of Teaching Aptitude (*Certificado de Aptitud Pedagógica/CAP*). Under the system established in 1970 this was done at a College of Education (*Instituto de Ciencias de la Educación/ICE*), attached to a university. However, these are currently being phased out. Their functions are being assumed by the regionally based Teachers' Centres (*Centros de (Encuentro de) Profesores*), which previously provided in-service training (*formación continua*) of various sorts. As in other Western countries, university teachers receive no formal training.

8.3.4 Further, continuing and special education

Several forms of further and continuing education are available in Spain. Some, like the people's universities [8.1.3], are community based; most, though, are provided by official bodies, at national, regional and municipal level. The central government has attempted to coordinate these in a national programme of adult continuing education (*educación permanente*), with limited success.

A major part of continuing education consists of distance-learning programmes designed to allow adults to achieve conventional qualifications.

Organizations dealing with the primary and secondary levels were set up during the Franco era. They were later joined by Spain's equivalent of the Open University (*Universidad Nacional de Educación a Distancia/UNED*). The Open University of Catalonia (*Universitat Oberta de Catalunya*) is a recently established, privately-run institution. In addition, special arrangements, including a separate entrance examination, exist for those aged 25 and over who wish to enter the conventional higher education system.

A more recent innovation is the concept of 'compensatory education'. This comprises a wide range of programmes aimed at individuals who require to make up lost educational ground in order to enter the job market. Target groups include drug addicts and those who, for whatever reason, failed to complete normal school education.

Special education, on the other hand, is concerned with overcoming learning disabilities of various sorts. Traditionally provision for children affected by such disabilities, where it existed at all, tended to be strictly separated from mainstream education, and often had little genuinely educational content. More recently the accent has been on overcoming such divisions. The Schools Integration Programme (*Programa de Integración Escolar*) aims at the teaching of disadvantaged children in mainstream classes wherever possible; only in extreme cases is separate provision now envisaged.

8.4 GLOSSARY

abandono m	dropping out
alfabetización f	basic literacy training
alumno m	(university) student; (school) pupil
asignatura f	subject
asociado m	teaching associate
aula f	classroom; lecture hall
autonomía universitaria f	university autonomy
ayudante m	junior lecturer; assistant
ayudante doctor m	lecturer
Bachillerato m	Baccalaureate
Bachillerato Unificado Polivalente (BUP) m	old-style selective Baccalaureate
beca f	student grant
carrera f	degree course
carrera corta f	three-year diploma course
casa de oficios f	craft training centre
cátedra f	professorial chair
catedrático m	professor
centro m	school
centro concertado m	grant-maintained school
centro no concertado m	non-maintained private school
centro piloto m	pilot school (for new teaching methods, etc.)
certificado de escolaridad m	old-style school-leaving certificate
ciclo m	stage (of school course); part (of degree course)
clase f	lecture; seminar; class

claustro m	university assembly
Colegio Mayor m	students' residence
colegio universitario m	university college
concierto m	maintenance agreement
consejo de gobierno m	university management board (since 2001)
Consejo de Universidades m	Universities' Council
Consejo Escolar m	School Council
Consejo Social m	(University) Court
cursillo m	short course
curso m	year of study
Curso de Orientación Universitaria (COU) m	pre-university year
desprestigio m	low reputation
diplomatura f	diploma (course)
director m	headteacher
distrito abierto/único m	system under which students may apply to any university, not merely those in their home region
docencia f	teaching
doctorado m	doctorate (course)
educación compensatoria f	compensatory education (allows adults to make good gaps in formal education)
educación especial f	special education
educación infantil f	nursery education
educación permanente f	continuing education
educación preescolar f	pre-school education
educación primaria f	new-style primary education
educación secundaria obligatoria (ESO) f	new-style secondary education
endogamia f	(academic) 'in-breeding', tendency for universities to recruit staff internally
enseñanza básica f	old-style basic education
enseñanza obligatoria f	compulsory education
enseñanza superior/terciaria f	higher/tertiary education
enseñanzas medias fpl	old-style secondary education
escolaridad f	school attendance
escolarización f	schooling; school attendance
escuela de párvulos f	infant school
escuela-taller f	training workshop
Escuela Técnica Superior f	Advanced Technical School
escuela universitaria f	university school
especialidad f	option
estudiante mf	student; (secondary school) pupil
expediente m	record of attainment
formación continua f	in-service training
formación profesional f	vocational training
fracaso escolar m	failure to complete compulsory education successfully
graduado en educación secundaria m	new-style secondary pass certificate

graduado escolar m	old-style basic-level pass certificate
gratuidad f	free provision
habilitación nacional f	single, Spain-wide examination of aptitude for university teaching
hora lectiva f	teaching/contact hour
ideario m	school's statement of educational philosophy
instituto m	secondary school
investigación f	research
jardín de infancia m	kindergarten
junta de gobierno f	university management board (until 2001)
libertad de cátedra f	academic freedom
licenciatura f	undergraduate degree (course)
maestro m	primary teacher
Magisterio m	primary teacher training
masificación f	overcrowding
master(s) m	postgraduate qualification offered without official government approval
matrícula f	(matriculation) fee
matriculación f	matriculation, registration
módulo m	module
nota f	mark
número de alumnos por aula m	class size
obligatoria (asignatura) f	compulsory class
optativa (asignatura) f	option class chosen from specified list
optativa de libre elección f	unrestricted option class
plan de estudios m	course structure
plan de humanidades m	arts subject syllabus (in particular, the history syllabus which the conservative government attempted to impose in 1997/98)
posgrado m	postgraduate
profesor m	schoolteacher; member of academic staff
profesor contratado m	senior lecturer
profesor no numerario (PNN) m	temporary lecturer
profesor titular m	permanent lecturer
promoción automática f	system under which pupils pass to the next level, irrespective of attainment
prueba de acceso f	entrance test/examination
rector m	vice-chancellor, principal
reválida f	national secondary school leaving examination
selectividad f	university entrance examination
separación por rendimiento f	streaming
subvención f	grant, subsidy
tasa f	fee
técnico m	qualified technician (new-style vocational qualification)
titulitis f	obsession with academic qualifications
título m	qualification, certificate, degree
troncal (asignatura) f	core subject
universidad f	university; the university system
universidad popular f	people's university

9

SOCIAL WELFARE

One of the fundamental principles of Spain's 1978 Constitution is that free market capitalism must be tempered by a concern for social issues [1.1.2]. Implicitly the resultant responsibility for welfare provision lies with the state. Opinion polls have repeatedly confirmed that Spaniards, to a markedly greater degree than most Europeans, support this view. It is, however, one at odds with their country's recent history, which saw only the most rudimentary of welfare states develop. Coupled with the rapid socio-economic changes of recent decades, this situation has posed a number of problems for the country. This chapter examines these, and the solutions that have emerged in terms of social security, health care and social services provision. The final section considers five groups in Spanish society who, in various ways, have particular need for such provision due to their disadvantaged social situation.

9.1 SOCIAL SECURITY

The origins of social security provision in Spain go back to the beginnings of the twentieth century. In 1900 compulsory insurance against accidents at work was introduced; in 1907 the National Social Insurance Agency (*Instituto Nacional de Previsión/INP*) was created. Later, under Primo de Rivera's dictatorship and the Second Republic, provision was extended in small ways. However, only under the Franco regime did a genuine social security system come into being. The unusual circumstances and nature of its development bequeathed substantial problems to the regime's democratic successors, which still plague the system to some extent today.

9.1.1 Francoism's legacy

Francoism's first attempt at establishing a unified system of social security came with the 1963 Social Security Framework Act (*Ley de Bases de la Seguridad Social*). This brought together a number of existing forms of benefit including old age, widows' and invalidity pensions (*pensiones de vejez, viudez e invalidez*). Most of these were far from generous; nor was there any mechanism for adjustment in line with inflation. In 1970, flushed with the economic success of the intervening years [0.2], the regime decided to make good these deficiencies.

The 1970 reforms improved a number of existing benefits (*prestaciones*) and extended coverage to new areas. In the medium term, their impact was disastrous. One reason was that they further accentuated the complexity and overlap which, despite supposed unification in 1963, characterized the Francoist system. It included numerous exceptional schemes (*regímenes especiales*) for particular groups of workers, as well as other anomalies. While significant sections of the population had no social security cover, some individuals were receiving multiple pensions from different parts of the system.

This bureaucratic complexity aggravated the second, and principal problem bequeathed by the 1970 reforms; their high cost. From 1973 on, economic boom turned to recession [6.1.1], causing a slump in the system's income, which was derived totally from the contributions (*cuotas*) paid by employers and employees. At the same time, the downturn also meant a rapid rise in the number of unemployed, for whom the 1970 reforms had increased the coverage and level of benefit.

The Franco regime's social security legacy thus turned out to be a considerable financial burden on its successors. In 1979 the system's outgoings exceeded its income for the first time. By 1986 its annual deficit had reached 24 per cent of budget. By European standards this figure was normal, or even low. In Spain, however, politicians and public were accustomed to the idea that the system should pay for itself.

The deficit accordingly gave rise to much talk of a 'crisis' in the social security system, and of a massive shortfall (*agujero*) in its finances. That there was, and is, a problem of how to finance the welfare state cannot be denied, but in essence it is one common to all developed countries. The distinctive issues facing the Spanish system in the early 1980s were, first, the alarming speed with which the financial situation was deteriorating and, second, the fact that welfare benefits remained relatively poor in a number of areas.

9.1.2 Reform and its limits

As in other areas, it was only when the Socialist Party (PSOE) reached power in 1982 that real steps were taken to tackle the social security 'crisis' [9.1.1]. Initially this was done by cutting some benefits, starting with the most costly of them: pensions. In 1985 some pension payments were reduced, and the number of years' contributions necessary to receive an old age pension increased. The government also sought to make savings on unemployment benefit by tightening up the requirements for entitlement and reducing the period of payment.

These changes focused attention on those jobless (over 60 per cent) who received no support. In 1989 a number of regional governments introduced a form of general income support, or social wage (*salario social*), to help them.

The central government, however, refused to countenance a country-wide scheme because of concern about its potential cost. Instead, it addressed the problem as part of an attempt to restructure overall provision.

This was the intention of the 1990 Social Security Act (*Ley de Seguridad Social*). Like earlier legislation, the Act distinguishes between financial benefits (*prestaciones económicas*) and benefits in kind (*prestaciones técnicas*). However, it also introduced a distinction between contributory benefits (*prestaciones contributivas*) and non-contributory ones. The intention was for the latter to be financed, not from contributions, but from general government revenue. The separation was finally completed in 1999.

Non-contributory benefits include all benefits in kind, of which by far the most important is health care. They also include subsistence payments to those who, for certain specific reasons, need support, but have not paid into the system for long enough to qualify for the relevant form of contributory benefit. The most important such payments provide income support for the unemployed (*subsidio de desempleo*), as well as basic pensions (*pensiones asistenciales*) for the old and permanent invalids. These latter are paid out of the National Social Welfare Fund (*Fondo Nacional de Asistencia Social/FONAS*) originally set up in 1960, responsibility for which passed to the National Social Services Agency in 1985 [9.3]. Non-contributory unemployment benefit, on the other hand, is administered by the National Employment Agency [6.2.4.1].

Contributory benefits are payable only to those who have made sufficient contributions to the system, on the basis of a number of defined circumstances (*contingencias*). The most important is pensionable status, which covers old age, permanent invalidity, and the condition of widow or orphan. Payments under this head account for over two-thirds of the total budget. The other main ones are unemployment, temporary incapacity for work (*incapacidad laboral transitoria*), and non-permanent invalidity and its aftermath (*invalidez provisional y recuperación*). Family support (*protección a la familia*), which is essentially child benefit, is also a contributory benefit.

These payments are administered by the National Social Security Agency (*Instituto Nacional de Seguridad Social/INSS*), which is attached to the Ministry of Employment. Because of the amounts involved, the system's accounts are kept separate from the general government budget and require parliamentary approval in their own right. While their situation was eased by the removal of non-contributory benefits, it was far from solved. Indeed, insofar as the reforms increased welfare coverage, they actually aggravated the financial situation to some extent.

Again pensions and unemployment benefit were the obvious places for the conservative government elected in 1996 to seek savings. With regard to the second, it has relied essentially on other economic measures reducing the number of unemployed, a strategy that is at last bearing some fruit [6.2.4.2]. On pensions, however, the government took a very different line; it sought to build on the cross-party Toledo Pact of 1995, in which the main political parties had agreed not to use pensions for electioneering purposes.

Accordingly, between 1996 and 2001 the government signed a series of further agreements with the trade unions [5.2.1] on means of rationalizing the pension system. These have certainly helped to stabilize the INSS budget, which even showed a surplus in 1999. Two years earlier the improving situation had enabled a much-needed cut in employers' contributions to the system [6.2.4.2]. Moreover, despite the continued existence of several exceptional schemes [9.1.1], basically those for farmworkers, domestic workers and the self-employed, the system is also much simpler.

However, considerable problems remain. Overall spending on benefits is comparatively low by international standards and still devoted disproportionately to the jobless. A number of needy groups, especially those of recent appearance such as single-parent families and young people living independently, are neglected by the system. Above all, given the rapidity with which Spain's population is ageing [9.4.1], pension costs are bound to rise in the future. Hence the current government's concern to extend provision through personal 'pension plans', possibly as part of company schemes, beyond their present rather rudimentary coverage.

9.2 HEALTH CARE

By the standards of developed countries Spain spends relatively little on health care (*asistencia sanitaria*) – around 7.5 per cent of GDP in 1998. Nevertheless, health spending represents a major burden on public finances, and one that is rising fast. Part of the cause, as in other countries, is the speed of medical advance. However, the problem has been particularly acute in Spain, because until recently the quality of health provision (*oferta sanitaria*) was extremely poor.

9.2.1 The Spanish NHS

It is true that the Franco regime introduced compulsory health insurance (*seguro obligatorio de enfermedad/SOE*) for ever larger groups of workers; by 1975 nearly 80 per cent of the population was covered by it. Yet the resultant system was complicated, wasteful and prone to abuses, in particular the practice of doctors holding posts in both the public and private sectors simultaneously (*pluriempleo*). What is more, only around a fifth of hospital facilities (*instalaciones hospitalarias*) were in public hands, most being run more or less directly by the Church. In 1978 a National Health Agency (*Instituto Nacional de la Salud/INSALUD*) was set up to coordinate provision. However, the move did not change the system's essential features: high dependence on private care and inadequate services.

For reasons of both ideology and efficiency this situation was unacceptable to the Socialist government elected in 1982. It therefore introduced a series of reforms, the framework for which was set out in the 1986 General Health Act (*Ley General de Sanidad/LGS*). The LGS provided for the creation of a National Health Service (*Servicio Nacional de Salud/SNS*) modelled, as the name suggests, on the British NHS rather than the contributory systems common in continental Europe.

Accordingly, the basic principle of the SNS is availability of care free of charge at the point of delivery. By the 1990s universality of free provision had effectively been achieved; only around 1 per cent of the wealthiest Spaniards are now required to pay for treatment under the SNS. However, users are required to bear 40 per cent of the cost of prescriptions (*recetas*), unless they are entitled to exemption. Charges also apply to dental and psychiatric care (*asistencia odontológica y psiquiátrica*).

The 1986 Act placed administration of the SNS in the hands of INSALUD. It provided for the creation of regional health services (*servicios autonómicos de salud*) and district health authorities (*Areas de Salud*), the latter serving a population of between 200,000 and 250,000. Each district is required to contain at least one district health complex (*Centro de Salud*), consisting of a general hospital and other facilities. In many cases these are based on the old health campuses (*ciudades hospitalarias*) in which various general and specialist hospitals were grouped together.

These arrangements apply to hospitals and other facilities run by INSALUD. For those run by private operators the Socialists adopted a similar solution to the one they had already applied in education [8.2.2.1]. Private hospitals may receive public funding, but only if they sign a maintenance agreement (*concierto*) with the health authorities covering the conditions under which they provide care. During the 1980s the government undertook a massive building programme which greatly reduced the importance of privately run facilities. Yet they still account for around 30 per cent of all hospitals, and about 20 per cent of available beds. Most have become maintained hospitals (*centros concertados*), but a significant minority continue to operate on a purely private basis.

Ironically, almost as soon as the SNS had been conceived its national character was undermined by the transfer of health care responsibilities to seven of the country's autonomous regions [3.1.3]. There the regional health services could not only exercise administrative functions but also acquired powers over policy and funding. At the end of 2001 agreement was reached on extending health devolution to the remaining regions [3.3.2].

In an attempt to ensure coordination, in 1987 the government set up the Joint National Health Council (*Consejo Interterritorial del Sistema Nacional de Salud*), which brings together representatives of central and regional governments. It has been unable to prevent a growing disparity in health resources between regions, generally to the detriment of the poorer ones. On the other hand, some see diversity in a more positive light, as a source of innovation. Catalonia has been particularly intent on going its own way, placing considerably greater emphasis on the role of private care than in Spain as a whole.

The conservative central government elected in 1996 has been similarly anxious to encourage the involvement of alternative providers. A year later it opened the way to the creation of health trusts (*fundaciones sanitarias*), as a means of doing so. Originally confined to new facilities, these may now also be formed to run existing ones. The best-known trust facility is the hospital at Alcorcón, near Madrid, but others are active in a wide range of care types, including general practice and preventive medicine. The range of trust sponsors is also wide, and includes medical associations as well as private companies.

9.2.2 Resource problems

Despite spending relatively little on health care, Spaniards enjoy excellent health according to the most commonly used indicators. The country's infant mortality rate, which as late as 1960 stood at 43 per thousand, is now under 9 per thousand – lower than in several EU countries as well as the USA. Life expectancy (*esperanza de vida*) is the highest in the EU, having reached almost 80 for women and over 73 for men. Yet for all the positive statistics, and despite the real achievements of recent years, the Spanish health service is regularly perceived as being in crisis.

The best-known symptom is the persistence of lengthy waiting lists (*listas de espera*) for many types of treatment. These caused renewed controversy in late 2001. During the negotiations on completing the devolution of health powers [3.3.2], a number of regional governments asserted that the lists provided by the central authorities for their regions grossly understated the true situation. Whatever the truth of those accusations – and it seems clear that a degree of manipulation had been taking place – the lists are indicative of significant resource difficulties in the system as a whole.

Thus there is a shortage of qualified nurses (*enfermeros titulados*) and nursing auxiliaries (*auxiliares de clínica*). Spain also continues to have insufficient hospital beds (*camas hospitalarias*) for its needs. Here a distinction must be drawn. Even excluding those in private hospitals, provision of acute beds (*camas de agudos*) is close to the EU average at around 3.5 per 1000 population. However, long-stay beds, especially for medical geriatric care, are in short supply. In addition, the available beds are unevenly distributed, being scarcer in rural areas and the south.

In the case of doctors, numbers are not a problem. In fact, Spain has proportionately more than any other developed country, a situation which reflects the massive increase in those studying medicine since 1980. Yet this same influx has aggravated the problem of poor training; many graduates feel the need to work abroad after qualifying to acquire the practical experience which is virtually non-existent in most medical faculties in Spain.

Expansion has led also to a maldistribution of specialists. Paediatricians are particularly abundant at a time when Spain's birth rate has plummeted. In addition doctors, like hospital beds, are poorly distributed across the country. And many are unemployed, because the system cannot afford to employ them. As a result, junior doctors especially have tended to be dissatisfied. Some of their senior colleagues, too, were offended by the 1987 ban on their occupying several posts simultaneously [9.2.1]; since then they have had to devote themselves to a single job (*dedicación exclusiva*).

The main resource problem, however, is the steady increase in health costs since the 1986 Act. For example, between 1988 and 1994 hospital medical staff increased by 30 per cent. Over the same period there was a 68 per cent rise in the number of hospital managers and administrators. Given the pressure to reduce public spending [6.1.2], the government had to act.

In 1992/93 it introduced a National Health Service Consolidation Plan (*Plan de Consolidación del SNS*), whose basic principle was a clear division between policy-making and the provision of care. Thus the Health Ministry now defines exactly the types of health care which Spaniards are entitled to receive free of charge. It also sets performance targets. These criteria are then incorporated in a services contract (*contrato-programa*) agreed with INSALUD [9.2.1], whose responsibility is to fulfil the targets and conditions set, within its assigned budget.

The Socialist government also moved to stem another source of rising costs, those for medicines. Unannounced, it raised prescription charges substantially, a move soon dubbed *medicamentazo*. After the conservatives came to power they repeated the tactic. But in 1997 they also managed to negotiate an agreement with the drug companies on the use of generic drugs, which previously had made up only around 1 per cent of the Spanish market as opposed to over 50 per cent in some Western countries.

Otherwise the conservatives' main prescriptions for the health service's resource problems have been to advocate an extension of private health provision, and to allow public hospitals greater management freedom. As yet they have shown no inclination to tackle a further important cause of upward pressure on health spending, the stress on expensive specialist care. In Spain, as elsewhere, this reflects the strong influence of doctors on health policy; indeed, the Spanish Medical Associations (*Colegios de Médicos*) act as expert advisers to the government.

9.2.3 Primary care

A further effect of the emphasis on specialist care [9.2.2] is that inadequate resources are directed to primary health care (*atención primaria de salud/APS*). Again, this is not a phenomenon unique to Spain. However, unlike in other Western countries, there was no established system of primary care in place before the rapid technological advances of recent decades. There has therefore been little in the way of a primary care lobby to protect the sector's interests.

The 1986 General Health Act [9.2.1] recognized the danger. Its aims explicitly included health awareness and the prevention of illness, and the Act stressed the importance of non-specialist care in achieving them. But these good intentions have been honoured more in the breach than the observance. Since 1986 the vast bulk of resources has continued to go on specialist care delivered in hospitals.

As a result, the local health centres (*ambulatorios*) through which primary care is delivered are underfunded by comparison with hospitals. Even more than the latter, they suffer from a lack of nursing staff. Moreover, few doctors wish to become GPs (*médicos de cabecera*). Until recently organization of primary care was also poor; even now that an appointment system (*cita previa*) has been introduced waiting times are frequently long, and consultations short. Small wonder that many Spaniards go directly to relatively well-equipped hospital accident and emergency units, thus increasing the pressures on them.

Such units, however, can do little to solve the biggest health problems facing Spain. They derive from the scope and depth of the social and economic changes the country has experienced over the last two or three decades. Alcohol consumption by the young has grown rapidly, as has the proportion of women who smoke. There has been a massive shift from manual labour to desk-bound employment. The country's traditional diet, thought to be the principal cause of good health and long life, is changing dramatically; young Spaniards now ingest as much cholesterol as their contemporaries in northern Europe.

The impact of these changes can be seen in a range of indicators, for example, the high incidence of circulatory and respiratory illness, and the large number of road deaths attributable to drunken driving. They mean that health awareness and illness prevention are even more vital than elsewhere as a factor in improving health levels, and, indeed, in maintaining existing ones. Yet, like other aspects of primary care, they continue to be the poor relations of the Spanish health system.

Like disparities in availability of doctors and facilities [9.2.2], neglect of primary care hits particularly hard at the worse-off in Spanish society, particularly rural dwellers and women. Moreover, research suggests that, in developed countries where health levels are already high, increased spending is generally reflected in the reduction of health inequalities. The poor are thus also likely to be the main losers from continuing downward pressure on health spending.

9.3 SOCIAL SERVICES

In some Western countries there is a long tradition of social welfare provision by charitable organizations (*sociedades benéficas*). In Spain, by contrast, the Church and the family remained virtually the sole providers into the 1970s. Since then, social and political change has radically reduced the social importance of both these institutions. Yet democracy has brought no significant flowering of interest or self-help groups [5.4]. As a result, it has been the public authorities which have been faced with the task of meeting rapidly increasing demand for social services.

Prior to 1975 public social provision was strictly limited, in both quantity and quality. Care facilities for the young, the old and the disabled or disadvantaged, where they existed, consisted almost entirely of large-scale institutions, reminiscent of the Victorian era in the UK. Significantly all tended to be referred to as asylums (*asilos*), a name which reflected the degree of isolation from the rest of society they implied. Such conditions clearly demanded reform. At the end of the 1970s the restored democratic local authorities led the way in establishing alternative forms of provision.

In 1978, to support and coordinate these efforts, the central government set up the the National Social Services Agency (*Instituto Nacional de Servicios Sociales/INSERSO*), but it took few initiatives of its own. In any case, as part of the devolution process responsibility for social services was transferred to the regions in two waves, the second in 1992 [3.3.2]. Since then there has been a noticeable trend for provision to vary from region to region.

Ironically, it was only once the central government had begun to shed its powers in this area that a separate Social Affairs Ministry was set up, in 1988. The new ministry at once took over responsibility for INSERSO, previously attached to the Ministry of Employment and Social Security. Three years previously the Agency had had its remit extended when it absorbed the National Social Welfare Agency (*Instituto Nacional de Asistencia Social/INAS*), responsible for the payment of non-contributory pensions [9.1.2].

Notwithstanding these changes, social services remain very much the Cinderella of the Spanish public sector. Spending continues to be dwarfed by that on health, and on the financial benefits provided by the social security system. Throughout its life the Social Affairs Ministry was the smallest of the central departments. In the first cabinet formed by the conservative government elected in 1996, the portfolio was re-joined to that of the Employment Ministry. The following year INSERSO became the National Immigration and Social Services Agency (IMSERSO), when it took on the task of supporting newly arrived immigrants.

9.4 DISADVANTAGED GROUPS

In any country, certain social groups suffer a degree of disadvantage (*discriminación*) relative to the population as a whole. In some cases these coincide with the major client groups who are the main recipients of welfare services. In others their disadvantage in part reflects the fact that provision largely fails to reach them. The concerns of five such groups structure much of the debate on social issues in Spain.

9.4.1 The elderly

Perhaps the most pressing demands which Spain's welfare services have had to face since 1975 result from the rapidity with which the country's population is ageing. Not only has life expectancy risen dramatically, the country's traditionally high birth rate is now among the world's lowest. One result is the urgent need for more geriatric hospital provision [9.2.2].

Equally great is the problem posed by the need for non-medical geriatric care. Not only are Spaniards living longer, but it is much less usual than in the past for younger relatives to be on hand. And even when they are, it seems that they – like their contemporaries elsewhere in Europe – are increasingly unwilling to assume the task of caring within the family home.

Precisely because that was previously the norm, Spain had until recently virtually no public provision for the elderly. One advantage of this is that most publicly run old people's homes (*residencias de tercera edad*) are relatively new and in good condition. Unfortunately these currently meet only some 40 per cent of the demand, the rest being covered by private homes of much more variable quality. Over a third of these latter are still run by religious orders; although generally of a higher standard than other private homes these are threatened by the sharp drop in the number of nuns [5.1.2.2].

Residential facilities have been supplemented by provision of various types of community-based care (*asistencia comunitaria*). They include sheltered housing (*viviendas tuteladas*), a home-help service (*servicio de ayuda a domicilio*) and helpline facilities (*tele-asistencia domiciliaria*). In addition the existing network of pensioners' day centres (*hogares del pensionista*) has been extended. More innovatively, the Socialist governments of 1982–96 introduced a substantial programme of subsidized holidays for the elderly (*vacaciones de tercera edad*) and health cures (*termalismo*). Given that their pensions have also been mainly unaffected by cutbacks since 1985 [9.1.2], all in all the elderly have been among the major beneficiaries of the expansion of social provision.

9.4.2 The young

Spain's young lack the electoral clout of the old. They are also probably the main victims of the massive rise in housing costs over the last two decades. Many have had little choice but to remain in the parental home until – and sometimes even after – marriage. Above all, the young have been disproportionately affected by the scourge of unemployment [6.2.4.1]. It is thus scarcely surprising that, while the situation of younger children (*menores*) has not as yet been a major source of public concern, teenagers and young adults represent perhaps the most problematic group in Spanish society.

A number of initiatives have been taken by governments to address their situation. In 1985 a National Youth Bureau (*Instituto de la Juventud*) was created, responsibility for which was passed to the Social Affairs Ministry when this was set up three years later. In 1991 an Integrated Youth Plan (*Plan Integral de Juventud*) was launched. Its main thrust was to improve training and qualification levels among the young, and so attack the chronic problem of youth unemployment. But, while such measures may increase young people's chances of securing such work as is available, they do not of themselves create jobs.

Youth unemployment, it would appear, is closely connected with another problem which particularly affects the young: drug addiction (*toxicomanía*).

Although notoriously difficult to measure, this seems to be especially wide-spread in Spain. Various causes have been suggested. Spain lies on the main routes into Europe of both marijuana (from Morocco) and cocaine (from Colombia). The Galician criminal families (*clanes*) who controlled the region's long-standing illicit trade in tobacco were well placed to move into the more lucrative business of narcotics smuggling. And the Socialist government elected in 1982 legalized all consumption, both public and private, a year later.

Perhaps rather more importantly it took a relaxed attitude, to say the least, to the provision of such things as clean needles, drug substitutes and rehabilitation facilities. The 1985 National Drugs Plan (*Plan Nacional sobre Drogas*) seemed to exist largely on paper. With the spectacular rise in the incidence of AIDS (*Síndrome de Inmunodeficiencia Adquirida/SIDA*), official concern grew and in 1992 public consumption of drugs was again made illegal.

However, at a time when even police authorities in some countries are arguing for decriminalization (*despenalización*) of consumption, that hardly seems likely to resolve the issue. Generally, policy seems to have missed the point that, for many young addicts, drugs are only one link in a cycle of despair that also includes unemployment, crime and prostitution. The government appears to have been under the impression that addiction can be handled in isolation from these other issues; it is indicative that the Drugs Plan remained the responsibility of the Health Minister, and was never transferred to the Social Affairs Ministry during its short life [9.3].

Another way in which young people's frustrations became apparent was in rejection of compulsory military service. Throughout the 1990s there was a steady rise in the numbers of conscientious objectors (*objetores de conciencia*), and a more dramatic increase in those refusing to perform even the alternative community service (*servicio social sustitutorio*). These latter, known as *insumisos*, were in breach of the law, and a number were imprisoned.

To some extent the stance of both groups reflected long-standing complaints about the *mili*; the frequent deaths and suicides of recruits, the humiliating and sometimes dangerous initiation rituals. But latterly objectors and, above all, *insumisos* seemed to be expressing a wider resentment among the young. It came as a general relief when the government decided to abolish the *mili* [5.1.1.2].

It is no coincidence that by far the highest incidence of refusal to perform either military or community service (*insumisión*) has been in the Basque Country and Navarre. Especially in the former, youth joblessness is particularly severe. And there, too, radical Basque regionalists close to the terrorist organization ETA [3.2.2.1] are ready and willing to channel resentment. For a decade now they have repeatedly been involved in vandalism, street violence and physical attacks on political opponents.

A number of observers have made the point that in behaviour and appearance many of those involved closely resemble those of seemingly very different groups in other parts of Spain. Gangs of skinheads (*cabezas rapadas*) are now an established phenomenon in the Madrid area, and in a number of other centres. They show clear signs of influence by neo-Nazi groups, but as yet no real political cohesion. Notwithstanding the presence of some better-off elements, the last social remnants of Francoism, most gang members are themselves victims of the marginalization affecting so many young people in Spain today.

9.4.3 Women

Until fairly recently the situation of women in Spanish society was in import-ant respects almost medieval. Until 1975 married women were legally required to obtain their husbands' permission before undertaking any activ-ity outside the home. On Franco's death later that same year both divorce and abortion remained banned. During the transition period divorce was a tricky political issue. In 1981 the then government took steps to legalize it, but split apart in the process [2.2.2]. Some aspects of the measure, but above all the attitudes of the overwhelmingly male Spanish judiciary in applying it, led to dissatisfaction among women's groups about its efficacy.

Abortion was legalized in 1985, although only under three specified cir-cumstances: danger to the life or health of the mother, rape, or physical dam-age to the foetus. A 1991 decision by the Supreme Court, however, seemed to establish the possibility of using social grounds as a further justification. Even so the conditions are the strictest in the EU outside Ireland. And they are enforced – gynaecologists are periodically prosecuted for ignoring them. In practice many doctors still refuse to perform even legal abortions.

As a result, Spain's official abortion rate is very low indeed, less than a third of that in the UK. One effect is the rising number of single mothers (*madres solteras*). However, the official rate does not tell the full story. Many Spanish women travel abroad to receive abortions. Furthermore, it is esti-mated that up to 70 per cent of the abortions performed in Spain are illegal. In the light of the associated health dangers, there has long been discussion of possible legislation based on time limits (*ley de plazos*).

As well as tackling the abortion issue, in 1987 the Socialists set up a National Women's Bureau (*Instituto de la Mujer*). The Bureau pioneered the establishment of centres for battered wives (*mujeres maltratadas*), around 60 of whom still die in Spain every year. It has also produced various Women's Equal Opportunities Plans (*Planes para la Igualdad de Oportunidades de las Mujeres*). Yet these have been characterized by a distinct lack of specific pro-posals, and it is hard to escape the conclusion that their main purpose was the improvement of the government's image among women.

Cynics might see the same tokenism behind the creation of the Social Affairs Ministry [9.3]. It was the smallest in the government and, after the transfer of social service powers to the regions, had few obvious responsibil-ities other than the Youth and Women's Bureaux. Throughout its short life, however, the Ministry accounted for half the female representation in the cab-inet through its successive political heads, Matilde Fernández and Cristina Alberdi.

Similarly, equal opportunity legislation has not, in practice, ended discrimination in the labour market. Women still tend to have lower paid jobs than similarly qualified males, and in the mid-1990s accounted for some 80 per cent of part-time workers. Especially worrying is the fact that little official effort has been devoted to changing the entrenched men's attitudes.

9.4.4 Disabled people

Under the Franco regime state provision for the disabled (*minusválidos*), other than that in 'asylums' [9.3], was limited to social security payments for those most seriously affected. The only major exception was the Spanish National Blind Association (*Organización Nacional de Ciegos Españoles/ONCE*), set up by Franco in 1938 to support those blinded fighting – on his side – in the Civil War.

However, the ONCE has never been a drain on the state, since its activities are more than adequately financed through its various highly popular lotteries. Indeed, for a time its earnings even allowed it to become an important player in the Spanish media sector [5.3.4]. Its activities have also extended to groups suffering from other forms of physical disability (*minusvalía*). In effect, it represents an alternative means of tax-raising to pay for disabled provision.

The current framework for this is provided by the Disabled Persons Integration Act (*Ley de Integración Social de los Minusválidos/LISMI*), passed in 1982. As well as extending the system of payments to the disabled, and increasing their size, the LISMI introduced support for carers (*terceras personas*) and a mobility allowance (*subsidio de movilidad*). The Act also set guidelines for disabled access to public premises.

Over the next decade various types of smaller care units were opened with the aim of providing specialist and more personalized care for particular groups. Some serve the severely mentally handicapped and physically disabled (*centros de atención a minusválidos psíquicos/físicos gravemente afectados/ CAMP/CAMF*). Others are rehabilitation centres for the physically disabled (*centros de recuperación de minusválidos físicos/CRMF*). Still others offer sheltered employment to those not in a position to deal with the world of work (*centros ocupacionales*).

More recently, the emphasis has been on the development of new forms of assistance for the disabled. IMSERSO [9.3] now runs the National Centre for Personal Independence and Technological Aids (*Centro Estatal de Autonomía Personal y Ayudas Técnicas/CEAPAT*). Spain has also participated in various EU programmes aimed at the disabled. Nevertheless, provision remains highly uneven in quantity and quality across the country.

9.4.5 Ethnic minorities

For centuries, dating back to the 'Reconquest' [0.1], many Spaniards' idea of their own nation has had strong overtones of racial purity. Franco, who deliberately likened his uprising against the country's legal government to the country's reconquest from the Moors, instituted an annual Day of the Spanish Race (*Día de la Raza*). After his death, however, any negative feelings associated with such ideas were swamped by enthusiasm for links with the outside world [0.2]. It became common to point to the relative racial tolerance characteristic of Spanish colonialism, and suggest that racism was foreign to the Spanish character.

A more accurate view might have been that Spain was largely unaffected by the factors underlying rising racial tension in other Western European countries during the 1960s and 1970s. It had long since gone through the process of decolonization; its economic backwardness made it a relatively unattractive destination for non-European immigrants, even after controls were relaxed after 1975. Today the country still has a comparatively small immigrant population by EU standards: an estimated 500,000 out of a total of 40 million, just under half of which comes from inside the EU.

In recent years, however, there has been a significant rise in immigration from the developing world [0.4.3]. As a result Spain is now host to a substantial community of North Africans (*magrebíes*), mainly from Morocco, as well as significant numbers of black Africans and Caribbeans. Many being in the country illegally, they are open to exploitation by unscrupulous employers. They are also resented by some Spaniards as a source of competition for scarce jobs [6.2.4], while in a few cases politicians have behaved irresponsibly, exaggerating the scale of immigration and inflaming emotions.

The result has been a degree of harassment and even violence, notably from the skinhead gangs which have appeared in some areas [9.4.2]. However, these were not concerned in the worst outbreak to date. It occurred at El Ejido, in Almería province, in February 2000. Following an alleged incident involving a Moroccan agricultural labourer, a substantial proportion of the town's indigenous population embarked on an orgy of violence and destruction directed against his compatriots, most of whom lived in shanty accommodation outside the town. Subsequently, El Ejido's conservative mayor was unrepentant. At national level, his party's response was to rush through legislation designed to discourage illegal immigration [0.4.3].

Such developments cast doubt on any notion of Spanish immunity to racism. In any case, one group which is effectively indigenous has long been the focus of tensions. Today gypsies still comprise Spain's largest ethnic minority, numbering over 300,000 in total. Popular antagonism towards them remains widespread, and in recent times has been given renewed vigour by the alleged involvement of gypsy gangs in drug dealing. In a number of cases this has led to reprisals against gypsy families or even whole communities.

In response to this situation, in 1988 the Social Affairs Ministry launched a Gypsy Development Programme (*Programa de Desarrollo Gitano*). Among other things it aims to integrate gypsies more closely into Spanish society, for example, by ensuring that all gypsy children receive the same education as other Spaniards, but also to preserve and promote gypsy culture and traditions. Unfortunately these laudable aims sometimes prove problematic and even contradictory.

Typically gypsies continue to live apart from non-gypsy society, often in shanty-like slums on the edges of towns and villages. Their traditional mode of life, which often involves a seasonal pattern of travelling determined by the farming year, can hamper efforts at integration. For instance, children's school attendance is frequently interrupted. And the desire to preserve gypsy traditions can come up against the uncomfortable reality that these may involve customs that seem to infringe contemporary norms, such as the treatment of women in gypsy society.

9.5 GLOSSARY

acogimiento familiar m	fostering
agujero m	deficit (in social security funding)
ambulatorio m	local health centre
Area de Salud f	district health authority
asilo m	asylum; old-style home (for children, the old, etc.)
asistencia comunitaria f	care in the community
asistencia odontológica f	dental care
asistencia sanitaria f	health care
asistencia social f	social welfare provision
atención especialista f	specialist (health) care
atención primaria de salud f	primary health care
auxiliar de clínica mf	nursing auxiliary
ayuda a domicilio f	home-help
cabeza rapada m	skinhead
cama de agudos f	acute bed
cama hospitalaria f	hospital bed
centro concertado m	private hospital publicly funded through a maintenance agreement
Centro de Salud m	district health complex
centro hospitalario m	hospital
centro no concertado m	private hospital
centro ocupacional m	sheltered training centre for the disabled
cita previa f	appointment
ciudad hospitalaria f	'health campus', old-style health complex
Colegio de Médicos m	Medical Association
concierto m	(hospital) maintenance agreement
consulta f	(medical) examination, consultation; doctor's surgery
contingencia f	circumstance (giving entitlement to benefit)
contrato-programa m	services contract
cotización f	(see *cuota*)
cuota f	social security contribution
dedicación exclusiva f	ban on (doctors) filling several salaried posts simultaneously
derecho m	right; entitlement
despenalización f	decriminalization
discriminación f	discrimination; disadvantage

enfermero(a) titulado(a) mf	qualified nurse
esperanza de vida f	life expectancy
familia monoparental f	single-parent family
fundación sanitaria f	health trust
gratuidad f	free provision (of services)
hogar del pensionista m	pensioners' day centre
incapacidad laboral (transitoria) f	(temporary) incapacity for work
instalaciones (hospitalarias) fpl	hospital facilities
insumisión f	refusal to perform military or community service
insumiso m	person who refuses to perform military or community service
invalidez provisional f	non-permanent disability
juventud f	youth; young people; teenagers
ley de plazos f	abortion legislation based on time limits
lista de espera f	waiting list
madre soltera f	single mother
magrebí mf	North African
médico de cabecera m	general practitioner
menor mf	child
minusvalía f	disability
minusválido físico/psíquico m	physically/mentally disabled person
mujer maltratada f	female victim of physical abuse; battered wife
objetor de conciencia m	conscientious objector (to military service)
oferta asistencial/hospitalaria/ sanitaria f	welfare/hospital/health provision
patera f	small boat (used by illegal immigrants from North Africa)
pensión asistencial f	basic non-contributory pension
pensión de invalidez f	disability pension
pensión de vejez f	old age pension
pensión de viudez f	widow's pension
plan de pensiones m	(company) pension scheme; (personal) pension plan
plan de previsión m	Basque Country only: (company) pension scheme; (personal) pension plan
pluriempleo m	simultaneous filling of several salaried posts
prestación f	(welfare) benefit
prestación contributiva f	contributory benefit
prestación económica f	financial benefit
prestación por desempleo f	(contributory) unemployment benefit
prestación técnica/no económica f	benefit in kind
previsión f	social insurance
protección a la familia f	family support, child benefit
racismo m	(see *xenofobia*)
receta f	prescription
recuperación f	recovery (from illness); rehabilitation (of the disabled)
régimen especial m	exceptional scheme
residencia f	home

residencia de ancianos/tercera edad f	old people's home
salario social m	social wage; basic income support
sanidad f	health; health care
servicio autonómico de salud m	regional health service
servicio de ayuda a domicilio m	home-help service
servicio social sustitutorio m	community service alternative to compulsory military service
Síndrome de Inmunodeficiencia Adquirida (SIDA) m	AIDS
sociedad benéfica f	charitable organization
subsidio de desempleo m	non-contributory unemployment benefit, income support
subsidio de movilidad m	mobility allowance
tele-asistencia domiciliaria f	helpline facility
tercera persona f	carer
termalismo m	health cure
toxicomanía f	drug addiction/dependence
vacaciones de tercera edad fpl	subsidized holidays for pensioners
vivienda tutelada f	sheltered housing (unit)
xenofobia f	racism

10

LAW AND ORDER

That Spain should be a 'state under the rule of law' is one of the three fundamental principles of the country's 1978 Constitution [1.1.2]. This chapter
begins by examining the guarantor of that condition, the country's legal system. The following sections look at the institutions charged with combating
threats to the rule of law: the various police forces and the prison service. Since
1978 these have faced an increase in the level of crime as well as a change in its
nature, and the last section considers the delicate relationship between protecting Spanish society from its effects and preserving civil liberties.

10.1 THE LEGAL SYSTEM

One aspect of Spain's limited experience of democratic politics [0.1] is that
its judiciary has historically tended to be more or less directly controlled by
the government of the day. Executive influence was especially widespread
under the Franco regime and took a number of forms. Offences that would in
most countries be considered a matter for the civilian courts fell under military jurisdiction; judges' career chances were under direct government control. As a result, the executive's role in the administration of justice was a
thorny issue facing democratic governments after 1975.

10.1.1 The General Council of the Judiciary

In order to ensure judicial independence the 1978 Constitution created a
General Council of the Judiciary (*Consejo General del Poder Judicial/CGPJ*),
modelled on similar bodies in France and Italy. Two years later detailed
arrangements for the Council's appointment and operation were set out in the
1980 Judiciary Act (*Ley Orgánica del Poder Judicial/LOPJ*). In essence, the CGPJ's
purpose was to remove from government control personnel decisions affecting the judiciary.

Thus under the 1980 Act it had sole responsibility for all such matters,
including the selection of members of the judicial service (*carrera judicial*),

appointment to particular posts, and promotion to higher courts. Its remit also includes conduct of any disciplinary proceedings relating to members of the judiciary, although – somewhat anomalously – its decisions in this regard can be challenged in the Supreme Court [10.1.3].

Furthermore, the CGPJ examines proposed legislation of all types, advising the government as to its compatibility with judicial procedures and the Constitution. It can itself propose changes in the organization of the judiciary and court system. It must be consulted by the government before the latter appoints a new Attorney-General [10.1.2], and it nominates two members of the Constitutional Court [1.1.3] as well as Supreme Court judges [10.1.3]. Finally, it is responsible for nominating from among its own members the Supreme Court's chair, who then automatically assumes that of the CGPJ itself.

In addition to its chairperson, the Council consists of 20 ordinary members (*vocales*) appointed for a five-year period. Eight must be lawyers with at least 15 years' professional experience; the remaining 12 are drawn from the judiciary itself. Under the 1980 Act the members were also elected in two different ways: 12 by the legal profession and eight by the two Houses of Parliament. As a result, control over the judiciary effectively remained in the hands of lawyers appointed by the Franco regime, most of whom were conservative, even reactionary in outlook.

After the Socialist Party (PSOE) reached power in 1982 it felt that the Council majority was blocking reforms which it had been democratically elected to carry out, both within the judicial system and more broadly, for instance over the limited legalization of abortion. In 1985 it therefore passed a second Judiciary Act. Among other measures, this removed from the CGPJ ultimate control over judicial appointments, which henceforth were required to be approved by the Ministry of Justice [10.1.2]. In 1993, however, a further reform reversed this change and returned sole control to the CGPJ.

The 1985 Act also changed the arrangements for appointing the Council itself, all of whose 20 ordinary members were now to be elected by Parliament with a three-fifths majority. The effect of this change was to politicize all appointments to the Council; indeed, as long as the PSOE enjoyed a sufficient parliamentary majority it appointed its own nominees at will. However, once its majority was eroded in the later 1980s vacancies could only be filled if there was agreement between government and opposition. After the 1993 general election this was not forthcoming and vacancies remained unfilled.

This unseemly deadlock, and the politicization it reflected, caused the Council's standing to fall badly in the mid-1990s. In addition, some individual members were involved in unprofessional practices of various sorts; one was even condemned by the Supreme Court as a result. Accordingly, after a minority conservative government came to power in 1996 the main parties finally agreed on candidates for the vacant seats. But the new administration nonetheless remained keen to reform the method of the Council's election – which, given the legislation's entrenched status [1.3.2], required agreement with the opposition. This was eventually achieved in May 2001, as part of a wider pact [10.1.4].

Under the new arrangements, eight Council members are to be elected by the two Houses of Parliament with a three-fifths majority. The remaining twelve will also be elected by MPs, but from a slate of 36 candidates presented by the legal profession. These candidates, in turn, will be presented by the various organizations representative of the legal profession, in proportion to their membership, or by non-affiliated lawyers and judges who can obtain sufficient signatures in support.

Rather than removing political influence, this delicate compromise is really an attempt to balance its different forms. For the various professional organizations are divided essentially along political lines, the larger ones being firmly conservative in outlook. As a result the Council too is made up of identifiably left- and right-wing factions, the latter clearly in the majority at present. In early 2002, when the Council was faced with the task of filling four vacancies on the Supreme Court, the conservative faction imposed its favoured candidates for all of them. Along with other partisan decisions, this dispelled any notion of the Council being apolitical, and both its role and formation seem certain to remain controversial.

10.1.2 Public interest

While judicial independence is crucial to the rule of law, democratic principles also require that the public interest in a correctly functioning legal system may somehow be asserted. This, too, is the subject of various constitutional provisions. First and foremost, the elected government of the day has a number of responsibilities in this area which, as in most continental European countries, are discharged through the Ministry of Justice.

The Ministry has a number of different roles. It drafts government legislation in consultation with various bodies, in particular the Lawyers' Association (*Colegio de Abogados*) to which all lawyers belong. It administers the legal system's physical infrastructure, such as court houses (*palacios de justicia*). And it runs the government's own legal service (*Servicio Jurídico del Estado*).

The Justice Minister is in an inherently delicate position when taking many decisions. As a member of an elected government he or she may, indeed must, bear in mind political criteria, while adhering strictly to the law as head of the legal authorities. Because of this special position the Justice portfolio is normally kept separate from other ministerial responsibilities. There was therefore considerable concern when, in 1994, it was amalgamated with the Interior Ministry [1.4.5]. The conservative government elected two years later opted to return to the practice of appointing a separate Justice Minister.

The second instrument of the public interest within the legal system is the government attorney service (*ministerio fiscal*). This body is responsible principally for acting as public prosecutor in criminal cases. As such, attorneys (*fiscales*) initiate the examination stage of cases [10.1.3], and thereafter cooperate with the police and the examining magistrate in assembling the evidence. At the subsequent trial they lead the prosecution case.

In addition, the attorney service has a general brief to monitor the functioning of the courts to ensure that verdicts are implemented and that procedures are properly carried out. Its members enjoy wide powers to intervene in cases where they have grounds to believe that the public interest is affected. The service is headed by the Attorney-General (*Fiscal General del Estado*), nominated by the government after consulting the General Council of the Judiciary.

Particularly after the 1985 reform of the Council [10.1.1], this arrangement inevitably placed a question mark over the Attorney-General's independence from government. Concern reached a peak in the early 1990s, when the then Socialist government appointed a known party supporter to the post, with the Council's approval – at a time when the succession of scandals involving government members [2.3.4] made his role as defender of the public interest particularly important. In the event his appointment was eventually overturned by the Constitutional Court on a technicality, and subsequently governments of both main parties have adopted a more sensitive attitude to the issue. On the other hand, they have also tended to shy away from their constitutional duty to call the Attorney-General, and the service as a whole, to account for its actions in general.

Finally, the Constitution also includes provisions for more direct public involvement in the judicial system, but these have been implemented only partially and with hesitation. Thus not until 1995 was a measure to regulate the operation of trial by jury (*jurado*) passed. Even then there was very little preparation in terms of public education, giving rise to considerable concern among both lawyers and the public about the practical effects. Similarly the constitutional right to instigate a private prosecution (*acción popular*) has had little practical effect because of the conditions surrounding its use. For only officially recognized legal representatives (*procuradores*) are permitted by law to present cases to a court. And the costs of litigation will be borne by the state only if sufficient public interest can be demonstrated, a very difficult task indeed.

10.1.3 Courts

Justice is dispensed in Spain, as in most countries, in the form of legally binding decisions made by courts. Prior to 1975 several types of institution enjoyed the power to impose these. They included Church courts (*tribunales eclesiásticos*), as well as the tribunals operated by certain professional organizations and by the military (*tribunales de honor*). The 1978 Constitution recognizes the jurisdiction of these latter within the specifically military sphere. With this single exception, however, it explicitly denies legal jurisdiction to all organs other than the courts of the state's own judicial system.

Along with civil and criminal courts, this comprises four other categories unknown in the United Kingdom which deal with specific areas of the law (see Table 10.1). In addition, the court system is structured on the basis of a conceptual division of the judicial process into stages. The central, indeed the only one in many cases (*causas*) is that of trial (*enjuiciamiento*). The approach

Table 10.1 Court types

Name	Type
juzgado de lo civil	civil court
juzgado de lo penal	criminal court
juzgado de lo social	employment court
juzgado de lo contencioso-administrativo	administrative court[a]
juzgado de vigilancia penitenciaria	prison supervision court[b]
tribunal tutelar de menores	children's court

Notes: [a] Deals with disputes between private individuals and state authorities.
[b] Deals with matters relating to the application of prison sentences imposed by the courts.

is investigative rather than adversarial: it is the presiding members of the judiciary, rather than the parties' representatives, who examine witnesses. The court may examine several witnesses together, as a means of resolving contradictions in their evidence (*careo*). If one of the parties has legitimate grounds to question the court's verdict (*sentencia*) or sentence (*condena*) the case may pass to a further stage, that of appeal (*recurso*).

In criminal cases the trial is preceded by another stage, that of examination (*instrucción*). During it the court authorities are responsible for gathering the relevant evidence, in the form of exhibits and statements. The results are then presented to the court trying the case, in a report (*sumario*). It is a fundamental principle of the system that, in a given case, no two of these stages should be handled by the same court.

The conceptual hierarchy of courts overlaps with a second, geographical one, higher levels of which cover larger areas as well as subsequent stages of procedure. It was subject to considerable reform by the 1988 Court Structure and Functions Act (*Ley de Demarcación y Planta Judicial*). The only tier left unaffected by the Act was the lowest, made up of the municipal courts (*juzgados de paz*) with jurisdiction over minor civil and criminal offences (*faltas*). They are presided over by a single Justice of the Peace (*juez de paz*), who is not required to have any legal training.

The fundamental change introduced by the 1988 Act was the establishment of new courts at the level of court districts (*partidos judiciales*) to replace the former district courts (*juzgados de distrito*). These so-called 'courts of the first instance and examination' deal with the bulk of cases. They act as appeal courts for cases tried before justices of the peace, a role in contradiction with their title. In other civil cases they act as a genuine court of the first instance, i.e. as the court by which the case is first heard. In most criminal cases they act as the examining court (*juzgado de instrucción*). These reformed district courts are again presided over by a single member of the judiciary (*juez*). Roughly equivalent to a Scottish sheriff, unlike JPs he or she must be a trained lawyer.

Another change brought about by the 1988 Act was the creation of special provincial criminal courts. They try lesser offences, that is, those subject to a maximum prison term of three years (*arresto menor*). Previously such trials had been heard by the district courts which had examined them, in violation of the principle that different stages of a case should be the responsibility of different courts. Along with the special provincial children's, prison, employment and administrative courts, they complete the category of lower courts.

Courts at higher levels of the system are distinguished in several ways. They are collegiate, that is, they are presided over by a bench composed of several judges (*magistrados*). They consist of several divisions (*salas*), concerned with different types of cases. And they also generally deal with appeals from lower courts rather than with first hearings. An important exception to this last distinction is provided by the provincial courts (*audiencias provinciales*) which, in addition to hearing appeals from below, also try criminal offences too serious to be heard by a lower court.

The next level consists of the Regional High Courts (*tribunales superiores de justicia*) established as a result of devolution in the 1980s, which replace the former regional courts (*audiencias territoriales*). For matters relating exclusively to the region concerned they provide the final court of appeal (*tribunal de última instancia*). In cases where country-wide issues are involved, further recourse may be had to the High Court (*Audiencia Nacional*), established in 1977. Its criminal division also tries cases in certain fields, including falsification of the coinage, contamination of foodstuffs and medicines, and drug trafficking. To allow it to do so it has three special examining courts.

Finally, the Supreme Court (*Tribunal Supremo*) is concerned with resolving appeals relating to the interpretation of legislation. Its decisions in such cases constitute a body of case law (*jurisprudencia*). This is collected and published by the General Council of the Judiciary [10.1.1] for use by lower courts as a source of guidance, additional but subordinate to legislation. The Court consists of five divisions, four of which deal with civil, criminal, administrative and employment matters. The final one is a military division (*sala de lo militar*), to which appeal may be made from the separate military courts.

10.1.4 A system in crisis

The workings of both the Central Council of the Judiciary [10.1.1] and the provisions for democratic control over the legal system [10.1.2] have given rise to considerable concern among experts in Spain. But the widespread popular perception of a system in crisis has a different cause. It is the courts' inability to deal with the cases which come before them within a reasonable time period. Examples are numerous, but perhaps the most notorious is the case, uncovered in 1981, of several hundred people who suffered poisoning as a result of consuming contaminated cooking oil (*síndrome tóxico*). Government officials allegedly involved in the scandal were eventually brought to trial fifteen years later, in 1996.

Various reasons can be identified for such grave delays. Crime has become more common and changed significantly in nature [10.4.1]; the volume of legislation has risen massively. The judicial system has been starved of resources. In 1982 Spain's spending under this heading was only a tenth of the EC average and, despite considerable increases in the interim, it remains relatively low. Consequently, and again despite considerable increases, the judiciary is understaffed by Western standards.

But delays also result from the complex nature of judicial procedure, in particular the division of functions between the public attorney, the examining court and that responsible for the trial [10.1.3]. Even simple cases can generate a lengthy interchange of judicial opinions (*autos*) between them. Yet another factor is the very steep rise in cases taken out against public authorities and coming before the administrative courts (see Table 10.1). This appears to reflect both a continuing and regrettable tendency for such bodies to treat individual members of the public as subjects rather than citizens [1.5.1], and also a growing unwillingness to submit to such treatment.

The Spanish courts also display an alarming propensity to commit errors, ranging from the loss of personal items submitted in evidence to wrongful imprisonment as the result of mistaken identity. Over the five-year period 1991–95 the Ministry of Justice received a total of 1038 claims for compensation in respect of these and other causes, 148 of which it found to be justified. In only one case did the Ministry attempt to recover the compensation paid from the member of the judiciary responsible. Several years later its claim was awaiting examination by a Barcelona court.

The cost of compensation for delays and other injustices is, in financial terms, insignificant. Much more important is the effect of such problems on public attitudes. It is common knowledge that punishment is highly unlikely for many offences, especially traffic offences or failure to obtain various forms of official licence. The result is that the courts, the judicial system and the law itself are all drawn into disrepute.

In order to address some of these issues, in 1992 the government introduced an Emergency Court Procedures Reform Act (*Ley de Medidas Urgentes de Reforma Procesal*). Implementing it proved difficult, however. For example, little progress was made in reducing the bench in higher administrative courts to a single judge, in order to allow more cases to be tried. As a result concern continued to mount. The situation had become so serious that the two main political parties were prepared to bury their differences to attempt a solution, and in May 2001, the conservative government and Socialist opposition finally reached an agreement. Included in it was a new formula for electing the General Council [10.1.1], but the main focus was on reforming the courts [10.1.3].

To that end, the pact contains five main proposals. First, the Supreme Court's workload is to be reduced by restricting access to the country's highest instance. In future it will hear appeals only from the High Court, or from cases it has itself judged. In order to take up the resultant slack, Regional High Courts will be allowed to hear criminal appeals. They will also take over a number of inspection and disciplinary powers. Thirdly, the map of court districts (*mapa judicial*) is to be redrawn to bring it more into line with contemporary population patterns, and so bring justice 'closer' to the mass of the people. In conjunction with that redistribution new district civil courts will be established. Presided over by a single member of the judiciary, they are intended to relieve the hopelessly overloaded general district courts introduced in 1988 [10.1.3].

Finally, new promotion criteria for the judiciary are to be introduced, based on qualifications and productivity (i.e. efficiency in dealing with cases). That change is intended primarily to reduce the importance of seniority (*antigüedad*) in deciding on appointments. But it also reflects another fear expressed in recent years, that some members of the judiciary are too close to particular interests or political parties for comfort.

The examining magistrate (*juez de instrucción*) Baltasár Garzón even sat briefly as a Socialist MP after 1993 [2.3.4]. However, he subsequently fell out badly with his party over his desire to crack down on corruption, while his tenacious investigation of the GAL affair eventually led to the imprisonment of a Socialist ex-Minister [10.4.2]. More recently, Garzón attempted to bring both the former Chilean dictator Augusto Pinochet and the current Italian Prime Minister Silvio Berlusconi to trial in Spain, the latter for alleged offences in relation to his media holdings [5.3.2]. In both cases the conservative government was clearly unhappy with his actions. If Garzón can be accused of anything, it is probably self-promotion rather than subservience to politicians.

On the other hand, the judgement of several of his colleagues does indeed seem to have been influenced by powerful businessmen, or by the government itself. The most notorious case was that of Javier Gómez de Liaño, who instigated proceedings against the PRISA group in a complex dispute involving pay-TV [5.3.4]. His action, which was in line with the government's known wishes, was later rejected by the Supreme Court, and he himself had to answer charges of perverting the course of justice (*prevaricación*).

10.2 THE FORCES OF PUBLIC ORDER

In Spain policing powers are exercised by a number of bodies. Under the Franco regime these included the country's military, and the overlap in functions was reflected by the prevalence of militarist and authoritarian attitudes throughout the various forces concerned. The 1978 Constitution drew a clear distinction between national security, a military responsibility, and the maintenance of public order. Nevertheless, vestiges of the past have remained.

10.2.1 Civil Guard

Spain's oldest public order force is the incongruously named Civil Guard (*Guardia Civil*). Set up in the nineteenth century to counter the problem of banditry on country roads, it retains a number of military characteristics. Not only do Civil Guard officers (*guardias*), like policemen in many countries, carry arms. They are deployed, often far from their home region, in barracks (*cuarteles*), and thus separated from the local population they serve.

Traditionally the Civil Guard's services to travellers in distress caused it to be known affectionately as *La Benemérita* (The Admirables). However, during and after the Franco era it became the subject of considerable public suspicion, because of doubts about its commitment to democracy. Mainly drawn from Spain's Military Academy, its officers have tended to share the reactionary views typical of their Army colleagues [5.1.1.1]. What is more, particularly in the early 1980s, the Civil Guard was the principal target of ETA terrorism [3.2.2.1].

These problems burst into the open with the participation of some Civil Guards in the 1981 attempted coup [0.3.3]. The Socialist government elected the following year placed the force under the command of Lieutenant-General Sáenz de Santa María, previously head of the National Police [10.2.2]. He was given the task of quelling unrest; once he was judged to have done so he was replaced by the Civil Guard's first ever civilian commander, Luis Roldán.

Only in time of war is the Civil Guard now responsible to the Defence Ministry, otherwise its political head is the Interior Minister. As a sop to officers' feelings – and in defiance of the EU's declared policy of phasing out all paramilitary police units – the Civil Guard's standing orders continue to reaffirm its military character. However, their detailed provisions are clearly closer to those of a police force.

These various moves have largely put a stop to overt insubordination, but not to all the Civil Guard's problems. They were aggravated by the activities of Roldán [10.4.1], which left the Civil Guard with an unnecessarily large and unwieldy central staff, infected with corruption. However, the force's problems go far beyond the influence of a single person.

Its officers have repeatedly been involved in human rights abuse of detainees, especially but not exclusively ETA suspects. The Intxaurrondo barracks in San Sebastián has been at the centre of a number of such allegations. In 1996 its former head, Lieutenant-General Rodríguez Galindo, was convicted in connection with the disappearance, torture and murder of two young Basques in the 1980s. Some of his subordinates, and officers elsewhere, have been found guilty of involvement in criminal activities, including drug trafficking. There is evidence, too, of politically motivated violence by Civil Guard officers, one of whom was charged with Spain's first race killing, of a young woman from the Dominican Republic.

In part the Civil Guard's problems can be traced to underemployment, now that relatively few Spaniards live in the rural areas that are its prime responsibility. The government has attempted to combat this problem by extending the force's activities, previously mainly concerned with patrolling traffic and Spain's external borders. Specialist units have been created to deal with coastal patrolling and with environmental problems such as forest fires, dumping of toxic wastes and protection of endangered species [7.3.1]. It must be open to question whether such changes will serve to harness fully the energies and loyalty of highly conservative officers who continue to see themselves as soldiers. So too must be their effectiveness as a response to overmanning, as they were accompanied by an increase in the force's manpower.

10.2.2 Police

Spain's largest purely civilian policing agency is the National Police Force (*Cuerpo Nacional de Policía/CNP*). It was formed in 1986 by amalgamating two existing forces, the General Force (*Cuerpo General*) and the National Police (*Policía Nacional*), until 1978 known as the Armed Police (*Policía Armada*). Both of these were established by the Franco regime, and the second in particular was closely associated with its repression of civil liberties.

Yet, unlike the Civil Guard [10.2.1], the CNP managed to throw off that aspect of its past fairly quickly. To a large extent that was thanks to the work of Lieutenant-General José Antonio Sáenz de Santa María, the force's commander from 1979 to 1982, under whose leadership it took an active part in suppressing the 1981 coup attempt [0.3.3]. Sáenz de Santa María also set up the Special Operations Group (*Grupo Especial de Operaciones/GEO*), which has a creditable record in ending terrorist sieges and similar operations.

Of course, the past had a certain weight. Inevitably, many senior positions continued to be held by officers promoted under the old regime. Indeed, for many years those known to hold more progressive ideas were persistently marginalized by the Interior Ministry, which has overall responsibility for the police. In 1994 Juan Alberto Belloch [2.3.4] took over as Interior Minister. As a lawyer, former judiciary member and also Minister of Justice, he was well aware of the problems caused by the lack of change in senior police personnel. Accordingly, he took action to put younger officers in charge.

But the most burdensome legacy of the Franco era, one which can still be felt, is the CNP's chronic undermanning and lack of resources. With fewer officers than the Civil Guard, the CNP has to deal with some four-fifths of crime, which itself has become much tougher to deal with in recent years [10.4.1]. Increasingly the CNP has been forced to concentrate on the growing problems of major crime, to the detriment of the pettier varieties which are most ordinary people's main concern.

Successive initiatives in neighbourhood and community policing (*policía de barrio/proximidad*) have done little to damp public disquiet. That, in turn, has served to further undermine the CNP's already low morale, which has occasionally been reflected in officers themselves turning to crime. It is also apparent in antagonism towards the Civil Guard; on occasion officers from the two forces have come to blows over successful drug hauls. More mundanely, there are problems of overlapping functions, not just with the Guard, but with the country's various other civilian forces.

The most numerous of these are the local police (*policía municipal*) who in larger towns are responsible for local by-laws, including parking regulations. Considerably wider responsibilities are wielded by the forces under the control of the Basque and Catalan governments (*Ertzaintza* and *Mossos d'Esquadre*), which have taken over much of the CNP's remit in their respective regions.

In the Basque Country the situation used to be further complicated by the existence of provincial police forces, but these have now been absorbed into the *Ertzaintza*.

10.3 THE PRISON SERVICE

Prisons in Spain are the responsibility of the Directorate-General of Prisons (*Dirección General de Instituciones Penitenciarias*), which forms part of the Interior Ministry. Down the years the country has produced a number of notable penal reformers, and in general prison conditions have been fairly good. In recent years, however, there has been growing concern, for a number of reasons.

Like the courts and the police, prisons (*centros penitenciarios*) have been placed under an increasing burden by the changing nature of crime [10.4.1]. One result of that has been a steep rise in the number of prison inmates (*reclusos*); between 1983 and 1991 alone this rose from under 15,000 to nearly 40,000. In a number of establishments the result has been severe overcrowding (*masificación*). Furthermore, there is a lack of adequate prison staff (*funcionarios de prisiones*). That in turn compounds the security problems posed by outdated facilities, which have led to a number of spectacular escapes from custody, most notably by businessman-turned-politician José María Ruiz Mateos [2.6] and former Civil Guard commander Luis Roldán [10.4.1].

The problems are aggravated by chronic delays in the court system [10.1.4], which means that prisons have to deal with many remand prisoners (*presos preventivos*). Their numbers first rose sharply during the transition period after 1975, due partly to a rise in offences. But the increase was also the result of a 1980 measure which greatly tightened up the conditions governing release on bail (*libertad bajo fianza*). Specialist remand facilities proved quite inadequate to cope with these twin pressures.

As a result, remand prisoners – substantial numbers of whom would later be acquitted – were held in unsatisfactory conditions, and alongside convicted prisoners (*condenados*). The same problem applied to juvenile offenders, and to first offenders (*primeros*), who, in theory, should be kept separate from previous offenders (*reincidentes*). In 1983 the new Socialist government revoked the 1980 amendment to the bail regulations and placed a limit on the time which prisoners might spend on remand (three years for those accused of serious crimes, 18 months in the case of minor offences).

The change led to a massive exodus from the prisons, thought to have contributed to a further rise in offences. Subsequently the government introduced a third change, increasing the limits on remand time (to four and two years, respectively). It has succeeded in stabilizing the situation to a considerable degree, although remand prisoners still account for around a third of the total.

The other main issues facing the prison system relate to inmates at the other end of the scale, that is, those convicted of serious crimes of violence.

Spain has one high-security prison (*centro de alta seguridad*), located at Herrera de la Mancha. However, few of the most controversial prisoners convicted of violent crimes are held there. These are ETA members convicted of terrorist offences [3.2.2.1]. ETA and its supporters claim to regard these as political prisoners (*presos políticos*), and persistently demand special treatment for them. The government's policy towards them has varied, tending sometimes towards concentrating them in a small number of prisons, sometimes towards dispersal among many.

This latter policy was designed to make it easier for individual ETA members to renounce violence and opt for reintegration into society (*reinserción social*). That approach has been criticized from the political right, since it involves early release of convicted terrorists. In the 1990s many conservatives demanded that the courts should be able to require sentences to be served in full (*cumplimiento íntegro de penas*). The resultant debate took on some of the symbolic significance of that in the UK over reintroduction of the death penalty (*pena de muerte*), which in Spain is forbidden by the 1978 Constitution.

The Socialist government of the time argued that the Constitution also outlaws full-term sentencing. Its argument was based on the constitutional principle that one of the aims of imprisonment should be rehabilitation of offenders (*resocialización*). For one thing, locking up prisoners for longer periods in itself works against rehabilitation. Moreover, early release is one of the most important of privileges (*beneficios penitenciarios*) which act as an incentive for prisoners to join actively in rehabilitation programmes.

On these grounds, the new Criminal Code passed in 1995 [10.4.3] left the question of privileges, including early release and parole (*libertad condicional*), in the hands of the prison supervision courts (see Table 10.1). The maximum prison term to be served in normal circumstances is set at 20 years. However, exceptions are allowed where consecutive sentences (*penas múltiples*) are involved, above all if any of the offences concerned is particularly serious. The 1995 Code also includes a number of steps designed to address the problems of overcrowding and reoffending, although their implementation has been dogged by resource problems.

10.4 CRIME AND CIVIL LIBERTIES

Declining respect for the law is a common complaint among some older Spaniards, and it is true that the number of offences rose sharply after Franco's death. On that basis it was sometimes argued that democracy had made Spain less safe and law-abiding. Yet, in so far as international comparisons are possible in a field where statistics are notoriously hard to interpret, the country's crime rate remains relatively low. Rather then the incidence, it is the nature of crime that has changed most radically, in ways that make it much more of a problem. On the other hand, rather less change than desirable has been observed in another area: the abuses of human rights and the law by public authorities, which were such a feature of the former regime.

10.4.1 Changing nature of crime

Certainly the number of offences (*delitos*) recorded in Spain rose substantially in the fifteen years after Franco's death. However, since then it has tended to level off. Today the official level of crime (*delincuencia*) is around one-third of that in the UK. Even allowing for under-reporting it seems clear that crime is not a major problem, although the fact that it was previously so little known inevitably conditions public perceptions of the present level. Whenever opinion pollsters ask Spaniards which issues most concern them, the notion of *inseguridad ciudadana* always features highly; in that sense the phrase has acquired roughly the connotations of 'law and order' in the British context.

What is meant is a generalized fear of offences affecting both individuals' property (e.g. house-breaking, car theft, bag-snatching) and their physical safety (muggings and other, more serious forms of assault). Such offences are concentrated in specific areas, particularly the depressed outlying parts of larger cities (*barrios periféricos*) and, to a lesser extent, tourist areas. The vast majority of offenders come from deprived backgrounds, turn to crime when young and then re-offend, in most cases repeatedly; many, especially the younger ones, are drug users. The problem is thus essentially one for the appropriate social services, which lack the resources necessary to deal with it [9.3].

Central government's response to public concern has tended to concentrate more on policing. In 1992 it introduced the Public Safety Act (*Ley de Seguridad Ciudadana*), better known as the 'Corcuera Act' after the then Interior Minister, the main aim of which was to clamp down on drug-related offences. However, the methods it proposed provoked considerable controversy, and it was eventually declared unconstitutional [10.4.2].

Two years later Corcuera's successor, Juan Alberto Belloch [10.2.2], announced a Civil Liberty and Public Safety Plan (*Plan de Libertad y Seguridad Ciudadanas*). The Plan's title betrayed the need to improve public perceptions of the police, and its central idea was to get more police on the streets in a preventive role. But neither such neighbourhood policing (*policía de barrio*), or a later scheme based on community policing (*policía de proximidad*), have enjoyed great success. Not surprisingly, given the lack of police manpower [10.2.2].

What is more, over the last decade the police have had to devote an increasing proportion of their scarce resources to various types of less frequent but much more serious offences. Thus there have been a number of extremely unpleasant attacks on women and children of the sort with which the UK has become depressingly familiar, but which were previously all but unknown in Spain. Even more worrying is the rise in organized crime, especially in Madrid and along the Mediterranean coast, a development thought to be associated with Mafia-type gangs. As elsewhere, their activities are often related to the drug trade, in which indigenous gangs such as the Galician clans have long been involved [9.4.2].

Organized crime is closely related to money-laundering (*blanqueo de dinero*), which the Spanish authorities claim to be especially rife in Gibraltar. But Spain, like other developed countries, is not immune from the problem, which in another sense is simply one aspect of the wider phenomenon of white collar crime (*criminalidad de cuello blanco*). The last two decades have seen various cases of large-scale financial fraud in the private sector. Perhaps the most notorious names are those of Mario Conde, one-time chairman of the *Banesto* bank, and Javier de la Rosa, who headed the Spanish operation of the Kuwait Investment Office (KIO).

Other cases have involved more or less senior figures in the public sector. One even involved the former Governor of the Bank of Spain, Mariano Rubio, who was found to have engaged in various forms of insider dealing. Another was that of the first civilian head of the Civil Guard, Luis Roldán [10.2.1], who was discovered to have made a fortune from rake-offs on tenders for building new barracks and other projects. The political parties, too, have been involved in such influence-peddling [2.1.3].

Politics is also linked, in a very different way, to another problem which soaks up valuable police resources, that of terrorism. Indeed, the activists and supporters of the Basque organization ETA would claim that it is a purely political phenomenon. While that might have been sustainable before 1975, the evolution of its activities since then marks them out as essentially criminal in nature [3.2.2.1]. As well as numerous members of the public, its victims have included public officials, local, regional and national politicians (one of them a former cabinet minister) of various persuasions, and Francisco Tomás y Valiente, a former chairman of the Constitutional Court.

Several times it has seemed that the police were on the point of destroying ETA, notably in the early 1990s [3.2.2.3]. More recently, in 1998/99, it maintained a ceasefire (*tregua*) for over a year. But sadly it continues to exist – and kill, now also journalists critical of its violence [3.2.2.4]. Gruesome as it is, that development is merely a new form of the intimidation with which ETA's opponents have long been familiar, especially in small rural communities. An important agent of this is the young camp-followers who are also responsible for regular outbursts of street violence (*kale borroka*) that involve burning buses, attacking police officers and similar activities. At a very different level, it seems certain that ETA has maintained links with the al-Qaeda international terrorist network.

ETA was not the only regionalist organization to turn to violence in the 1970s. However, neither the Catalan group Free Homeland (*Terra Lliure*) nor the Galician People's Guerilla Army (*Ejército Guerrilleiro do Pobo Galego*) have been active for many years. A further grouping known as GRAPO (*Grupos Revolucionarios Antifascistas Primero de Octubre*) carried out sporadic actions, mainly kidnappings, into the 1990s. Its nature was never fully clear; some observers suspected it of being a front organization for elements in the security forces, a belief given credibility by revelations about state-sponsored counter-terrorism in the Basque Country [10.4.2].

10.4.2 Civil liberties

The 'dirty war' against ETA is undoubtedly the most severe breach of civil liberties to have occurred in Spain since its return to democracy. It was carried on by a shadowy organization known as the Anti-terrorist Liberation Groups (*Grupos Antiterroristas de Liberación/GAL*), which killed 27 people and injured over 30 others, almost all in the French Basque Country, between 1983 and 1987. Few of their victims were important or even proven ETA activists; several were French citizens with no ETA connections whatsoever.

The first GAL members captured were mercenaries and common criminals, but in 1991 two Spanish police officers were convicted of recruiting and organizing these, the superior being José Amedo. Their subsequent confessions, above all Amedo's, incriminated not only their immediate superiors but politically appointed administrators in the Basque Country and the Ministry of the Interior. Other evidence established links to the secret service (CESID) and to the Civil Guard, especially the notorious Intxaurrondo barracks in San Sebastian [10.2.1].

In 1998 twelve senior government servants were convicted of involvement in one GAL operation, the botched kidnapping of a French citizen Segundo Marey. Among them was José Barrionuevo, Interior Minister at the time, who was subsequently given a 10-year jail sentence. Two years later five more officials, including Intxaurrondo's commander Lieutentant-General Rodríguez Galindo, were sentenced in a second case [10.2.1], and investigation of others continues. Accusations that 'Mister X', the GAL's supreme commander, was actually Felipe González, Socialist Prime Minister from 1982 to 1996, were never substantiated.

The GAL affair's significance is hard to exaggerate. For one thing, it has undoubtedly made ending ETA's violence significantly more difficult [3.2.2.3]. Its negative impact in the Basque Country was greatly increased by an aspect almost as disturbing as the GAL's actions themselves: the persistent attempts by central government to obstruct investigations by journalists and individual judges, notably Baltasár Garzón [10.1.4].

Such obstruction did not even cease when the Socialists fell from power in 1996. Against the advice of the Central Council of the Judiciary [10.1.1], the new conservative administration refused to release government documents essential to the case without even submitting them for judicial review (*control*) to establish their degree of sensitivity. This belated solidarity – the GAL affair had been a major plank of the conservatives' campaign to unseat González – was a timely reminder that the 'dirty war' almost certainly started under the centre-right governments of 1976–82, through the agency of the 'Basque-Spanish Battalion'.

At the same time, civil rights abuses in the fight against terrorism have stretched well beyond the GAL affair. Sadly, there have been repeated instances of maltreatment, torture and even death in detention. A number of senior officials have been implicated; in 1997 revelations about the treatment of an ETA suspect by the name of Elejalde led to the dismissal of the chief of police in San Sebastian, and the Civil Governor of Guipúzcoa province [1.5.3].

Many such cases have been concerned with the application of the Anti-terrorist Act (*Ley Antiterrorista*). Originally introduced in 1977 by the then centrist administration as an emergency measure, in 1985 it was normalized by the Socialist government in power at the time. The Act allows for the suspension of normal safeguards for the rights of detainees, such as access to a lawyer, where they are suspected of terrorist offences. In 1988, however, police officers were convicted of having used it in the case of a common criminal known as *El Nani*, who died in custody after suffering severe maltreatment.

Worries about police malpractice of this sort were at the root of opposition to the 1992 Corcuera Act [10.4.1]. It proposed to give the police greatly increased powers to enter private premises in search of drugs; the phrase universally associated with it was 'kicking the door in' (*patada en la puerta*). Its opponents referred the measure to the Constitutional Court [1.1.3], which eventually found that it did indeed infringe constitutional safeguards for individual liberties and declared it invalid.

More generally, the governments of the post-Franco era have shown little desire to rein in or even investigate abuses by the security forces. Several scandals have occurred due to illegal telephone tapping (*escuchas telefónicas*) by national and regional police forces, and by the Defence Intelligence Service (*Centro Superior de Información de la Defensa/CESID*), the main Spanish secret service. In 1993 one such case forced the resignation of the Deputy Prime Minister, Narcis Serra, and six years later the Service's former head, Emilio Manglano, was jailed for his part in the affair.

The treatment of suspected illegal immigrants is another area of concern. The Aliens Act (*Ley de Extranjería*) in force up to 1999 gave the Spanish authorities wide powers of deportation without recourse to the courts. Its replacement, passed in 2000 by the conservative government against the opposition of all other significant political forces, denies those suspected of entering the country illegally certain basic civil freedoms, such as the right of association or to join a trade union. And, in the spring of 2002, reports emerged of the appalling conditions in two centres on the Canaries used to house Africans who had crossed clandestinely to the islands.

10.4.3 The 1995 Criminal Code

A need long recognized by all shades of political opinion in Spain was a thorough revision of the country's criminal code (*código penal*), which in essence dated from the previous century. It was a theme of the 1982 election campaign which brought the Socialist Party (PSOE) to power. The following year the PSOE introduced changes covering about a sixth of the relevant provisions, including the decriminalization (*despenalización*) of soft drug usage. However, it was not for over a decade that a full revision was carried out, in 1995.

The substantial changes introduced by the new code reflect changes in the nature of crime [10.4.1], as well as the consolidation of democratic values over the foregoing 20 years. Thus a new category of corporate offences (*delitos societarios*) was introduced, in an attempt to counter white-collar crime. They relate to company directors and carry a maximum penalty of three years' imprisonment, as well as heavy fines. Specifically covered are the falsification of company accounts, and the use of a majority holding to decide on actions contrary to the interest of other shareholders.

In the area of political corruption [2.1.3], the new code mainly increases the penalties for existing offences. Those involved in bribery of public employees (*cohecho*) may receive a fine and six-year prison term, as well as disqualification from public office (*inhabilitación*) for up to 12 years. One new provision relates to conflict of interest; public employees who act as advisers to private persons or companies may now be heavily fined and barred from office for three years.

Other changes introduced by the code relate particularly to young offenders [10.4.1], and place the emphasis on preventing reoffending rather than punishment. Incapacity due to drug or alcohol addiction can now, under certain circumstances, exempt individuals from criminal responsibility, thus opening the way to rehabilitation outside prison. Those who refused to perform compulsory military or community service in the last years before their abolition [5.1.1.2] were more likely to be fined than imprisoned.

The new code also includes a number of measures designed to reduce prison overcrowding and aid rehabilitation by keeping offenders out of prison as far as possible [10.3]. They extend the opportunities for courts to impose a suspended sentence (*suspensión de pena*), a possibility first introduced in 1983. A completely new concept is that of weekend imprisonment (*arrestos de fin de semana*), which may replace terms of up to two years at the rate of two weekends per week of sentence. With the agreement of the offender, fines or community service (*trabajos en beneficio de la comunidad*) may also be substituted.

Finally, the new code widens significantly the civil responsibility of the state for the actions of its employees. Compensation to members of the public for the errors and omissions of public bodies is now payable under much less stringent conditions. No longer must a claimant prove the direct responsibility of a particular employee, but need merely show that he or she was prejudiced by the 'operation of public services'. Moreover, responsibility is no longer limited to intentional acts (*delitos dolosos*) but extends to unintended ones (*delitos culposos*). This last change was introduced during the code's passage through Parliament, against the government's will. That, like the provision itself, was a welcome check on the executive [1.4.1], and a reassuring indication of Spanish democracy's good health.

10.5 GLOSSARY

acción popular f	private prosecution
antecedentes penales mpl	criminal record

antigüedad f	seniority
arresto de fin de semana m	weekend imprisonment
arresto mayor m	custodial/prison sentence of over three years
arresto menor m	custodial/prison sentence of up to three years
Audiencia Nacional f	high court
audiencia provincial f	provincial court
audiencia territorial f	old-style regional court
auto m	judicial opinion
barrio periférico m	(deprived) outlying area of city
beneficios penitenciarios mpl	privileges granted to prisoners
Benemérita f	Civil Guard
blanqueo de dinero m	money-laundering
careo m	simultaneous examination by a court of several witnesses
carrera judicial f	judicial service
causa f	case
centro de alta seguridad m	high-security prison
centro penitenciario m	prison
código civil/penal m	civil/criminal code
cohecho m	bribery of public employee
Colegio de Abogados m	Lawyers' Association
condena f	sentence
condenado m	convicted prisoner
Consejo General del Poder Judicial (CGPJ) m	General Council of the Judiciary
contencioso m	case, legal dispute
control judicial m	judicial review
criminalidad f	crime; criminality
criminalidad de cuello blanco f	white-collar crime
Cuerpo Nacional de Policía (CNP) m	National Police Force
cumplimiento íntegro de penas m	full-term sentencing
delincuencia f	crime
delito m	offence
delito culposo m	unintentionally prejudicial act
delito doloso m	intentionally prejudicial act
delito societario m	corporate offence
despenalización f	decriminalization
destino m	post (in judicial service)
director m	governor (of prison)
enjuiciamiento m	(process of) trial
Ertzaintza f	Basque police force
escuchas telefónicas fpl	phone-tapping
falta f	minor offence
fiscal m	state attorney
Fiscal General del Estado m	Attorney-General
funcionario de prisiones m	member of prison staff; prison warder
Grupo Especial de Operaciones (GEO) m	Special Operations Group (of National Police)

guardia (civil) m	civil guard officer
Guardia Civil f	Civil Guard
inhabilitación f	disqualification (from office)
inseguridad ciudadana f	lack of public safety
instrucción f	examination (stage of legal process)
juez m	member of judiciary
juez de instrucción m	examining magistrate
juez de paz m	justice of the peace
juicio m	trial (of a particular case)
jurado m	jury
jurisprudencia f	jurisprudence, case law
juzgado m	court
juzgado de lo civil m	civil court
juzgado de lo contencioso-administrativo m	administrative court
juzgado de distrito m	old-style district court
juzgado de lo penal m	criminal court
juzgado de lo social m	employment court
juzgado de paz m	municipal court
juzgado de primera instancia m	court of the first instance
juzgado de primera instancia e instrucción m	new-style district court
juzgado de última instancia m	final court of appeal
juzgado de vigilancia penitenciaria m	prison supervision court
kale borroka f	campaign of street violence by younger ETA supporters
lavado de dinero m	(see *blanqueo de dinero*)
libertad bajo fianza f	release on bail
libertad ciudadana f	civil liberty
libertad condicional f	parole
magistrado m	judge
mapa judicial m	division of country into court districts
masificación de presos f	prison overcrowding
ministerio fiscal m	government attorney service
Mossos d'Esquadre mpl	Catalan police force
órgano colegial m	court presided by bench with several members
órgano unipersonal m	court presided by single-person bench
palacio de justicia m	court house
partido judicial m	court district
pena f	sentence
pena de muerte f	death sentence
penas múltiples fpl	consecutive sentences
poder judicial m	judiciary
policía de barrio f	neighbourhood policing
policía de proximidad f	community policing
preso m	prison inmate, prisoner
preso preventivo m	remand prisoner
prevaricación f	perverting the course of justice
primero m	first offender

procurador m	officially recognized legal representative
recluso m	(see *preso*)
recurso m	appeal
reincidente mf	reoffender
reinserción social f	reintegration into society; rehabilitation of offenders
resocialización f	rehabilitation of offenders
sala f	division (of court)
sala de lo militar f	division of Supreme Court dealing with appeals from military courts
sentencia f	verdict
Servicio Jurídico del Estado m	government legal service
suburbio m	(see *barrio periférico*)
sumario m	report from examining court/magistrate
suspensión de pena f	suspended sentence
trabajos en beneficio de la comunidad mpl	community work
tregua f	(ETA) ceasefire
tribunal m	(see *juzgado*)
tribunal de honor m	military court; tribunal of professional association
tribunal eclesiástico m	Church court
Tribunal Superior de Justicia m	regional high court
Tribunal Supremo m	Supreme Court
tribunal tutelar de menores m	children's court
vocal mf	ordinary member (of committee, council, etc.)

11

THE REGIONS

This chapter gives pen-portraits of Spain's seventeen autonomous regions (*Comunidades Autónomas*/CCAA) and two 'autonomous cities'. They include the principal geographic and demographic features of each region, its politics, economy and media landscape, as well as any distinctive cultural character-istics. In addition, a number of basic statistics are summarized at the end of the chapter, in Table 11.1. It should be noted that the focus here is on regions' internal affairs. The impact on Spanish politics as a whole of regionalists – regionally-based parties which aim to protect regional interests – is dealt with in Chapter 3 [3.2.1–3].

11.1 ANDALUSIA

Regional capital: Seville (*Sevilla*)
Main population centres: Seville (701,000), Málaga (532,000), Córdoba (313,000), Granada (244,000), Jerez de la Frontera (184,000), Almería (169,000), Huelva (141,000), Cádiz (140,000), Jaén (111,000), Marbella (106,000), Algeciras (104,000), Dos Hermanas (97,000)
Official name of regional government: *Junta de Andalucía*
Regional prime minister: Manuel Chaves (PSOE)
Composition of parliament following most recent regional election (2000): Andalusian Socialist Party (PSOE-A) 52; People's Party (PP) 46; Andalusian United Left-Greens (IULV-CA) 6; Andalusian Regionalist Party (PA) 5
Leading daily newspapers (readership as percentage of all newspaper readers):
Abc (15%), *Ideal* (13%), *Diario Sur* (11%), *Diario de Cádiz* (8%)

With some 40 per cent more inhabitants than Denmark, Andalusia (*Andalucía*) is Spain's most populous region and its second-largest by area. Andalusia's people live overwhelmingly in relatively large settlements – it has more cities with over 100,000 inhabitants than any other region – between which lie vast tracts of virtually uninhabited land. While the broad, low-lying valley of the Guadalquivir river forms the region's heart, it also includes such major mountain ranges as the Sierra Morena and the Sierra Nevada, the latter of which includes mainland Spain's highest peak, the Mulhacén. And, whereas Andalusia is blessed by a generally Mediterranean climate and magnificent scenery, both coastal and inland, it also suffers severe environmental problems, in the form of desertification [7.2.2] and the pollution caused by mining activities [7.1.2].

Many of the traditions and customs popularly associated with Spain, such as bullfighting and flamenco dancing, are in fact essentially Andalusian. This distinctive character has various roots, notably the region's lengthy occupation by the Moors – its name comes from the Arabic *al-Andalus* – and the strong gypsy presence there. With the prospect of devolution in the late 1970s feelings of regional identity acquired a new strength and coherence, ensuring that Andalusia joined the group of regions endowed with a higher level of autonomy [3.1.2].

One aspect of this awakening was the establishment of the Andalusian Regionalist Party (*Partido Andalucista/PA*) [3.2.3.1], which has remained a feature of the region's political landscape ever since. Indeed, since 1996 the PA has been a junior partner in the region's coalition government. Its success has been strictly limited, though, not least by constant friction between supporters in different cities and provinces. In particular, the PA has suffered from a lengthy and public feud between its Seville-based party leader Alejandro Rojas Marcos and the long-time Mayor of Jerez, Pedro Pacheco.

As a result the regional government continues to be effectively controlled by the Socialist Party (PSOE), as it has been since its foundation. Regional premier Manuel Chaves, a former central government minister, has been in office since 1991, and is one of the PSOE's most powerful 'barons' [2.3.6]. His party's dominance has been based on the support of the rural poor, and has been gradually eroded by a series of scandals similar to those which affected the party nationally [2.3.4]. The communist-led United Left (IU), which engaged in a bitter feud with the PSOE over exactly such issues [2.5.2], has also seen its backing severely reduced. Conversely, through the 1990s the conservative People's Party gained ground steadily; at the 2000 general election it actually outpolled the Socialists in four of the region's eight provinces.

Andalusia has two public television channels of its own, *Canal Sur* and *Canal 2 Andalucía*, which between them command an audience share of around one fifth. Newspaper readership is low, especially when one considers that the region is one of only two where the top-selling daily is the specialist sports title *Marca*. It is also atypically distributed in Spanish terms. Thus Andalusia is the only region where the most-read news daily is the conservative *Abc* [5.3.3], which was originally based in Seville. At the same time, though, papers produced in the region account for almost three-quarters of total readership. Yet none is a truly regional daily; each essentially serves its own city and province. The most important are *Diario Sur* and *Ideal*, both now owned by the Correo group [5.3.4] and printed in Málaga and Granada respectively, while *Diario de Cádiz*, *Córdoba* and *Diario de Sevilla*, the last a newcomer, all have significant readerships.

Farming remains central to Andalusia's economy, and indeed the region is the country's leading agricultural producer. But with isolated exceptions, such as the market gardeners of Almería and Huelva [6.3.1], the sector is far from efficient, partly due to the legacy of large, unproductive estates (*latifundios*). It is also over-dependent on individual crops, notably olives. The Franco regime attempted to foster industry through the creation of growth poles (*polos de desarrollo*), which led to the development of chemical production in Huelva, shipbuilding around Cádiz bay and vehicle production at Linares, near Jaén. Yet precisely these industries were then disproportionate victims of industrial restructuring in the 1980s [6.1.2].

Consequently, Andalusia has been particularly hard hit by Spain's chronic unemployment problem [6.2.4.1]. At its worst in the early 1990s joblessness in the region stood at around 30 per cent, with as many as three-quarters of young people out of work. The figures have improved somewhat of late, but remain by some distance the worst in Spain, while Andalusia still has virtually the lowest living standards of all seventeen regions. Massive investment in infrastructure, much of it co-financed by the European Union [4.3.2], and in the 1992 Expo held in Seville appear to have had little impact. Without tourism and the public sector the situation would be bleak indeed. At least the sherry producers of Jerez and Sanlúcar de Barrameda, at one time under severe threat due to changing market trends, seem to have evaded crisis by skilful adaptation.

11.2 ARAGON

Regional capital: Saragossa (*Zaragoza*)
Main population centres: Saragossa (605,000)
Official name of regional government: *Diputación General*
Regional prime minister: Marcelino Iglesias (PSOE)
Composition of parliament following most recent regional election (1999):
   People's Party (PP) 28; Socialist Party (PSOE) 23; Aragonese Regionalist Party (Par) 10; Aragonese Regionalist Committee (CHA) 5; United Left (IU) 1
Leading daily newspapers (readership as percentage of all newspaper readers):
   Heraldo de Aragón (70%), *El Periódico* (14%), *El País* (6%)

Much of Aragon (*Aragón*) is mountainous and inhospitable – although often scenically beautiful, especially in the Pyrenean north – and has suffered severe depopulation over the last half century, a fact reflected in its very low population density. Moreover, given that almost a third of Aragonese live in Saragossa, the only settlement with a population of over 50,000, the average figure disguises the emptiness that characterizes much of Aragon.

The present-day region of Aragon formed only one, relatively unimportant part of the medieval 'Crown of Aragon', Castile's rival for the position of leading power in the Iberian peninsula. But it did form a distinct unit with considerable self-government within what was, in modern terms, a sort of federation. The experience has left a deeply-rooted feeling of identity among its inhabitants (known colloquially as *maños* and renowned for their constancy – or obstinacy, depending on one's viewpoint). It is reflected today in the pattern of newspaper readership, in which the *Heraldo de Aragón* far outranks all the Madrid-based titles.

Nonetheless, Aragon was granted only the standard level of autonomy in the first devolution round of the early 1980s [3.1.2]. This slight led to an upsurge of popular resentment later in the decade, effectively triggering a second round as part of which Aragon's powers were greatly extended [3.3.2]. Moreover, in the region's revised Statute of Autonomy, Aragon is explicitly given the status of a 'nationality', previously reserved for the so-called 'historic nationalities' [3.1.1].

As part of these developments, the Aragonese Regionalist Party (*Partido Aragonés Regionalista/Par*) [3.2.3.2] rose to become the second force in regional politics behind the Socialist PSOE. It was even able to claim the post of regional PM for a time as the price of helping the conservative People's Party (PP) to unseat the PSOE. Thereafter, however, the Par lost some support and influence, while the regionalist vote was split by the emergence of a second, more left-wing grouping, the Aragonese Regionalist Committee (*Chunta Aragonesista/CHA*). As a result, the PP was able to consolidate itself as Aragon's largest party and the dominant force in its government. However, following the 1999 regional election the Par joined forces with the Socialists to unseat the PP and form a PSOE-led coalition.

Blessed by few natural advantages, Aragon was for centuries a rather poor region. In recent years, however, the Ebro valley which forms its heart has emerged as an important development axis [6.3.5], with Saragossa as a key transport nexus within it. As a result the region now has one of the country's lowest jobless rates and has seen a considerable increase in living standards, at least for the great majority of Aragonese living in the relatively small area affected. Their prosperity is nonetheless heavily dependent on a few major employers, notably the General Motors vehicles plant outside Saragossa.

11.3 ASTURIAS

Regional capital: Oviedo
Main population centres: Gijón (267,000), Oviedo (200,000), Avilés (84,000)
Official name of regional government: *Principado de Asturias*
Regional prime minister: Vicente Alvarez Areces (PSOE)
Composition of parliament following most recent regional election (1999):
  Socialist Party (PSOE) 24; People's Party (PP) 15; United Left (IU) 3;
  Asturian Modernizing Union (*URAS*) 3

Leading daily newspapers (readership as percentage of all newspaper readers):
La Nueva España (60%), *El Comercio* (32%), *La Voz de Asturias* (20%)

Asturias is the cradle of the Spanish nation, since it was here that the long process of reconquest from the Moors began [1.1], specifically at Covadonga in the Picos de Europa mountains. Yet the same range divides Asturias geographically from the old Kingdom of Castile, of which it formed part, while the local dialect of Castilian (*bable*) is claimed by some to be a separate language – reasons enough for Asturias's status as one of Spain's traditional regions.

In modern times, the region's most distinctive feature was its industrial nature, the coal mines of its central valleys and the associated steel industry making it one of Spain's best-off areas. Since the 1970s, though, both sectors have been in crisis, leaving the region with grave economic problems and, in the former steel centre of Avilés, severe air pollution [7.1.1]. Since Spain's accession to the EU the situation has been aggravated by the difficulties of the previously important dairy industry [6.3.1]. The region's problems are compounded by lack of good communications and remoteness from major European markets, and Asturias has slid down the league table of regional living standards to a position above only the poorest regions of the south.

The Asturian miners and steelworkers were traditionally staunch socialists, and their votes helped the PSOE to dominate regional politics in the 1980s. Conversely the decline of their industries severely hit the party [2.3.3], which lost control of the regional government to the conservative People's Party (PP) in 1991. However, the PP's Asturian leaders soon fell out with their Madrid leadership. They eventually formed a breakaway grouping known as the Asturian Modernizing Union (*Unión Renovadora Asturiana/URAS*), whose modest success at the 1999 regional election helped return the Socialists to power. The older Asturian Regionalist Party (Bable: *Partíu Asturianista/PAS*) is currently not represented in parliament.

The regional institutions are located in Oviedo, one of the major population centres along with Gijón and the – now largely former – mining areas. The two main cities are very different in character, one an administrative centre, the other an industrial port, and have long been rivals. Each has its own daily: *La Nueva España*, the more widely read, being printed in Oviedo and *El Comercio* in Gijón. Both of them, and also *La Voz de Asturias*, recently acquired by the Zeta group [5.3.4], outsell all the Madrid titles and between them dominate the market.

11.4 BALEARIC ISLANDS

Regional capital: Palma (*Palma de Mallorca*)
Main population centres: Palma (334,000)
Official name of regional government: *Govern de les Illes Balears* (Catalan)
Regional prime minister: Francesc Antich (PSOE)

Composition of parliament following most recent regional election (1999):
People's Party (PP) 28; Socialist Party (PSOE) 13; Majorcan Socialist Party–Nationalist Front (PSM-EN) 5; Majorcan Union (UM) 3; United Left (EU) 3; Other local parties 7

Leading daily newspapers (readership as percentage of all newspaper readers):
Ultima Hora (47%), *Diario de Mallorca* (30%), *El Mundo* (13%)

In area terms the smallest of Spain's autonomous regions is that made up of the Balearic Islands (Catalan: *Illes Balears*). It consists of four islands, Majorca (*Mallorca*), Minorca (*Menorca*), Ibiza (*Eivissa*) and Formentera, of which Majorca is by far the most significant, containing some 80 per cent of the population. The islands, with their attractive climate, are fairly densely but evenly populated, with Palma as the only large city. Historically the archipelago formed part of the 'Crown of Aragon' [11.2] and has a consequent tradition of self-rule, both as a unit and at the level of the individual islands, each of which has its own elected assembly (*consell*).

Most people on the islands speak a form of Catalan, which has official status in the region. The region has no TV station of its own, but around 10 per cent of its audience is accounted for by regional stations in Catalonia itself and Valencia [11.10, 11.17]. The two main regional dailies, which comfortably outsell their rivals from the mainland, both appear in Castilian, however.

The islands boast several political parties of their own, the most important being the Majorcan Socialist Party–Nationalist Front (*Partido Socialista Mallorquín-Entesa Nacionalist/PSM-EN*) and the more right-wing Majorcan Union (*Unió Mallorquín/UM*). In fact they have a strong conservative tradition, and the regional government was controlled by the right from 1983 to 1999, when the People's Party was once again the largest party by some distance. Subsequently, however, UM and PSM-EN, as well as smaller groupings from Ibiza and Formentera known as PACTE and COP respectively, joined with the PSOE to oust the PP and form a coalition government.

Economically the Balearics have enjoyed considerable success over recent decades, and are now among Spain's most prosperous regions. Their advance has been based almost entirely on tourism, which makes up some 80 per cent of the economy by value, and the associated construction sector. There is awareness of the need to diversify both within and away from tourism, but efforts to do so have been hampered by the shortage of water on the islands, which at times has to be supplied by tanker from the mainland.

11.5 BASQUE COUNTRY

Regional capital: Vitoria (Basque: *Gasteiz*)

Main population centres: Bilbao (354,000), Vitoria (217,000), San Sebastian (Basque: *Donostia*) (180,000), Barakaldo (97,000), Getxo (84,000), Irún (57,000), Portugalete (53,000)

Official name of regional government: *Eusko Jaurlaritza* (Basque)/*Gobierno Vasco*
Regional prime minister: Juan José Ibarretxe (PNV)
Composition of parliament following most recent regional election (2001):
   Basque Nationalist Party (PNV)/Basque Solidarity (EA) 33; People's Party (PP) 19; Basque Socialist Party (PSE-EE) 13; Alliance for the Basque Nation (EH) 7; Basque United Left (EB-IU) 3
Leading daily newspapers (readership as percentage of all newspaper readers):
   El Correo (51%), *El Diario Vasco* (31%), *Deia* (10%), *Gara* (8%)

The Basque Country (Basque: *Euskadi*) lies at the meeting point of three very different parts of Spain: the Pyrenees, the Cantabrian coastal strip, and the Ebro valley on the edge of Spain's central tableland. Between them lies a region with a dramatic coastline of cliffs and coves, and consisting mainly of hill country rent by steep valleys. Today, though, few Basques live on the traditional upland farmsteads (*caseríos*). Instead the great majority are urban dwellers, in the Bilbao metropolitan area (*Gran Bilbao*), in the other cities and in numerous smaller centres.

The region may make up less than 1.5 per cent of Spain's territory – its three provinces are the country's smallest by area – yet it generates a very high proportion of foreign media coverage. The focus of attention is, of course, the area's strong nationalist movement. The impression often created is that the Basques are not really Spaniards at all – ironically, the nationalist argument in its most extreme form. As so often, the true picture is much more complex than that.

On the one hand there can be no doubt, not just that the region is different from the rest of Spain in many respects, but that most of its people feel a strong sense of common and distinct identity. But equally, when asked, the majority say that they feel both Basque and Spanish. And, at the same time, there are important differences within the region itself and among its inhabitants, so that it is often impossible to talk about what 'Basques' think or want.

Thus the Basque language (*euskera*) is nothing if not distinctive, being unrelated not just to Castilian Spanish but to any known tongue. But until recently the related culture was largely oral, its best-known expression a range of highly distinctive sports. By the 1950s the language's use was confined almost entirely to the countryside, while it was also divided into several very different dialects. From the 1960s on, attempts have been made to revive it on the basis of a specially constructed common form (*batua*), first through the creation of independent Basque-language schools (*ikastolak*) and later by the autonomous regional authorities. They have enjoyed considerable success. But even today most people in the Basque Country habitually use Spanish, especially in the region's southernmost province, Alava, where Basque cultural influence in general is very weak.

To a large extent it is the provinces that form the basis of Basque distinctiveness. Into the nineteenth century they enjoyed certain traditional rights (*fueros*), the best known being those of Vizcaya, associated with the town of Guernica (Basque: *Gernika*) and its Assembly Hall (*Casa de Juntas*). These included exemption from Spanish customs duties, and meant in effect that the Basque provinces (*Vascongadas*) were economically separate from the rest of Spain. What is more, even after the rights were suppressed in 1876 the provinces continued to collect their own taxes before remitting part of them as a reverse block grant (*cupo*) to the central government, as stipulated in regular financial agreements (*conciertos económicos*). In the case of Alava, which largely supported Franco's 1936 uprising [0.2], this privilege was retained even under his rule. And all three provinces continue to play an important part in Basques' perceptions and loyalties today.

In the arrangements for devolution made after Franco's death, the Basque Country's special situation was recognized by giving it privileged access to autonomy, the details of which were set out in its Statute of Autonomy [3.1.1]. Known as the Statute of Guernica, it was overwhelmingly approved by referendum in 1979, a result that underlined the strength of common Basque sentiment. Yet in a number of respects the Statute's provisions clearly reflected the special situation of the three provinces.

Thus devolution revived the system of financial agreements with Madrid, made, not by the region, but with the individual provinces. Moreover, and uniquely in Spain, each of these has its own directly elected assembly (*Juntas Generales*) to oversee the provincial government (*Diputación Foral*). In the Basque Parliament, each of the three has equal representation, even though their populations differ widely. And, along with the other main institutions, the parliament is located in Vitoria, the capital of Alava, even though Bilbao is both the region's chief city and the cradle of its nationalist movement. The purpose was to give the Alavese a stake in a project for which many had no great enthusiasm.

Their feelings were exploited by a new political party, Alavese Unity (*Unidad Alavesa/UA*), which for a time in the 1990s attracted considerable support (see Table 3.2). However, by 2000 UA had effectively re-joined the mainstream conservative People's Party (PP) from which it had originally broken away. The PP is now the region's second political force, having moderated its initial sharp opposition to Basque self-rule and accepted the region's autonomous status [2.4.4]. By contrast the Basque Socialists (PSE-EE), who traditionally enjoyed strong support, have seen it eroded, despite absorbing the regionalist grouping Basque Left (*Euskadiko Ezkerra/EE*) [3.2.2.1].

Instead, the region's political agenda has been set by the nationalist movement, the main representative of which is the Basque Nationalist Party (*Partido Nacionalista Vasco/PNV*) [3.2.2.2]. The PNV has topped the poll at virtually every election, Spanish, regional or local, since 1977. Up to 1986 it ran the region alone, and subsequently it has been the senior partner in a series of coalitions, until 1998 almost always including the PSE-EE.

Since then, however, the PNV has ruled together with Basque Solidarity (*Eusko Alkartasuna/EA*), and currently also with one minister from Basque United Left (*Ezker Batua/EB-IU*) [2.5.2]. EA split away from the PNV in 1986 but now seems on the way to rejoining the fold; at the 2001 regional election the two campaigned jointly [3.2.2.4]. They won a notable victory, not least because of the sharp decline in support for ETA's political wing, People's Unity (*Herri Batasuna/HB*) [3.2.2.1], now running under the mantle of Alliance for the Basque People (*Eusko Herritarrok/EH*). In response to this and other setbacks HB was relaunched in 2001 merely as Unity (*Batasuna*).

Economically the Basque Country was distinguished by a rapid process of industrialization that began in the late nineteenth century. Industrialization acted as the trigger for nationalism [3.2.2.2], one of its offshoots being a separate Basque trade union organization [5.2.1.1]. Based originally on local iron ore reserves, it outlasted the exhaustion of the mines and saw the development of important steel and shipbuilding sectors in Bilbao and along the left bank (*margen izquierda*) of the Nervión estuary. In the 1960s industry spread out beyond this heartland to the valleys of Guipúzcoa and to Vitoria, which benefited from Alava's favourable location and financial privileges.

By the 1980s the farming and fishing so important to regionalists' view of the Basque Country were of only marginal importance. They were also hit badly by Spanish accession to the EU, while the traditional heavy industries were decimated by industrial restructuring [6.1.2]. Subsequently the region has suffered badly from unemployment, especially among the young, and from a small but steady outflow of population. However, in recent years the efforts of successive regional governments have helped generate a gradual recovery, based partly on established industries, particularly machine tools, but also on the development of services; the modernized port of Bilbao has also played a significant part.

Finally, the Basque media landscape reflects many of the factors already mentioned. The two television channels run by the Durango-based Basque Television Service (*Euskal Telebista/ETB*) have an audience share of almost a quarter. However, that of the Basque-language channel ETB-1 is only around 7 per cent, the remainder being accounted for by ETB-2, which broadcasts in Spanish.

One daily paper, *Euskaldunon Egunkaria*, appears in Basque, but its circulation is low. Two more contain some copy in the language but largely as a gesture; *Deia* is close to the PNV, and *Gara* (formerly *Egin*) is the mouthpiece of ETA's supporters. Both are more widely read than any of the Madrid-based press, but both also lag far behind the regional market leaders, the Bilbao-based *Correo* – Spain's sixth ranking daily and now the head of a country-wide media group [5.3.4] – and its San Sebastian stablemate *El Diario Vasco*.

11.6 CANARY ISLANDS

Regional capital: Las Palmas (*Las Palmas de Gran Canaria*)/Santa Cruz (*Santa Cruz de Tenerife*)

Main population centres: Las Palmas (359,000), Santa Cruz (215,000), La Laguna (127,000), Telde (88,000)

Official name of regional government: *Gobierno Canario*

Regional prime minister: Ramón Rodríguez (CC)
Composition of parliament following most recent regional election (1999):
Canary Islands Alliance (CC) 24; Socialist Party (PSOE) 19; People's Party
(PP) 15; El Hierro Independents (AHI) 1
Leading daily newspapers (readership as percentage of all newspaper readers):
La Provincia (34%), *Canarias-7* (32%), *El Día* (17%)

Located some 1000 kilometres from mainland Spain but a mere 100 from the
coast of Africa, the Canary Islands (*Islas Canarias*) are unique among Spain's
regions by dint of pure geography. As well as various uninhabited islets, the
archipelago consists of Gran Canaria, Tenerife, Lanzarote, Fuerteventura, La
Gomera, La Palma and El Hierro. Its considerable ecological value is attested
by the fact that it contains no less than four of Spain's twelve National Parks
[7.3.1]. They contain a wealth of spectacular scenery, in particular various
live volcanoes on Lanzarote and the extinct cone of Teide on Tenerife, Spain's
highest point.

The islands' favourable climate supports a high density of population,
most of which is concentrated on Gran Canaria and Tenerife. The two are
traditional rivals, a situation reflected in the complex arrangements made for
the regional institutions. Thus the regional parliament is located in Santa Cruz
and the office of the Government Representative [1.5.2] in Las Palmas, while
the regional PM's residence shuttles between the two cities every two years.
In practice the regional ministries have offices in both cities, as does the
islands' television station, TVA. Their two best-selling dailies, *La Provincia* and
Canarias-7, are printed in Las Palmas, the third, *El Día*, in Santa Cruz. All three
have considerably larger readerships than the Madrid-based press.

Inter-island differences are also a feature of the Canaries' strong but hybrid
regionalist movement. Some of its roots lie in left-wing activism during the
1970s, which was centred on Gran Canaria and at one point spawned an
armed group, the 'Movement for the Self-Determination and Independence
of the Canaries Archipelago' (MPAIAC). On Tenerife, by contrast, demands
for autonomy came principally from centrist politicians.

Since 1986 these and factions from other islands have been united in the
Canary Islands Alliance (*Coalición Canarias/CC*) [3.2.3.1], with only the El
Hierro Independents (*Agrupación Herreña Independiente/AHI*) remaining separate. Certainly tensions remain within CC, but they also plague the Madrid-
based parties. They have not prevented CC from establishing itself as the
leading force in the regional parliament, and for some years it has also been
the senior partner in a government coalition with the People's Party.

Long poor compared with mainland Spain, since the 1970s the islands have
experienced a considerable increase in their relative prosperity, based heavily
on the tourist industry. A further factor has been recognition of the archipelago's unique situation in the form of special economic and fiscal arrangements.
These involve exemption from certain taxes, as well as liberty of import and
export.

11.7 CANTABRIA

Regional capital: Santander
Main population centres: Santander (184,000), Torrelavega (56,000)
Official name of regional government: *Diputación Regional*
Regional prime minister: José Martínez Sieso (PP)
Composition of parliament following most recent regional election (1999):
People's Party (PP) 19; Socialist Party (PSOE) 14; Cantabrian Regionalist Party (PRC) 6
Leading daily newspapers (readership as percentage of all newspaper readers):
Diario Montañés (84%), *El País* (6%), *El Mundo* (4%)

Historically an integral part of Old Castile, Cantabria is nevertheless geographically separate from Spain's central, Castilian plateau, perched on the northern slopes of the Picos de Europa and oriented towards the sea. The distinctive nature of its terrain is reflected in the popular term for the area – the Highlands (*La Montaña*). The name has been adopted by Cantabria's main daily, which utterly dominates the regional market, a further indication of the distinctiveness that led to the creation of the second-smallest of Spain's regions by population.

In line with its conservative traditions, Cantabria was one of only two regions governed throughout the 1980s by the Right, led latterly by the controversial figure of Juan Hormaechea. Having been ejected from the People's Party, Hormaechea formed his own Cantabrian Progress Union (*Unión para el Progreso de Cantabria/UPCA*), which for a time proved strong enough to significantly destabilize regional politics. However, at the 1999 election the UPCA lost its last parliamentary seats, and the region's government is once more firmly in the PP's hands. Meanwhile the Cantabrian Regionalist Party (*Partido Regionalista de Cantabria/PRC*) has survived the turmoil; it won around one seventh of the vote in 1999.

Up until the 1970s dairying and a substantial steel industry brought the region a degree of prosperity. However, since the 1980s both these sectors have suffered severe problems and the region has slipped down the league of regional rankings. Recent years have seen signs of recovery but – as for the other regions of the north coast – it is held back by poor communications and relative remoteness from major European markets. In terms of overall well-being Cantabria, though, tends to rank near the top, mainly due to a high level of social provision.

11.8 CASTILE-LA MANCHA

Regional capital: Toledo
Main population centres: Albacete (150,000), Talavera de la Reina (74,000), Toledo (69,000), Guadalajara (66,000), Ciudad Real (60,000), Puertollano (50,000)

Official name of regional government: *Junta de Comunidades*
Regional prime minister: José Bono (PSOE)
Composition of parliament following most recent regional election (1999):
Socialist Party (PSOE) 26; People's Party (PP) 21
Leading daily newspapers (readership as percentage of all newspaper readers):
El País (17%), *Abc* (16%), *El Mundo* (15%)

Consisting of the arid southern half of Spain's central plateau, Castile-La Mancha (*Castilla-La Mancha*) is the most sparsely populated region of what is, by European standards, a rather empty country. A natural geographical unit, it has little historical basis – it is made up of New Castile but without its heart, Madrid, together with Albacete province, whose traditional links were with Murcia. As a result, it lacks a true centre. It is the only Spanish region without a significant daily newspaper of its own. Indeed, as in Andalusia, the sports daily *Marca* tops the readership rankings, with much of the remaining audience shared among the three main Madrid titles [5.3.3].

Castile-La Mancha is one of only two regions where no regionalist party has ever been represented in parliament. Indeed currently only the two largest Spanish parties have such representation, the first time this has occurred in any region. As it has been since its establishment the regional government is headed by the Socialist José Bono, who as a result has become one of the PSOE's leading 'barons' [2.3.6]. Only in 1995 was his overall majority even remotely threatened.

Castile-La Mancha has long been poor, and has suffered severe depopulation as a result. Its economy remains based on a rather inefficient agricultural sector, with the petrochemical complex at Puertollano representing its only major industry. Of late, however, parts of Toledo and Guadalajara provinces have obtained some spillover benefits from economic development around Madrid. Together with better marketing of local food products these have brought an improvement in performance and moved the region away from the very foot of the regional prosperity league.

11.9 CASTILE-LEON

Regional capital: Valladolid
Main population centres: Valladolid (319,000), Burgos (163,000), Salamanca (159,000), Leon (138,000), Palencia (81,000), Zamora (65,000), Ponferrada (63,000)
Official name of regional government: *Junta de Comunidades*
Regional prime minister: Juan Herrera Campo (PP)
Composition of parliament following most recent regional election (1999):
People's Party (PP) 48; Socialist Party (PSOE) 30; Leonese People's Union (UPL) 3; United Left of Castile-Leon (IU-CyL) 1; Castilian Nationalist Party (TC-PNC) 1

Leading daily newspapers (readership as percentage of all newspaper readers):

El Norte de Castilla (28%), *El Mundo* (15%), *Diario de León* (13%)

The region of Castile-Leon (*Castilla y León*) is not only Spain's largest by area but the most extensive such unit in the entire European Union; indeed, it is bigger than Portugal and seven other EU member states. It consists of the northern half of Spain's central plateau, essentially the upper basin of the River Duero. Drained by emigration between 1950 and 1975 its population today is spread thinly and unevenly, concentrated mainly in the capitals of its various provinces.

A number of these, notably Burgos and, above all, Salamanca, are fine historic centres. They provide the main attraction of a growing tourist industry which has become a major factor in the regional economy. Traditionally that was based on cereals and these remain important today, although the main crop is now barley rather than wheat. The main industrial centre is Valladolid, which has managed to build on its designation by the Franco regime as a growth pole (*polo de desarrollo*) and to benefit from the establishment by the French car maker Renault of a major plant there.

The establishment of Castile-Leon, which combines most of New Castile with the historically distinct – and older – region of Leon, was the cause of some controversy. Even once the merger was agreed the question of its headquarters remained, the new unit having no obvious natural or traditional capital. Eventually Valladolid's sheer size carried the day and all the region's political institutions were sited there, with its High Court located in Burgos as a concession to feeling there.

The lack of an undisputed regional centre continues to be reflected today in the pattern of newspaper readership. This is headed by the Valladolid-based *El Norte de Castilla*, now owned by the Correo group [5.3.4], but with a considerably lower share than the leading titles in most other regions. The second most popular daily is the Madrid-based *El Mundo* – the other two nationwide papers also sell fairly well – while the third is the *Diario de León*. A number of other titles printed in the various provincial capitals also command significant market shares.

After a brief period of Socialist rule up to 1987 the region has been governed continuously by the Right, of which it is a traditional stronghold. An early regional PM was the future People's Party leader and Spanish Prime Minister, José María Aznar. Ever since the region's establishment the Leonese People's Union (*Unión del Pueblo Leonés/UPL*) has articulated resentment at Leon's incorporation into Castile, and in the province of that name won almost a fifth of the votes at the 1999 regional election. At that time the UPL was joined in the regional parliament by a single representative of the Castilian Nationalist Party (*Tierra Comunera-Partido Nacionalista Castellano/TC-PNC*), which also operates – with less success – in Castile-La Mancha.

11.10 CATALONIA

Regional capital: Barcelona

Main population centres: Barcelona (1,496,000), L'Hospitalet de Llobregat (242,000), Badalona (209,000), Sabadell (184,000), Terrassa (172,000), Santa Coloma de Gramenet (117,000), Tarragona (114,000), Lleida (112,000), Mataró (105,000), Reus (89,000), Cornella de Llobregat (81,000), Girona (74,000)

Official name of regional government: *Generalitat de Catalunya* (Catalan)

Regional prime minister: Jordi Pujol (CiU)

Composition of parliament following most recent regional election (1999): Convergence and Union (CiU) 56; Catalan Socialist Party–Citizens for Change–Initiative for Catalonia–Greens (PSC-CIPC) 55; People's Party (PP) 12; Catalan Republican Left (ERC) 12

Leading daily newspapers (readership as percentage of all newspaper readers):

El Periódico (37%), *La Vanguardia* (29%), *El País* (7%)

Catalonia (*Cataluña*/Catalan: *Catalunya*) is Spain's largest regional economy, with a GDP superior to that of several EU member states. Its population, second only to Andalusia, is unevenly distributed, being concentrated along the coast, above all in Barcelona and its surrounding satellite towns, and in a number of smaller inland centres such as Girona (Spanish: *Gerona*) and Lleida (Spanish: *Lérida*), both of which are now officially known by their Catalan names. The region lies across the most direct route into Spain from the EU's economic core area. In geographic terms, it resembles a microcosm of the country itself, the range of its landscapes passing from the high Pyrenees, through lower mountain ranges and a section of inland plateau, to the Mediterranean coast and the wetlands of the Ebro delta [7.3.1].

At the same time, however, Catalonia is also a highly distinctive region where support for autonomy has long extended across most of the political spectrum [3.2.1.1]. As a result it was given privileged access to devolution, its Statute of Autonomy – known as the Statute of Vic – receiving overwhelming popular support in 1979 [3.1.1]. Since the initial election the following year the regional government has been controlled without a break by the regionalist grouping Convergence and Union (*Convergència i Unió/CiU*), and headed by CiU's founder and leader Jordi Pujol [3.2.1.2]. A persistent concern of his party has been to establish Catalonia's traditional districts (*comarques*) as the only intermediate administrative tier within the region. As yet, however, the central government has refused to consider abolishing the provinces [1.6.2].

The main opposition in the regional parliament is provided by the Catalan Socialists (*Partit dels Socialistes Catalans/PSC*). The PSC is an enthusiastic advocate of Catalan self-government and itself enjoys considerable autonomy within its parent party, the PSOE [3.2.1.1]. At the most recent regional election, in 1999, it formed a ground-breaking alliance with two non-Socialist groups, the non-party movement known as Citizens for Change (*Ciutadans per Canví*) and Initiative for Catalonia (*Iniciativa per Catalunya/IC*). IC has its origins in the independent Catalan Communist Party PSUC [3.2.1.1], but broke away altogether from the Communist-led United Left (IU) in 1997. Subsequently it has formed a close alliance with the Catalan Greens, and describes itself as an 'ecosocialist' party.

The two remaining parties in the Catalan parliament represent the two extremes of the region's political spectrum. Catalan Republican Left (*Esquerra Republicana de Catalunya/ERC*) is an old-established regionalist party which for a time in the 1990s abandoned its traditional moderation and openly backed independence, before reverting to support for strong autonomy. This prompted ERC's more radical wing to leave and form a separate Pro-independence Party (*Partit Independentista*), but this has since vanished. Meanwhile ERC has moved towards the PSC's orbit, in the hope of ousting CiU from power [3.2.1.3]. At the same time the Catalan section of the People's Party (*Partit Popular/PP*), which for long viewed regionalism and autonomy with grave suspicion, has also moderated its stance, and has come to accept Catalan distinctiveness.

Its essential basis, and that of Catalan regionalism, is the existence of a distinct culture with its own language (*català*). Unlike Basque, Catalan has a long literary tradition and has always enjoyed high status, being used by large sections of the region's economic elites. It is also relatively easily learnt by incomers to the region – again in contrast to Basque – and is widely used today, despite attempts to stamp it out by the Franco regime. Understandably, following his death the new regional authorities felt the need to consolidate Catalan's situation, and introduced legislation to 'normalize' the language. It provided for increased use of Catalan by public authorities and within the education system, and enjoyed broad support.

Towards the end of the century, however, the CiU regional government introduced a further set of 'normalization' measures which further downgraded the use of Castilian Spanish in schools. Along with alleged discrimination in access to public sector jobs, this was seized upon by the PP's then leader in the region, Aleix Vidal-Quadras, as a means of rallying support from the region's non-Catalan speakers. But the other opposition parties backed the proposals, and Vidal-Quadras was eventually obliged to resign by the PP's own Madrid leadership, thus restoring the broad consensus on language matters in the region.

The other main dimension of Catalan distinctiveness is economic. Long the powerhouse of the Spanish economy, it has been further favoured by Spain's involvement in the process of European integration and parades its self-confidence through membership of the so-called Four Motors, a loose association with similarly dynamic regions in France, Germany and Italy. Catalonia's economic importance dates back to Barcelona's emergence as a major port and commercial centre in the Middle Ages. The contrast with Spain as a whole was accentuated from the mid-nineteenth century on by industrialization in and around the capital, a process centred on the textile and, later, metal industries.

More recently both of these industries have experienced some decline but, overall, Catalonia was relatively unscathed by the economic difficulties of the 1980s. New industries have emerged as leaders of the regional economy, notably petrochemicals, while the strength of the region's energy sector, with abundant supplies of both hydroelectric and nuclear power, has been another advantage. Above all, Catalonia has built on its traditional strength in trade and commerce to develop a thriving services sector within which both tourism and business and financial services play significant parts.

Finally, Catalonia has its own flourishing media sector concentrated in Barcelona. The publicly-run Catalan Television Service (TVC) broadcasts on two conventional channels, *TV-3* and *Canal 33*, of which the former is much the more popular with an audience share of around 25 per cent. Both broadcast in Catalan, but have been criticized for ignoring indigenous productions in favour of dubbed English-language material. The same is true of the cable channel *K3*. Two daily newspapers produced in Catalan, *Avui* and *El Punt*, printed in Girona, have respectable readerships, although they are outsold by *El País*. It, in turn, lags far behind the two market leaders, *El Periódico* and *La Vanguardia*, the flagships of the Catalan-based Zeta and Godó groups, two of Spain's largest [5.3.4].

11.11 EXTREMADURA

Regional capital: Mérida
Main population centres: Badajoz (136,000), Cáceres (82,000), Mérida (50,000)
Official name of regional government: *Junta de Extremadura*
Regional prime minister: Juan Carlos Rodríguez Ibarra (PSOE)
Composition of parliament following most recent regional election (1999): Socialist Party (PSOE) 34; People's Party (PP) 28; United Left–Alliance for Extremadura (IU-CE) 3
Leading daily newspapers (readership as percentage of all newspaper readers):
Hoy-Diario de Extremadura (62%), *El País* (9%), *El Mundo* (8%)

Separated by mountains from the main Castilian plateau and pressed against the Portuguese border, Extremadura is something of a backwater. That, and its mostly inhospitable climate, have condemned it to centuries of emigration and poverty. Indeed by most measures it still enjoys the dubious distinction of being the poorest of Spain's regions, as well as being one of the most thinly populated. On the other hand, and partly as a result, it possesses a richness of landscape and fauna unrivalled in Western Europe [7.2.3].

As in Andalusia, large unproductive estates (*latifundios*) are a feature of Extremadura's countryside. Partly as a result, while agriculture continues to employ around 30 per cent of the workforce it contributes under half that proportion to the regional economy in value terms. With industrial development limited mainly to the processing of local food products, the public sector is crucial to economic survival. However, in one sector, energy, the region does play a significant role, as an important producer of both hydroelectric and nuclear power.

Rivalry between the capitals of Extremadura's two constituent provinces, the two most extensive in Spain, led its devolved institutions to be located in the smaller centre of Mérida. It has been run without a break by the Socialist PSOE under Juan Carlos Rodríguez Ibarra, who is well-known for criticizing the ongoing devolution process as being unfair to Spain's poor regions in general, and Extremadura in particular. The region has two small regionalist parties, one of the which – Extremadura United (EU) – has now lost its place in parliament. The other, Alliance for Extremadura (*Coalición Extremeña/CE*), managed to preserve its representation in 1999 by allying with United Left (IU).

11.12 GALICIA

Regional capital: Santiago de Compostela
Main population centres: Vigo (286,000), Corunna (Galician: *A Coruña*) (242,000), Ourense (109,000), Santiago de Compostela (94,000), Lugo (88,000), Ferrol (81,000), Pontevedra (75,000)
Official name of regional government: *Xunta de Galiza* (Galician)
Regional prime minister: Manuel Fraga (PP)
Composition of parliament following most recent regional election (2001):
  People's Party (PP) 41; Galician National Alliance (BNG) 17; Galician Socialist Party (PSdeG-PSOE) 17
Leading daily newspapers (readership as percentage of all newspaper readers):
  Voz de Galicia (55%), *Faro de Vigo* (20%), *La Región* (11%)

In many ways Galicia (Galician: *Galiza*) is Spain's most distinctive region. It is a land of rolling hills and steep river valleys fed by high rainfall. Its coastline is punctuated by the long, shallow inlets known as *rías* and makes up one third of the entire Spanish total. Separated from the rest of the country by mountains, the region's natural geographical links are with northern Portugal rather than Spain. The same is true of the Galician language (Galician: *galego*), while the lively indigenous culture is not Iberian in nature at all, but Celtic.

For these reasons Galicia had already been granted limited self-government under the Second Republic [0.1], and as a result was accorded the status of a 'historic nationality' in the 1978 Constitution. That gave it rapid access to relatively extensive autonomy [3.1.2], although Galicians themselves showed no marked enthusiasm; in the devolution referendum the turnout was a mere 30 per cent. The region has no undisputed centre, while its two largest cities, Vigo and Corunna, are old rivals. As a result, and given its historical significance, the new regional institutions were located in the much smaller Santiago de Compostela.

The lack of any great regionalist pressure in Galicia was, in fact, just one aspect of its general political and social backwardness. More than those of any other region its politics had been controlled by corrupt party bosses (*caciques*) and, in sharp contrast to the Basque Country and Catalonia, it had experienced no significant industrialization before 1975. Not surprisingly, it has been the Right's most secure stronghold since then. For over a decade now its Prime Minister has been Manuel Fraga, the doyen of contemporary Spanish conservatism, who is himself a native of the region.

The only break in the domination of the People's Party (PP) and its predecessor, People's Alliance (AP), came in the late 1980s, when AP suffered the breakaway of a grouping known as Galician Alliance (*Coalición Galega/CG*). With CG's support the local Socialists were briefly able to form a government, but at the next regional election in, 1989, the PP swept back to power and CG melted away. In essence it was a vehicle for personal ambitions rather than a genuine expression of regionalist sentiment.

More recently, however, this situation has changed substantially with the rise of the Galician National Alliance (*Bloque Nacional Galego/BNG*) [3.2.3.2]. The BNG is an amalgamation of diverse left-wing groups, some in a moderate tradition stretching back to the 1930s, others born out of 1970s revolutionary ideas. These were skilfully welded together by Xosé Manoel Beiras, a leader whose personal charisma has itself contributed much to the BNG's success. At the 1997 regional election BNG overtook the Socialist PSOE to become the main opposition in the region's parliament. Four years later it once again outpolled the Socialists, albeit narrowly; with their support it also runs several major towns, including Vigo.

Galician is securely implanted at popular level – it is more widely spoken even than its counterpart in Catalonia – and is widely used by authors of literature. The region's public television station, TVG, broadcasting in Galician, commands almost a quarter of the regional audience, although the only two newspapers published in Galician have small circulations. Yet Galicia has its own press, the penetration of the Madrid-based press being very low indeed. Instead Galicians opt for dailies produced in the region, and even in their own province. While *La Voz de Galicia*, printed in Corunna and Spain's seventh most popular title, heads the readership ranking by some way, the *Faro de Vigo* and *La Región*, produced in Ourense, both account for substantial shares.

Galicia's agricultural potential is limited by the high proportion of uncultivated land, at 60 per cent among the highest in Europe, and by a landownership structure dominated by unviably small holdings (*minifundios*). The result, historically, was poverty and massive emigration, above all to Latin America [0.4.2]. Nonetheless agriculture has always been the backbone of its economy, with fishing also of major importance (the Galician fleet accounts for half the Spanish total and exceeds that of any other EU country). Changes in recent decades, not least Spanish accession to the EU, have hit both sectors hard, as well as what was the region's main industry – shipbuilding, based primarily in Ferrol. Despite its relative lack of industry, however, the region does have its own trade union organization [5.2.1.1].

Given the added difficulties of an extremely isolated situation in European terms, and poor communications, the region has continued to experience rather slow growth. However, some newer industries have prospered, such as the Citroën vehicles plant at Vigo and aluminium production in Lugo. The trend away from pure beach holidays has also helped the substantial tourist sector. Moreover, there has been a considerable – although obviously unmeasured – flow of money into the region as the result of smuggling, both of tobacco and of other harder drugs [10.4.1]. These factors have enabled Galicia to catch up somewhat with the rest of Spain, but it remains a relatively poor region. Moreover, rankings of overall well-being tend to place the Galician provinces very low indeed, with Lugo and Ourense right at the foot, due to their continuing low level of infrastructure and services.

11.13 MADRID

Regional capital: Madrid

Main population centres: Madrid (2,883,000), Móstoles (196,000), Fuenlabrada (174,000), Leganés (172,000), Alcalá de Henares (166,000), Getafe (146,000), Alcorcón (145,000), Torrejón de Ardoz (94,000), Alcobendas (90,000), Coslada (77,000), Parla (74,000), Pozuelo de Alarcón (66,000)

Official name of regional government: *Gobierno de la Comunidad*

Regional prime minister: Alberto Ruiz Gallardón (PP)

Composition of parliament following most recent regional election (1999): People's Party (PP) 55; Socialist Party (PSOE) 39; United Left (IU) 8

Leading daily newspapers (readership as percentage of all newspaper readers): *El País* (30%), *Abc* (24%), *El Mundo* (22%)

Traditionally part of New Castile; when Spain's new regional map was drawn in the early 1980s the province of Madrid was established as a separate region (*Comunidad Autónoma de Madrid/CAM*) due to its radically different demographic and economic structure. Although its western and northern fringes take in the high peaks of the Gredos and Guadarrama mountains, the new region is by far the most densely populated in the country. The population is concentrated above all in the capital itself, Spain's largest city, but also in the satellite towns to its south-west and north-east that have grown with astonishing rapidity since the 1960s, when most were little more than villages.

Unlike other European capitals, Madrid long remained in essence a purely administrative centre, relatively unimportant in economic terms. Today, however, it is Spain's leading business centre. Its region lies second only to Catalonia in its contribution to the national economy, and its people are on average the best off in the country.

This growth has been based on a number of factors, in particular the advantage of a central location at the focus of the country's transport system and the growing importance of service industries, for which capital cities are favoured locations. These, particularly financial services as well as public administration, now form the mainstay of the regional economy, although there has also been substantial light industrial development, especially in the satellite towns (*cinturón industrial*). Finally, Madrid was a particular beneficiary of Spain's entry into the European Union.

Politically the region was initially governed by the Socialists. Subsequently, however, it has followed the countrywide pattern of a swing to the Right but to a particularly marked degree. As a result, the early Communist strength, particularly in some of the satellite towns, has largely evaporated. Madrid itself was the stronghold of the New Left Democratic Party (PDNI) that broke away from the communist-led United Left in the late 1990s to join the PSOE [2.5.2], a move from which the Socialists expected significant dividends. But in the event they suffered another heavy defeat in the 1999 election, which confirmed the People's Party's comfortable overall majority in the regional parliament. Predictably this contains no regionalist representatives, although it did briefly include one in the 1980s.

As regards media, the CAM has its own television station, *Telemadrid*, which holds a respectable audience share of around 18 per cent. Its press is dominated by the three main country-wide titles, of which *El País* is by some distance the most widely read, although since 2000 it also has its own daily, known as *Madrid y Mas*.

11.14 MURCIA

Regional capital: Murcia

Main population centres: Murcia (357,000), Cartagena (180,000), Lorca (72,000)

Official name of regional government: *Consejo de Gobierno*

Regional prime minister: Ramón Valcárcel (PP)

Composition of parliament following most recent regional election (1999): People's Party (PP) 26; Socialist Party (PSOE) 18; United Left of Murcia (IURM) 1

Leading daily newspapers (readership as percentage of all newspaper readers):
La Verdad (78%), *El País* (4%), *El Mundo* (3%)

On the map Murcia looks somewhat of an anomaly, a small wedge between the much larger regions of Andalusia, Castile-La Mancha and Valencia. Nor does it have any obvious distinguishing characteristics in terms of geography or culture. In fact, though, it is one of Spain's traditional regions, admittedly in conjunction with the neighbouring province of Albacete. But the latter's allocation to Castile-La Mancha when the new regions were created in the early 1980s responded fully to geographic logic, and if anything served to increase Murcia's own internal cohesion.

Traditionally, too, the region was plagued by the rivalry between its capital and the second city, Cartagena. The latter, a fine natural harbour and Spain's chief Mediterranean naval base, long sought the creation of its own, separate province. The issue now seems buried, however, at least to judge by the very high readership penetration enjoyed by the Murcia-based daily *La Verdad*. It dwarfs not just the region's other, more local titles, but also the country-wide ones.

The region's population is heavily concentrated along a coastal strip, the remainder of the terrain being mountainous and fairly inhospitable. In the past Murcia was notoriously one of the poorest parts of Spain, and lost heavily through emigration, above all to Catalonia where 'Murcian' became a general term for all poor incomers. Its economy depended almost exclusively on mining, which has left the landscape around Cartagena and La Unión badly scarred [7.1.2], and agriculture. Since the 1950s, however, Murcia has experienced a modest but consistent improvement in performance. Its bases have been tourism and soft-fruit canning, the latter in turn made viable by the transfer of water resources from the Ebro to the region's main river, the Segura.

Ensuring that further such transfers go ahead [7.3.2] is, understandably, a vital priority for the region's political leaders. As in a number of other regions, these underwent a change of colour in the 1990s, when the People's Party (PP) replaced the Socialist PSOE in the regional government. In another respect, though, Murcia is atypical, being one of only two regions where no regionalist party has ever sat in parliament.

11.15 NAVARRE

Regional capital: Pamplona (Basque: *Iruña*)
Main population centres: Pamplona (183,000)
Official name of regional government: *Gobierno de Navarra*
Regional prime minister: Miguel Sanz (UPN)
Composition of parliament following most recent regional election (1999):
   Navarrese People's Union (UPN) 22; Navarrese Socialist Party (PSN-
   PSOE) 11; Alliance for the Basque Nation (EH) 8; United Left (IU/EB) 3;
   Navarrese Democratic Convergence (CDN) 3; Basque Solidarity (EA) 3
Leading daily newspapers (readership as percentage of all newspaper readers):
   Diario de Navarra (82%), *Gara* (5%), *El Mundo* (3%)

The region of Navarre (*Comunidad Foral de Navarra*) may be relatively small, but it ranks second to none in the complexity of its nature and affairs. While the rivers of its wet, mountainous north drain to the Atlantic, the south forms part of the dry Ebro valley which runs down to the Mediterranean. In the former the Basque language (*euskera*) and its associated culture have a strong presence that is completely lacking in the more heavily populated south. In the centre lies a zone of transition which includes the Navarrese capital, Pamplona, the region's largest settlement by far. Yet, at the same time, few regions have a stronger and more cohesive sense of identity than Navarre.

The reasons are essentially historical. Navarre was once an independent kingdom extending north of the Pyrenees. Even after its incorporation into Spain, like the neighbouring Basque Country it enjoyed traditional rights (*fueros*) that effectively separated it from the rest of the country [11.5]. Even after the rights were suppressed in 1876 Navarre retained certain financial privileges, including the right to collect its own taxes. Moreover, these were maintained even under Franco, in recognition of enthusiastic Navarrese support for his 1936 uprising [0.1].

Thus when devolution got under way after his death, Navarre was unique among the new regions in already having a degree of self-rule. Its representatives insisted that the autonomy now to be granted be seen, not as a new departure, but as a direct continuation of existing arrangements. Consequently, it is the only region not to have a Statute of Autonomy as such. Instead its constitutional status is defined by the 1982 Act reaffirming its historic rights (*Ley Orgánica de Reintegración y Amejoramiento del Régimen Foral de Navarra*), known usually as the *Amejoramiento Foral*. In particular, this confirms the system of regular financial agreements (*convenios económicos*) under which Navarre collects almost all taxes before remitting a certain sum, or reverse block grant (*aportación*), to the central government.

A further complication was introduced by the fact that Basque regionalists claim Navarre as an integral part of the Basque Country; the 1978 Constitution even included special provision for the two regions to amalgamate [1.1.2]. While that is now recognized by all but extremists as a remote aspiration at best, Basque parties operate in Navarre and currently make up over a fifth of its parliament. The most successful has been ETA's political wing, People's Unity (HB) [3.2.2.1], which currently stands at elections under the mantle of the Alliance for the Basque Nation (*Eusko Herritarrok/EH*).

Navarre's main political tradition is of militant conservatism, embodied by the Carlist movement [0.1]. However, in the 1980s Carlism's collapse enabled the Socialist PSOE to emerge as the region's first governing party. It was helped also by a split between mainstream Spanish conservatives and the Navarrese People's Union (*Unión del Pueblo Navarro/UPN*) [3.2.3.1], whose chief concern was to protect the region's separate identity. In 1991, though, the UPN took over the regional government with support from the People's Party (PP), before itself suffering a breakaway by the less conservative Navarrese Democratic Convergence (*Convergencia de Demócratas de Navarra/CDN*). For a time in the mid-1990s this joined a Socialist-led coalition also involving Basque Solidarity (*Eusko Alkartasuna/EA*) [11.5]. Nonetheless, in 1999 the UPN, which has persuaded the PP to allow it a free run in regional elections, reasserted its leading role, admittedly in a regional parliament that remains highly fragmented.

Perhaps surprisingly given the complexities and even turbulence of its politics, economically Navarre has been one of Spain's major success stories in recent decades. Previously somewhat poor, from the 1960s on the region has undergone a massive but relatively painless process of industrialization, achieving some of the country's highest growth rates on the way. It also has – by Spanish standards – a very low level of joblessness. Expansion was based partly on the region's advantageous location *vis-à-vis* European markets, but also on its privileged financial status which has enabled it to develop high quality communications and other infrastructure. Indeed, such facilities mean that in terms of overall well-being rather than just material prosperity, Navarre ranks first among all the Spanish regions – and that, despite the security problems posed by ETA's activities.

Before 1960 the regional economy was overwhelmingly agricultural. Today farming accounts for only a small share, although specialization in high-value crops such as asparagus means that it continues to make a significant contribution. Industry, most but by no means all of which is centred on Pamplona, is very diverse in nature. Metal industries of various sorts, including a major car plant near the capital, are most strongly represented, with vegetable canning and bottling also important.

In cultural terms, Navarre's diversity is acknowledged by official recognition for the Basque language. The two television channels controlled by the Basque government [11.5] have a 10 per cent share of the region's television audience, and its second paper in terms of readership is *Gara*, which is controlled by ETA's supporters. The content of these media is overwhelmingly in Spanish, however, while by far the largest readership is enjoyed by the local *Diario de Navarra*, to the virtual exclusion of Madrid-based papers.

11.16 THE RIOJA

Regional capital: Logroño
Main population centres: Logroño (128,000)
Official name of regional government: *Consejo de Gobierno*
Regional prime minister: Pedro Sanz Alonso (PP)
Composition of parliament following most recent regional election (1999):
    People's Party (PP) 18; Socialist Party (PSOE) 13; Party of the Rioja (PR) 2
Leading daily newspapers (readership as percentage of all newspaper readers):
    La Rioja (84%), *El País* (6%), *Diario de Navarra* (6%)

The Rioja is the least extensive of Spain's mainland regions, and the smallest of all in demographic terms. Yet it is surprisingly diverse; much of the south is mountainous and empty, while the population is concentrated in small towns along the Ebro valley and, above all, in the capital, Logroño. Historically the area formed part of Old Castile, and includes the monastery at San Millán de la Cogolla, usually regarded as the cradle of the Castilian language.

However, it is geographically separate from the Castilian plateau and the main local daily utterly dominates the local press – in a region with more readers than the average. The region has even given birth to its own political formation, the Party of the Rioja (*Partido Riojano/PR*), which on occasion has held the balance of power in its parliament and been a junior partner in governments. The leading role in these, however, has been played by the major Spanish parties: in the 1980s mainly the Socialists, since 1991 the conservative PP.

Economically the Rioja is stable and prosperous. Its well-balanced economy includes an efficient and profitable agricultural sector, centred on cereals and the intensive production of fruit and vegetables, and a diversity of mainly light industries. Several of these use as their inputs local agricultural produce, the most famous being, of course, wine production.

11.17 VALENCIA

Regional capital: Valencia (Valencian: *València*)
Main population centres: Valencia (739,000), Alicante (Valencian: *Alacant*) (277,000), Elche (Valencian: *Elx*) (196,000), Castellón de la Plana (Valencian: *Castelló de la Plana*) (142,000), Torrent (65,000), Alcoy (Valencian: *Alcoi*) (60,000), Gandia (59,000), Sagunto (Valencian: *Sagunt*) (57,000), Benidorm (54,000), Orihuela (53,000), Elda (52,000)
Official name of regional government: *Generalitat Valenciana* (Valencian)
Regional prime minister: Eduardo Zaplana (PP)
Composition of parliament following most recent regional election (1999): People's Party (PP) 49; Socialist Party (PSOE) 35; United Left of Valencia (EUPV) 5
Leading daily newspapers (readership as percentage of all newspaper readers):
Levante (34%), *Las Provincias* (22%), *Información de Alicante* (18%)

Long before the Rioja was a name known in the English-speaking world, Valencia was indelibly linked in the popular mind with oranges. They are still important for the present-day region of that name (*Comunidad Valenciana*), which produces 70 per cent of Spain's citrus fruit. Within the country it is associated above all with the irrigated market gardens known as *huertas*, whose products include rice as well as fruit and vegetables. And, in fact, almost 45 per cent of Spanish farm exports come from Valencia.

Today, however, the region's economy is by no means exclusively agricultural. As part of the favoured Mediterranean coastal strip [6.3.5] it has developed and diversified, and now has substantial services and manufacturing sectors. Some industrial employers are large, such as the Ford car plant near the capital, but most businesses are small or medium-sized and are spread over a range of light industries, such as tiles, concentrated around Castellón, and footwear. Fine beaches have also made for a substantial tourist industry, with Benidorm the best-known resort. This mix of activities includes several particularly affected by the underground economy [6.2.3], so that living standards in the region may well be higher than suggested by the relatively modest official figures.

Both economic activity and population are concentrated in and around the city of Valencia – the fourth largest in Spain – and in the medium-sized towns which dot the coastal strip. By Spanish standards this is a lush area, which benefits from the sometimes controversial transfer of water from the Ebro to its main river, the Segura [7.3.2]. Behind it lie ranges of hills, not particularly high but often forbidding; the Maestrazgo in the north of the region is a byword for difficult terrain.

The Valencian region has a long history as a distinct unit, initially within the medieval 'Crown of Aragon' [11.2], while its capital is a long-established port and trading centre, the traditional rival of Barcelona. Linguistically, too, it lies outside the Castilian orbit, with most of its people speaking what for most scholars is a dialect of Catalan. However, officially Valencian is now regarded as a distinct tongue. The regional government has gone so far as to withdraw from joint language-promotion programmes with its Catalan (and Balearic) counterparts in such areas as teacher training.

These political decisions were taken as a result of pressure from sectors of the lower middle class suspicious of all things Catalan. In the 1980s they were the driving force behind the rise of a new political party, Valencian Union (*Unió Valenciana/UV*) [3.2.3.1], which for a time attracted sufficient support to become a major player in regional politics and formed part of coalition governments. Initially is main impact, though, was to split the right-wing vote; the result was that the Socialist PSOE ran the region throughout the 1980s. More recently, UV's sharp decline has had the opposite effect of ensuring a solid majority for the People's Party (PP).

Valencia has its own public broadcasting service which runs two channels. The older, *Canal 9*, commands an audience share of over 20 per cent; the other, *Punt 2*, was introduced only in 2000 and as yet has much lower figures. Both broadcast material in Valencian. The language's presence is rather lower in the daily press, which is characterized by its diversity. On the one hand, the Madrid-based titles are relatively widely read. On the other, the three leading dailies are all regional, the two largest being printed in the capital and the third in Alicante.

11.18 CEUTA AND MELILLA

Ceuta and Melilla are two small enclaves on the Moroccan coast, both of which have formed part of Spain since the sixteenth century. Ceuta (population 75,000) lies just inside the Straits of Gibraltar, Melilla (population 66,000) rather further east, roughly opposite Almería. For administrative purposes Melilla's territory includes Spain's minuscule Mediterranean possessions, the Chafarinas Islands and the rocky islets of Alhucemas and Vélez de la Gomera.

Table 11.1 Regional indicators

	Area (sq km)	Population	Pop. density (per sq km)	Gross Added Value[a] (EUR bn)	Per capita GAV[b] (EUR)	Unemployment[c] (%)
Andalusia	87,560	7,340,000	84	69.1	9,500	24.9
Aragon	47,720	1,190,000	25	18.0	15,300	7.0
Asturias	10,604	1,077,000	102	12.5	11,600	15.5
Balearic Is	4,992	846,000	169	15.6	19,200	4.5
Basque Co	7,235	2,099,000	290	32.7	15,600	11.9
Canary Is	7,447	1,716,000	230	23.4	14,100	13.2
Cantabria	5,231	531,000	102	6.6	12,600	13.0
Cast-La Man	79,462	1,734,000	22	18.8	10,900	11.6
Cast-Leon	94,224	2,479,000	26	31.0	12,600	13.5
Catalonia	32,114	6,262,000	195	107.1	17,400	8.2
Extremadura	41,635	1,069,000	26	10.1	9,400	23.0
Galicia	29,575	2,732,000	92	31.8	11,700	14.4
Madrid	8,028	5,205,000	648	97.8	19,300	11.2
Murcia	11,314	1,149,000	102	12.6	11,200	13.8
Navarre	10,391	544,000	52	9.0	16,900	6.1
Rioja	5,045	264,000	52	4.4	16,600	8.1
Valencia	23,255	4,121,000	177	57.3	14,100	11.1
Ceuta/Melilla	32	142,000	9944	1.4	10,700	22.4
Spain	505,864	40,500,000	80	559.2	14,000	13.7

Notes: [a] 2000 figure (nearest thousand). Source: National Statistical Office (*Instituto Nacional de Estadística*).
[b] Annual figure for 1999. Source: *Anuario El País 2001*.
[c] Third quarter 2000 (unadjusted). Source: *Anuario El País 2001*.

Both cities are relatively poor, their per capita income amounting to some three-quarters of the Spanish average, although in recent years they have improved their position somewhat. Both are ports, Ceuta one of the most important in the Mediterranean thanks to its free port status, whereas Melilla's economy depends mainly on its large military garrison.

The two, which are a constant source of low-level friction with Morocco [0.4.3], were made 'autonomous cities' in 1995. Their politics have tended to be dominated by the issue of immigration, which has been exploited cynically but successfully by the Independent Liberal Group (*Grupo Independiente Liberal/GIL*) headed by Marbella's controversial mayor Jesús Gil [2.6].

11.19 GLOSSARY

Amejoramiento Foral m	law establishing Navarre's autonomous status
aportación f	sum paid by Navarre in respect of services provided by central government
bable m	Asturian dialect of (Castilian) Spanish
batua m	recently constructed common form of Basque language
cacique m	(historically) corrupt local political boss, especially common in Galicia
Casa de Juntas f	building in Guernica where historically Spanish monarchs swore to respect Vizcayan rights
caserío m	Basque farmsteading
cinturón industrial m	ring of satellite towns round Madrid and other major cities
comarque f	district (in Catalonia)
Comunidad Autónoma f	autonomous region
concierto económico m	financial agreement between central government and each of the Basque provinces
Consejo de Gobierno m	regional government (Murcia, the Rioja)
convenio económico m	financial agreement between central government and Navarre
cupo m	sum paid by each of the Basque provinces in respect of services provided by central government
Diputación Foral f	provincial government of each of the Basque provinces
Diputación General f	regional government (Aragon)
Diputación Regional f	regional government (Cantabria)
euskera m	Basque language
Eusko Jaurlaritza m	Basque regional government
fueros mpl	traditional privileges enjoyed by each of the Basque provinces and Navarre
galego m	Galician language
Generalitat f	regional government (Catalonia, Valencia)
Govern m	regional government (Balearic Islands)
huerta f	irrigated market garden typical of Valencia region
ikastola f	Basque-language school

Junta f	regional government (Andalusia, Extremadura)
Junta de Comunidades f	regional government (Castile-La Mancha, Castile-Leon)
Juntas Generales fpl	elected assembly of each of the Basque provinces
latifundio m	large estate, often underutilized, typical of southern regions
margen izquierda f	industrial area on left bank of River Nervión below Bilbao
minifundio m	uneconomically small farm unit, especially common in Galicia
Montaña, La f	popular name for Cantabria
polo de desarrollo m	growth pole (under Franco regime)
Principado m	regional government (Asturias)
ría f	long shallow inlet typical of Galician coast
Vascongadas, Provincias fpl	Basque provinces (term used under Franco regime)
Xunta f	regional government (Galicia)

FURTHER READING

INTRODUCTION

Brenan, G. 1990 *The Spanish labyrinth.* Cambridge, Cambridge University Press.
Esdaile, C. 2000 *Spain in the Liberal Age.* Oxford, Oxford University Press.
Gillespie, R. and Youngs, R. (eds) 2001 *Spain: the European and international challenges.* London, Frank Cass.
Preston, P. 1986 *The triumph of democracy in Spain.* London, Methuen.
Ross, C. 2000 *Spain 1812–1996.* London, Arnold.

CHAPTER 1

Heywood, P. 1991 Governing a new democracy: the power of the Prime Minister in Spain. *West European Politics* 14 (2).
Heywood, P. 1995 *The government and politics of Spain.* London, Macmillan (Chaps 2, 4, 8).
Newton, M. T. 1997 *Institutions of modern Spain: a political and economic guide.* Cambridge, Cambridge University Press (Chaps 1–6, 8).
Román, P. (ed.) 1995 *Sistema político español.* Madrid, McGraw Hill (Chaps 2, 3, 5–8, 11).
Sánchez Goyanes, E. 1989 *Constitución española comentada.* Madrid, Paraninfo.

CHAPTER 2

Bell, D. (ed.) 1993 *Western European Communists and the collapse of Communism.* London, Berg (Chap. 6).
Fysh, P. and Hughes, N. 2001 Explaining the Populares' majority: the Spanish general election of 12 March 2000. *International Journal of Iberian Studies* 14 (1).
Heywood, P. 1995 *The government and politics of Spain.* London, Macmillan (Chaps 8, 9).
Hopkin, J. 1993 Reflections on the disintegration of UCD. *Journal of Association for Contemporary Iberian Studies* 6 (2).
Tusell, J. and Sinova, J. 1992 *La década socialista: el ocaso de Felipe González.* Madrid, Espasa.

Tussell, J. (ed.) 2000 *El gobierno de Aznar: balance de una gestión, 1996–2000.* Barcelona, Crítica.

Chapter 3

Amodia, J. (ed.) 1994 *The resurgence of nationalist movements in Europe.* Bradford, Bradford University Press (Chaps 10, 11).

Atkinson, D. 2000 Language legislation in Catalonia: the politics of normalization. *International Journal of Iberian Studies* 13 (2).

Balcells, A. 1996 *Catalan nationalism: past and present.* London, Macmillan.

Heiberg, M. 1989 *The making of the Basque nation.* Cambridge, Cambridge University Press.

Hollyman, J. 1995 The tortuous road to regional autonomy in Spain. *Journal of Association for Contemporary Iberian Studies* 8 (1).

Roller, E. 2000 The October 1999 elections in Catalonia: the end of nationalist dominance in Catalan politics? *International Journal of Iberian Studies* 13 (2).

Ross, C. 1996 Nationalism and party competition in the Basque Country and Catalonia. *West European Politics* 16 (3).

Sullivan, J. 1999 Forty years of ETA. *History Today* 49 (4).

Chapter 4

Cooper, T. 2001 '¡Aleluya por Europa!' Press treatment of the European Union in Spain and the United Kingdom. *International Journal of Iberian Studies* 14 (2).

Gillespie, R. and Youngs, R. (eds) 2001 *Spain: the European and international challenges.* London, Frank Cass.

Moreno Juste, A. 1998 *España y el proceso de construcción europea.* Barcelona, Ariel.

Squires, J. 1999 Catalonia, Spain and the European Union: a tale of a region's 'empowerment'. *International Journal of Iberian Studies* 12 (1).

Chapter 5

Berger, S. and Broughton, D. (eds) 1995 *The force of labour: the Western European labour movement and the working class in the twentieth century.* London, Berg (Chap. 7).

Bustamante, E. 2000 Spain's interventionist and authoritarian communication policy: Telefónica as political battering ram of the Spanish Right. *Media, Culture and Society* 22 (4).

Deacon, P. 1994 *The press as the mirror of the new Spain.* Bristol, Bristol University Press.

Hernández, A. 1995 *El quinto poder: la iglesia de Franco a Felipe.* Madrid, Temas de hoy.

Román, P. (ed.) 1995 *Sistema político español.* Madrid, McGraw Hill (Chap. 10).

CHAPTER 6

Harrison, J. 1995 *The Spanish economy: from the Civil War to the European Community.* Cambridge, Cambridge University Press.

Longhurst, C. A. 1995 The Spanish labour market. In Cooper, T. (ed.) *Spain in Europe.* Leeds, All Saints College.

Longhurst, C. A. 1997 Poverty amidst affluence in contemporary Spain: a case of 'the poor you shall always have with you'? *International Journal of Iberian Studies* 10 (3).

Murphy, B. 1998 Real and nominal convergence: Spain on the threshold of EMU. *International Journal of Iberian Studies* 11 (3).

Salmon, K. 1995 *The modern Spanish economy.* London, Pinter.

Salmon, K. 2001 Spanish foreign direct investment, transnationals and the redefinition of the Spanish business realm. *International Journal of Iberian Studies* 14 (2).

Tamames, R. 2000 *Estructura económica española.* Barcelona, Bosch.

Tamames, R. 1996 *La economía española de la transición a la unión monetaria.* Madrid, Temas de hoy.

CHAPTER 7

Bangs, P. 1995 The European Union and the Spanish environment. In Cooper, T. (ed.) *Spain in Europe.* Leeds, All Saints College.

Brooksbank-Jones, A. 1998 (Un)covering the environment: some Spanish perspectives. *International Journal of Iberian Studies* 11 (1).

CHAPTER 8

Boyd-Barrett, O. and O'Malley, P. (eds) 1995 *Education reform in democratic Spain.* London, Routledge.

CHAPTER 9

Brooksbank-Jones, A. 1997 *Women in contemporary Spain.* Manchester, Manchester University Press.

Comisión Europea Contra El Racismo Y La Intolerancia 1999 *Informe sobre España.* Equipo Nizkor.

European Observatory on Health Care Systems 2000 *Health care systems in transition: Spain.*

CHAPTER 10

Merino-Blanco, E. 1996 *The Spanish legal system.* London, Sweet & Maxwell.

Román, P. (ed.) 1995 *Sistema político español.* Madrid, McGraw Hill (Chap. 7).

Woodworth, P. 2001 *Dirty war, clean hands: ETA, the GAL and Spanish democracy*. Cork, Cork University Press.

CULTURE AND SOCIETY

Graham, H. and Labanyi, J. (eds) 1995 *Spanish cultural studies: an introduction*. Oxford, Oxford University Press (Chaps 18, 20).
Hooper, J. 1995 *The new Spaniards*. Harmondsworth, Penguin.
Richardson, B. 2001 *Spanish studies: an introduction*. London, Arnold.

CURRENT DEVELOPMENTS AND STATISTICS

Anuario El País (annual produced by newspaper of same name).
International Journal of Iberian Studies.

USEFUL WEB SITES

www.la-moncloa.es – official Spanish government site, giving access to those of individual ministries and regional governments.
www.congreso.es; www.senado.es – official sites of the two Houses of Parliament.
www.admiweb.org – compendium of information on the Spanish public sector as a whole, with search facility.
www.areaplural.com – portal to wide range of political information (parties, regionalism, etc.).
www.ine.es – Spanish National Statistics Office.
www.elpais.es; www.el-mundo.es; www.abc.es – leading Spain-wide daily newspapers.
www.elperiodico.es; www.lavanguardia.es – leading newspapers in Catalonia.
www.diario-elcorreo.es – leading newspaper in the Basque Country.
www.oecd.org/eco/surv/esu-spa.htm – contains latest edition of OECD's annual economic survey.

INDEX

The index includes Spanish abbreviations and acronyms, for which the full (Spanish) form and an English translation are supplied. Otherwise translations are given only where required to identify some of the references shown. Page numbers shown in bold type indicate sections devoted specifically to the term concerned.